The Methodology of Positive Economics

Milton Friedman's 1953 essay "The methodology of positive econom-ics" remains the most cited, influential, and controversial piece of meth-odological writing in twentieth-century economics. Since its appearance, the essay has shaped the image of economics as a scientific discipline, both within and outside academia. At the same time, there has been an ongoing controversy over the proper interpretation and normative eval-uation of the essay. Perceptions have been sharply divided, with some viewing economics as a scientific success thanks to its adherence to Friedman's principles, others taking it as a failure for the same reason. In this book, a team of world-renowned experts in the methodology of economics cast new light on Friedman's methodological arguments and practices from a variety of perspectives. It provides the twenty-first-century reader with an invaluable assessment of the impact and contem-porary significance of Friedman's seminal work.

Uskali Mäki is Academy Professor at the Academy of Finland. He has written extensively on the philosophy and methodology of economics and is editor of a number of books, including *The Economic World View* (Cambridge University Press, 2001), *Fact and Fiction in Economics* (Cambridge University Press, 2002), and *Handbook of the Philosophy of Economics* (2009).

The Methodology of Positive Economics

Reflections on the Milton Friedman legacy

Edited by
Uskali Mäki

CAMBRIDGE
UNIVERSITY PRESS

CAMBRIDGE UNIVERSITY PRESS

Cambridge, New York, Melbourne, Madrid, Cape Town, Singapore, São Paulo, Delhi

Cambridge University Press
The Edinburgh Building, Cambridge CB2 8RU, UK

Published in the United States of America by Cambridge University Press, New York

www.cambridge.org
Information on this title: www.cambridge.org/9780521686860

© Cambridge University Press 2009

First published 2009

Printed in the United Kingdom at the University Press, Cambridge

A catalogue record for this publication is available from the British Library

ISBN 978-0-521-86701-6 hardback
ISBN 978-0-521-68686-0 paperback

For INEM

Contents

Figures

Tables

Contributors

ROGER E. BACKHOUSE is Professor of the History and Philosophy of Economics at the University of Birmingham. He is author of *The Penguin History of Economics / The Ordinary Business of Life* (2002) and many books and articles on the history of economics in the twentieth century and on economic methodology. He has edited several volumes on economic methodology and is a former editor of the *Journal of Economic Methodology*. He is past Chair of the International Network for Economic Method.

MARK BLAUG is Professor Emeritus of the University of London and Buckingham University, UK, and Visiting Professor of Economics at the University of Amsterdam and Erasmus University of Rotterdam, the Netherlands. He is a Fellow of the British Academy and a Foreign Honorary Member of the Royal Netherlands Academy of Arts and Sciences. His principal fields of interest are economic methodology and the history of economic thought. His publications include *Introduction to the Economics of Education* (1970), *The Methodology of Economics* (1980), *Great Economists since Keynes* (1985), *Economic History and the History of Economics* (1987), *The Economics of Education and the Education of an Economist* (1987), *Economic Theories. True or False?* (1990), *Not Only an Economist. Recent Essays* (1997), *Who's Who in Economics*, ed. (1999).

KEVIN D. HOOVER is Professor of Economics and Philosophy at Duke University. He received his D.Phil from Oxford University. He was previously a Research Fellow at Nuffield College, Oxford, and a lecturer at Balliol College and Lady Margaret Hall, Oxford, as well as a research associate and visiting economist at the Federal Reserve Bank of San Francisco. He is the author of *Causality in Macroeconomics* and *The Methodology of Empirical Macroeconomics* (both Cambridge University Press, 2001), and of numerous articles in macroeconomics, monetary economics, economic methodology, and the philosophy of science. He is also the editor of *Macroeconometrics: Developments, Tensions, and Prospects* (1995) and *Real Business Cycle: A Reader* (1998). Hoover is past President of the History of Economics Society, past Chairman of the International Network for Economic Methodology and a former editor of the *Journal of Economic Methodology*. Hoover is best known for his work on causality and on the new classical macroeconomics. The latter work began with "Two types of monetarism" (*Journal of Economic Literature*, 1984), which contained a careful examination of Milton Friedman's economics and methodology, trying to locate why Friedman disassociated himself from his apparent followers such as Lucas and Sargent. These themes were further developed in *The New Classical Macroeconomics* (1988).

J. DANIEL HAMMOND is Professor of Economics at Wake Forest University, Winston-Salem, NC. He received his PhD from the University of Virginia, and has published in monetary economics, economic methodology, and history of economics. He has written extensively on the history of University of Chicago economics, including *Theory and Measurement: Causality Issues in Milton Friedman's Monetary Economics* (Cambridge University Press, 1996), *Making Chicago Price Theory: Friedman-Stigler Correspondence 1945–1957* (editor with Claire H. Hammond, Routledge, 2006), and "An interview with Milton Friedman on methodology," *Research in the History of Economic Thought and Methodology* (1992). Hammond has served as an elected member of the executive committee of the History of Economics Society, and in 2001–2 as the Society's president.

D. WADE HANDS is Professor of Economics at the University of Puget Sound in Tacoma, WA. He has published widely on various topics in the history of economic thought and economic methodology. Some of his published work is about the history and methodology of the Chicago school, of which Milton Friedman is a member. His most recent book is *Reflection Without Rules* (Cambridge University Press, 2001). He is also one of the editors (along with John Davis and Uskali Mäki) of *The Handbook of Economic Methodology* (1998). His textbook *Introductory Mathematical Economics* is in its second edition (2003). He is an editor of the *Journal of Economic Methodology*.

USKALI MÄKI is Academy Professor at the Academy of Finland and former Professor at the Erasmus Institute for Philosophy and Economics. He has published on the assumptions issue, realism and realisticness, idealizations and models, causation, explanation, the rhetoric, sociology, and economics of economics, and the foundations of New Institutional and Austrian economics; in journals such as the *Journal of Economic Literature, Philosophy of the Social Sciences, Studies in the History and Philosophy of Science, Perspectives on Science, Erkenntnis, Kyklos, Journal of Economic Methodology, History of Political Economy, Economics and Philosophy, Cambridge Journal of Economics*. He is editor of *The Economic World View: Studies in the Ontology of Economics* (Cambridge University Press, 2001); *Fact and Fiction in Economics: Models, Realism, and Social Construction* (Cambridge University Press, 2002); and a co-editor of *The Handbook of Economic Methodology* (1998); *Economics and Methodology. Crossing Boundaries* (1998); *Rationality, Institutions and Economic Methodology* (1993). He is Chair of the International Network for Economic Method and a former editor of the *Journal of Economic Methodology*.

THOMAS MAYER was born in Vienna in 1927, emigrated to England in 1938 and to the United States in 1944. He received his BA from Queens College, CUNY, in 1948 and his PhD from Columbia University in 1953. He taught at West Virginia University, University of Notre Dame, Michigan State University, University of California at Berkeley, and for most of his professional life as professor at the University of California at Davis from which he retired in 1992. His initial interests were macroeconomics, monetary theory, and policy, where he could best be classified either as an eclectic or a moderate monetarist. Much of his work has addressed Friedman's monetarist thinking. Shortly before retirement he shifted mainly to methodology where he advocated a de-emphasis on formalist economics. During this period, he has published on Friedman's methodology. He is the author of *Permanent Income, Wealth and Consumption*; *The Structure of Monetarism* (with others); *Money, Banking and the Economy* (with J. Duesenberry and R. Aliber); *Monetarism and Monetary Policy*; *Truth vs. Precision in Economics*; *Doing Economic Research*; *Monetary Policy*; and *The Great Inflation in the United States*. He lives in Berkeley, California, and is a citizen of the USA.

MELVIN W. REDER is Gladys G. and Isidore Brown Professor of Urban and Labor Economics Emeritus at the Graduate School of Business at the University of Chicago; previously Professor of Economics at Stanford University. Book publications include *Economics: the Culture of a Controversial Science* (1999), *Rationality in Psychology and Economics* (coeditor) (1986), *Labor in a Growing Economy* (1957), *Studies in the Theory of Welfare Economics* (1947).

CHRIS STARMER is Professor of Experimental Economics at the University of Nottingham, UK. Starmer was awarded a PhD for an experimental investigation of decision under risk in 1992 from the University of East Anglia (UEA). He worked as Lecturer then Senior Lecturer at UEA and was visiting Associate Professor at Caltech before moving to Nottingham in 2000. His main research interests have focused on experimental economics, theories of decision making and economic methodology. This combination makes him the best expert on Friedman's work on expected utility and on methodology. Starmer has published articles on these topics in *American Economic Review*, *Econometrica*, *Economic Journal*, *Economica*, *Journal of Economic Literature*, *Journal of Economic Methodology*, *Quarterly Journal of Economics*, and *Review of Economic Studies*. Starmer is currently Director of the Centre for Decision Research and Experimental Economics (CeDEx) at the University of Nottingham.

DAVID TEIRA SERRANO is associate professor in the Department of Logic, History and Philosophy of Science (UNED, Madrid) and research associate of the Urrutia Elejalde Foundation. His PhD thesis, *Azar, economía y política en Milton Friedman*, won the best dissertation award of the Spanish Society for Logic and Philosophy of Science for the period 2001–3. He has published papers in the *Journal of Economic Methodology*, *History of Political Economy* and *Studies in History and Philosophy of Science*, among other journals.

JACK VROMEN is professor of the philosophy of science at the Faculty of Philosophy of the Erasmus University Rotterdam, where he is also part of EIPE (Erasmus Institute for Philosophy and Economics). His main research interest is in philosophy of economics, with a special focus on conceptual and meta-theoretical aspects of the relation between evolutionary biology and evolutionary theorizing in economics. He has published on Friedman's and Alchian's evolutionary argument in the theory of the firm. Recent publications include "Ontological commitments of evolutionary economics," in *The Economic World View* (ed. Uskali Mäki, Cambridge University Press, 2001), and "Stone Age minds and group selection – what difference do they make?" in *Constitutional Political Economy* (2002) and "Cognitive theory meets evolutionary theory – what promise does evolutionary psychology hold out for economics?" in *Cognitive Developments in Economics* (ed. S. Rizzello, 2003). He is a past member of the Executive Board of INEM (The International Network for Economic Methodology) and Book Review Editor of the *Journal of Economic Methodology*.

OLIVER P. WILLIAMSON is Professor of the Graduate School and Edgar F. Kaiser Professor Emeritus of Business, Economics, and Law at the University of California, Berkeley. Williamson is a member of the National Academy of Sciences (USA) and a Fellow of the American Academy of Arts and Sciences and the Econometric Society. He is a past president of the American Law and Economics Association, the Western Economics Association, and the International Society for New Institutional Economics. His books include *Markets and Hierarchies* (1975), *The Economic Institutions of Capitalism* (1985), and *The Mechanisms of Governance* (1996).

JESÚS P. ZAMORA BONILLA is PhD in Philosophy and in Economics, professor of Philosophy of Science at Universidad Nacional de Educacion a Distancia (Madrid, Spain), as well as Academic Coordinator of the Urrutia Elejalde Foundation (devoted to the study of the connections between Economics and Philosophy). His main research has been in the fields of scientific realism, verisimilitude, economic methodology, and the economics of scientific knowledge. Some recent papers by him are "Verisimilitude and the scientific strategy of economic theory" (*Journal of Economic Methodology*, 1999), "Scientific inference and the pursuit of fame" (*Philosophy of Science*, 2002), and "Meaning and testability in the structuralist theory of science" (*Erkenntnis*, 2003), as well as a special issue (as invited editor) on "Darwinism in Economics" in the journal *Theoria*. He is a member of the Executive Board of the International Network for Economic Method, of the Executive Board of the Spanish Society for Logic and Philosophy of Science, and was a founder of the Iberian American Society for Economic Methodology.

MICHEL DE VROEY is Professor of Economics at Université catholique de Louvain, Belgium. He has written extensively on the history of economic thought. His particular research interest is the history of macroeconomics. He is also a member of the editorial board for *European Journal of Economic Thought* and a founding member of the European Association for the History of Economic Thought. His latest book is *Involuntary Unemployment: The Elusive Quest for a Theory* (2004).

Preface

Milton Friedman is known for a variety of contributions. Professional economists acknowledge his work in monetary economics and some other fields of economic inquiry. Many others recognize his name in connection with the late twentieth-century free market ideology – an ideology advising how to conduct economic policy and how to organize social life more generally. His writings in these areas are numerous, influential, and controversial.

Friedman has also contributed to what may be called the ideology of science – an ideology advising how to conduct economic inquiry and how to organize academic life in general. On this topic, his recognized writings are less numerous, often considered reducible to one piece, "The methodology of positive economics," that was published as the lead essay in his *Essays in Positive Economics* in 1953 (dubbed throughout this volume as "F53"). The essay was to become the most cited, the most influential, the most controversial piece of methodological writing in twentieth-century economics. It is also poorly understood – and indeed hard to understand, given its richness and obscurities. And it remains highly topical for the foundational debates in and around economics in the early twenty-first century. These are among the ingredients of a classic.

These features of F53 gave sufficient grounds for organizing a conference around it. The conference, organized by the Erasmus Institute for Philosophy and Economics, took place in Rotterdam, the Netherlands, on 12–13 December 2003. The occasion of the conference was the fiftieth anniversary of the publication of F53. Prior to the conference, in January 2003, there was a panel session on F53 at the ASSA meetings in Washington, DC, organized by Thomas Mayer. Milton Friedman was connected to the panel via a telephone connection – he had an opportunity to comment on our ideas and to reply to our questions. Papers originating from that panel were subsequently published in the *Journal of Economic Methodology* later that year. The Erasmus conference was an ambitious expansion of that panel.

Papers for the conference were commissioned from what was close to the best possible team of scholars on the theme. They were asked to highlight a number of well-circumscribed issues that are contained in F53 or that F53 has given rise to. The assignment given to the contributors was broad and simple. They were asked to put themselves in the shoes of a twenty-first-century reader wishing to check by himself or herself what to make of F53: in the light of (1) the text of the essay, (2) the historical and intellectual context of the essay, and (3) the later developments of economics and its methodology – what is the twenty-first-century reader advised to think of the contents of F53 and their descriptive and prescriptive adequacy? The assignment was indeed broad, but each contributor was invited to approach it from a separate limited angle. Taken together, the responses, reported in the chapters of the present book, provide a rather comprehensive account of F53 for the twenty-first-century reader.

The harvest is no doubt thus far the most ambitious collective attempt to examine and assess F53 in its various contexts. The flow of commentaries, criticisms, utilizations, and debates over the credentials of F53 has continued for half a century now. I dare claim that the volume you're holding in your hands makes significant progress towards a deeper understanding of F53 and the difficult issues that it set out to address in the mid twentieth century and that economists and their critics keep arguing about half a century later.

I invited Milton Friedman to join us in Rotterdam, but at the age of 91, he was not eager to travel. Revealing his enduring interest in methodological issues, he did read the contributions and wrote a brief note that is included at the end of this volume. To my knowledge, this is the first time that he has publicly spelled out his views about what others have written about his essay, but unsurprisingly perhaps, he keeps his statement very general and polite (while in private correspondence and conversations, he has been active in reacting to various criticisms and suggestions in more substantive ways). He had decided to stick to his old private rule according to which he will let the essay live its own life. It remains a challenge to the rest of us to live our academic lives together with the methodological essay that he left behind. This is the challenge the current volume sets out to meet.

Special thanks go to Frank Hindriks, Caterina Marchionni, and Giorgos Papadopoulos for great help in preparing and running the conference, and to Samuli Pöyhönen for splendid assistance in preparing the volume.

We would also like to thank the University of Chicago Press for allowing us to reproduce F53 in its full and original form.

USKALI MÄKI

Part 1

The classical essay in twentieth-century economic methodology

The Methodology of Positive Economics*

IN HIS admirable book on *The Scope and Method of Political Economy* John Neville Keynes distinguishes among "a *positive science* . . . [,] a body of systematized knowledge concerning what is; a *normative* or *regulative science* . . . [,] a body of systematized knowledge discussing criteria of what ought to be . . . ; an *art* . . . [,] a system of rules for the attainment of a given end"; comments that "confusion between them is common and has been the source of many mischievous errors"; and urges the importance of "recognizing a distinct positive science of political economy."[1]

This paper is concerned primarily with certain methodological problems that arise in constructing the "distinct positive science" Keynes called for—in particular, the problem how to decide whether a suggested hypothesis or theory should be tentatively accepted as part of the "body of systematized knowledge concerning what is." But the confusion Keynes laments is still so rife and so much of a hindrance to the recognition that economics can be, and in part is, a positive science that it seems well to preface the main body of the paper with a few remarks about the relation between positive and normative economics.

I. THE RELATION BETWEEN POSITIVE AND NORMATIVE ECONOMICS

Confusion between positive and normative economics is to some extent inevitable. The subject matter of economics is regarded by almost everyone as vitally important to himself and within the range of his own experience and competence; it is

* I have incorporated bodily in this article without special reference most of my brief "Comment" in *A Survey of Contemporary Economics,* Vol. II (B. F. Haley, ed.) (Chicago: Richard D. Irwin, Inc., 1952), pp. 455–57.

I am indebted to Dorothy S. Brady, Arthur F. Burns, and George J. Stigler for helpful comments and criticism.

1. (London: Macmillan & Co., 1891), pp. 34–35 and 46.

the source of continuous and extensive controversy and the occasion for frequent legislation. Self-proclaimed "experts" speak with many voices and can hardly all be regarded as disinterested; in any event, on questions that matter so much, "expert" opinion could hardly be accepted solely on faith even if the "experts" were nearly unanimous and clearly disinterested.[2] The conclusions of positive economics seem to be, and are, immediately relevant to important normative problems, to questions of what ought to be done and how any given goal can be attained. Laymen and experts alike are inevitably tempted to shape positive conclusions to fit strongly held normative preconceptions and to reject positive conclusions if their normative implications—or what are said to be their normative implications—are unpalatable.

Positive economics is in principle independent of any particular ethical position or normative judgments. As Keynes says, it deals with "what is," not with "what ought to be." Its task is to provide a system of generalizations that can be used to make correct predictions about the consequences of any change in circumstances. Its performance is to be judged by the precision, scope, and conformity with experience of the predictions it yields. In short, positive economics is, or can be, an "objective" science, in precisely the same sense as any of the physical sciences. Of course, the fact that economics deals with the interrelations of human beings, and that the investigator is himself part of the subject matter being investigated in a more intimate sense than in the physical sciences, raises special difficulties in achieving objectivity at the same time that it provides the social scientist with a class of data not available to the physical sci-

2. Social science or economics is by no means peculiar in this respect—witness the importance of personal beliefs and of "home" remedies in medicine wherever obviously convincing evidence for "expert" opinion is lacking. The current prestige and acceptance of the views of physical scientists in their fields of specialization—and, all too often, in other fields as well—derives, not from faith alone, but from the evidence of their works, the success of their predictions, and the dramatic achievements from applying their results. When economics seemed to provide such evidence of its worth, in Great Britain in the first half of the nineteenth century, the prestige and acceptance of "scientific economics" rivaled the current prestige of the physical sciences.

entist. But neither the one nor the other is, in my view, a fundamental distinction between the two groups of sciences.[3]

Normative economics and the art of economics, on the other hand, cannot be independent of positive economics. Any policy conclusion necessarily rests on a prediction about the consequences of doing one thing rather than another, a prediction that must be based—implicitly or explicitly—on positive economics. There is not, of course, a one-to-one relation between policy conclusions and the conclusions of positive economics; if there were, there would be no separate normative science. Two individuals may agree on the consequences of a particular piece of legislation. One may regard them as desirable on balance and so favor the legislation; the other, as undesirable and so oppose the legislation.

I venture the judgment, however, that currently in the Western world, and especially in the United States, differences about economic policy among disinterested citizens derive predominantly from different predictions about the economic consequences of taking action—differences that in principle can be eliminated by the progress of positive economics—rather than from fundamental differences in basic values, differences about which men can ultimately only fight. An obvious and not unimportant example is minimum-wage legislation. Underneath the welter of arguments offered for and against such legislation there is an underlying consensus on the objective of achieving a "living wage" for all, to use the ambiguous phrase so common in such discussions. The difference of opinion is largely grounded on an implicit or explicit difference in predictions about the efficacy of this particular means in furthering the agreed-on end. Proponents believe (predict) that legal minimum wages diminish poverty by raising the wages of those receiving less than the minimum wage as well as of some receiving more than the

3. The interaction between the observer and the process observed that is so prominent a feature of the social sciences, besides its more obvious parallel in the physical sciences, has a more subtle counterpart in the indeterminacy principle arising out of the interaction between the process of measurement and the phenomena being measured. And both have a counterpart in pure logic in Gödel's theorem, asserting the impossibility of a comprehensive self-contained logic. It is an open question whether all three can be regarded as different formulations of an even more general principle.

minimum wage without any counterbalancing increase in the number of people entirely unemployed or employed less advantageously than they otherwise would be. Opponents believe (predict) that legal minimum wages increase poverty by increasing the number of people who are unemployed or employed less advantageously and that this more than offsets any favorable effect on the wages of those who remain employed. Agreement about the economic consequences of the legislation might not produce complete agreement about its desirability, for differences might still remain about its political or social consequences; but, given agreement on objectives, it would certainly go a long way toward producing consensus.

Closely related differences in positive analysis underlie divergent views about the appropriate role and place of trade-unions and the desirability of direct price and wage controls and of tariffs. Different predictions about the importance of so-called "economies of scale" account very largely for divergent views about the desirability or necessity of detailed government regulation of industry and even of socialism rather than private enterprise. And this list could be extended indefinitely.[4] Of course, my judgment that the major differences about economic policy in the Western world are of this kind is itself a "positive" statement to be accepted or rejected on the basis of empirical evidence.

If this judgment is valid, it means that a consensus on "correct" economic policy depends much less on the progress of normative economics proper than on the progress of a positive economics yielding conclusions that are, and deserve to be, widely accepted. It means also that a major reason for dis-

4. One rather more complex example is stabilization policy. Superficially, divergent views on this question seem to reflect differences in objectives; but I believe that this impression is misleading and that at bottom the different views reflect primarily different judgments about the source of fluctuations in economic activity and the effect of alternative countercyclical action. For one major positive consideration that accounts for much of the divergence see "The Effects of a Full-Employment Policy on Economic Stability: A Formal Analysis," *infra*, pp. 117–32. For a summary of the present state of professional views on this question see "The Problem of Economic Instability," a report of a subcommittee of the Committee on Public Issues of the American Economic Association, *American Economic Review*, XL (September, 1950), 501–38.

tinguishing positive economics sharply from normative economics is precisely the contribution that can thereby be made to agreement about policy.

II. Positive Economics

The ultimate goal of a positive science is the development of a "theory" or "hypothesis" that yields valid and meaningful (i.e., not truistic) predictions about phenomena not yet observed. Such a theory is, in general, a complex intermixture of two elements. In part, it is a "language" designed to promote "systematic and organized methods of reasoning."[5] In part, it is a body of substantive hypotheses designed to abstract essential features of complex reality.

Viewed as a language, theory has no substantive content; it is a set of tautologies. Its function is to serve as a filing system for organizing empirical material and facilitating our understanding of it; and the criteria by which it is to be judged are those appropriate to a filing system. Are the categories clearly and precisely defined? Are they exhaustive? Do we know where to file each individual item, or is there considerable ambiguity? Is the system of headings and subheadings so designed that we can quickly find an item we want, or must we hunt from place to place? Are the items we shall want to consider jointly filed together? Does the filing system avoid elaborate cross-references?

The answers to these questions depend partly on logical, partly on factual, considerations. The canons of formal logic alone can show whether a particular language is complete and consistent, that is, whether propositions in the language are "right" or "wrong." Factual evidence alone can show whether the categories of the "analytical filing system" have a meaningful empirical counterpart, that is, whether they are useful in analyzing a particular class of concrete problems.[6] The simple example of "supply" and "demand" illustrates both this point and the pre-

5. Final quoted phrase from Alfred Marshall, "The Present Position of Economics" (1885), reprinted in *Memorials of Alfred Marshall,* ed. A. C. Pigou (London: Macmillan & Co., 1925), p. 164. See also "The Marshallian Demand Curve," *infra,* pp. 56–57, 90–91.

6. See "Lange on Price Flexibility and Employment: A Methodological Criticism," *infra,* pp. 282–89.

ceding list of analogical questions. Viewed as elements of the language of economic theory, these are the two major categories into which factors affecting the relative prices of products or factors of production are classified. The usefulness of the dichotomy depends on the "empirical generalization that an enumeration of the forces affecting demand in any problem and of the forces affecting supply will yield two lists that contain few items in common."[7] Now this generalization is valid for markets like the final market for a consumer good. In such a market there is a clear and sharp distinction between the economic units that can be regarded as demanding the product and those that can be regarded as supplying it. There is seldom much doubt whether a particular factor should be classified as affecting supply, on the one hand, or demand, on the other; and there is seldom much necessity for considering cross-effects (cross-references) between the two categories. In these cases the simple and even obvious step of filing the relevant factors under the headings of "supply" and "demand" effects a great simplification of the problem and is an effective safeguard against fallacies that otherwise tend to occur. But the generalization is not always valid. For example, it is not valid for the day-to-day fluctuations of prices in a primarily speculative market. Is a rumor of an increased excess-profits tax, for example, to be regarded as a factor operating primarily on today's supply of corporate equities in the stock market or on today's demand for them? In similar fashion, almost every factor can with about as much justification be classified under the heading "supply" as under the heading "demand." These concepts can still be used and may not be entirely pointless; they are still "right" but clearly less useful than in the first example because they have no meaningful empirical counterpart.

Viewed as a body of substantive hypotheses, theory is to be judged by its predictive power for the class of phenomena which it is intended to "explain." Only factual evidence can show whether it is "right" or "wrong" or, better, tentatively "accepted" as valid or "rejected." As I shall argue at greater length below, the only relevant test of the *validity* of a hypothesis is

7. "The Marshallian Demand Curve," *infra*, p. 57.

comparison of its predictions with experience. The hypothesis is rejected if its predictions are contradicted ("frequently" or more often than predictions from an alternative hypothesis); it is accepted if its predictions are not contradicted; great confidence is attached to it if it has survived many opportunities for contradiction. Factual evidence can never "prove" a hypothesis; it can only fail to disprove it, which is what we generally mean when we say, somewhat inexactly, that the hypothesis has been "confirmed" by experience.

To avoid confusion, it should perhaps be noted explicitly that the "predictions" by which the validity of a hypothesis is tested need not be about phenomena that have not yet occurred, that is, need not be forecasts of future events; they may be about phenomena that have occurred but observations on which have not yet been made or are not known to the person making the prediction. For example, a hypothesis may imply that such and such must have happened in 1906, given some other known circumstances. If a search of the records reveals that such and such did happen, the prediction is confirmed; if it reveals that such and such did not happen, the prediction is contradicted.

The validity of a hypothesis in this sense is not by itself a sufficient criterion for choosing among alternative hypotheses. Observed facts are necessarily finite in number; possible hypotheses, infinite. If there is one hypothesis that is consistant with the available evidence, there are always an infinite number that are.[8] For example, suppose a specific excise tax on a particular commodity produces a rise in price equal to the amount of the tax. This is consistent with competitive conditions, a stable demand curve, and a horizontal and stable supply curve. But it is also consistent with competitive conditions and a positively or negatively sloping supply curve with the required compensating shift in the demand curve or the supply curve; with monopolistic conditions, constant marginal costs, and stable demand curve, of the particular shape required to produce this result; and so on indefinitely. Additional evidence with which the

8. The qualification is necessary because the "evidence" may be internally contradictory, so there may be no hypothesis consistent with it. See also "Lange on Price Flexibility and Employment," *infra,* pp. 282–83.

hypothesis is to be consistent may rule out some of these possibilities; it can never reduce them to a single possibility alone capable of being consistent with the finite evidence. The choice among alternative hypotheses equally consistent with the available evidence must to some extent be arbitrary, though there is general agreement that relevant considerations are suggested by the criteria "simplicity" and "fruitfulness," themselves notions that defy completely objective specification. A theory is "simpler" the less the initial knowledge needed to make a prediction within a given field of phenomena; it is more "fruitful" the more precise the resulting prediction, the wider the area within which the theory yields predictions, and the more additional lines for further research it suggests. Logical completeness and consistency are relevant but play a subsidiary role; their function is to assure that the hypothesis says what it is intended to say and does so alike for all users—they play the same role here as checks for arithmetical accuracy do in statistical computations.

Unfortunately, we can seldom test particular predictions in the social sciences by experiments explicitly designed to eliminate what are judged to be the most important disturbing influences. Generally, we must rely on evidence cast up by the "experiments" that happen to occur. The inability to conduct so-called "controlled experiments" does not, in my view, reflect a basic difference between the social and physical sciences both because it is not peculiar to the social sciences—witness astronomy— and because the distinction between a controlled experiment and uncontrolled experience is at best one of degree. No experiment can be completely controlled, and every experience is partly controlled, in the sense that some disturbing influences are relatively constant in the course of it.

Evidence cast up by experience is abundant and frequently as conclusive as that from contrived experiments; thus the inability to conduct experiments is not a fundamental obstacle to testing hypotheses by the success of their predictions. But such evidence is far more difficult to interpret. It is frequently complex and always indirect and incomplete. Its collection is often arduous, and its interpretation generally requires subtle analysis and involved chains of reasoning, which seldom carry real conviction. The denial to economics of the dramatic and direct evidence of the "crucial" experiment does hinder the adequate testing of hypotheses; but this is much less significant than the difficulty it places in the way of achieving a reasonably prompt and wide consensus on the conclusions justified by the available evidence. It renders the weeding-out of unsuccessful hypotheses slow and difficult. They are seldom downed for good and are always cropping up again.

There is, of course, considerable variation in these respects. Occasionally, experience casts up evidence that is about as direct, dramatic, and convincing as any that could be provided by controlled experiments. Perhaps the most obviously important example is the evidence from inflations on the hypothesis that a substantial increase in the quantity of money within a relatively short period is accompanied by a substantial increase in prices. Here the evidence is dramatic, and the chain of reasoning required to interpret it is relatively short. Yet, despite numerous instances of substantial rises in prices, their essentially one-to-one correspondence with substantial rises in the stock of money, and the wide variation in other circumstances that might appear to be relevant, each new experience of inflation brings forth vigorous contentions, and not only by the lay public, that the rise in the stock of money is either an incidental effect of a rise in prices produced by other factors or a purely fortuitous and unnecessary concomitant of the price rise.

One effect of the difficulty of testing substantive economic hypotheses has been to foster a retreat into purely formal or tautological analysis.[9] As already noted, tautologies have an extremely important place in economics and other sciences as a specialized language or "analytical filing system." Beyond this, formal logic and mathematics, which are both tautologies, are essential aids in checking the correctness of reasoning, discovering the implications of hypotheses, and determining whether supposedly different hypotheses may not really be equivalent or wherein the differences lie.

But economic theory must be more than a structure of tautol-

9. See "Lange on Price Flexibility and Employment," *infra, passim.*

ogies if it is to be able to predict and not merely describe the consequences of action; if it is to be something different from disguised mathematics.[10] And the usefulness of the tautologies themselves ultimately depends, as noted above, on the acceptability of the substantive hypotheses that suggest the particular categories into which they organize the refractory empirical phenomena.

A more serious effect of the difficulty of testing economic hypotheses by their predictions is to foster misunderstanding of the role of empirical evidence in theoretical work. Empirical evidence is vital at two different, though closely related, stages: in constructing hypotheses and in testing their validity. Full and comprehensive evidence on the phenomena to be generalized or "explained" by a hypothesis, besides its obvious value in suggesting new hypotheses, is needed to assure that a hypothesis explains what it sets out to explain—that its implications for such phenomena are not contradicted in advance by experience that has already been observed.[11] Given that the hypothesis is

10. See also Milton Friedman and L. J. Savage, "The Expected-Utility Hypothesis and the Measurability of Utility," *Journal of Political Economy, LX* (December, 1952), 463–74, esp. pp. 465–67.

11. In recent years some economists, particularly a group connected with the Cowles Commission for Research in Economics at the University of Chicago, have placed great emphasis on a division of this step of selecting a hypothesis consistent with known evidence into two substeps: first, the selection of a class of admissible hypotheses from all possible hypotheses (the choice of a "model" in their terminology); second, the selection of one hypothesis from this class (the choice of a "structure"). This subdivision may be heuristically valuable in some kinds of work, particularly in promoting a systematic use of available statistical evidence and theory. From a methodological point of view, however, it is an entirely arbitrary subdivision of the process of deciding on a particular hypothesis that is on a par with many other subdivisions that may be convenient for one purpose or another or that may suit the psychological needs of particular investigators.

One consequence of this particular subdivision has been to give rise to the so-called "identification" problem. As noted above, if one hypothesis is consistent with available evidence, an infinite number are. But, while this is true for the class of hypotheses as a whole, it may not be true of the subclass obtained in the first of the above two steps—the "model." It may be that the evidence to be used to select the final hypothesis from the subclass can be consistent with at most one hypothesis in it, in which case the "model" is said to be "identified"; otherwise it is said to be "unidentified." As is clear from this way of describing the concept of "identification," it is essentially a special case of the more general

consistent with the evidence at hand, its further testing involves deducing from it new facts capable of being observed but not previously known and checking these deduced facts against additional empirical evidence. For this test to be relevant, the deduced facts must be about the class of phenomena the hypothesis is designed to explain; and they must be well enough defined so that observation can show them to be wrong.

The two stages of constructing hypotheses and testing their validity are related in two different respects. In the first place, the particular facts that enter at each stage are partly an accident of the collection of data and the knowledge of the particular investigator. The facts that serve as a test of the implications of a hypothesis might equally well have been among the raw material used to construct it, and conversely. In the second place, the process never begins from scratch; the so-called "initial stage" itself always involves comparison of the implications of an earlier set of hypotheses with observation; the contradiction of these implications is the stimulus to the construction of new

---

problem of selecting among the alternative hypotheses equally consistent with the evidence—a problem that must be decided by some such arbitrary principle as Occam's razor. The introduction of two substeps in selecting a hypothesis makes this problem arise at the two corresponding stages and gives it a special cast. While the class of all hypotheses is always unidentified, the subclass in a "model" need not be, so the problem arises of conditions that a "model" must satisfy to be identified. However useful the two substeps may be in some contexts, their introduction raises the danger that different criteria will unwittingly be used in making the same kind of choice among alternative hypotheses at two different stages.

On the general methodological approach discussed in this footnote see Tryvge Haavelmo, "The Probability Approach in Econometrics," *Econometrica*, Vol. XII (1944), Supplement; Jacob Marschak, "Economic Structure, Path, Policy, and Prediction," *American Economic Review*, XXXVII (May, 1947), 81–84, and "Statistical Inference in Economics: An Introduction," in T. C. Koopmans (ed.), *Statistical Inference in Dynamic Economic Models* (New York: John Wiley & Sons, 1950); T. C. Koopmans, "Statistical Estimation of Simultaneous Economic Relations," *Journal of the American Statistical Association*, XL (December, 1945), 448–66; Gershon Cooper, "The Role of Economic Theory in Econometric Models," *Journal of Farm Economics*, XXX (February, 1948), 101–16. On the identification problem see Koopmans, "Identification Problems in Econometric Model Construction," *Econometrica*, XVII (April, 1949), 125–44; Leonid Hurwicz, "Generalization of the Concept of Identification," in Koopmans (ed.), *Statistical Inference in Dynamic Economic Models*.

hypotheses or revision of old ones. So the two methodologically distinct stages are always proceeding jointly.

Misunderstanding about this apparently straightforward process centers on the phrase "the class of phenomena the hypothesis is designed to explain." The difficulty in the social sciences of getting new evidence for this class of phenomena and of judging its conformity with the implications of the hypothesis makes it tempting to suppose that other, more readily available, evidence is equally relevant to the validity of the hypothesis—to suppose that hypotheses have not only "implications" but also "assumptions" and that the conformity of these "assumptions" to "reality" is a test of the validity of the hypothesis *different from* or *additional to* the test by implications. This widely held view is fundamentally wrong and productive of much mischief. Far from providing an easier means for sifting valid from invalid hypotheses, it only confuses the issue, promotes misunderstanding about the significance of empirical evidence for economic theory, produces a misdirection of much intellectual effort devoted to the development of positive economics, and impedes the attainment of consensus on tentative hypotheses in positive economics.

In so far as a theory can be said to have "assumptions" at all, and in so far as their "realism" can be judged independently of the validity of predictions, the relation between the significance of a theory and the "realism" of its "assumptions" is almost the opposite of that suggested by the view under criticism. Truly important and significant hypotheses will be found to have "assumptions" that are wildly inaccurate descriptive representations of reality, and, in general, the more significant the theory, the more unrealistic the assumptions (in this sense).[12] The reason is simple. A hypothesis is important if it "explains" much by little, that is, if it abstracts the common and crucial elements from the mass of complex and detailed circumstances surrounding the phenomena to be explained and permits valid predictions on the basis of them alone. To be important, therefore, a hypothesis must be descriptively false in its assumptions; it

12. The converse of the proposition does not of course hold: assumptions that are unrealistic (in this sense) do not guarantee a significant theory.

takes account of, and accounts for, none of the many other attendant circumstances, since its very success shows them to be irrelevant for the phenomena to be explained.

To put this point less paradoxically, the relevant question to ask about the "assumptions" of a theory is not whether they are descriptively "realistic," for they never are, but whether they are sufficiently good approximations for the purpose in hand. And this question can be answered only by seeing whether the theory works, which means whether it yields sufficiently accurate predictions. The two supposedly independent tests thus reduce to one test.

The theory of monopolistic and imperfect competition is one example of the neglect in economic theory of these propositions. The development of this analysis was explicitly motivated, and its wide acceptance and approval largely explained, by the belief that the assumptions of "perfect competition" or "perfect monopoly" said to underlie neoclassical economic theory are a false image of reality. And this belief was itself based almost entirely on the directly perceived descriptive inaccuracy of the assumptions rather than on any recognized contradiction of predictions derived from neoclassical economic theory. The lengthy discussion on marginal analysis in the *American Economic Review* some years ago is an even clearer, though much less important, example. The articles on both sides of the controversy largely neglect what seems to me clearly the main issue—the conformity to experience of the implications of the marginal analysis—and concentrate on the largely irrelevant question whether businessmen do or do not in fact reach their decisions by consulting schedules, or curves, or multivariable functions showing marginal cost and marginal revenue.[13] Perhaps these

13. See R. A. Lester, "Shortcomings of Marginal Analysis for Wage-Employment Problems," *American Economic Review*, XXXVI (March, 1946), 62–82; Fritz Machlup, "Marginal Analysis and Empirical Research," *American Economic Review*, XXXVI (September, 1946), 519–54; R. A. Lester, "Marginalism, Minimum Wages, and Labor Markets," *American Economic Review*, XXXVII (March, 1947), 135–48; Fritz Machlup, "Rejoinder to an Antimarginalist," *American Economic Review*, XXXVII (March, 1947), 148–54; G. J. Stigler, "Professor Lester and the Marginalists," *American Economic Review*, XXXVII (March, 1947), 154–57; H. M. Oliver, Jr., "Marginal Theory and Business Behavior," *American Economic Review*, XXXVII (June, 1947), 375–83; R. A. Gordon,

two examples, and the many others they readily suggest, will serve to justify a more extensive discussion of the methodological principles involved than might otherwise seem appropriate.

III. CAN A HYPOTHESIS BE TESTED BY THE REALISM OF ITS ASSUMPTIONS?

We may start with a simple physical example, the law of falling bodies. It is an accepted hypothesis that the acceleration of a body dropped in a vacuum is a constant—g, or approximately 32 feet per second per second on the earth—and is independent of the shape of the body, the manner of dropping it, etc. This implies that the distance traveled by a falling body in any specified time is given by the formula $s = \frac{1}{2} gt^2$, where s is the distance traveled in feet and t is time in seconds. The application of this formula to a compact ball dropped from the roof of a building is equivalent to saying that a ball so dropped behaves *as if* it were falling in a vacuum. Testing this hypothesis by its assumptions presumably means measuring the actual air pressure and deciding whether it is close enough to zero. At sea level the air pressure is about 15 pounds per square inch. Is 15 sufficiently close to zero for the difference to be judged insignificant? Apparently it is, since the actual time taken by a compact ball to fall from the roof of a building to the ground is very close to the time given by the formula. Suppose, however, that a feather is

---

"Short-Period Price Determination in Theory and Practice," *American Economic Review*, XXXVIII (June, 1948), 265–88.

It should be noted that, along with much material purportedly bearing on the validity of the "assumptions" of marginal theory, Lester does refer to evidence on the conformity of experience with the implications of the theory, citing the reactions of employment in Germany to the Papen plan and in the United States to changes in minimum-wage legislation as examples of lack of conformity. However, Stigler's brief comment is the only one of the other papers that refers to this evidence. It should also be noted that Machlup's thorough and careful exposition of the logical structure and meaning of marginal analysis is called for by the misunderstandings on this score that mar Lester's paper and almost conceal the evidence he presents that is relevant to the key issue he raises. But, in Machlup's emphasis on the logical structure, he comes perilously close to presenting the theory as a pure tautology, though it is evident at a number of points that he is aware of this danger and anxious to avoid it. The papers by Oliver and Gordon are the most extreme in the exclusive concentration on the conformity of the behavior of businessmen with the "assumptions" of the theory.

dropped instead of a compact ball. The formula then gives wildly inaccurate results. Apparently, 15 pounds per square inch is significantly different from zero for a feather but not for a ball. Or, again, suppose the formula is applied to a ball dropped from an airplane at an altitude of 30,000 feet. The air pressure at this altitude is decidedly less than 15 pounds per square inch. Yet, the actual time of fall from 30,000 feet to 20,000 feet, at which point the air pressure is still much less than at sea level, will differ noticeably from the time predicted by the formula— much more noticeably than the time taken by a compact ball to fall from the roof of a building to the ground. According to the formula, the velocity of the ball should be gt and should therefore increase steadily. In fact, a ball dropped at 30,000 feet will reach its top velocity well before it hits the ground. And similarly with other implications of the formula.

The initial question whether 15 is sufficiently close to zero for the difference to be judged insignificant is clearly a foolish question by itself. Fifteen pounds per square inch is 2,160 pounds per square foot, or 0.0075 ton per square inch. There is no possible basis for calling these numbers "small" or "large" without some external standard of comparison. And the only relevant standard of comparison is the air pressure for which the formula does or does not work under a given set of circumstances. But this raises the same problem at a second level. What is the meaning of "does or does not work"? Even if we could eliminate errors of measurement, the measured time of fall would seldom if ever be precisely equal to the computed time of fall. How large must the difference between the two be to justify saying that the theory "does not work"? Here there are two important external standards of comparison. One is the accuracy achievable by an alternative theory with which this theory is being compared and which is equally acceptable on all other grounds. The other arises when there exists a theory that is known to yield better predictions but only at a greater cost. The gains from greater accuracy, which depend on the purpose in mind, must then be balanced against the costs of achieving it.

This example illustrates both the impossibility of testing a theory by its assumptions and also the ambiguity of the concept "the assumptions of a theory." The formula $s = \frac{1}{2} gt^2$ is valid for bodies falling in a vacuum and can be derived by analyzing the behavior of such bodies. It can therefore be stated: under a wide range of circumstances, bodies that fall in the actual atmosphere behave *as if* they were falling in a vacuum. In the language so common in economics this would be rapidly translated into: the formula assumes a vacuum. Yet it clearly does no such thing. What it does say is that in many cases the existence of air pressure, the shape of the body, the name of the person dropping the body, the kind of mechanism used to drop the body, and a host of other attendant circumstances have no appreciable effect on the distance the body falls in a specified time. The hypothesis can readily be rephrased to omit all mention of a vacuum: under a wide range of circumstances, the distance a body falls in a specified time is given by the formula $s = \frac{1}{2} gt^2$. The history of this formula and its associated physical theory aside, is it meaningful to say that it assumes a vacuum? For all I know there may be other sets of assumptions that would yield the same formula. The formula is accepted because it works, not because we live in an approximate vacuum—whatever that means.

The important problem in connection with the hypothesis is to specify the circumstances under which the formula works or, more precisely, the general magnitude of the error in its predictions under various circumstances. Indeed, as is implicit in the above rephrasing of the hypothesis, such a specification is not one thing and the hypothesis another. The specification is itself an essential part of the hypothesis, and it is a part that is peculiarly likely to be revised and extended as experience accumulates.

In the particular case of falling bodies a more general, though still incomplete, theory is available, largely as a result of attempts to explain the errors of the simple theory, from which the influence of some of the possible disturbing factors can be calculated and of which the simple theory is a special case. However, it does not always pay to use the more general theory because the extra accuracy it yields may not justify the extra cost of using it, so the question under what circumstances the simpler theory works "well enough" remains important. Air pressure is one, but only one, of the variables that define these circumstances; the shape of the body, the velocity attained, and still other variables are relevant as well. One way of interpreting the variables other than air pressure is to regard them as determining whether a particular departure from the "assumption" of a vacuum is or is not significant. For example, the difference in shape of the body can be said to make 15 pounds per square inch significantly different from zero for a feather but not for a compact ball dropped a moderate distance. Such a statement must, however, be sharply distinguished from the very different statement that the theory does not work for a feather because its assumptions are false. The relevant relation runs the other way: the assumptions are false for a feather because the theory does not work. This point needs emphasis, because the entirely valid use of "assumptions" in *specifying* the circumstances for which a theory holds is frequently, and erroneously, interpreted to mean that the assumptions can be used to *determine* the circumstances for which a theory holds, and has, in this way, been an important source of the belief that a theory can be tested by its assumptions.

Let us turn now to another example, this time a constructed one designed to be an analogue of many hypotheses in the social sciences. Consider the density of leaves around a tree. I suggest the hypothesis that the leaves are positioned as if each leaf deliberately sought to maximize the amount of sunlight it receives, given the position of its neighbors, as if it knew the physical laws determining the amount of sunlight that would be received in various positions and could move rapidly or instantaneously from any one position to any other desired and unoccupied position.[14] Now some of the more obvious implications of this hypothesis are clearly consistent with experience: for example, leaves are in general denser on the south than on the north side of trees but, as the hypothesis implies, less so or not at all on the northern

14. This example, and some of the subsequent discussion, though independent in origin, is similar to and in much the same spirit as an example and the approach in an important paper by Armen A. Alchian, "Uncertainty, Evolution, and Economic Theory," *Journal of Political Economy*, LVIII (June, 1950), 211–21.

slope of a hill or when the south side of the trees is shaded in some other way. Is the hypothesis rendered unacceptable or invalid because, so far as we know, leaves do not "deliberate" or consciously "seek," have not been to school and learned the relevant laws of science or the mathematics required to calculate the "optimum" position, and cannot move from position to position? Clearly, none of these contradictions of the hypothesis is vitally relevant; the phenomena involved are not within the "class of phenomena the hypothesis is designed to explain"; the hypothesis does not assert that leaves do these things but only that their density is the same *as if* they did. Despite the apparent falsity of the "assumptions" of the hypothesis, it has great plausibility because of the conformity of its implications with observation. We are inclined to "explain" its validity on the ground that sunlight contributes to the growth of leaves and that hence leaves will grow denser or more putative leaves survive where there is more sun, so the result achieved by purely passive adaptation to external circumstances is the same as the result that would be achieved by deliberate accommodation to them. This alternative hypothesis is more attractive than the constructed hypothesis not because its "assumptions" are more "realistic" but rather because it is part of a more general theory that applies to a wider variety of phenomena, of which the position of leaves around a tree is a special case, has more implications capable of being contradicted, and has failed to be contradicted under a wider variety of circumstances. The direct evidence for the growth of leaves is in this way strengthened by the indirect evidence from the other phenomena to which the more general theory applies.

The constructed hypothesis is presumably valid, that is, yields "sufficiently" accurate predictions about the density of leaves, only for a particular class of circumstances. I do not know what these circumstances are or how to define them. It seems obvious, however, that in this example the "assumptions" of the theory will play no part in specifying them: the kind of tree, the character of the soil, etc., are the types of variables that are likely to define its range of validity, not the ability of the leaves to do complicated mathematics or to move from place to place.

A largely parallel example involving human behavior has been used elsewhere by Savage and me.[15] Consider the problem of predicting the shots made by an expert billiard player. It seems not at all unreasonable that excellent predictions would be yielded by the hypothesis that the billiard player made his shots *as if* he knew the complicated mathematical formulas that would give the optimum directions of travel, could estimate accurately by eye the angles, etc., describing the location of the balls, could make lightning calculations from the formulas, and could then make the balls travel in the direction indicated by the formulas. Our confidence in this hypothesis is not based on the belief that billiard players, even expert ones, can or do go through the process described; it derives rather from the belief that, unless in some way or other they were capable of reaching essentially the same result, they would not in fact be *expert* billiard players.

It is only a short step from these examples to the economic hypothesis that under a wide range of circumstances individual firms behave *as if* they were seeking rationally to maximize their expected returns (generally if misleadingly called "profits")[16] and had full knowledge of the data needed to succeed in this attempt; *as if*, that is, they knew the relevant cost and demand functions,

15. Milton Friedman and L. .J. Savage, "The Utility Analysis of Choices Involving Risk," *Journal of Political Economy,* LVI (August, 1948), 298. Reprinted in American Economic Association, *Readings in Price Theory* (Chicago: Richard D. Irwin, Inc., 1952), pp. 57–96.

16. It seems better to use the term "profits" to refer to the difference between actual and "expected" results, between *ex post* and *ex ante* receipts. "Profits" are then a result of uncertainty and, as Alchian (*op. cit.,* p. 212), following Tintner, points out, cannot be deliberately maximized in advance. Given uncertainty, individuals or firms choose among alternative anticipated probability distributions of receipts or incomes. The specific content of a theory of choice among such distributions depends on the criteria by which they are supposed to be ranked. One hypothesis supposes them to be ranked by the mathematical expectation of utility corresponding to them (see Friedman and Savage, "The Expected-Utility Hypothesis and the Measurability of Utility," *op. cit.*). A special case of this hypothesis or an alternative to it ranks probability distributions by the mathematical expectation of the money receipts corresponding to them. The latter is perhaps more applicable, and more frequently applied, to firms than to individuals. The term "expected returns" is intended to be sufficiently broad to apply to any of these alternatives.

The issues alluded to in this note are not basic to the methodological issues being discussed, and so are largely by-passed in the discussion that follows.

calculated marginal cost and marginal revenue from all actions open to them, and pushed each line of action to the point at which the relevant marginal cost and marginal revenue were equal. Now, of course, businessmen do not actually and literally solve the system of simultaneous equations in terms of which the mathematical economist finds it convenient to express this hypothesis, any more than leaves or billiard players explicitly go through complicated mathematical calculations or falling bodies decide to create a vacuum. The billiard player, if asked how he decides where to hit the ball, may say that he "just figures it out" but then also rubs a rabbit's foot just to make sure; and the businessman may well say that he prices at average cost, with of course some minor deviations when the market makes it necessary. The one statement is about as helpful as the other, and neither is a relevant test of the associated hypothesis.

Confidence in the maximization-of-returns hypothesis is justified by evidence of a very different character. This evidence is in part similar to that adduced on behalf of the billiard-player hypothesis—unless the behavior of businessmen in some way or other approximated behavior consistent with the maximization of returns, it seems unlikely that they would remain in business for long. Let the apparent immediate determinant of business behavior be anything at all—habitual reaction, random chance, or whatnot. Whenever this determinant happens to lead to behavior consistent with rational and informed maximization of returns, the business will prosper and acquire resources with which to expand; whenever it does not, the business will tend to lose resources and can be kept in existence only by the addition of resources from outside. The process of "natural selection" thus helps to validate the hypothesis—or, rather, given natural selection, acceptance of the hypothesis can be based largely on the judgment that it summarizes appropriately the conditions for survival.

An even more important body of evidence for the maximization-of-returns hypothesis is experience from countless applications of the hypothesis to specific problems and the repeated failure of its implications to be contradicted. This evidence is extremely hard to document; it is scattered in numerous memorandums, articles, and monographs concerned primarily with specific concrete problems rather than with submitting the hypothesis to test. Yet the continued use and acceptance of the hypothesis over a long period, and the failure of any coherent, self-consistent alternative to be developed and be widely accepted, is strong indirect testimony to its worth. The evidence *for* a hypothesis always consists of its repeated failure to be contradicted, continues to accumulate so long as the hypothesis is used, and by its very nature is difficult to document at all comprehensively. It tends to become part of the tradition and folklore of a science revealed in the tenacity with which hypotheses are held rather than in any textbook list of instances in which the hypothesis has failed to be contradicted.

IV. THE SIGNIFICANCE AND ROLE OF THE "ASSUMPTIONS" OF A THEORY

Up to this point our conclusions about the significance of the "assumptions" of a theory have been almost entirely negative: we have seen that a theory cannot be tested by the "realism" of its "assumptions" and that the very concept of the "assumptions" of a theory is surrounded with ambiguity. But, if this were all there is to it, it would be hard to explain the extensive use of the concept and the strong tendency that we all have to speak of the assumptions of a theory and to compare the assumptions of alternative theories. There is too much smoke for there to be no fire.

In methodology, as in positive science, negative statements can generally be made with greater confidence than positive statements, so I have less confidence in the following remarks on the significance and role of "assumptions" than in the preceding remarks. So far as I can see, the "assumptions of a theory" play three different, though related, positive roles: (*a*) they are often an economical mode of describing or presenting a theory; (*b*) they sometimes facilitate an indirect test of the hypothesis by its implications; and (*c*), as already noted, they are sometimes a convenient means of specifying the conditions under which the theory is expected to be valid. The first two require more extensive discussion.

A. THE USE OF "ASSUMPTIONS" IN STATING A THEORY

The example of the leaves illustrates the first role of assumptions. Instead of saying that leaves seek to maximize the sunlight they receive, we could state the equivalent hypothesis, without any apparent assumptions, in the form of a list of rules for predicting the density of leaves: if a tree stands in a level field with no other trees or other bodies obstructing the rays of the sun, then the density of leaves will tend to be such and such; if a tree is on the northern slope of a hill in the midst of a forest of similar trees, then . . . ; etc. This is clearly a far less economical presentation of the hypothesis than the statement that leaves seek to maximize the sunlight each receives. The latter statement is, in effect, a simple summary of the rules in the above list, even if the list were indefinitely extended, since it indicates both how to determine the features of the environment that are important for the particular problem and how to evaluate their effects. It is more compact and at the same time no less comprehensive.

More generally, a hypothesis or theory consists of an assertion that certain forces are, and by implication others are not, important for a particular class of phenomena and a specification of the manner of action of the forces it asserts to be important. We can regard the hypothesis as consisting of two parts: first, a conceptual world or abstract model simpler than the "real world" and containing only the forces that the hypothesis asserts to be important; second, a set of rules defining the class of phenomena for which the "model" can be taken to be an adequate representation of the "real world" and specifying the correspondence between the variables or entities in the model and observable phenomena.

These two parts are very different in character. The model is abstract and complete; it is an "algebra" or "logic." Mathematics and formal logic come into their own in checking its consistency and completeness and exploring its implications. There is no place in the model for, and no function to be served by, vagueness, maybe's, or approximations. The air pressure is zero, not "small," for a vacuum; the demand curve for the product of a competitive producer is horizontal (has a slope of zero), not "almost horizontal."

The rules for using the model, on the other hand, cannot possibly be abstract and complete. They must be concrete and in consequence incomplete—completeness is possible only in a conceptual world, not in the "real world," however that may be interpreted. The model is the logical embodiment of the half-truth, "There is nothing new under the sun"; the rules for applying it cannot neglect the equally significant half-truth, "History never repeats itself." To a considerable extent the rules can be formulated explicitly—most easily, though even then not completely, when the theory is part of an explicit more general theory as in the example of the vacuum theory for falling bodies. In seeking to make a science as "objective" as possible, our aim should be to formulate the rules explicitly in so far as possible and continually to widen the range of phenomena for which it is possible to do so. But, no matter how successful we may be in this attempt, there inevitably will remain room for judgment in applying the rules. Each occurrence has some features peculiarly its own, not covered by the explicit rules. The capacity to judge that these are or are not to be disregarded, that they should or should not affect what observable phenomena are to be identified with what entities in the model, is something that cannot be taught; it can be learned but only by experience and exposure in the "right" scientific atmosphere, not by rote. It is at this point that the "amateur" is separated from the "professional" in all sciences and that the thin line is drawn which distinguishes the "crackpot" from the scientist.

A simple example may perhaps clarify this point. Euclidean geometry is an abstract model, logically complete and consistent. Its entities are precisely defined—a line is not a geometrical figure "much" longer than it is wide or deep; it is a figure whose width and depth are zero. It is also obviously "unrealistic." There are no such things in "reality" as Euclidean points or lines or surfaces. Let us apply this abstract model to a mark made on a blackboard by a piece of chalk. Is the mark to be identified with a Euclidean line, a Euclidean surface, or a Euclidean solid?

Clearly, it can appropriately be identified with a line if it is being used to represent, say, a demand curve. But it cannot be so identified if it is being used to color, say, countries on a map, for that would imply that the map would never be colored; for this purpose, the same mark must be identified with a surface. But it cannot be so identified by a manufacturer of chalk, for that would imply that no chalk would ever be used up; for his purposes, the same mark must be identified with a volume. In this simple example these judgments will command general agreement. Yet it seems obvious that, while general considerations can be formulated to guide such judgments, they can never be comprehensive and cover every possible instance; they cannot have the self-contained coherent character of Euclidean geometry itself.

In speaking of the "crucial assumptions" of a theory, we are, I believe, trying to state the key elements of the abstract model. There are generally many different ways of describing the model completely—many different sets of "postulates" which both imply and are implied by the model as a whole. These are all logically equivalent: what are regarded as axioms or postulates of a model from one point of view can be regarded as theorems from another, and conversely. The particular "assumptions" termed "crucial" are selected on grounds of their convenience in some such respects as simplicity or economy in describing the model, intuitive plausibility, or capacity to suggest, if only by implication, some of the considerations that are relevant in judging or applying the model.

B. THE USE OF "ASSUMPTIONS" AS AN
INDIRECT TEST OF A THEORY

In presenting any hypothesis, it generally seems obvious which of the series of statements used to expound it refer to assumptions and which to implications; yet this distinction is not easy to define rigorously. It is not, I believe, a characteristic of the hypothesis as such but rather of the use to which the hypothesis is to be put. If this is so, the ease of classifying statements must reflect unambiguousness in the purpose the hypothesis is designed to serve. The possibility of interchanging theorems and axioms in an abstract model implies the possibility of interchanging "implications" and "assumptions" in the substantive hypothesis corresponding to the abstract model, which is not to say that any implication can be interchanged with any assumption but only that there may be more than one set of statements that imply the rest.

For example, consider a particular proposition in the theory of oligopolistic behavior. If we assume (a) that entrepreneurs seek to maximize their returns by any means including acquiring or extending monopoly power, this will imply (b) that, when demand for a "product" is geographically unstable, transportation costs are significant, explicit price agreements illegal, and the number of producers of the product relatively small, they will tend to establish basing-point pricing systems.[17] The assertion (a) is regarded as an assumption and (b) as an implication because we accept the prediction of market behavior as the purpose of the analysis. We shall regard the assumption as acceptable if we find that the conditions specified in (b) are generally associated with basing-point pricing, and conversely. Let us now change our purpose to deciding what cases to prosecute under the Sherman Antitrust Law's prohibition of a "conspiracy in restraint of trade." If we now assume (c) that basing-point pricing is a deliberate construction to facilitate collusion under the conditions specified in (b), this will imply (d) that entrepreneurs who participate in basing-point pricing are engaged in a "conspiracy in restraint of trade." What was formerly an assumption now becomes an implication, and conversely. We shall now regard the assumption (c) as valid if we find that, when entrepreneurs participate in basing-point pricing, there generally tends to be other evidence, in the form of letters, memorandums, or the like, of what courts regard as a "conspiracy in restraint of trade."

Suppose the hypothesis works for the first purpose, namely, the prediction of market behavior. It clearly does not follow that it will work for the second purpose, namely, predicting whether there is enough evidence of a "conspiracy in restraint of trade"

17. See George J. Stigler, "A Theory of Delivered Price Systems," *American Economic Review*, XXXIX (December, 1949), 1143–57.

to justify court action. And, conversely, if it works for the second purpose, it does not follow that it will work for the first. Yet, in the absence of other evidence, the success of the hypothesis for one purpose—in explaining one class of phenomena—will give us greater confidence than we would otherwise have that it may succeed for another purpose—in explaining another class of phenomena. It is much harder to say how much greater confidence it justifies. For this depends on how closely related we judge the two classes of phenomena to be, which itself depends in a complex way on similar kinds of indirect evidence, that is, on our experience in other connections in explaining by single theories phenomena that are in some sense similarly diverse.

To state the point more generally, what are called the assumptions of a hypothesis can be used to get some indirect evidence on the acceptability of the hypothesis in so far as the assumptions can themselves be regarded as implications of the hypothesis, and hence their conformity with reality as a failure of some implications to be contradicted, or in so far as the assumptions may call to mind other implications of the hypothesis susceptible to casual empirical observation.[18] The reason this evidence is indirect is that the assumptions or associated implications generally refer to a class of phenomena different from the class which the hypothesis is designed to explain; indeed, as is implied above, this seems to be the chief criterion we use in deciding which statements to term "assumptions" and which to term "implications." The weight attached to this indirect evidence depends on how closely related we judge the two classes of phenomena to be.

Another way in which the "assumptions" of a hypothesis can facilitate its indirect testing is by bringing out its kinship with other hypotheses and thereby making the evidence on their validity relevant to the validity of the hypothesis in question. For example, a hypothesis is formulated for a particular class

18. See Friedman and Savage, "The Expected-Utility Hypothesis and the Measurability of Utility," *op. cit.*, pp. 466–67, for another specific example of this kind of indirect test.

of behavior. This hypothesis can, as usual, be stated without specifying any "assumptions." But suppose it can be shown that it is equivalent to a set of assumptions including the assumption that man seeks his own interest. The hypothesis then gains indirect plausibility from the success for other classes of phenomena of hypotheses that can also be said to make this assumption; at least, what is being done here is not completely unprecedented or unsuccessful in all other uses. In effect, the statement of assumptions so as to bring out a relationship between superficially different hypotheses is a step in the direction of a more general hypothesis.

This kind of indirect evidence from related hypotheses explains in large measure the difference in the confidence attached to a particular hypothesis by people with different backgrounds. Consider, for example, the hypothesis that the extent of racial or religious discrimination in employment in a particular area or industry is closely related to the degree of monopoly in the industry or area in question; that, if the industry is competitive, discrimination will be significant only if the race or religion of employees affects either the willingness of other employees to work with them or the acceptability of the product to customers and will be uncorrelated with the prejudices of employers.[19] This hypothesis is far more likely to appeal to an economist than to a sociologist. It can be said to "assume" single-minded pursuit of pecuniary self-interest by employers in competitive industries; and this "assumption" works well in a wide variety of hypotheses in economics bearing on many of the mass phenomena with which economics deals. It is therefore likely to seem reasonable to the economist that it may work in this case as well. On the other hand, the hypotheses to which the sociologist is accustomed have a very different kind of model or ideal world, in which single-minded pursuit of pecuniary self-interest plays a much less important role. The indirect evidence available to the sociologist on

19. A rigorous statement of this hypothesis would of course have to specify how "extent of racial or religious discrimination" and "degree of monopoly" are to be judged. The loose statement in the text is sufficient, however, for present purposes.

this hypothesis is much less favorable to it than the indirect evidence available to the economist; he is therefore likely to view it with greater suspicion.

Of course, neither the evidence of the economist nor that of the sociologist is conclusive. The decisive test is whether the hypothesis works for the phenomena it purports to explain. But a judgment may be required before any satisfactory test of this kind has been made, and, perhaps, when it cannot be made in the near future, in which case, the judgment will have to be based on the inadequate evidence available. In addition, even when such a test can be made, the background of the scientists is not irrelevant to the judgments they reach. There is never certainty in science, and the weight of evidence for or against a hypothesis can never be assessed completely "objectively." The economist will be more tolerant than the sociologist in judging conformity of the implications of the hypothesis with experience, and he will be persuaded to accept the hypothesis tentatively by fewer instances of "conformity."

V. Some Implications for Economic Issues

The abstract methodological issues we have been discussing have a direct bearing on the perennial criticism of "orthodox" economic theory as "unrealistic" as well as on the attempts that have been made to reformulate theory to meet this charge. Economics is a "dismal" science because it assumes man to be selfish and money-grubbing, "a lightning calculator of pleasures and pains, who oscillates like a homogeneous globule of desire of happiness under the impulse of stimuli that shift him about the area, but leave him intact";[20] it rests on outmoded psychology and must be reconstructed in line with each new development in psychology; it assumes men, or at least businessmen, to be "in a continuous state of 'alert,' ready to change prices and/or pricing rules whenever their sensitive intuitions . . . detect a change in demand and supply conditions";[21] it

20. Thorstein Veblen, "Why Is Economics Not an Evolutionary Science?" (1898), reprinted in *The Place of Science in Modern Civilization* (New York, 1919), p. 73.

21. Oliver, *op. cit.*, p. 381.

assumes markets to be perfect, competition to be pure, and commodities, labor, and capital to be homogeneous.

As we have seen, criticism of this type is largely beside the point unless supplemented by evidence that a hypothesis differing in one or another of these respects from the theory being criticized yields better predictions for as wide a range of phenomena. Yet most such criticism is not so supplemented; it is based almost entirely on supposedly directly perceived discrepancies between the "assumptions" and the "real world." A particularly clear example is furnished by the recent criticisms of the maximization-of-returns hypothesis on the grounds that businessmen do not and indeed cannot behave as the theory "assumes" they do. The evidence cited to support this assertion is generally taken either from the answers given by businessmen to questions about the factors affecting their decisions—a procedure for testing economic theories that is about on a par with testing theories of longevity by asking octogenarians how they account for their long life—or from descriptive studies of the decision-making activities of individual firms.[22] Little if any evidence is ever cited on the conformity of businessmen's actual market behavior—what they do rather than what they say they do—with the implications of the hypothesis being criticized, on the one hand, and of an alternative hypothesis, on the other.

22. See H. D. Henderson, "The Significance of the Rate of Interest," *Oxford Economic Papers,* No. 1 (October, 1938), pp. 1–13; J. E. Meade and P. W. S. Andrews, "Summary of Replies to Questions on Effects of Interest Rates," *Oxford Economic Papers,* No. 1 (October, 1938), pp. 14–31; R. F. Harrod, "Price and Cost in Entrepreneurs' Policy," *Oxford Economic Papers,* No. 2 (May, 1939), pp. 1–11; and R. J. Hall and C. J. Hitch, "Price Theory and Business Behavior," *Oxford Economic Papers,* No. 2 (May, 1939), pp. 12–45; Lester, "Shortcomings of Marginal Analysis for Wage-Employment Problems," *op. cit.*; Gordon, *op. cit.* See Fritz Machlup, "Marginal Analysis and Empirical Research," *op. cit.*, esp. Sec. II, for detailed criticisms of questionnaire methods.

I do not mean to imply that questionnaire studies of businessmen's or others' motives or beliefs about the forces affecting their behavior are useless for all purposes in economics. They may be extremely valuable in suggesting leads to follow in accounting for divergencies between predicted and observed results; that is, in constructing new hypotheses or revising old ones. Whatever their suggestive value in this respect, they seem to me almost entirely useless as a means of *testing* the validity of economic hypotheses. See my comment on Albert G. Hart's paper, "Liquidity and Uncertainty," *American Economic Review,* XXXIX (May, 1949), 198–99.

A theory or its "assumptions" cannot possibly be thoroughly "realistic" in the immediate descriptive sense so often assigned to this term. A completely "realistic" theory of the wheat market would have to include not only the conditions directly underlying the supply and demand for wheat but also the kind of coins or credit instruments used to make exchanges; the personal characteristics of wheat-traders such as the color of each trader's hair and eyes, his antecedents and education, the number of members of his family, their characteristics, antecedents, and education, etc.; the kind of soil on which the wheat was grown, its physical and chemical characteristics, the weather prevailing during the growing season; the personal characteristics of the farmers growing the wheat and of the consumers who will ultimately use it; and so on indefinitely. Any attempt to move very far in achieving this kind of "realism" is certain to render a theory utterly useless.

Of course, the notion of a completely realistic theory is in part a straw man. No critic of a theory would accept this logical extreme as his objective; he would say that the "assumptions" of the theory being criticized were "too" unrealistic and that his objective was a set of assumptions that were "more" realistic though still not completely and slavishly so. But so long as the test of "realism" is the directly perceived descriptive accuracy of the "assumptions"—for example, the observation that "businessmen do not appear to be either as avaricious or as dynamic or as logical as marginal theory portrays them"[23] or that "it would be utterly impractical under present conditions for the manager of a multi-process plant to attempt . . . to work out and equate marginal costs and marginal revenues for each productive factor"[24]—there is no basis for making such a distinction, that is, for stopping short of the straw man depicted in the preceding paragraph. What is the criterion by which to judge whether a particular departure from realism is or is not acceptable? Why is it more "unrealistic" in analyzing business behavior to neglect the magnitude of businessmen's costs than the

23. Oliver, *op. cit.*, p. 382.

24. Lester, "Shortcomings of Marginal Analysis for Wage-Employment Problems," *op. cit.*, p. 75.

color of their eyes? The obvious answer is because the first makes more difference to business behavior than the second; but there is no way of knowing that this is so simply by observing that businessmen do have costs of different magnitudes and eyes of different color. Clearly it can only be known by comparing the effect on the discrepancy between actual and predicted behavior of taking the one factor or the other into account. Even the most extreme proponents of realistic assumptions are thus necessarily driven to reject their own criterion and to accept the test by prediction when they classify alternative assumptions as more or less realistic.[25]

The basic confusion between descriptive accuracy and analytical relevance that underlies most criticisms of economic theory on the grounds that its assumptions are unrealistic as well as the plausibility of the views that lead to this confusion are both strikingly illustrated by a seemingly innocuous remark in an article on business-cycle theory that "economic phenomena are varied and complex, so any comprehensive theory of the business cycle that can apply closely to reality must be very complicated."[26] A fundamental hypothesis of science is that appearances are deceptive and that there is a way of looking at or interpreting or organizing the evidence that will reveal superficially disconnected and diverse phenomena to be manifestations of a more fundamental and relatively simple structure. And the test of this hypothesis, as of any other, is its fruits—a test that science has

25. E.g., Gordon's direct examination of the "assumptions" leads him to formulate the alternative hypothesis generally favored by the critics of the maximization-of-returns hypothesis as follows: "There is an irresistible tendency to price on the basis of average total costs for some 'normal' level of output. This is the yardstick, the short-cut, that businessmen and accountants use, and their aim is more to earn satisfactory profits and play safe than to maximize profits" (*op. cit.*, p. 275). Yet he essentially abandons this hypothesis, or converts it into a tautology, and in the process implicitly accepts the test by prediction when he later remarks: "Full cost and satisfactory profits may continue to be the objectives even when total costs are shaded to meet competition or exceeded to take advantage of a sellers' market" (*ibid.*, p. 284). Where here is the "irresistible tendency"? What kind of evidence could contradict this assertion?

26. Sidney S. Alexander, "Issues of Business Cycle Theory Raised by Mr. Hicks," *American Economic Review*, XLI (December, 1951), 872.

so far met with dramatic success. If a class of "economic phenomena" appears varied and complex, it is, we must suppose, because we have no adequate theory to explain them. Known facts cannot be set on one side; a theory to apply "closely to reality," on the other. A theory is the way we perceive "facts," and we cannot perceive "facts" without a theory. Any assertion that economic phenomena *are* varied and complex denies the tentative state of knowledge that alone makes scientific activity meaningful; it is in a class with John Stuart Mill's justly ridiculed statement that "happily, there is nothing in the laws of value which remains [1848] for the present or any future writer to clear up; the theory of the subject is complete."[27]

The confusion between descriptive accuracy and analytical relevance has led not only to criticisms of economic theory on largely irrelevant grounds but also to misunderstanding of economic theory and misdirection of efforts to repair supposed defects. "Ideal types" in the abstract model developed by economic theorists have been regarded as strictly descriptive categories intended to correspond directly and fully to entities in the real world independently of the purpose for which the model is being used. The obvious discrepancies have led to necessarily unsuccessful attempts to construct theories on the basis of categories intended to be fully descriptive.

This tendency is perhaps most clearly illustrated by the interpretation given to the concepts of "perfect competition" and "monopoly" and the development of the theory of "monopolistic" or "imperfect competition." Marshall, it is said, assumed "perfect competition"; perhaps there once was such a thing. But clearly there is no longer, and we must therefore discard his theories. The reader will search long and hard—and I predict unsuccessfully—to find in Marshall any explicit assumption about perfect competition or any assertion that in a descriptive sense the world is composed of atomistic firms engaged in perfect competition. Rather, he will find Marshall saying: "At one extreme are world markets in which competition acts directly from all parts of the globe; and at the other those secluded

27. *Principles of Political Economy* (Ashley ed.; Longmans, Green & Co., 1929), p. 436.

markets in which all direct competition from afar is shut out, though indirect and transmitted competition may make itself felt even in these; and about midway between these extremes lie the great majority of the markets which the economist and the business man have to study."[28] Marshall took the world as it is; he sought to construct an "engine" to analyze it, not a photographic reproduction of it.

In analyzing the world as it is, Marshall constructed the hypothesis that, for many problems, firms could be grouped into "industries" such that the similarities among the firms in each group were more important than the differences among them. These are problems in which the important element is that a group of firms is affected alike by some stimulus—a common change in the demand for their products, say, or in the supply of factors. But this will not do for all problems: the important element for these may be the differential effect on particular firms.

The abstract model corresponding to this hypothesis contains two "ideal" types of firms: atomistically competitive firms, grouped into industries, and monopolistic firms. A firm is competitive if the demand curve for its output is infinitely elastic with respect to its own price for some price and all outputs, given the prices charged by all other firms; it belongs to an "industry" defined as a group of firms producing a single "product." A "product" is defined as a collection of units that are perfect substitutes to purchasers so the elasticity of demand for the output of one firm with respect to the price of another firm in the same industry is infinite for some price and some outputs. A firm is monopolistic if the demand curve for its output is not infinitely elastic at some price for all outputs.[29] If it is a monopolist, the firm is the industry.[30]

As always, the hypothesis as a whole consists not only of this abstract model and its ideal types but also of a set of rules, mostly

28. *Principles,* p. 329; see also pp. 35, 100, 341, 347, 375, 546.

29. This ideal type can be divided into two types: the oligopolistic firm, if the demand curve for its output is infinitely elastic at some price for some but not all outputs; the monopolistic firm proper, if the demand curve is nowhere infinitely elastic (except possibly at an output of zero).

30. For the oligopolist of the preceding note an industry can be defined as a group of firms producing the same product.

implicit and suggested by example, for identifying actual firms with one or the other ideal type and for classifying firms into industries. The ideal types are not intended to be descriptive; they are designed to isolate the features that are crucial for a particular problem. Even if we could estimate directly and accurately the demand curve for a firm's product, we could not proceed immediately to classify the firm as perfectly competitive or monopolistic according as the elasticity of the demand curve is or is not infinite. No observed demand curve will ever be precisely horizontal, so the estimated elasticity will always be finite. The relevant question always is whether the elasticity is "sufficiently" large to be regarded as infinite, but this is a question that cannot be answered, once for all, simply in terms of the numerical value of the elasticity itself, any more than we can say, once for all, whether an air pressure of 15 pounds per square inch is "sufficiently" close to zero to use the formula $s = \frac{1}{2}gt^2$. Similarly, we cannot compute cross-elasticities of demand and then classify firms into industries according as there is a "substantial gap in the cross-elasticities of demand." As Marshall says, "The question where the lines of division between different commodities [i.e., industries] should be drawn must be settled by convenience of the particular discussion."[31] Everything depends on the problem; there is no inconsistency in regarding the same firm as if it were a perfect competitor for one problem, and a monopolist for another, just as there is none in regarding the same chalk mark as a Euclidean line for one problem, a Euclidean surface for a second, and a Euclidean solid for a third. The size of the elasticity and cross-elasticity of demand, the number of firms producing physically similar products, etc., are all relevant because they are or may be among the variables used to define the correspondence between the ideal and real entities in a particular problem and to specify the circumstances under which the theory holds sufficiently well; but they do not provide, once for all, a classification of firms as competitive or monopolistic.

An example may help to clarify this point. Suppose the problem is to determine the effect on retail prices of cigarettes of an

---

31. *Principles,* p. 100.

increase, expected to be permanent, in the federal cigarette tax. I venture to predict that broadly correct results will be obtained by treating cigarette firms as if they were producing an identical product and were in perfect competition. Of course, in such a case, "some convention must be made as to the" number of Chesterfield cigarettes "which are taken as equivalent" to a Marlborough.[32]

On the other hand, the hypothesis that cigarette firms would behave as if they were perfectly competitive would have been a false guide to their reactions to price control in World War II, and this would doubtless have been recognized before the event. Costs of the cigarette firms must have risen during the war. Under such circumstances perfect competitors would have reduced the quantity offered for sale at the previously existing price. But, at that price, the wartime rise in the income of the public presumably increased the quantity demanded. Under conditions of perfect competition strict adherence to the legal price would therefore imply not only a "shortage" in the sense that quantity demanded exceeded quantity supplied but also an absolute decline in the number of cigarettes produced. The facts contradict this particular implication: there was reasonably good adherence to maximum cigarette prices, yet the quantities produced increased substantially. The common force of increased costs presumably operated less strongly than the disruptive force of the desire by each firm to keep its share of the market, to maintain the value and prestige of its brand name, especially when the excess-profits tax shifted a large share of the costs of this kind of advertising to the government. For this problem the cigarette firms cannot be treated *as if* they were perfect competitors.

Wheat farming is frequently taken to exemplify perfect competition. Yet, while for some problems it is appropriate to treat cigarette producers as if they comprised a perfectly competitive industry, for some it is not appropriate to treat wheat producers as if they did. For example, it may not be if the problem is the differential in prices paid by local elevator operators for wheat.

Marshall's apparatus turned out to be most useful for problems in which a group of firms is affected by common stimuli,

32. Quoted parts from *ibid.*

and in which the firms can be treated *as if* they were perfect competitors. This is the source of the misconception that Marshall "assumed" perfect competition in some descriptive sense. It would be highly desirable to have a more general theory than Marshall's, one that would cover at the same time both those cases in which differentiation of product or fewness of numbers makes an essential difference and those in which it does not. Such a theory would enable us to handle problems we now cannot and, in addition, facilitate determination of the range of circumstances under which the simpler theory can be regarded as a good enough approximation. To perform this function, the more general theory must have content and substance; it must have implications susceptible to empirical contradiction and of substantive interest and importance.

The theory of imperfect or monopolistic competition developed by Chamberlin and Robinson is an attempt to construct such a more general theory.[33] Unfortunately, it possesses none of the attributes that would make it a truly useful general theory. Its contribution has been limited largely to improving the exposition of the economics of the individual firm and thereby the derivation of implications of the Marshallian model, refining Marshall's monopoly analysis, and enriching the vocabulary available for describing industrial experience.

The deficiencies of the theory are revealed most clearly in its treatment of, or inability to treat, problems involving groups of firms—Marshallian "industries." So long as it is insisted that differentiation of product is essential—and it is the distinguishing feature of the theory that it does insist on this point—the definition of an industry in terms of firms producing an identical product cannot be used. By that definition each firm is a separate industry. Definition in terms of "close" substitutes or a "substantial" gap in cross-elasticities evades the issue, introduces fuzziness and undefinable terms into the abstract model where they have no place, and serves only to make the theory analytically meaningless—"close" and "substantial" are in the same category

33. E. H. Chamberlin, *The Theory of Monopolistic Competition* (6th ed.; Cambridge: Harvard University Press, 1950); Joan Robinson, *The Economics of Imperfect Competition* (London: Macmillan & Co., 1933).

as a "small" air pressure.[34] In one connection Chamberlin implicitly defines an industry as a group of firms having identical cost and demand curves.[35] But this, too, is logically meaningless so long as differentiation of product is, as claimed, essential and not to be put aside. What does it mean to say that the cost and demand curves of a firm producing bulldozers are identical with those of a firm producing hairpins?[36] And if it is meaningless for bulldozers and hairpins, it is meaningless also for two brands of toothpaste—so long as it is insisted that the difference between the two brands is fundamentally important.

The theory of monopolistic competition offers no tools for the analysis of an industry and so no stopping place between the firm at one extreme and general equilibrium at the other.[37] It is therefore incompetent to contribute to the analysis of a host of important problems: the one extreme is too narrow to be of great interest; the other, too broad to permit meaningful generalizations.[38]

VI. Conclusion

Economics as a positive science is a body of tentatively accepted generalizations about economic phenomena that can be used to predict the consequences of changes in circumstances.

34. See R. L. Bishop, "Elasticities, Cross-elasticities, and Market Relationships," *American Economic Review*, XLII (December, 1952), 779–803, for a recent attempt to construct a rigorous classification of market relationships along these lines. Despite its ingenuity and sophistication, the result seems to me thoroughly unsatisfactory. It rests basically on certain numbers being classified as "large" or "small," yet there is no discussion at all of how to decide whether a particular number is "large" or "small," as of course there cannot be on a purely abstract level.

35. *Op. cit.*, p. 82.

36. There always exists a transformation of quantities that will make either the cost curves or the demand curves identical; this transformation need not, however, be linear, in which case it will involve different-sized units of one product at different levels of output. There does not necessarily exist a transformation that will make both pairs of curves identical.

37. See Robert Triffin, *Monopolistic Competition and General Equilibrium Theory* (Cambridge: Harvard University Press, 1940), esp. pp. 188–89.

38. For a detailed critique see George J. Stigler, "Monopolistic Competition in Retrospect," in *Five Lectures on Economic Problems* (London: Macmillan & Co., 1949), pp. 12–24.

Progress in expanding this body of generalizations, strengthening our confidence in their validity, and improving the accuracy of the predictions they yield is hindered not only by the limitations of human ability that impede all search for knowledge but also by obstacles that are especially important for the social sciences in general and economics in particular, though by no means peculiar to them. Familiarity with the subject matter of economics breeds contempt for special knowledge about it. The importance of its subject matter to everyday life and to major issues of public policy impedes objectivity and promotes confusion between scientific analysis and normative judgment. The necessity of relying on uncontrolled experience rather than on controlled experiment makes it difficult to produce dramatic and clear-cut evidence to justify the acceptance of tentative hypotheses. Reliance on uncontrolled experience does not affect the fundamental methodological principle that a hypothesis can be tested only by the conformity of its implications or predictions with observable phenomena; but it does render the task of testing hypotheses more difficult and gives greater scope for confusion about the methodological principles involved. More than other scientists, social scientists need to be self-conscious about their methodology.

One confusion that has been particularly rife and has done much damage is confusion about the role of "assumptions" in economic analysis. A meaningful scientific hypothesis or theory typically asserts that certain forces are, and other forces are not, important in understanding a particular class of phenomena. It is frequently convenient to present such a hypothesis by stating that the phenomena it is desired to predict behave in the world of observation *as if* they occurred in a hypothetical and highly simplified world containing only the forces that the hypothesis asserts to be important. In general, there is more than one way to formulate such a description—more than one set of "assumptions" in terms of which the theory can be presented. The choice among such alternative assumptions is made on the grounds of the resulting economy, clarity, and precision in presenting the hypothesis; their capacity to bring indirect evidence to bear on the validity of the hypothesis by suggesting some of its implications that can be readily checked with observation or by bringing out its connection with other hypotheses dealing with related phenomena; and similar considerations.

Such a theory cannot be tested by comparing its "assumptions" directly with "reality." Indeed, there is no meaningful way in which this can be done. Complete "realism" is clearly unattainable, and the question whether a theory is realistic "enough" can be settled only by seeing whether it yields predictions that are good enough for the purpose in hand or that are better than predictions from alternative theories. Yet the belief that a theory can be tested by the realism of its assumptions independently of the accuracy of its predictions is widespread and the source of much of the perennial criticism of economic theory as unrealistic. Such criticism is largely irrelevant, and, in consequence, most attempts to reform economic theory that it has stimulated have been unsuccessful.

The irrelevance of so much criticism of economic theory does not of course imply that existing economic theory deserves any high degree of confidence. These criticisms may miss the target, yet there may be a target for criticism. In a trivial sense, of course, there obviously is. Any theory is necessarily provisional and subject to change with the advance of knowledge. To go beyond this platitude, it is necessary to be more specific about the content of "existing economic theory" and to distinguish among its different branches; some parts of economic theory clearly deserve more confidence than others. A comprehensive evaluation of the present state of positive economics, summary of the evidence bearing on its validity, and assessment of the relative confidence that each part deserves is clearly a task for a treatise or a set of treatises, if it be possible at all, not for a brief paper on methodology.

About all that is possible here is the cursory expression of a personal view. Existing relative price theory, which is designed to explain the allocation of resources among alternative ends and the division of the product among the co-operating resources and which reached almost its present form in Marshall's *Principles of Economics,* seems to me both extremely fruitful and deserving of much confidence for the kind of economic system that characterizes Western nations. Despite the appearance of considerable controversy, this is true equally of existing static monetary theory, which is designed to explain the structural or secular level of absolute prices, aggregate output, and other variables for the economy as a whole and which has had a form of the quantity theory of money as its basic core in all of its major variants from David Hume to the Cambridge School to Irving Fisher to John Maynard Keynes. The weakest and least satisfactory part of current economic theory seems to me to be in the field of monetary dynamics, which is concerned with the process of adaptation of the economy as a whole to changes in conditions and so with short-period fluctuations in aggregate activity. In this field we do not even have a theory that can appropriately be called "the" existing theory of monetary dynamics.

Of course, even in relative price and static monetary theory there is enormous room for extending the scope and improving the accuracy of existing theory. In particular, undue emphasis on the descriptive realism of "assumptions" has contributed to neglect of the critical problem of determining the limits of validity of the various hypotheses that together constitute the existing economic theory in these areas. The abstract models corresponding to these hypotheses have been elaborated in considerable detail and greatly improved in rigor and precision. Descriptive material on the characteristics of our economic system and its operations have been amassed on an unprecedented scale. This is all to the good. But, if we are to use effectively these abstract models and this descriptive material, we must have a comparable exploration of the criteria for determining what abstract model it is best to use for particular kinds of problems, what entities in the abstract model are to be identified with what observable entities, and what features of the problem or of the circumstances have the greatest effect on the accuracy of the predictions yielded by a particular model or theory.

Progress in positive economics will require not only the testing and elaboration of existing hypotheses but also the construction of new hypotheses. On this problem there is little to say on a formal level. The construction of hypotheses is a creative act of inspiration, intuition, invention; its essence is the vision of something new in familiar material. The process must be discussed in psychological, not logical, categories; studied in autobiographies and biographies, not treatises on scientific method; and promoted by maxim and example, not syllogism or theorem.

Part 2

Reading and writing a classic

1   Reading *the* methodological essay in twentieth-century economics: map of multiple perspectives

Uskali Mäki

Even outrageously unrealistic assumptions are just fine insofar as the theory or model involving them performs well in predicting phenomena of interest. Most economists and many non-economists will attribute this principle to Milton Friedman. Many will consider the principle itself outrageous, while others praise Friedman for having formulated it so persuasively.

Friedman's "The methodology of positive economics" was published in 1953 as the opening chapter of his *Essays in Positive Economics*. There is no doubt that this short essay of forty pages became *the most cited, the most influential, and the most controversial* piece of methodological writing in twentieth-century economics. The power and diversity of its impact and reception are evident. The essay (henceforth "F53") has helped shape many economists' conceptions of how to do good economics and how to defend certain ways of doing economics. It has also provoked many others to voice their disagreement with the claims of the essay, to argue that the view of science suggested by F53 is deeply flawed, even dangerous for the cognitive aspirations and social responsibilities of economics. These disagreements have not diminished in the course of the years since the publication of F53. Whenever someone makes reference to "Friedman's methodological view" (perhaps using other expressions such as "Friedman's as-if methodology" or "Friedman's instrumentalism"), the context typically reveals that the expression is used either approvingly or disapprovingly, and often uncompromisingly so.

The legacy of F53 has led a double life. In the last half a century, F53 has prompted numerous scholarly commentaries and criticisms in an attempt to understand and (mostly) to resist its message. But the influence of F53 evidently reaches far beyond such explicit commentaries. In fact its effective impact may have flown along its own separate ways, uninfluenced by the various criticisms that have been leveled against the essay. There has been a *popular legacy* of F53, based on a vague understanding of its key ideas, sustained and transmitted without any detailed analysis or reflection on the text of the essay, often without citation or reference. The popular legacy manifests itself in introductory chapters of economics textbooks in which it is explained to students why the assumptions of economic models do not need to be realistic, and in oral communication at seminars and conference sessions when reference is made to "as-if methodology" or the importance of predictive implications in testing models. Parallel to this popular legacy, and surely motivated by it, there has been a tradition of more or less systematic "F53 studies" aiming at detailed critical scrutiny of the claims and arguments of the essay. This has constituted what may be called the *reflective legacy* of F53. Numerous studies have been published in journals and books, critically analyzing and interpreting and explaining F53 from a variety of angles, focusing on its different aspects, and drawing conclusions that rival or complement one another. The present volume adds many important and novel insights and analyses to this body of reflective literature. It is hoped that they will have consequences for the contents of the popular legacy.

In both of these incarnations of its legacy, the popular and the reflective, F53 has been highly influential. It has shaped the perceptions of the economist-of-the-street, and it has provoked specialists in economic methodology to engage in serious scholarly studies in hermeneutic interpretation and analytical criticism. I should add the important observation that its influence is not restricted to the economics profession: F53 has shaped the image of economics also amongst other social scientists. One often comes across statements about the nature of economic reasoning that make reference to F53, thereby suggesting that F53 gives a relatively accurate picture of how economics is being done by economists. In most such situations, the image is not intended as a flattering one. Indeed, many social scientists other than economists take it as evident that a discipline dependent on working with highly unrealistic assumptions is of dubious scientific value, thus a methodology seeking to justify such a practice must be at least equally suspect as a theory of science. To the extent that the broader public image of economics derives from F53, it is usually not one of praise and celebration.

Yet another very important motivating observation is that F53 seems to have been *poorly understood*. One might be surprised by this claim: given its strong impact, and given the large number of reflective commentaries that have appeared, one would expect F53 to be well understood by now. But this is surely not the case. On the one hand, strong impact, as in the popular legacy, is perfectly compatible with a poor understanding of what exactly makes that impact. Even more embarrassingly, poor understanding sometimes *helps* a piece of writing to make a popular impact. On the other hand, even though one might have higher expectations in regard to the explicitly reflective commentaries, they too may have failed to generate sufficiently solid understanding of F53 for understandable reasons. Some of these reasons derive from the fact that F53 is inherently very hard to understand. This difficulty is not only due to its richness, but also to its obscurities, ambiguities, and inconsistencies. One may even take these characteristics to support the radical conclusion that there is no single correct way of interpreting F53, rather there are multiple justifiable readings. Another possible reason for failure, or imperfect success, is the familiar mismatch between one's interpretive concepts (employed by readers) and one's target (the text). Any reflective commentary of a text approaches its target equipped with conceptual tools and philosophical frames, and these may not be appropriate for the task of getting the meaning of the text right. No doubt F53 has been approached from angles that are too limited or even plainly misguided to result in a solid understanding given the richness and complexity of F53 itself.

F53 was published more than half a century ago, but the interest in understanding and assessing the essay is not at all just historical. Its key claims remain as topical as ever: they are repeatedly being invoked by economists, generation after generation. Nowadays, they have special contemporary relevance in the context of the new debates around economic theory and method. In its own time, F53 was motivated by empirically based attacks against marginalist profit maximization. As Roger Backhouse explains in his chapter below, F53 can only be understood against the background of the so-called marginalist controversy in the 1940s. Together with Fritz Machlup's methodological polemics (Machlup 1946, 1955), F53 became a major defensive statement that sought to undermine the empirical criticisms that were leveled against marginalist maximization assumptions. Today, we are again witnessing massive attacks against the standard assumptions of rationality, and there are new attempts to replace them by more realistic assumptions. The difference is that in the late 1930s and early 1940s, the critical strategy was one based on field survey, simply asking business managers what they were doing, while nowadays the critical conclusions derive from experiment and brain scan, with psychologists and neuroscientists contributing to the collection of critical evidence. Even though F53 itself badly underestimated the role of experiment in economics, the topicality of its methodological arguments is evident.

F53 also set out to defend perfect competition against developments in the theory of monopolistic competition that it described as an entirely misguided pursuit of greater realisticness. As Oliver Williamson's chapter below shows, post-F53 developments in theories of the firm and market structure have not been obedient to these proscriptions; they have rather taken the theories toward opening the black box of the business firm and thereby toward more realistic images of motivation and procedure within firms. Monopolistic competition has also recently made a comeback packaged with increasing returns in explaining phenomena of growth and agglomeration. The challenge is to assess these developments in terms of F53 – and to assess F53 in terms of these developments.

The topicality of F53 is also fortified by the chronic difficulties in running reliable predictive tests in economics. The core principle endorsed by F53 appears to require that there be a set of well-defined and agreed-upon objective rules for measuring predictive success – given that predictive success is supposed to be all that matters in testing a theory. F53 itself does not formulate such rules, and as we know, economists constantly struggle with the consequences of not having such rules. Naturally, there are established practices of prediction and testing, but they are not – and cannot – be completely governed by explicit rules. Testing by prediction is far from anything straightforward and uncontestable. Paradoxically perhaps, F53 itself supports this claim, as I point out in chapter 3 below. Indeed, there is a line of thought in F53 that seems to have been missed by most readers: predictive tests are not fully objective and reliable, they unavoidably involve subjective judgment and social convention. Whether or not this makes F53 a self-undermining piece of writing, it is obvious that it does imply a call for greater caution in appealing to predictive tests, and for greater attention to the details of the structure of actual predictive tests.

The above are among the features of F53 that taken together give sufficient grounds for organizing a collective reconsideration of the essay half a century after its publication. Contributions were commissioned from scholars with complementary interests and competences to offer insight into the conundrums of F53 from a variety of perspectives. The assignments were designed with the goal of having a number of analyses complementing one another, while avoiding excessive overlap between the contributions. Each contribution would have a separate focus, and together they would provide a comprehensive and rich – but still incomplete – picture of F53 in context. The contributors were asked to help a twenty-first-century reader to have a reasoned opinion of F53, its contents, and their descriptive and prescriptive adequacy. Meeting this challenge would be based on examining the text of the essay, its historical and intellectual context, and the developments of economics and its methodology after 1953.

Just like the various commentaries of F53 that have been published during the last half a century, the contributions to this volume approach F53 from different angles, addressing different questions and pursuing the answers by following different strategies. In order to assess the various contributions one has to understand what they seek to accomplish, what their goals and constraints and other presuppositions are. It may therefore be useful to outline a map of approaches to F53, providing the beginnings of a typology of readings or interpretations. Such a map should help assess the readings in their own terms and to compare their merits and ambitions.

In the remainder of this chapter, I propose to organize the various ways of reading and examining F53, each of them giving rise to different types of project. I am thinking of a map that is on five dimensions. The first dimension is related to the functions of reading F53, from taking it as a target of critical examination to using it without examining it, for example as a source of information or inspiration. The second dimension consists of a range of internal characteristics of F53, from those of its elements that focus on the logical aspects of economic theorizing to those that highlight its ontological, semantic, and social aspects. The third dimension is constituted by a variety of external contexts of F53, from the context of its writing to the context of its reading and reception. The fourth dimension consists of perspectives that range from normatively assessing various features of F53 to analyzing and explaining those features. The fifth dimension is concerned with the sources of various labels attached to F53, from extra-economics to intra-economics, and more.

I will expand on this map and will illustrate by locating various contributions to "F53 studies" that have appeared in the course of the last half a century, including those published in the present volume.

1   Examining and using

The first dimension has to do with the foci and functions of reading F53, ranging from examining it to using it. At one end, one may approach F53 as itself the primary target of study, examining and explaining it, analyzing and scrutinizing it, contextualizing and criticizing it, and so on. At the other end of the spectrum, the reader of F53 may take it as a source or means of information and inspiration, of persuasive argument and authoritative judgment, of reproach and ridicule. Here, without examining F53 itself, one may quote or cite it, and then proceed to focus on other things, such as the nature of economic models, contemporary debates in economic theory and method, issues around the public image of economics, or challenges of economics education.

There is no dichotomy here, but rather a continuum of foci along this dimension. For example, many reflective readers of F53 nowadays examine the text of the essay in order to use the findings as evidence for an account of the methodological outlook of the author of F53 more broadly.

In this case, one examines F53 without drawing conclusions about F53 only, but may use the outcome of such investigations together with other sources of evidence for portraying Milton Friedman's methodology of doing economic research. This strategy appears in several studies, including the book on Friedman by Abraham Hirsch and Neil De Marchi (1990), Daniel Hammond's and Thomas Mayer's various works, as well as the chapter below by Kevin Hoover.

This observation gives us an important distinction between examining F53 in order to understand it, and examining F53 in order to understand Friedman's economics and its methodology. It is important to be explicit about the difference between the two goals of reading, given that they are not always kept distinct. Both are legitimate tasks, but they require different standards to be appropriately assessed. For example, in considering an interpretive attempt to understand F53 alone, one should not judge the attempt straightforwardly in terms of its success or failure to provide understanding of Friedman's economics. A good account of F53 may not be a good account of Friedman's methodology, in some cases not even part of it. Indeed, *Friedman's methodology* and *the methodology of F53* are not one and the same thing, even though the two are likely to be connected. That they are not the same thing is exemplified, among other things, by incongruences between the dictates of F53 and Friedman's statements and practices elsewhere, such as unrealisticness of assumptions considered irrelevant here, but relevant there. It is notable that prior to the 1980s, virtually all commentary on F53 focused on F53 without any interest in Friedman's methodology. The situation has since then changed, perhaps due to the changes in Milton Friedman's status within economics: next to straight F53 studies, we now also have studies of Friedman's methodology.

Given that all the other dimensions on my map lean towards the examination side of the first dimension, I will not say more about this here, but will instead focus on the use side. The popular legacy of F53 is a matter of use without examination. As an example in this category, textbook authors sometimes make reference to F53 when explaining to the students why they should not worry about unrealistic assumptions.

In the present volume, all contributions are within the reflective legacy, but in some of them the use component is more pronounced than the examination component.

Melvin Reder's chapter deals with the role of visions or general "frames" in economic theorizing, offering an extensive discussion of contemporary debates over involuntary unemployment and sticky wages and other methodological issues concerned with what qualifies as evidence in economics. In these parts of Reder's chapter, F53 is not so much examined itself as used for launching the broader discussion. Also dealing with issues of evidence, the focus of Chris Starmer's chapter is on the articles on expected utility jointly authored by Friedman and Savage, published in the neighborhood of F53, namely in 1948 and 1952. Pointing out parallels and incongruences between the methodological positions revealed in these articles and F53, Starmer raises critical questions about using normative appeal as indirect evidence in support of the expected-utility hypothesis. Starmer puts his observations also in the context of current debates over the assumptions of rationality.

The mixture of examination and use is similar in Oliver Williamson's chapter, which discusses some key ideas of F53 in the context of the post-1953 developments away from the neoclassical theory of the firm defended by F53. These developments lead away from just one theory toward many theories, and from the unrealistic image of theories as production functions with profit maximization toward increasing realisticness in motivation, then in process. Jack Vromen's chapter can be seen as a combination of examination and use: tracing various pre-F53 and post-F53 versions of the evolutionary argument as designed and used by various economists, he manages to help us see the distinct characteristics of the argument as presented in F53 itself – while at the same time informing us about the variety of such arguments available in economics.

2   Internal characteristics of F53

The second dimension on my map consists of a range of internal characteristics of F53 noticed by the reader, namely what F53 itself is taken to say about economic theories and scientific reasoning, and how it says it. The accounts of F53 here focus on interpreting and assessing its stated or implied view of economics as a scientific discipline. The text of F53 serves as the main source of evidence for these accounts, while the goal is to identify and examine the claims and arguments of the essay. Given the richness of the internal characteristics of F53, any reading is bound to be somewhat selective among them – some more, some less – and there are many ways of making one's selections.

At one end, readers may focus narrowly on just how F53 deals with *"assumptions," "predictive implications" and "data" as well as their logical relationships in economic theorizing.* Most commentaries from the 1950s to the 1970s were largely constrained by this perspective, from Rotwein (1959) through Samuelson (1963) and Simon (1963) to Melitz (1965), Bear and Orr (1967), Brunner (1969), Wong (1973), and Boland (1979). F53 was read as stating that the truth of the assumptions of economic theories is irrelevant, and their falsehood is just fine, thus it makes no sense to try to test them against empirical data, while the assumptions entail predictive implications that are to be checked against the data, and this constitutes an appropriate test of the theory itself. Commentators then critically examined the logic of this argument about the logic of testing economic theory. Some of them recognized the ambiguity of "assumption" in F53 and elsewhere, and checked the consequences with alternative specifications of the meaning of the term. Among the premises shared by many such narrowly logical accounts of F53 were the ideas that unrealisticness (of an assumption, or model) amounts to falsehood; that the falsehood of its assumptions amounts to the falsehood of a theory or model; and that assumptions are considered mainly from the point of view of their role in yielding predictions. Obviously, these premises enable creating a very limited image of F53.

The portrayal of F53 can then be enriched by adding a mixed variety of further characteristics to its description, including how F53 depicts *the ontological, semantic, and social aspects of scientific reasoning.* As for the ontological aspects, what does F53 suggest regarding what is presupposed about the constitution of economic reality in economic theorizing? For example, does the profit maximization assumption presuppose something about the deliberations and purposeful activities of business managers or owners, or rather about the real pressures of the selection mechanisms of competitive markets? How is one to interpret Friedman's suggestion that the assumption of profit maximization summarizes the conditions of firm survival through natural selection in the competitive market? These questions have been discussed since Koopmans (1957) and Winter (1964). Jack Vromen's chapter below joins this tradition in his extended analysis of Friedman's selection argument in support of the maximization assumption. Chris Starmer devotes a section to this sort of argument in his chapter on expected utility. Kevin Hoover's discussion below on Friedman's poorly articulated attitudes towards real-world causation is another example of addressing ontological issues. Mere logical relations between sentences in a model are insufficient for capturing real causal connections.

Moreover, rather than just taking the truth-values of "assumptions" and "predictions" as given, and then examining their logical relationships, we may ask: what does F53 suggest regarding what it is for a theory and its assumptions to be true, or fail to be so? What functions do true and false assumptions serve in a model? How should we interpret the as-if formulation from the point of view of truth and falsehood, and what epistemic purpose is being served? What other ways are there for a theory or model to be realistic or unrealistic? These questions require attention to the precise claims about the world that theories and their components are used for making. For example, an assumption may appear false when formulated as a straightforward assertion about the world (the air pressure is nil, the market is perfect), but may have a chance of being true when rephrased as a claim about the negligibly small effect of some factor (the air pressure is negligibly small, the deviation from market perfection is negligible). This is a theme that was not perfectly lucid in F53, but was later introduced by Alan Musgrave (1981) and followed up in Mäki (2000). There is another important idea that was not explicitly developed by F53, but on generous interpretation may be viewed as compatible with it. This is the idea that a model may appear false due to its narrowness and its containment of false assumptions, yet it may be used for making true claims about some significant facts about the world (Mäki 1992). This idea is further developed in my second chapter to this volume, as are the semantics and ontology of the as-if locution. Furthermore, next to truth and falsehood, there are other kinds of realisticness and unrealisticness that play important implicit roles in F53's reasoning, such as those related to observationality and partiality.

As to the social aspect of economic theorizing, what does F53 say or imply about the ways in which theorizing is shaped by various social factors within academia and outside it? These factors range from the enabling and constraining roles of academic communities and conventions to the pressures from economic policy and ideology. This has been a strikingly neglected theme in the legacy of F53, both popular and reflective. The chapter by Teira and Zamora in this volume looks at one aspect of F53 from the point of view of a contract between the "agents" (economists) and "principals" (consumers) of economic knowledge. My own work has stressed the central role of social shaping of economics in the reasoning of F53 and combines this with the rest of the spectrum, namely the logical, ontological, epistemological, and semantic perspectives (e.g. Mäki 1986, 1992, 2000).

3   External contexts of F53

My map has another important dimension along which readings and commentaries of F53 are located. This third dimension consists of the range of external contexts of F53. "External" here means external to F53, ranging from academic or intellectual contexts (such as the situation within economics and the philosophy of science) to political and broader cultural contexts in society at large – and both of these at the more particular level of Friedman's individual biography and at the more general level of academic and other social institutions. One may discuss F53 as a response to developments in economics and the philosophy of science, and one may examine its later impact on these developments. Most of the systematic commentary on F53, when paying attention to external contexts at all, has thus far focused on such more narrowly academic contexts. This is also the case in the present volume, even though observations about the economist expert (by Teira and Zamora) and free market ideology (by Reder) reach beyond the narrow academic horizons.

Let us make the discussion on external context more focused by drawing a distinction between the context of production and the context of consumption. At one end, the focus is put on *the context of writing*: the intellectual challenges and inspirations that provoked and shaped the production of F53 – such as the marginalist controversy triggering the textual production of F53, and the Marshallian tradition guiding it, as well as Friedman's own work as an economist and as a policy adviser. A prime example of these accounts is the book on Friedman's economics by Abraham Hirsch and Neil De Marchi (1990). Among other things, they suggest ways in which Wesley Mitchell's methodological views may have influenced those of Friedman while at the NBER, and they point out what they claim to be close affinities between Friedman's methodology and John Dewey's pragmatist account of inquiry. Daniel Hammond's extensive work on Friedman's methodology and its origins is another major example in this category (e.g. Hammond 1996; on the idea of contexts, see Hammond 1992b).

These authors have been driven by the ambition of identifying Friedman's authentic convictions in economic methodology. They believe the internal characteristics of F53 alone do not suffice as evidence for those convictions, and that only when combined with lots of other evidence related to Friedman's work in economics and his broader intellectual background can reliable conclusions be drawn about Friedman's real methodological beliefs. Hammond's contribution to the present volume, tracing the development of the early drafts of F53, examines the context of writing in almost as fine detail as it can get. Roger Backhouse's chapter examines the well-known role of the marginalist controversy in the context of writing F53. Complementing Hammond's story, Backhouse offers new information on the peculiar characteristics of F53 as a statement on theories of the firm and market structure by consulting the correspondence between Friedman and Don Patinkin in the late 1940s. Michel De Vroey's chapter deals with Friedman's convictions in relation to the Marshallian and Walrasian traditions. Chris Starmer casts new illumination on the methodological issues in Friedman and Savage's joint work on expected utility and its role in inspiring some of the arguments in F53 – such as the use of "as if" in formulating assumptions and the use of predictive tests in assessing theories. Teira and Zamora argue that the first section of F53 on the positive–normative distinction was motivated by Friedman's experience with policy advice. Painting with a broader brush, Melvin Reder's chapter situates F53 in the long tradition of the "frame" of the Invisible Hand of the free market.

At the other end, the focus is on *the context of reading*: of consumption rather than production, of *ex post* influence and reception rather than *ex ante* inspiration and creation. The context is that of the career of F53 once it was born. There are weak and strong versions of these "consumptionist" accounts. The *weak versions* deal with the (actual, possible, desirable, inadvisable) reception and influence while at the same time keeping an eye on the author's beliefs and intentions. The *strong versions* bracket the author's attitudes entirely. Thomas Mayer's and Wade Hands's chapters below are largely in the weak consumptionist category. Their main interest lies in the reception and influence of F53, but they contrast this with what they view as Friedman's true beliefs and intentions. They raise questions about whether F53 has been read appropriately, whether its reception and influence are justified from the point of view of Friedman's authentic methodological convictions. For example, one may ask whether F53 licensed the "formalist revolution" as Wade Hands does and then answers in the negative (whereas a section in my second chapter suggests that F53 itself encouraged a "torso version" of its overall message, and that the torso version can easily be used for licensing formalism).

On the other hand, the strong consumptionist is only interested in the reader's reception rather than the author's intention. The goal is to read a methodological text from the point of view of its (actual or possible) reception by the relevant audiences, including its (actual or possible) interpretations and influences – while completely ignoring questions about the author's beliefs and goals. This is what I call "reception methodology" in analogy with reception aesthetics. My own second chapter purports to be a more or less pure exercise in reception methodology. The important difference between my chapter and those of Mayer and Hands lies in the fact that Mayer and Hands provide a role for the authentic beliefs and intentions of the author of F53, while I am bracketing them off altogether and discussing the text of F53 only. A further difference is that Mayer and Hands write about the actual reception by others in historical terms, while I am offering my own novel reading of the essay. Theirs is a project of contrasting some other people's readings of F53 with their own reading of it, where their own reading is supposed to yield access to the views that the author of F53 really held. My project cannot be contrastive in that way since here I pay no attention to Friedman's true beliefs and intentions.

Powerful support seems to be available to such a strong receptionist approach: Milton Friedman himself has refrained from commenting on the commentators of F53 in public, and he has done so deliberately. He made an early decision to let F53 live its own life, leaving it at the mercy of its readers as it were. This is confirmed in his "final word" at the end of the present volume. He has enjoyed watching the readings of, and debates over, F53 and has only privately provided feedback to its various inter-pretations. All this seems to offer strong support to the receptionist approach from the most authoritative source. There is a tension here, though. Reception methodology was supposed to ignore the author's beliefs and intentions, so it might seem inappropriate to appeal to this same author's stated intentions in defense of reception methodology. The obvious way of relieving the tension simply points out that one should not conflate the two levels of appeal to the author's attitudes: the levels of the justification of a reading and of the justification of a strategy of reading. The receptionist reading of F53 makes no appeal to the author's inten-tions, while it is at most the justification of the receptionist strategy that makes higher-order appeal to the author's attitudes. Further relief is due to the fact that, in the end, the former is not dependent on the latter: we may adopt a receptionist strategy without Friedman's permission.

Another way of justifying a receptionist reading of F53 is based on the recognition that this is how most readers view F53 anyway. This is very much part of the popular legacy of F53, and this is part of much of the reflective legacy as well. Most readers are not in the least interested in Milton Friedman's peculiar intellectual trajectories or his authentic meth-odological convictions. They rather read F53 as a source of insights and arguments that they can put into use when themselves dealing with trou-bling methodological issues in economics. When connecting the meth-odological arguments of F53 to the practice of economics, readers do not usually connect them to Friedman's practice but rather to that of their own and of others, whenever it seems useful as issues of justification and critique of that practice arise.

The above remarks have dealt with the intra-academic context of F53. It should also be possible to put F53 in a broader extra-academic context. One could read it as being embedded in the cultural and political currents of its time, both reflecting and shaping them. Not only would this mean examining the image that F53 conveys of economics – and of the econo-mist expert as a politically powerful role – amongst the sciences, but also in society more broadly. The contribution by Teira and Zamora to this volume takes some steps toward this direction.

Further steps could be taken by locating F53 in a historically and politically unique external context. I have in mind a way of reading that has not been practiced yet (not at least systematically), but that is not only a possible approach but also one that I anticipate will be attempted in the near future. This is based on recognizing a larger societal context in which the production and consumption of F53 have taken place. This larger context has to do with the overall transformations in the social sciences (and the philosophy of science) that took place in the 1950s and that have been linked with the broader sociopolitical conditions of the time, including the Cold War and the role of powerful funding agencies and research institutes (for examples, see Amadae 2003; Mirowski 2002; Reisch 2005). "Cold War history of science" is already a major stream of scholarly work, and it will not be surprising if there is another small current of it within the flow of F53 studies.

4   Evaluating and explaining

The fourth dimension of my map has to do with whether F53 is being read from a normative or from an explanatory perspective. At one end, one sets out to *evaluate* the soundness of the claims and arguments put forth in the essay. Most evaluations in the reflective legacy have been critical of the contents of F53. These include commentaries such as those by Koopmans (1957), Rotwein (1959), Samuelson (1963), Melitz (1965), Caldwell (1980), Blaug (1980), and Hausman (1992a).

Many of these criticize F53 for failing to see that good science not only pursues predictive success but also asks and answers explanatory why-questions about the phenomena investigated – and in answering such questions, the assumptions cannot be too much off the mark. Others point out that even an economist interested in reliable predictions should prefer realistic assumptions. Some question the objectivity of the reliance on the predictive performance of economic theories without spelling out very precise standards in terms of which to measure such performance. Many critics also complain about the apologetic and complacent attitude endorsed by F53: its arguments seek to justify a dogmatic commitment to perfect competition and profit maximization against empirical challenges. Another class of criticisms claims to identify mistaken statements in F53 (such as claiming that the Walrasian rendering of monopolistic competition theory is motivated by photographic accuracy). Yet another set of complaints (my favorite) points out the strategic function of ambiguities and inconsistencies in the reasoning of F53, as well as incompatibilities between F53 and Friedman's practice as an economist (such as defending unrealistic assumptions in some situations and criticizing them in other contexts; suggesting reliance on the objectivity of predictive tests while denying their objectivity; holding dogmatic attitudes while advocating strong fallibilism).

So the mainstream of evaluative readings has been critical, and indeed only a minority of reflective readings, such as Karl Brunner's (1969), has been supportive, usually with qualifications. Many evaluations are mixtures of approval and disapproval. In his chapter below, Williamson criticizes F53 for an anti-pluralist endorsement of a single all-purpose theory of the firm while admitting that the central idea of F53, namely testing theories by predictions, is basically right. My own reading of F53 is a mixture of praise and blame. The popular legacy is a different story again: the proportion of favorable evaluations of F53 has been larger than within the reflective legacy. Evaluations in this class typically do not come with qualifications; they express simple attitudes in terms of yes–yes, or no–no.[1]

In all evaluative judgments of F53, one invokes, explicitly or implicitly, a set of standards. Such standards are concerned with the desirability and possibility of things such as truth, reliability, explanation, causal knowledge, predictive success, epistemic progress, consistency, consensus, and value-freedom. Further investigations are needed to turn such standards explicit whenever they are implicit, to specify the various meanings of such key terms whenever there is vagueness and ambiguity, and to identify and critically examine further presuppositions whenever there is conflict between, or disagreement over, those standards. For example, one needs to subscribe to the standard of consistency between scientific disciplines regarding their theories and empirical results if one sets out to blame an economist or an economic theory for ignoring evidence produced by experimental psychology.

While evaluation is one project, another task is to *explain* F53. We can exploit the ambiguity of "explain" here and divide this into two types of exercise. The *first* kind of exercise aims at explaining what the various phrases and arguments in F53 mean, how they are best understood (this can also be called an analytical activity). Naturally, this is a task that must be taken before evaluation. One must understand what one wants to evaluate before actually evaluating it. But this principle is not always respected. The obvious suspicion is that within the popular legacy,

---

[1] In his "final word" at the end of this volume, Milton Friedman exercises some playful self-criticism, saying that had F53 been more lucid, commentators would have silenced by now. This contrasts with his spoken statement, conveyed via a telephone connection at the panel discussion on the occasion of the fiftieth anniversary of F53 at the ASSA Meetings (in Washington, DC, January 2003). He said he recently reread F53 and found its claims basically right. Had he been a perfect "receptionist" about F53 himself, he would have said neither of these things.

normative judgment is easily passed without any solid understanding of the arguments and claims of F53. This is understandable as it is almost definitive of the popular legacy that no deep and detailed reflective understanding is sought to support the assessment. But it is clear that the reflective legacy has also failed to produce consistently sound understandings of the message of F53. This is evident, among other things, in the multiplicity of incompatible philosophical labels attached to F53. It is also notable that while Boland (1979) claimed that all previous critics have failed to understand F53, it can be argued that Boland himself is in that same boat.

The *second* use of "explain" is in terms of answering various why- and how-questions about F53. Why and how was the essay written the way it actually came about? Why and how was it received, or could have been received? For example, combining this with the focus on the context of writing, one may argue: this is how Friedman came to hold these views, and/or this is what he intended to mean by what he wrote. Dan Hammond's work exemplifies this approach. The work of many others, including my own, is a combination of the normative and explanatory perspectives.

Using these categories, one may envision a distinction between reading F53 philosophically and reading it historically. In reading F53 *philosophically* one adopts the first kind of explanatory perspective that aims at interpreting and analyzing intended or possible meanings and arguments in F53, and based on some interpretation, the reader may adopt an evaluative perspective, assessing the soundness of its claims. In reading F53 *historically*, one adopts the second kind of explanatory perspective, describing and explaining the temporal trajectory of relevant ideas – those in F53 as well as those that have shaped it and those that it has shaped – at personal and social levels. These two ways of reading complement one another usefully, and can also be combined with one another.

5   Extra-economic and intra-economic labels

It is only natural that the message of a complex text such as F53 will be simplified in terms of supposedly informative labels that help classify and characterize its message as distinctive. Since the 1970s, labeling the message of F53 has been a major task undertaken by its reflective readers. The labels have mostly come from extra-economic sources, namely philosophy: F53 has been classified as exemplifying this or that particular position in the philosophy of science. A few others have characterized Friedman's position as "Marshallian," using an intra-economic label. And there are other possibilities. This is the final dimension on my map.

A number of philosophical labels have been ascribed to Friedman and F53 (mostly by readers who are professional economists). The view has been labeled as positivist, falsificationist, conventionalist, pragmatist, and instrumentalist – and as realist, social constructivist, and radical fallibilist in my own unconventional reading of F53. Of these, "instrumentalism" has become the most popular label attached to F53. Very roughly, according to an instrumentalist conception of scientific theory, a theory is an instrument or tool for some purpose, such as problem solving or organizing the empirical data. Such instrumental purposes must be other than truthfully representing the way in which the phenomena of interest come about – the latter is how realism would see the tasks of theorizing. Given that Friedman argues that it is all right for the assumptions of a theory to be false as long as the theory predicts well, instrumentalism has appeared to be his philosophy of economic theory.

Insofar as I have been able to determine, "instrumentalism" was first explicitly used by Bear and Orr (1967) in characterizing Friedman's views. Later on, it was used by commentators such as Wong (1971), Boland (1979), Blaug (1980), and Caldwell (1980, 1999). However, the priority on this matter should perhaps go to philosopher of science Ernest Nagel. His authoritative treatise *The Structure of Science* appeared in 1961. The book contained a substantial discussion on conceptions of scientific theory, classifying them into what he called "descriptivist," "instrumentalist," and "realist" views (Nagel 1961). In December 1962, the American Economic Association Meetings included a panel session devoted to F53, featuring Paul Samuelson, Herbert Simon, Andreas Papandreou, Sherman Krupp, Fritz Machlup, and Nagel. In that session, Nagel (1963) suggested a possible interpretation of F53 as largely instrumentalist, but he did not use the term "instrumentalism" (even though he used the expression "theory as a useful instrument"). I presume he could easily have done so, but my guess is that because he was addressing an audience mainly consisting of economists, he did not want to burden his account with unnecessary philosophical labels.

But is the instrumentalist reading right? This still remains a legitimate question. Contributing to the establishment of the instrumentalist interpretation of F53, Larry Boland's 1979 paper in the *Journal of Economic Literature* put forth the claim that F53 is a coherent defense of an instrumentalist conception of economics. This claim has two components in it, one about coherence and the other about instrumentalism. Since the publication of Boland's paper, I have disputed both of these claims. I have argued that what F53 offers is far from a coherent and unambiguous argument for any well-defined position, and also that the most plausible interpretation of F53 (and perhaps Friedman's methodology in general) is based on the opposite of instrumentalism, namely realism (Mäki 1986, 1992, 2000). My contribution to this volume provides a detailed reading of F53 in realist terms. The key to this revisionist reading is to reconsider the functions of falsehood in economic models. Also in this volume, Kevin Hoover gives further support to the realist reading of Friedman's methodology by offering evidence from Friedman's work in monetary economics. The instrumentalist interpretation of F53 used to be the dominant one, but may have to give way to a diametrically opposing realist reading.

The broad variety of attributions is likely to be partly due to incompetent or relaxed use of the philosophical labels, but part of the reason may be rooted just in the ambiguities and inconsistencies of F53 itself. For example, to claim that F53 is a positivist statement simply because of its adherence to the positive/normative distinction might be taken as an example of philosophical incompetence if no other evidence is offered (or else it might be just a matter of using the label in a very narrow sense). There are a few other "positivist" elements in F53 (see Mäki 1986), but they are not dominant (at the same time we should grant that the label "positivist" has itself become disturbingly vague and uninformative). Similarly, there is a falsificationist element in F53 (the notion of failure to be contradicted by evidence), but it appears just in passing. Social constructivist features – such as the emphasis on the role of disciplinary culture in shaping scholarly judgment – are far more central to the argument of F53, even though they have been mostly ignored by the readers.

It has been suggested that Friedman was not a professional philosopher and therefore F53 should not be interpreted and judged in philosophical terms. This suggestion has been made by commentators such as Daniel Hammond, Thomas Mayer, and Kevin Hoover, also in this volume. When viewed through philosophical lenses, F53 may emerge as uninformed and obscure. The suggestion is that Friedman's methodology should instead be inferred from his work as an economist and as being embedded in the tradition of economics. This approach then is argued to suggest that the proper label for characterizing Friedman's methodology is "Marshallian" – a label that is *intra-economic* in that it derives from within the tradition of economics itself rather than being imposed from outside economics, using philosophical labels such as "positivist" and "instrumentalist."

I have three responses to this suggestion. First, I believe it will be fruitful to consider the intra-economic and extra-economic perspectives as complements rather than substitutes. They usefully complement and cross-check one another rather than exclude each other as incompatible rivals. Second, while it is obvious that F53 is not to be celebrated for its elaborate philosophical clarity and systematicity, I do think F53 is a delightfully useful piece of writing from a philosophical point of view. It is a rich pool of philosophically intriguing insights that pose difficult challenges to the philosophical analysis of economic theorizing and reasoning. Moreover, published in 1953, many of its ideas anticipated later "post-positivist" ideas and arguments in the philosophy of science (such as the centrality of disciplinary community and culture, the theory-ladenness of observations, and the underdetermination of theories by data). Pointing this out has been a theme in my contributions to F53 studies and it is also one theme in my second chapter to this volume. Third, while it is obvious that due to the ambiguities of F53 the message of the essay is hard to characterize using a single philosophical label, it may be equally problematic to identify Friedman's methodology as "Marshallian" due to the simple fact that "Marshallian" is far from an unambiguous label itself, with fixed and well-defined contents.

Friedman himself drew a distinction between "Marshallian" and "Walrasian" ways of doing economics and elsewhere – not in F53 – identified his own approach with the Marshallian mode. He actively portrayed his position in negative terms by leveling criticisms against what he depicts as the unacceptable "Walrasian" approach. As pointed out by Michel De Vroey in this volume, Friedman's understanding of "Walrasian" was not fully coherent and historically accurate. It would not be surprising if the opposing "Marshallian" label were to suffer from similar unclarities.

Hence, whether using philosophical labels (such as "instrumentalism") or intra-economics labels (such as "Marshallian"), one cannot escape the hard task of offering further detailed specifications and elaborations. One has to look into the details of F53 and Friedman's economics (and whatever other things are relevant) to make progress in understanding Friedman's methodology (or in just understanding F53, were this to be the goal). Interaction and collaboration between philosophical concepts and those derived from within economics (while granting that there is no strict boundary line between the two) will be advisable in future investigations.

An extreme conclusion would be to label Friedman's methodological position simply as "Friedmanian." This *"intra-Friedmanite"* strategy would have the advantage of evading the problems of extra-economic and intra-economic labels of the above kind. Yet the task would not be easy. How would one go about selecting the relevant features of the various methodological statements and practices that can be ascribed to Friedman? Would one include a comprehensive and complex set of details and peculiarities, throughout his intellectual career and across various rhetorical contexts, not forgetting about the numerous inconsistencies within and between those statements and practices? This would single out the position as unique and unlike any other position actually or potentially held by others. Or should one rather pursue a generous interpretation that would ignore the ambiguities and inconsistencies and try to capture the simple and abstract "essence" of Friedman's methodological position, perhaps by way of comparing and contrasting his statements with those of relevant others? This, too, might end up with describing a unique position. (Note that one may also choose to include some of the inconsistencies in one's depiction of the simple essence of Friedman's position – or the position of F53.) On top of such strategic choices, this line also involves the challenge of collecting and processing masses of textual and other evidence that contributes to the contents of the label "Friedmanian" methodology.[2] Anyhow, when pursued on a broad front in search for Friedman's methodology, this line has mainly historical relevance. In contrast, a reception methodologist reading F53 only from the point of view of its later receptions and functions is relatively uninterested in the contents of "Friedmanian methodology," provided they have no major consequences for the reception of F53.

Finally, it is also possible to use *intra-F53* labels when characterizing the message of F53. One such possibility would be to say F53 exemplifies a "predictivist" position. Indeed, even though the very term "predictivism" does not appear in the text of F53, it seems an appropriate derivative of the repeated emphasis in F53 on the role of prediction as the goal and standard of economic theorizing. Another intra-F53 label is to say that it endorses an "as-if methodology". This might appear even more accurate given that F53 formulates many hypotheses in terms of the "as-if" locution.

Again, the intra-F53 strategy of labeling is no less problematic than the other three strategies. This is because neither of the labels, "predictivism" or "as-if methodology," is able to fix a well-defined and distinctive methodological position. Indeed, many different and rival methodological views put stress on prediction, and likewise the as-if locution can be employed to express a number of different ideas with a number of different philosophical commitments. Just as with the other three labeling strategies, this gives rise to the further need to provide more detailed analyses, this time of the different meanings and uses of both prediction and the as-if. Thus to say that the central message of F53 is the importance

---

[2] That the task would not be easy is revealed by Hammond's (1992a) interview with Friedman on the latter's methodology: the interview is revealing in that it manages to reveal so little, suggesting that perhaps there is little more there to be revealed concerning the "essence" of Friedman's consciously held methodology.

of testing theories by their predictive implications, as Williamson does in his chapter, is not yet detailed enough to distinguish Friedman or F53 from many other similar but rival views.

My response to all four strategies of labeling – extra-economic, intra-economic, intra-Friedmanite, intra-F53 – has been the same. Labels are useful and necessary, but if unsuccessful, they can be uninformative and even misleading. To make them accurate and informative, more details and qualifications are needed about the targets they are used for naming, and about the purposes these labels are intended to serve. Providing such details and qualifications is the task of careful empirical and conceptual inquiry into the available textual and other evidence. The present volume sets out to contribute to just such inquiry.

References

Amadae, S. M. (2003). *Rationalizing Capitalist Democracy. The Cold War Origins of Rational Choice Liberalism*. Chicago: University of Chicago Press

Bear, D. V. T. and Daniel Orr (1967). Logic and expediency in economic theorizing. *Journal of Political Economy*, 75, 188–96

Blaug, Mark (1980). *The Methodology of Economics*. Cambridge: Cambridge University Press

Boland, Larry (1979). A critique of Friedman's critics. *Journal of Economic Literature*, 17, 503–22

Brunner, Karl (1969). "Assumptions" and the cognitive quality of theories. *Synthese*, 20, 501–25

Caldwell, Bruce J. (1980). A critique of Friedman's methodological instrumentalism. *Southern Economic Journal*, 47, 366–74

(1992). Friedman's predictivist methodological instrumentalism – a modification. *Research in the History of Economic Thought and Methodology*, 10, 119–28

Friedman, Milton (1953). The methodology of positive economics. In *Essays in Positive Economics*. Chicago: Chicago University Press, pp. 3–43

Hammond, J. Daniel (1992a). An interview with Milton Friedman on methodology. *Research in the History of Economic Thought and Methodology*, 10, 91–118

(1992b). The problem of context for Friedman's methodology. *Research in the History of Economic Thought and Methodology*, 10, 129–47

(1996). *Theory and Measurement: Causality Issues in Milton Friedman's Monetary Economics*. Cambridge: Cambridge University Press

Hausman, Daniel (1992). "Why look under the hood?" In *Essays in Philosophy and Economic Methodology*. Cambridge: Cambridge University Press

Hirsch, Abraham and De Marchi, Neil (1990). *Milton Friedman: Economics in Theory and Practice*. Hertfordshire: Harvester Wheatsheaf

Koopmans, Tjalling C. (1957). *Three Essays on the State of Economic Science*. New York: McGraw-Hill

Machlup, Fritz (1946). Marginal analysis and empirical research. *American Economic Review*, 36, 519–54
  (1955). The problem of verification in economics. *Southern Economic Journal*, 22, 1–21
Mäki, Uskali (1986). Rhetoric at the expense of coherence: a reinterpretation of Milton Friedman's methodology. *Research in the History of Economic Thought and Methodology*, 4, 127–43
  (1992). Friedman and realism. *Research in the History of Economic Thought and Methodology*, 10, 171–95
  (2000). Kinds of assumptions and their truth: Shaking an untwisted F-twist. *Kyklos*, 53, 303–22
Melitz, Jack (1965). Friedman and Machlup on the significance of testing economic assumptions. *Journal of Political Economy*, 73, 37–60
Mirowski, Philip (2002). *Machine Dreams: Economics Becomes a Cyborg Science.* Cambridge: Cambridge University Press
Musgrave, Alan (1981). "Unreal assumptions" in economic theory. *Kyklos*, 34, 377–87
Nagel, Ernest (1961). *The Structure of Science.* London: Routledge and Kegan Paul
  (1963). Assumptions in economic theory. *American Economic Review*, 53, 211–19
Reisch, George A. (2005). *How the Cold War Transformed Philosophy of Science.* Cambridge: Cambridge University Press
Rotwein, Eugene (1959). On "The methodology of positive economics." *Quarterly Journal of Economics*, 73, 554–75
Samuelson, Paul (1963). Problems of methodology – discussion. *American Economic Review, Papers and Proceedings*, 53, 231–6
Simon, Herbert (1963). Problems of methodology – discussion. *American Economic Review, Papers and Proceedings*, 53, 229–31
Winter, Sidney G. (1964). Economic "natural selection" and the theory of the firm. *Yale Economic Essays*, 4, 225–72
Wong, S. (1973). The "F-twist" and the methodology of Paul Samuelson. *American Economic Review*, 63, 312–25

2　Early drafts of Friedman's methodology essay

J. Daniel Hammond

1　Introduction

Milton Friedman's essay, "The methodology of positive economics" (F53), has been many things to many people since it was published in 1953 as the "Introduction" to *Essays in Positive Economics*. Generations of graduate students have learned a lesson (*the* lesson for most) in what it means for economics to be a science. Philosophers and methodologists have seen it as Friedman's apologetic for this or that philosophy of science. Some have used it as a whipping boy to expose the philosophical naiveté of economists. Others have used it to frame the parameters of the "Chicago school."[1]

For close to four decades after its publication those who have used the essay treated it as the beginning and end of Friedman's methodology. More recently this has changed as interpreters and critics have looked to other works by Friedman, on methodology and on economics, and into the context from which he wrote it for insights to the essay's substance.[2]

A 1988 interview with Milton Friedman (Hammond 1992a) began to uncover the unpublished historical background for Friedman's methodology. However, while he talked at length in the interview about his methodology and speculated about its intellectual roots, Friedman was unable to shed any light on the history of the essay itself. He said, 'I don't really remember why I wrote that article to tell you the truth … What I don't know is whether the idea of the collection of essays came first, or the essay came first' (Hammond 1992a, 106). This history, the history of the

---

[1] A few examples from the voluminous literature will suffice. Wong (1973) was the first of a number of readers including Boland (1979) and Caldwell (1980, 1982, 1992) who interpreted Friedman's methodology as instrumentalism. Alan Walters (1987) claims that Friedman introduced Popper's philosophy of science to economists. McCloskey (1983, 1985) tags the essay as one of the "main texts" of "modernism," for which he uses the Chicago school as a primary exemplar. See Hammond (1992b) for more on the various interpretations.

[2] My contributions to this include Hammond (1992b) and (1996) See also Hirsch and De Marchi (1990).

making of the essay, is important for our understanding of the text in the narrow sense and Friedman's methodology in the broader sense. In the Friedman Papers at the Hoover Institution are two preliminary drafts of the essay along with other unpublished documents that shed considerable light on why Friedman wrote the essay and what he intended the message to be. The remainder of this chapter sketches the evolution of the essay through the two preliminary drafts into the final published version. This history of the essay's making helps us see not only from whence the essay came but also what was central and what peripheral in Friedman's argument as presented in *Essays in Positive Economics*.

2   Draft one: "Descriptive validity vs. analytical relevance in economic theory"

The earliest draft of Friedman's methodology essay that I have been able to identify (which I will label draft one) has the title "Descriptive validity vs. analytical relevance in economic theory." To judge from the citations and from Friedman's correspondence it would appear that he began writing it in late 1947 or early 1948 and finished in the summer of 1948.[3] The paper is twenty-four typescript pages. Friedman opens with the remark that theories are often judged by two criteria: the validity of their assumptions and the validity of their implications. Neoclassical theory that assumes perfect competition is judged "unrealistic" by the first criterion, and business cycle theories are rejected by the second. Friedman says he will demonstrate that this view "is fundamentally wrong and is productive of much mischief" (Descrip, 1). He explains what he means in a manner that has become familiar to readers of the 1953 essay, that "the two tests, when examined critically, reduce to one, since the only relevant criterion for judging whether the assumptions are sufficiently good approximations for the purpose in hand is whether they lead to valid conclusions" (Descrip, 1). He distinguishes between "mere" validity of a theory, and significance or importance, arguing that significant theories have assumptions that are "inaccurate representations of reality." This is

---

[3] The paper contains a reference to R. A. Gordon's June 1948 *American Economic Review* article, "Short-period price determination in theory and practice." There is, on the other hand no reference to A. G. Hart's paper for the 1948 American Economic Association meeting. As a discussant, Friedman criticized Hart's suggestion that economists should use survey evidence. This dating of draft one is also suggested by the fact that Friedman wrote to George Stigler in November 1947, "I have gotten involved for various irrelevant reasons in a number of discussions of scientific methodology related to the kind of thing you are talking about. In the course of these I have been led to go further than I had before in distinguishing between description and analysis" (MF to GS, November 19, 1947).

because a significant theory necessarily abstracts the crucial elements from the complex mass of circumstances surrounding the phenomenon under explanation.

Friedman suggests that this insight will likely appear "trite and hardly worth explicit formulation and discussion" (Descrip, 2). Friedman may well have thought that on abstract methodological grounds he would find no opposition to his argument. Or this may be a rhetorical gambit used to establish credibility before actually making the argument. But, whether the methodology could be made self-evident or not, there was in Friedman's mind a serious problem, for economics was proceeding down the wrong methodological path. He draws on two examples to illustrate this: monopolistic (imperfect) competition, which was a reaction against the assumptions of "pure competition" and "pure monopoly," and a series of *American Economic Review* (*AER*) articles criticizing and defending marginal analysis. Friedman indicates that he considers the second example the clearer but less important of the two. He postpones detailed treatment of the two cases until after discussion of the methodological issues.

This discussion opens with the familiar example of the formula $s = \frac{1}{2} gt^2$, used to relate the distance a body falls in a vacuum (s) to the force of gravity (g) and the time the body is falling (t).[4] Friedman interprets applications of the hypothesis represented by this equation as being made under the "as-if" condition. A ball falls from the roof of a building "as if" it were in a vacuum. He considers the outcome of different applications: a feather dropped from the building's roof, and the ball dropped from an airplane at 30,000 feet. He claims that the example illustrates the impossibility of testing a hypothesis by its assumptions, and moreover the inherent ambiguity in the very idea of "the assumptions of a theory." Air pressure is only one of several factors that determine how well the formula works. What are commonly regarded as the assumptions of a theory are in fact parts of the specification of conditions under which the theory is expected to work. And the only way to see which conditions are critical or at what point any of them become critical in the context of the others is to test the theory by its implications. Thus Friedman concludes that "the formula is accepted because it works, not because we live in an approximate vacuum – whatever that means" (Descrip, 4–5).

---

[4] In the November 19, 1947 letter to Stigler Friedman used the distance formula to introduce Stigler to his idea that the only way to determine how closely assumptions correspond to reality is by checking the theory's predictions. The main purpose of this letter was to respond to a draft of Stigler's essay on Chamberlin (1949). Friedman says, "I thoroughly agree with you … The main additional point I would like to make is that you do not really go at all far enough" (MF to GS, November 19, 1947).

Friedman next turns to an example taken from Friedman and Savage (1948) – the billiards player. One might conceivably construct a complicated mathematical formula that would determine the best shot for any given arrangement of the balls on the table. This formula then could be used to predict the shots made by the billiards player "as if" he made the appropriate calculations with the formula. Our confidence in the formula would be based on our ability to use it to predict his shots, not on our belief that he knew the mathematics and was actually able to make the calculations. "In this case it seems highly unlikely that even the description of the area of validity of the hypothesis would employ directly any of the 'assumptions' of the hypothesis" (Descrip, 7). Friedman argues that it is but a short step from these two examples to the hypothesis that businessmen behave "as if" they calculate marginal cost and marginal revenue to maximize profit.

Next, he introduces the natural selection argument, saying that the businessman's situation is like the billiards player's. The latter will not be an expert at billiards unless he can make shots "as if" he did the calculations. The businessman likewise will not long stay in business unless he reaches the same result that marginal theory implies. Any alternative theory that *does not* imply the same behavior as the profit maximization hypothesis *does* imply abundant opportunities for easy profit, and according to Friedman this is clearly not the kind of world in which we live. Since this implication of the alternative theories is false they must be rejected in favor of the profit maximization hypothesis for a wide range of circumstances. Expressing the idea differently, Friedman suggests that even if firms chose their output randomly, but once and for all, and if their funding was from internal sources only, the outcome via natural selection would be the same as that implied by profit maximization.

As he continues explaining his position Friedman insists that the "as if" profit maximization construct does not imply that we actually view businessmen as "selfish, coldly-calculating, and heartless" any more than the formula $s = \frac{1}{2} gt^2$ implies that we live in a vacuum. Rather, each pulls parts of reality that are more essential away from those which are less essential *in the circumstances*. So, Friedman points out, the profit maximization hypothesis should not be expected to be equally useful in all aspects of human behavior.

This brings Friedman to what he considers the real but largely neglected problem of profit maximization – determining the limits of the hypothesis, "the circumstances under which, and the problems for which, it gives reasonably good predictions" (Descrip, 11). He speculates that the hypothesis will prove to be of no great use in explaining the behavior of individual firms. Its strength is that it identifies a force that operates on firms from the outside. For any given firm there will likely be aberrations, but across firms these should cancel out, so that the hypothesis will work best for industries.[5]

Friedman then shifts to the other issue at stake in the debates over monopolistic competition and Marshall's industry analysis. This is the assumption of perfect competition. He claims that critics are wrong in attributing to Marshall the "assumption" that real-world industries in fact are perfectly competitive. With several page citations from *Principles* he claims that "Marshall took the world as it was, he sought to construct an 'engine' to analyze it, not a photographic reproduction of it" (Descrip, 13). Marshall used perfect competition in the "as if" mode, and then only for situations in which the common forces from outside such as changes in demand for firms' product are dominant. For this kind of analysis it is not possible to once and for all divide firms into industries by measures such as cross-elasticity. Quoting Marshall, "The question where the lines of division between different commodities (i.e. industries) should be drawn must be settled by convenience of the particular discussion" (Descrip, 14; Marshall 1920, 100).

Friedman uses examples of a Federal cigarette tax (where perfect competition is appropriate) and war-time price controls on cigarettes (where it is not) to illustrate how "everything depends on the problem; and there is no inconsistency in regarding firms as if they were perfect competitors for one problem, and perfect monopolists for another" (Descrip, 14). In the first case Friedman speculates that the firms will respond as if they produced identical products in perfect competition. For the second there was evidence from World War II that firms increased rather than reduced production, presumably in order to maintain market share.

Friedman acknowledges that it would be desirable to have a general theory of which perfect competition is a special case. But the standards for this theory are that it have "content and substance; it must have implications; and it must have some capable of empirical contradiction and some of substantive interest and importance" (Descrip, 17). The theory of monopolistic competition might be thought of as a general theory, but it has none of the essential features. It is based on the presumption that good theories are "realistic" representations of reality in their assumptions and that the differences between firms and their products are of essential importance. Thus any attempt to apply this theory in the domain of "the real problems of the world," where common forces influence groups of firms, requires that the theory be scuttled. Disciples of Chamberlin and

---

[5] The usefulness of Marshallian industries was the central issue in Friedman's 1941 review of Triffin's *Monopolistic Competition and General Equilibrium Theory*.

Robinson, notably Triffin (1940), have recognized this impasse and chosen fealty to the assumptions over applicability.

Friedman reiterates that a more general theory is to be sought, and characterizes the work of von Neumann and Morgenstern on game theory as such an attempt. Their advantage is in not confusing descriptive validity and analytical relevance. However Friedman has doubts that the experiment will prove successful.

He next turns to the controversy over marginal analysis, suggesting that the best example is the most recent article in the series, by R. A. Gordon (1948). He quotes from Gordon:

There is still need to examine critically the assumptions underlying the conventional theory of the firm and the extent to which these assumptions meet the test of business practice. The following pages elaborate upon a long felt belief that conventional price theory has held to unnecessarily unrealistic assumptions, with the result that our analytical tool box is not as useful as it should be. (Descrip, 18–19; Gordon 1948, 265).

Friedman says that this passage indicates that Gordon is on a dead-end trail, for it presumes that we can directly examine the validity of a theory's assumptions, and it takes descriptive accuracy and comprehensiveness as a standard for theory choice. Friedman makes his point by invoking the notion of a completely representative theory of the wheat market. This would have to account for a multitude of non-essential features such as the types of money and credit used in trading, the color of hair and eyes of traders, as well as their education, the type of soil on which the wheat is grown, and so on. So the converse of Gordon's statement, that if the assumptions are slavishly realistic the theory is not useful, is closer to the truth.

What Gordon has failed to do is to test for the importance of the "unreality" of the assumptions in terms of how the theory's implications accord with reality, and in comparison with an alternative theory. That is, in terms of the example given earlier, Gordon is checking with the billiards player to see how much math he knows. He is not observing his game. Gordon's view that theory is a description of what businessmen actually do is "thoroughly false." A "sophisticated" view of theory is that however businessmen may make their decisions "for a wide class of problems, the results are what they would be *if* businessmen engaged in rational and informed profit maximization" (Descrip, 21; emphasis his). Friedman strings together a number of quotations from Gordon's paper to show the argument. One of these is, "There is an irresistible tendency to price on the basis of average total cost for some 'normal' level of output. This is the yardstick, the short-cut, that businessmen and accountants use, and their aim is more to earn satisfactory profits and play safe than to maximize profits" (Descrip, 22; Gordon 1948,

275). Friedman remarks in a footnote that he has never been able to understand this kind of argument, that behavior is the outcome of an "irresistible" tendency, in the face of observable and clearly false implications. His interpretation of how economists such as Gordon deal with this situation is that they either eliminate all content from their theory, making it tautological, or interpret it in a way that makes it de facto equivalent to the "usual" theory.

Friedman concludes his paper with a response to Gordon's closing section, which has the title "The need for greater realism." The main point Friedman makes here is that he has no dispute with Gordon's account of the lack of descriptive realism in standard theory. His quarrel is over implications. Gordon thinks greater realism would make theory more useful; Friedman does not. But Gordon offers no evidence that a more realistic theory is more useful. In the absence of such evidence the greater complexity is a burden with no counterweight. Friedman tries to make clear that he is not arguing that marginal theory is useful, though he thinks it is. He is arguing over the grounds for determining this. In his final statement Friedman suggests an appropriate role for descriptive studies of business behavior. This is in deriving new hypotheses, an activity which is distinct from testing existing hypotheses. Construction of new hypotheses depends on "intuition," "inspiration," and "invention," and is not subject to formal methodological analysis.[6]

---

[6] This became a point of dispute between Friedman and George Stigler and Arthur Burns. In September 1948 Stigler wrote to Friedman:

> Personally I would like to see it published (in part because I've paraphrased the argument in two paragraphs of my Chamberlin essay, and would like to give a more specific reference). But I keep feeling that you arouse skepticism and opposition by stopping where you do. Because surely in some sense an assumption can be more promising than another ... It is surely possible to say something about some assumptions being more promising than others, and yet not to take back any of the things you are saying at present. If you can pierce this muddy frontier of your article, it would be a great improvement. (GS to MF, September 1948)

Friedman responded:

> I think part of the difficulty you have on the methodology problem arises out of the fact that the issues it deals with pertain only to one small part of all work in economics. One might, I suppose, separate out four kinds of things that economists and other scientists do: first, the collection of data to provide something to generalize from; second, the derivation of hypotheses to generalize the empirical uniformities discovered in the data; third, the testing of these hypotheses; and fourth, the utilization of them. My strictures apply only to the third of these steps ... The real problem that you raise arises, I take it, when somebody proposes a theory which we haven't as yet been able to test, and the question arises, shall we use it instead of some alternative. It's at this point that one is most likely to say that he is judging the theory by its assumptions and to say that he will have some confidence in it if the assumptions are reasonable, and he will not if they are not. This is the kind of point Arthur was raising most strenuously this summer against it. (MF to GS, October 4, 1948)

3   Draft two: "The relevance of economic analysis to prediction and policy"

The next draft has a different title, "The relevance of economic analysis to prediction and policy," and considerable new content. At forty-seven pages, it is almost exactly twice as long as the first. The manuscript is undated, but we can place it in the fall of 1952. The copy that I am working from has a holographic note on the first page from Friedman to Arthur Burns identifying this as "the piece I spoke of," and Burns wrote a November 26, 1952 letter in reaction to the paper.[7] Also, the paper opens with a footnote explaining that "I have incorporated bodily in this article without special reference most of my brief Comment (1952a) in *A Survey of Contemporary Economics*," which was published in 1952.

Friedman opens with what is now familiar to readers of the published version of "The methodology of positive economics," a reference to J. N. Keynes's "admirable book" on *The Scope and Method of Political Economy*, which Friedman uses to distinguish positive from normative science and to make the point that there is confusion between the two. Friedman claims that this confusion will arise so long as there are self-proclaimed "experts" with their own agendas.[8] He writes of the distinctions between positive and normative economics and of the influence which properly runs one way, from positive to normative economics. He identifies the task of positive economics as "to make correct predictions about the consequences of any change in circumstances," and claims that its performance is to be judged by "the precision, scope, and conformity with experience of the predictions it yields" (Friedman 1952b, 2). He judges that most disputes over economic policy are the result of differences on positive

---

[7] Burns wrote, "In accepting the heart of your argument, I do not, however, accept the details of your exposition. I have made perhaps four or five comments on the margin, whereas forty of four hundred are probably called for" (AB to MF, November 26, 1952). Burns thought that Friedman had not explored sufficiently the bases on which confidence rests in not yet tested theories. Thus he criticized Friedman for not making, or not making clearly enough, the very sort of distinction that Friedman began to make in his letter to Stigler about draft one, and which he attempted in draft two.

    Burns also thought the illustrations from economic theory were too sketchy, that none were presented with the precision required for scientific testing. He suggested that the proper time for stating precisely the circumstances under which the hypothesis is expected to hold is before its testing.

[8] I have come across several pages of text that seem to have been intended as part of a draft of Friedman's essay, in which he reproduces Keynes's quotation from F. A. Walker that gives the ubiquity of quackery as reason for concern with economic methodology. Friedman indicates more faith than Keynes in the public's ability to discriminate genuine science from quackery. He contends that the more important reason methodology is valuable is the special difficulty in economics of producing clear-cut evidence for or against theories.

analysis, "different predictions about the consequences of taking action," rather than differences in values. The minimum wage, the role of trade unions, price controls, tariffs, regulation of business, and even socialism are given as examples. He concludes that making progress in positive economics is of more importance than making progress in normative economics proper. This introduction in draft two is different only in minor details from that of the published essay. It has the same title, "The relation between positive and normative economics." But the introduction, with its references to Keynes and positive and normative science, is not in draft one.

The second section of draft two likewise has a title that is carried over into the published version, "Positive economics." The section opens with the distinction, now familiar to readers of Friedman's essay but new in draft two, between theory as "language" and as "substantive hypotheses." Friedman gives citations from Marshall's "The present position of economics" ([1885] 1925), and from his own "The Marshallian demand curve" (1949), and "Lange on price flexibility and employment" (1946). As a language (a set of tautologies) theory is to be judged by criteria "appropriate to a filing system," which are partly logical and partly factual. As a body of substantive hypotheses it is judged by "its predictive power for the class of phenomena which it is intended to 'explain' " (Friedman 1952b, 7). He addresses the question of choice among hypotheses that are equally consistent with the evidence, suggesting that the appropriate criteria are "simplicity" and "fruitfulness." He discusses the restricted latitude for controlled experiments in the social sciences, but suggests that often history provides evidence as conclusive as one would get from a controlled experiment.[9] Inflation is suggested as one phenomenon for which the evidence is very clear. Yet even here the inability to produce the "crucial" experiment makes weeding out unsuccessful hypotheses very difficult.

Friedman speculates that the difficulty of testing hypotheses has encouraged "a retreat into purely formal or tautological analysis." Here economics becomes little more than "disguised mathematics." Properly seen, tautologies are to be judged ultimately by how well they facilitate

[9] In 1946 the University of Chicago received a grant from the Volker Fund to initiate a "Program of Factual Research into Questions Basic to the Formulation of a Liberal Economic Policy" ("Free Market Study"), with Aaron Director as director of the study. Friedman was a member of the Executive Committee. The prospectus for the program indicates the goal of modeling the studies after the experimental natural sciences. "Studies such as these are of the nature of experiments in the physical sciences, most of which are unsuccessful" (University of Chicago, "A Program...", 5). It also is based on the same presumption that Friedman stated in the methodology essay, that "Disagreement about the appropriate economic policy for the United States arises in considerable measure from disagreement about facts rather than from differences in objectives" ("A Program...", 1).

empirical analysis. However, the more serious outcome of the difficulty of testing hypotheses is misunderstanding of the role of empirical evidence, as seen in the idea that theories can be tested by their assumptions. Here Friedman breaks the role of empirical evidence into two "methodologically distinct" but temporally overlapping roles – construction of new hypotheses and testing of existing hypotheses.

The difficulty in the social sciences of getting new evidence for this class of phenomena (that which the hypothesis is designed to explain) and of judging its conformity with the implications of the hypothesis makes it tempting to suppose that other, more readily available evidence, is equally relevant to the validity of the hypotheses; to suppose that hypotheses have not only "implications" but also "assumptions," and that the conformity of these "assumptions" to "reality" is a test of the validity of the hypothesis *different from* or *additional to* the test by implications." (Friedman 1952b, 12; emphasis his)

Friedman continues with the argument that because explanatory theory necessarily abstracts from complex reality "in general, the more significant the theory, the more unrealistic the assumptions" (Friedman 1952b, 13). The key is not whether assumptions are descriptively "realistic," "but whether they are sufficiently good approximations for the purpose at hand. And this question can be answered only by seeing whether they work, which means whether the theory yields sufficiently accurate predictions. The supposedly two independent tests thus reduce to one" (Friedman 1952b, 13).

Up to this point the material in the section headed "Positive economics" is new to draft two, and with two exceptions identical to the section with the same title in the published version.[10] The exceptions are two passages added to the final version. Just after making the distinction between theory as language and as substantive hypotheses Friedman adds a paragraph to the published version including past events not yet observed in what he means by "predictions" (F53, 9). He adds another passage nearby that gives an example (excise tax) of a situation where predictions do not allow the investigator to choose between theories, making it necessary to fall back on "simplicity" and "fruitfulness" for theory choice.

The final paragraph of the section on "Positive economics" in draft two introduces the reader to the two outcomes of muddled methodology that Friedman treats, monopolistic competition and the *AER* debate over

---

[10] By "new to draft two" I mean the material is not in draft one. Friedman had made similar arguments elsewhere, as indicated by his references to "Lange on price flexibility and employment" (1946), "The Marshallian demand curve" (1949), and Friedman and Savage's "The expected-utility hypothesis and the measurability of utility" (1952).

marginalism. This paragraph is identical to the concluding paragraph on pp. 15–16 in the published version. Aside from the lengthy footnote citing the *AER* articles (footnote 13 in the published version), it is similar to material on pp. 2–3 of draft one. So here, fourteen pages into draft two and fifteen pages into the published version the discussion comes to the point at which draft one begins.

Section III contains discussion of the distance formula and the billiards player taken from pages 3 through 8 of draft one. It also matches up for the most part with section III in the published draft; in both versions the section's title is "Can a(n) hypothesis be tested by the realism of its assumptions?"

The opening paragraph lays out the distance formula and the applications: a compact ball dropped from a roof; a feather dropped from the same roof; and the ball dropped from an airplane. Each of these circumstances produces a different result. The next paragraph poses the question of how much difference between the predicted and measured distance is sufficient to conclude that the formula "does not work." This depends, according to Friedman, on the accuracy of the predictions from an alternative hypothesis and on the relative costs of using the two hypotheses.

This discussion is virtually word for word the same as the published version. The first paragraph is rewritten from draft one and the second paragraph is new. The copy of draft one that I am working from has penciled changes which mostly match up with the text in this second draft, but they do not match up wholly. This suggests that there was still another draft with at least minor changes between what I am treating as draft one and draft two.

Friedman's use of the distance formula is completed with his argument that the real task for use of the formula is to determine the circumstances under which it works, or how well it works under different circumstances. Here he makes the contrast between more and less general theories. But, he contends, specifying the conditions under which the less general and simpler hypothesis works, or the errors obtained with certain values for the disturbing factors, is quite different from testing the hypothesis by determining whether the assumptions are true or false. This discussion is the same as the published version except for two brief passages added to the latter.[11] These are the statement on p. 18 of the published version which claims that this specification cannot be separated from the hypothesis itself, and the special emphasis drawn on p. 19 to the difference between

---

[11] These appear to be in response to Burns's criticism in the November 26, 1952 letter.

the specification Friedman is concerned with here and the use of assumptions to *determine* the circumstances for which the hypothesis holds.

Friedman then moves to the example of the positioning of leaves around a tree, which is not in draft one. The text is the same as that in the published version. Explanation is given in a footnote that Friedman's use of the example is "though independent in origin, ... similar to and in much the same spirit" as that used by Armen Alchian in his June 1950 *Journal of Political Economy* article.[12] The comparison is drawn between a simple hypothesis that leaves are positioned *as if* they sought out and maximized the amount of sunlight they receive, and the more general theory that sunlight contributes to growth and survivability of leaves. The choice between these theories rests, once again, not in a comparison of assumptions with reality but in their ability to predict accurately over a wide variety of circumstances.

The billiards player example, originally in Friedman and Savage (1948), is rewritten from the first draft, and identical to the published version through the example's end in draft two. The point is made that our confidence in the hypothesis that the expert billiards player makes shots *as if* he could calculate angles and solve the mathematical formulas that describe the optimal shot comes from the fact that unless he can achieve roughly the same result he will not in fact *be* an expert billiards player. We judge the formula on the basis of how well it predicts his shots, not on how he says he makes his shots.

Thereafter the published version has material that is pulled forward from further into draft two (section 6, "The present state of positive economics") and rewritten. This is the final two paragraphs of section 3 in the published version. Here Friedman returns to the maximization of returns hypothesis to draw the parallel between the examples from outside economics and the economic issue; natural selection ensures that successful (surviving) businessmen's behavior is *as if* they maximized returns. The second paragraph that Friedman pulls forward points to the difficulty of documenting the success of the maximization of returns hypothesis since the "experience from countless applications of the hypothesis to specific problems" is "scattered in numerous memorandums, articles, and monographs concerned primarily with specific concrete problems rather than with submitting the hypothesis to test" (F53, 22–3).

Section IV of draft two has the same title ("The significance and role of the "assumptions" of a theory") and subsections as the published version. The essential content is the same, though there are a number of changes

---

[12] Friedman read and criticized several drafts of Alchian's paper in 1949 and 1950 before it was accepted for the *Journal of Political Economy*.

and additions to the published version. But in relation to draft one this section is wholly new. The discussion is Friedman's attempt to identify some constructive use for "assumptions," given "the strong tendency we all have to speak of the assumptions of a theory and to compare the assumptions of alternative theories" (Friedman 1952b, 20), and in response to the criticisms of Stigler and Burns. Friedman warns, however, that he is less confident in the positive comments that follow than he is in the negative comments that make up much of the rest of the essay.

He identifies three positive roles for assumptions: (1) economical presentation of a theory; (2) facilitation of indirect tests of the hypothesis by its implications; and (3) specification of conditions under which the hypothesis is expected to hold. As the third has been covered in earlier parts of the essay, Friedman devotes the balance of this section to the first two.

The beginning of the discussion of the role of assumptions in stating a theory is identical in draft two and the published version. The assumptions sort out in a short-hand manner factors that are expected to influence the phenomenon under explanation into those that are more and those that are less important. A hypothesis has two parts, the abstract model and the rules which define the class of phenomena for which the model is taken to be an adequate representation and which specify the correspondence between variables in the model and observable phenomena. The model is abstract and complete; the rules are concrete and necessarily incomplete. In the two paragraphs where Friedman lays out these differences between the parts of hypotheses (pp. 24–5 in F53) there are several changes made between draft two and the final. A sentence, "At this stage (the abstract model), such qualifications (e.g. that air pressure is 'small', not zero) are signs of sloppiness and fuzzy-mindedness, not of practicality or realism," is dropped. This would appear to be the result of Arthur Burns's marginal notation, "to me!" Friedman also adds a sentence stressing the importance of making the rules explicit in the interest of making science as objective as possible.

The example of Euclidian geometry as an abstract model with pure but "unrealistic" lines and the application of this model with a chalk mark on a blackboard is the same in this draft as in the final. So is the final paragraph in the subsection, which sums up the use of assumptions for stating key elements of the abstract model.

The next subsection discusses the use of assumptions as an indirect test of a theory.[13] The first three paragraphs of the published version are not in

[13] Friedman sketched the outlines of this argument in his October 4, 1948 letter to George Stigler. Stigler responded, "I like your general position but want you to enlarge it, –

draft two, which starts off by directly pointing out that assignment of parts of a theory into "assumptions" and "implications" is a matter of convention. Implications can be treated as assumptions and vice versa. The evidential value of this reversibility is limited, however, when the "assumptions" refer to a class of phenomena different from those the theory is intended to explain. Here a brief elaboration in draft two is cut for the final.

A second and closely related way in which assumptions can facilitate indirect testing is when the kinship of two hypotheses can be demonstrated by restating them in terms of the same assumption, and evidence for the implications of one provides indirect support for the other. Friedman gives as an example the use of the self-interest assumption along with market power to explain different degrees of racial discrimination across industries or regions. Here the economist's expectation that this "economic" hypothesis will account for the discrimination is based on success in using it to explain other behavior. Friedman's changes here between draft two and the final again bear the mark of Arthur Burns's comments. The section concludes with observations on the choice of hypotheses in the absence of a crucial test of the implications, and the role of the scientist's background in influencing the amount of evidence he requires before making a judgment for or against a hypothesis. Here two sentences are added to the published version that roughly double the length of the final paragraph. They point out the frequent need for a conclusion in advance of a satisfactory test and the impossibility of completely "objective" choice among hypotheses.

In section V, "Some implications for economic issues," Friedman turns to the methodologically charged economic issues that dominate the first draft but in draft two are encountered twenty-six pages into the manuscript (twenty-seven pages into the published version). Section V shows considerable editing and rearranging between draft two and the published version, including the folding in of material from section VI, a section which is dropped in the final.

Friedman quotes Veblen and H. M. Oliver to put the "unrealistic assumptions" before his readers. He immediately thereafter pulls material forward from section VI of draft two for the published version. This is the comparison of criticism of "orthodox" theory on the basis of survey evidence (e.g. Hall and Hitch 1939) with asking octogenarians how they

precisely as you are enlarging it in your letter to me. While some elaboration along these lines will take some of the paradox out of your thesis (and in a certain sense weaken its message unless you write very carefully), it will create sympathy for and receptiveness to your thesis and make the paper much more influential" (GS to MF, undated [October 1948]).

account for long life. The first two references in footnote 22 of the published version are added to the corresponding footnote in draft two.

Friedman recalls from earlier discussion of the distance formula ($s = \frac{1}{2} gt^2$) that complete realism as demanded by the critics is impossible, a point he illustrates here with another example indicating the absurdity of a "realistic" theory of the wheat market. This example is taken from p. 19 of draft one. Friedman admits that he is attacking a straw man, since no reasonable critic would demand a thoroughly realistic theory of business behavior, but he argues that the critics themselves offer no basis for stopping short of the straw man. They must either go all the way or fall back on predictive accuracy as the test of how much realism is enough.

An allusion to the purported complexity of business cycle phenomena dictating a complex theory is found at this point in draft two, as it is in the final version. This and a reference to Sydney Alexander's 1951 *AER* paper are new in draft two, but the shadow of draft one's title is found in the opening sentence of this (and the next) paragraph, where Friedman refers to the confusion between descriptive accuracy and analytical relevance.

Friedman next argues that the misguided effort to make abstract models descriptively accurate is illustrated clearly in the charge that Marshall assumed the world was made up of perfectly competitive industries. Friedman challenges Marshall's critics to find in *Principles* an assumption that industries are perfectly competitive. What they will find, according to Friedman, is that Marshall "took the world as it is." This discussion is taken with minor changes from draft one, beginning on p. 12. Marshall's view as interpreted by Friedman is that grouping firms into industries cannot be done once and for all. It is contingent on their being subject to a common external stimulus and on the analytical purpose at hand. The most prominent change in Friedman's explanation from draft one to draft two (and the published version) is his use of the distinction between the abstract model, in which there are the ideal types of perfect competition, infinitely elastic demand curves for identical products, etc., and the rules for classification in real-world applications. Otherwise Friedman's interpretation of Marshall is the same as in draft one.

The critics' mistake is to suppose that finding the abstract model's ideal types in the real world is necessary for applications. Friedman draws on the distance formula and chalk mark examples to emphasize the error in this supposition. He also appeals to the example used in draft one to illustrate how the cigarette industry can be treated as competitive or monopolistic, depending on the problem at hand.

Friedman leads into his criticism of the theory of monopolistic competition by granting that it would be desirable to have a theory more general than Marshall's. But to be useful "it must have implications susceptible to empirical contradiction and of substantive interest and importance" (Friedman 1952b, 34). Monopolistic competition is, according to Friedman, a failed attempt to construct such a theory. The failure is seen most clearly in this theory's inability to treat problems involving groups of firms. Proponents of the theory find themselves on the horns of a dilemma; they must either introduce "fuzziness and undefinable terms into the abstract model where they have no place" (Friedman 1952b, 35), or forego the opportunity of treating problems faced by groups of firms, retreating into the economics of the individual firm. In draft two (and draft one) there is a concluding paragraph for section 5 which is dropped in the published version. It suggests that the von Neumann–Morgenstern theory of games is more likely than monopolistic competition to provide a general theory within which Marshallian analysis will be a special case. Friedman doubts that even this attempt to develop the more general theory will succeed; "yet it is not doomed from the start by a confusion between descriptive realism and analytical relevance" (Friedman 1952b, 36).[14]

The title of section VI in draft two is "The present state of positive economics." This section is dropped in the published version. As mentioned above, some of the material is folded into section V. Other parts are rewritten and placed in the "Conclusion" of the published version. Some of that discussion, in which Friedman attempts to be more specific about the confidence warranted for different branches of contemporary economic theory, is apparently taken from an early draft of Friedman's essay on Wesley Mitchell.[15] Friedman begins with the caveat, "all that is possible here is a cursory expression of a personal view, together with a somewhat more extensive examination of a particular hypothesis to exemplify the kind of evidence that exists" (Friedman 1952b, 36–7). The corresponding

---

[14] In draft one Friedman says, "I have real doubts that it will succeed." In draft two his prognosis is, "It may not succeed in furnishing a fruitful construction within which the Marshallian analysis can find its place as a special case ..."

[15] In the Friedman Papers at the Hoover Institution there are fragments of two early drafts of Friedman's review of Mitchell's contributions to economics (1950). In a section of one draft entitled "The present state of economic theory," the same title as section VI of draft two of the methodology essay, Friedman writes:

Finally, Mitchell was not only a great scientific worker, but he also was a distinguished essayist. His numerous essays are always well organized and beautifully written, but they are on a different level from his fundamental scientific work. They are far less profound and often implicitly at variance with his own work. In particular, I feel that the remarks on methodology in his essays are, to say the least, unfortunate; and have been the source of much misunderstanding – his scientific instincts, incorporated in his own work, are sounder than his rationalizations of them. (Friedman Papers, Box 53, folder unlabeled)

The paragraph concludes with, "Section 5 discusses briefly this point." In the margin there is the holographic notation, "Have not written such a section. Should I?"

discussion begins three paragraphs into the "Conclusion" of the published version, on p. 41.

Friedman divides economic theory into relative price theory, "which is designed to explain the allocation of resources among alternative ends and the division of the product among the cooperating resources" and monetary theory, "which is designed to explain the absolute level of prices, aggregate output, and other variables for the economy as a whole" (Friedman 1952b, 37). This division itself is based on an "as if"; it is made "as if" money was a "veil" that can largely be ignored when explaining relative prices, and real factors can be ignored when explaining the price level, etc. Friedman then divides these two types of theory into statics and dynamics.

He argues that "the neo-classical theory of relative prices, which reached almost its present form in Alfred Marshall's *Principles of Economics* is, in my opinion, both extremely fruitful and deserving of much confidence for the kind of economic system that characterizes Western nations" (Friedman 1952b, 37). In a statement that is dropped from the published version he contends that

The essence of this theory is that the phenomena with which it deals can be explained or predicted by supposing men to behave as if they sought single-mindedly and successfully to pursue their own interests and as if their interests were predominantly to maximize the money income they could wring from a hostile environment – though so bald and simplified a statement does less than justice to the subtlety of the theoretical structure and the range of phenomena it is capable of illuminating. (Friedman 1952b, 37–8)

The weakness of relative price theory is in capital theory, according to Friedman. The quantity theory of money is deserving of confidence as an explanation of monetary statics. However in monetary dynamics "it is difficult or impossible to single out any theory that can be regarded as deserving of much confidence" (Friedman 1952b, 39). There have been high hopes for Keynesian theories but their predictions have not been confirmed.

Here Friedman returns to the maximization of returns hypothesis to indicate the types of evidence in its favor. There are three. The first is that, if there is natural selection among firms, the hypothesis isolates the condition for survival. This harks back to the illustrations of the billiards player and leaves around a tree in section III. In the published version this discussion is moved to section III. The discussion is also in draft one.

The second and more important type of evidence is the record of successful applications of the hypothesis to specific problems. However, this is hard to document as it is scattered through various publications and because the evidence is generated in the course of applications rather than by a "crucial test." The third type of evidence is the knowledge we have that indicates businessmen's pursuit of profit. This is the "indirect" evidence obtained by reversing the place of assumptions and implications, and is of a lesser order of importance.

Friedman points out that most criticism directed at the maximization of returns hypothesis concerns the third, and least important, class of evidence. He compares the use of surveys of businessmen to determine how they set prices and quantities with the use of surveys of octogenarians for testing theories of longevity. This discussion, as we have seen, is moved forward to the beginning of section V in the published version. Friedman allows a role for survey evidence, but this is in constructing new hypotheses and revising old ones when their predictive power is weak. He repeats that this evidence is not a test of the hypothesis.

He then turns to Gordon's *AER* paper with its consideration of an alternative to the maximization of returns hypothesis. This is that "There is an irresistible tendency to price on the basis of average total costs for some 'normal' level of output" (Friedman 1952b, 43; Gordon 1948, 275). Friedman's challenge is (as on pp. 22–3 of draft one) that this hypothesis is contradicted by observable implications. The counterevidence includes "bargain sales, reductions in price associated with rises in 'average total costs for some "normal" level of output,' increased or reduced prices associated with no changes in costs" (Friedman 1952b, 43). The contradictions can be avoided by defining "average total costs for some "normal" level of output" in a way that makes it depend on demand. But this is no resolution of the problem, it either reduces the hypothesis to a tautology or makes it indistinguishable from the maximization of returns hypothesis.

Section V of draft two concludes with discussion taken from pp. 10–11 in draft one. Here Friedman returns to the more general point that the maximization of returns hypothesis is an "as if" proposition that is supposed to isolate the crucial aspect of behavior for the problem at hand. Its successful application does not suppose or depend on actual behavior that is "selfish, coldly and calculatingly heartless, or all-wise and all-knowing in any descriptive sense, any more than using the formula $s = \frac{1}{2} gt^2$ means 'assuming' we live in a vacuum" (Friedman 1952b, 44). Furthermore, the hypothesis cannot be expected to explain equally well behavior in all settings. "Precisely because it selects one from many aspects of human behavior as central, it is both useful and limited in its applicability" (Friedman 1952b, 44). The challenge that remains for economists regarding the hypothesis is to determine the limits of its applicability. Friedman is skeptical that it will prove applicable to the problems of the individual firm, focusing as it does on forces that operate on firms from the outside.

Section VI is the "Conclusion" of draft two. This is different from the conclusion in the published version, which is almost totally new. In draft two Friedman begins the concluding section with the observation we find at the end of the published conclusion. This is that progress in positive economics depends on both testing existing hypotheses and construction of new hypotheses. Of the latter task there is very little that can be said in formal methodological terms. This is one reason Friedman focuses on testing hypotheses. The other reason is that the obstacles to "crucial tests" lead economists to wrongly reject the principle of testing by implications. This methodological confusion has:

> fostered mathematical economics, with its emphasis on Walrasian general equilibrium analysis as an escape from the *ceteris paribus* of partial equilibrium analysis; it explicitly motivated monopolistic competition analysis and explains its popularity; it encouraged emphasis on arithmetical rather than economic considerations in all branches of economic analysis, it was the battle cry of institutionalism and the closely related emphasis on extensive statistical studies of economic phenomena; it is a major source of the naïve yet recurring notion that the progress of positive economics depends critically on the progress of psychology; it has been manifested most recently in the belief that a theory can be tested by asking questions of consumers, producers, and the like. (Friedman 1952b, 46)

These tendencies have not been wholly without beneficial results, but have impeded the testing of hypotheses. "Alfred Marshall's emphasis on the construction of an 'engine for the discovery of concrete truth' has tended to be submerged under the urge for descriptive realism" (Friedman 1952b, 47).

4   Conclusion

Friedman worked on the methodology essay over a period of several years, most likely from late 1947 into 1953 when *Essays in Positive Economics* was published. During the period form the mid 1940s through the mid 1950s Friedman was heavily engaged in economic methodology. Methodology is prominent in much of what he wrote during this period. And up to at least 1957 he gave a number of seminars on methodology.[16] There is also

---

[16] There are at least eleven sets of notes for lectures in the Milton Friedman Papers and in his personal files. Some are dated and identified as to the place of the lecture and others are not. The earliest that is dated is March 22, 1950 at Vanderbilt University and the latest is April 23, 1957 at Purdue University.

evidence, in the form of an outline, that at some point Friedman planned to write a book on methodology.

Taking the first draft as its heart, the central methodological message of the essay is that theory necessarily leaves out elements of reality, and consilience of a theory's implications with evidence of the phenomena it is supposed to explain is the only test of how crucial omitted factors are. Apart from this, the very meaning of "the assumptions" of a theory is ambiguous. Friedman used the distance formula and billiards player examples to illustrate these points with theory that abstracts from reality in the "as if" mode in non-economic settings.

As for the connections between methodology and economic theory – and Friedman's concern was always methodology within the context of economic theory issues – the essay was a defense of Marshall's economics from two attacks. One of these was the monopolistic competition of Chamberlin and Triffin, where Marshall's analytical tools of industries, perfect competition, and pure monopoly were attacked. The other was the critique of profit maximization and marginalism by Gordon and others. Friedman thought the limits of the applicability of Marshall's approach had not been determined.

Friedman was imbued with Marshall. His label for his methodology, a label he actually used in some of his methodological writings, was "Marshallian." But for Friedman Marshallian methodology and Marshallian theory went hand in hand. He told students in the opening lecture of Economics 300a at the University of Chicago at about the time he was writing the methodology essay, "Marshall's "Principles" viewed contemporaneously, i.e., as if he were writing today instead of a century ago, is still the best book available in economic theory. This is a sad commentary on the economics of our time. Marshall's superiority is explained primarily by his approach to economics as contrasted with the modern approach" (Lecture Notes, p. 1).

Draft two of the essay and the final published version bear the marks of Burns's and Stigler's responses to draft one. They were particularly concerned that Friedman would lose his readers by appearing to take an overly extreme position on the realism of assumptions. They urged and he responded with two changes. One was to emphasize that his concern was only with the stage of the research enterprise at which one is testing theory. He thought that there was little to say about the "derivation" of theory.[17] The other was to consider positive roles for assumptions.

---

[17] By derivation Friedman means something other than logical derivation from a set of axioms. For him theory derivation is making use of existing theory and data to come up with new hypotheses.

The natural selection example of leaves' position around a tree is new in draft two, fitting in with the two examples carried over from draft one. The idea of natural selection, however, is not new, having been illustrated with the billiards player example. The positive–normative distinction and reference to J. N. Keynes's *The Scope and Method of Political Economy* are new in draft two and largely peripheral to the heart of the essay. Friedman's addition of this introduction to the essay has not been without effects, for some readers of the essay have taken away the association of Friedman and the essay with philosophical positivism. A more apt title in retrospect might have been "The methodology of Marshallian economics."

References

Alchian, Armen A. (1950). Uncertainty, evolution, and economic theory. *Journal of Political Economy*. 58, 211–21

Alexander, S. (1951). Issues in business cycle theory raised by Mr. Hicks. *American Economic Review*, 41, 861–78

Boland, Lawrence (1979). A critique of Friedman's critics. *Journal of Economic Literature*, 17, 503–22

Burns, A. F. (1952). Letter to Milton Friedman, November 26, Box 43, Milton Friedman Papers, Hoover Institution, Stanford University

Caldwell, Bruce J. (1980). A critique of Friedman's methodological instrumentalism. *Southern Economic Journal*, 47, 366–74

  (1982). *Beyond Positivism*. London: Allen and Unwin

  (1992). Friedman's predictivist methodological instrumentalism – a modification. In W. J. Samuels (ed.), *Research in the History of Economic Thought and Methodology*, vol. 10. Greenwich, CT: JAI Press, 119–28

Friedman, Milton (1941). Review of *Monopolistic Competition and General Equilibrium Theory* by Robert Triffin. *Journal of Farm Economics*, 23, 389–90

  (1946). Lange on price flexibility and employment. *American Economic Review*. 36, 613–31

  (1947). Letter to G. J. Stigler, November 19. In Hammond and Hammond (2006)

  (1948a). Descriptive validity vs. analytical relevance in economic theory, mimeo, undated [1948], Box 43, Milton Friedman Papers, Hoover Institution, Stanford University

  (1948b). Letter to G. J. Stigler, October 4. In Hammond and Hammond (2006)

  (1949). The Marshallian demand curve. *Journal of Political Economy*, 57, 463–95

  (1950). Wesley C. Mitchell as an economic theorist. *Journal of Political Economy*, 58, 465–93

  (1952a). Comment. In B. F Haley (ed.), *A Survey of Contemporary Economics*, Chicago: Richard D. Irwin, 455–7

  (1952b). The relevance of economic analysis to prediction and policy, mimeo, undated, Box 43, Milton Friedman Papers, Hoover Institution, Stanford University

(1953). The methodology of positive economics. In his *Essays in Positive Economics*. Chicago: University of Chicago Press, 3–43

(Undated). Lecture notes "Price Theory." Undated, Box 76, Milton Friedman Papers, Hoover Institution, Stanford University

Friedman, Milton and Leonard Savage (1948). The utility analysis of choices involving risk. *Journal of Political Economy*, 56, 270–304

(1952). The expected utility hypothesis and the measurability of utility. *Journal of Political Economy*, 60, 463–74

Gordon, R. A. (1948). Short-period price determination in theory and practice. *American Economic Review*, 38, 265–88

Hall, R. J. and C. J. Hitch (1939). Price theory and business behavior. *Oxford Economic Papers*, 2, 12–45

Hammond, J. Daniel (1992a). An interview with Milton Friedman on method-ology. In W. J. Samuels (ed.), *Research in the History of Economic Thought and Methodology*, vol. 10, Greenwich, CT: JAI Press, 91–118

(1992b). The problem of context for Friedman's methodology. In W. J. Samuels (ed.), *Research in the History of Economic Thought and Methodology*, vol. 10, Greenwich, CT: JAI Press, 129–47

(1996). *Theory and Measurement: Causality Issues in Milton Friedman's Monetary Economics*. Cambridge and New York: Cambridge University Press

Hammond, Claire H. and J. Daniel Hammond (2006). *Making Chicago Price Theory: Friedman-Stigler Correspondence, 1945–1958*. London: Routledge

Hirsch, Abraham and Neil De Marchi (1990). *Milton Friedman: Economics in Theory and Practice*. Ann Arbor: University of Michigan Press

Keynes, John Neville (1891). *The Scope and Method of Political Economy*. London: Macmillan

Marshall, Alfred (1920). *Principles of Economics*, 8th edition London: Macmillan

([1885] 1925). The present position of economics. Reprinted in A. C. Pigou (ed.), *Memorials of Alfred Marshall*. London: Macmillan

McCloskey, D. N. (1983). The rhetoric of economics. *Journal of Economic Literature*, 21, 481–517

(1985). *The Rhetoric of Economics*. Madison: University of Wisconsin Press

Stigler, George J. (1948). Letter to Milton Friedman, undated (September 1948). In Hammond and Hammond (2006)

(1948). Letter to Milton Friedman, undated (October 1948). In Hammond and Hammond (2006)

(1949). Monopolistic competition in retrospect. In his *Five Essays on Economic Problems*. New York: Longmans, Green Co.

Triffin, Robert (1940). *Monopolistic Competition and General Equilibrium Theory*. Cambridge, MA: Harvard University Press

University of Chicago. A program of factual research into questions basic to the formulation of a liberal economic policy. Box 79, Milton Friedman Papers, Hoover Institution, Stanford University

Walters, Alan (1987). Friedman, Milton. In *The New Palgrave Dictionary of Economics*, vol. 2. London: Macmillan

Wong, Stanley (1973). The "F-twist" and the methodology of Paul Samuelson. *American Economic Review*, 63, 312–25

3 Unrealistic assumptions and unnecessary confusions: rereading and rewriting F53 as a realist statement

Uskali Mäki

1 Introduction

Depending on the reader's intellectual preferences and capacities, the experience of reading Milton Friedman's 1953 essay on economic methodology (F53 for short) tends to be either one of relief and conviction or one of irritation and provocation – or perhaps some mixture of these feelings. Many practicing economists have found the message of the essay appealing and liberating, and its arguments convincing. Most specialists in economic methodology, and some practicing economists, have found F53 entirely defective, presenting a dangerously misguided doctrine of scientific theory and method. Both of these responses may be based on an incomplete understanding of the essay, or so I want to argue.

I will argue for two sets of general claims. First, there is no unambiguous doctrine or argument presented in F53. The essay presents no unproblematically identifiable single methodology of economic theorizing. The message of F53 *cannot* be captured by popular phrases like "Friedman's instrumentalism" or "Friedman's as-if methodology" or "Friedman's argument in support of unrealistic assumptions" or the "F-twist". This is because F53 also contains strong anti-instrumentalist elements; because "as if" is itself highly flexible and compatible with a variety of philosophical outlooks; and because F53 argues for unrealistic (and sometimes for realistic) assumptions from sets of mutually incompatible premises. What the reader is served is an *F-mix*, a mixture of ingredients many of which are ambiguous and some of which are hard to reconcile with one another. In consequence, a variety of readers with different intellectual tastes will be

This is an expanded and revised version of a paper presented at the conference on F53 at Erasmus University of Rotterdam in December 2003. And that version was a much expanded version of the one presented at the ASSA meetings in Washington, DC, in January 2003. After the Erasmus conference, it was presented at the universities of Aix-en-Provence, Freiburg, Athens, and Lund. Useful comments from the various audiences are acknowledged. In his characteristically generous fashion, Milton Friedman offered some written comments that have been consequential.

able to find in F53 their own selection of ideas that they will endorse or oppose.

Second, the flexibility and malleability of the textual material creates room for alternative readings of F53 that challenge its current reified textbook image. In particular, it is possible to develop non-traditional interpretations that might bring many former friends and foes of F53 – or, more precisely, of what has been believed to be the message of F53 – closer to one another, if not unite them entirely. In what follows, I will remove some unnecessary confusions and ambiguities in F53, and by doing so, hope to pave the way for a new sensible reading that will be found much less objectionable by many more readers, practitioners and methodologists alike. To the extent that my *rereading* fails to be a matter of unbiased discovery of what is already there, hidden in the text of F53, it can also be taken as a project of *rewriting* the essay. It is a matter of rewriting by selection and correction so as to eliminate its flaws and to make it more agreeable to a variety of audiences. On this rereading (or rewriting) F53 emerges as a realist (rather than instrumentalist) manifesto with strong fallibilist and social constructivist sensitivities (in contrast to standard textbook positivism).[1]

One might object by saying that my rereading F53 as a realist and social constructivist statement amounts to a reformulation beyond recognition, or at least to a forced interpretation that does not come naturally. In contrast, my conviction is that what I am about to offer is an obvious interpretation that does come very naturally indeed. My interpretation is more forced when ignoring parts of what F53 seems to be saying, while it is less forced when based just on highlighting elements in F53 that have been overlooked by other readers. But I must grant there is a possible source of bias: the image of economics that emerges in F53 as it is being reread and rewritten here is one that I myself endorse. I am rebuilding F53 as a statement that captures and conveys this rebuilder's own methodological convictions.

A remark is needed on the strategy and motivation of this chapter by way of locating it on the map of the various readings of F53 (the map was outlined in chapter 1 above). First, mine is primarily an examination of F53 itself rather than explicitly using F53 for some other purpose (though I think it wonderfully serves other useful purposes). Second, my reading goes beyond the narrow logical accounts (in terms of the relationship between "assumptions" and "predictions") and incorporates ontological, semantic, and social ingredients in the image that F53 conveys of

---

[1] This chapter follows the line of, and draws on, earlier work such as Mäki 1986, 1989, 1992, 2000, 2003. These papers document my career in the F53 exegesis as one of swimming against the stream.

economics. Third, the reading combines normative and descriptive perspectives in that it suggests remedying some flaws of F53 so as to identify and reconstruct its sensible core ideas. Fourth, it attaches extra-economic labels to F53, borrowed from philosophy and science studies. Finally, and importantly, my reading is an exercise in what I called reception methodology: the focus lies on the context of consumption of F53 rather than its production by its author. The context is that of the reader's reception rather than that of the author's intention. Reception methodology here amounts to reading F53 from the point of view of its actual and possible interpretations and influences among the relevant audiences.

It is part of my receptionist reading of the essay that I make no claims about the author's intentions: I am not after Friedman's authentic convictions or anything related to "what Friedman really meant" (in fact I am not convinced there are such things there to be discovered, at least in F53 alone).[2] The focus here is on the text of F53 while the author's intentions and beliefs are bracketed. As a technical expression of this I am not referring to the author but rather to the text: I am not saying "here Friedman argues..." but rather, "F53 claims..."; not "Friedman's opinion seems to be..." but rather, "F53 can be read as...," and so on. My attempt to "rewrite" F53 so as to make it more acceptable to various audiences is also independent of anything that Milton Friedman the author might have believed or intended, or of whether he would accept the rewritten version of F53 as sound (even though I believe he would have ample reason to accept it).

Let it be added that the receptionist reading of F53 is also consistent with, and supported by, Milton Friedman's personal strategy in relation to F53, as repeated in his statement at the end of this volume: he has chosen not to respond to any commentaries on F53 by others, but has rather let the text live its own life in the intellectual realm, at the mercy of its readers, as it were.

2   Assumptions and predictions, and the non-predictivist torso

If there is one basic thesis conveyed by F53, it is this: *economic theories should not be judged by their assumptions but by their predictive implications –* and in particular, *the unrealisticness of the assumptions of a theory is no reason*

---

[2] The only way to determine what Friedman's possible authentic methodological convictions are is to read F53 together with his other methodological remarks conjoined with a scrutiny of the implicit methodology of his work in economics. This is a very legitimate historical and analytical project, but it does not lie at the heart of my reception methodology.

for complaint or worry about the theory. The methodological advice given to economists by F53 appears simple: when assessing a theory, don't pay separate attention to its assumptions, instead focus on the predictions it yields. As the much-cited statement puts it, "the only relevant test of the *validity* of a hypothesis is comparison of its predictions with experience. The hypothesis is rejected if its predictions are contradicted ("frequently" or more often than predictions from an alternative hypothesis); it is accepted if its predictions are not contradicted" (F53, 8–9). This passage makes three important points about testing scientific theories: testing is by predictive implications, not by assumptions; failed predictions play a key role: acceptances are just failures to be rejected; and testing is comparative: what matters is the predictive performance of a theory relative to that of alternative theories.[3]

It is clear that the main focus of attention of the text of F53 is on assumptions, not on predictions. The historical context of F53 essentially contained various attacks against some of the key assumptions of marginalist theory, blaming them for harmful unrealisticness. F53 sets out to convince the skeptical or hesitant reader that unrealistic assumptions are just fine, and the arguments of F53 revolve around this idea. Yet, in some cases the reader would expect to be shown the full force of the basic thesis in its entirety, including the role of comparative predictive performance.

Consider the treatment of Edward Chamberlin's theory of monopolistic competition. F53 does not hide its hostility towards Chamberlin's theory – an inferior theory that economics does not need at all in addition to the superior simple models of perfect competition and perfect monopoly. The argument of F53 is straightforward: the creation of the theory of monopolistic competition was "explicitly motivated, and its wide acceptance and approval largely explained, by the belief that the assumptions of 'perfect competition' or 'perfect monopoly' said to underlie neoclassical economic theory are a false image of reality" (15), and it is this misguided motivation and flawed basis of acceptance that speaks against the theory. What is noteworthy is that there is no appeal here to the superior predictive capacity of Friedman's favorite theories in contrast to the predictive failures of Chamberlin's theory. The realisticness or unrealisticness of assumptions was not supposed to matter, but it seems they do, after all. The key thesis of F53 is thereby turned into a modified non-predictivist

---

[3] In these formulations, one may choose to hear echoes of Popper's doctrine of refutation based on failed predictions as well as Lakatos's doctrine of comparative and dynamic predictive performance. The English translation of Popper's *Logik der Forschung* appeared in 1959 (Popper 1959), while Lakatos's relevant essays were published a decade or so later (e.g. Lakatos 1970). Friedman had learnt about Popper's falsificationist views when personally meeting him in the late 1940s.

torso: *hail unrealistic assumptions, proscribe against the pursuit of realistic assumptions.*

This I believe is how many practicing economists have received the message of F53. This explains its emancipatory effect on economists: it helps liberate those employing models with unrealistic assumptions from a sense of unease (see Mayer 1993). This also suggests why there is an easy link between F53 and the defense of "blackboard economics" that is mathematically highly refined and rigorous but accused of being unconnected to real-world facts and issues (cf. Hands 2003 and in this volume). Whatever the methodological preferences of the author of F53 – in fact we know Friedman is an opponent of formalistic blackboard economics – it is not surprising to see appeals to F53 in justification of the assumptions that help create the model worlds on the blackboard. From the point of view of the context of consumption, it is the reception and use of F53 that matters. A tension between the author's intended methodology and the use of the torso version of the basic thesis of F53 does not lie within the purview of reception methodology.

3   Unrealisticness as irrelevant and as a virtue

Friedman's claim about unrealistic assumptions appears in at least two versions: one is in terms of irrelevance, the other is in terms of virtue. The weaker version is the claim that unrealisticness is irrelevant for the goodness of theory: that it does not matter even if a theory's assumptions are unrealistic. Now it is important to see that a consistent irrelevance thesis would have to imply that the actual degree of *both unrealisticness and realisticness* does not matter. In other words, no matter how unrealistic or realistic the assumptions of a theory, this is irrelevant to the assessment of the theory, since those properties are not among the ones we should measure when evaluating a theory. But the bulk of F53 is not symmetric in this way, thus not in line with the weak version: the essay keeps stressing that it is high degrees of *un*realisticness that do not matter. As the attack in F53 against more realistic behavioral assumptions and the theory of monopolistic competition indicates, the pursuit of high degrees of realisticness is regarded as a serious demerit of both a theorist who does so and of a theory that is pursued. This contradicts the weak thesis in terms of irrelevance.

The strong version acknowledges the asymmetry of F53 and does it in a radicalized manner: it is the claim that unrealisticness is a virtue, that the better the theory, the more unrealistic it is in its assumptions. Many readers have found the strong version unacceptable, even outrageous. Indeed, as a general rule, it must be mistaken. Even in some cases where violating the truth may seem recommendable – such as in assuming a vacuum for falling cannon balls and assuming profit maximization for certain purposes – the strong version goes too far. F53's examples of excellent scientific theories assume zero air pressure and profit maximization. The strong version suggests that there might be even better theories that assume that air pressure is infinitely large and that businessmen aim at maximizing their losses – these assumptions would be more unrealistic than the ordinary ones. But obviously, such unrealistic assumptions would not be epistemically virtuous, thus the strong version is questioned.

There are obvious cases in which both versions appear questionable. In the study of the used cars market, it is neither irrelevant nor virtuous for a theory to falsely assume that information is symmetric, and in the study of the computer software industry, one is not well advised to assume diminishing returns. Qualifications and further conditions are needed: neither version of Friedman's thesis can be defended as a general principle. I will have more to say about this in later sections.

4   Indirectly testing approximation to the truth

On closer scrutiny, it appears that F53 does not subscribe to either of the above versions of the thesis consistently or without qualifications. Indeed, the truth of assumptions appears as a relevant issue after all. F53 indicates an interest in truth when suggesting that truth is something to be estimated: indeed, predictive tests serve as indirect tests of the approximate truth of assumptions. The required degree of approximation is not simply to be maximized (or minimized!) but is relative to the purposes that the theory is supposed to serve: "the relevant question to ask about the 'assumptions' of a theory is ... whether they are sufficiently good approximations for the purpose at hand" (15). So there is a relevant question to ask about assumptions, and the question is about their approximate truth. The way to measure whether the required degree of approximation has been achieved is to put the theory to the predictive test:

Complete "realism" [realisticness] is clearly unattainable, and the question whether a theory is realistic "enough" can be settled only by seeing whether it yields predictions that are good enough for the purpose in hand or that are better than predictions from alternative theories. (41)

This implies that the unrealisticness of assumptions is not an irrelevant issue at all, something to be ignored. On the contrary, one is advised to pay attention to their actual degree of realisticness and to judge whether it is sufficiently high for the purposes at hand. It appears that two kinds of considerations shape these judgments: pragmatic and ontological.

Pragmatic considerations enter in the form of purposes: the appropriate degree of (un)realisticness is relative to the purposes for which the theory is put. Ontological considerations are concerned with the causal powerfulness of various factors: some factors are too weak to be included in the model, while others play major causal roles and should be included. In other words, it all depends on the difference those factors make:

> Why is it more "unrealistic" in analyzing business behavior to neglect the magnitude of businessmen's costs than the color of their eyes? The obvious answer is because the first makes more difference to business behavior than the second; but there is no way of knowing that this is so simply by observing that businessmen do have costs of different magnitude and eyes of different color. Clearly it can only be known by comparing the effect on the discrepancy between actual and predicted behavior of taking the one factor or the other into account. (33)

Indeed, not only is it "more unrealistic" to ignore the magnitude of businessmen's costs than the color of their eyes, but such unrealisticness also *matters* a great deal. It is advisable to consider costs – but not the eye color – because they make a difference for the phenomena being explained. And to determine whether or not they make a difference relative to some purpose requires checking the predictive implications. Another way of putting these ideas is to say that some of the assumptions of a theory are to be paraphrased as statements about the negligibility of a factor, and that predictive tests are a way of assessing such claims about negligibility (Musgrave 1981; Mäki 2000). I will return to this idea in a later section.

5   Testing by assumptions and testing by predictions

F53 itself, and indeed most of the commentators on the issue, draw a distinction between testing a theory by its assumptions and testing it by its predictions. Accordingly, the participants in the debate are classified as the "assumptionists" and the "predictivists," the latter often also called instrumentalists (I'll come back to the uses and abuses of this label later). The assumptionists are supposed to test the assumptions "directly" and thereby to test the theory, while the predictivists test the theory "indirectly" via its predictive implications.

Without qualifications, this is a misleading distinction. No "direct" testing of assumptions is available. This should be easy to see: when one seeks to test an assumption, one has to construe an argument in which that assumption serves as one of the major premises and which entails a predictive implication that one then compares with evidence. When testing the assumption of transitive preferences, one conjoins it with several other assumptions and draws implications concerning choice behavior, and then checks those implications against, say, experimental data.

I think the intended difference is between two or more domains of testing by implications. Economists hold different views as to the relevant domain of data that should be consulted as evidentially relevant. Thus, some hold the view that the maximization assumption is to be tested against the data concerning the individual behavior of business managers. Others believe the assumption, and the theory of which it is a constitutive element, should only be tested by drawing implications concerning market data. In both cases, one tests by predictive implications.

6   The whole truth and nothing but the truth

F53 uses a variety of expressions to refer to species of unrealisticness. These include "descriptively false," "descriptively unrealistic," and "descriptively inaccurate" (pp. 14–15). None of them is being defined in F53 other than through examples. But the examples reveal fatal ambiguities. In particular, F53 conflates falsehood proper (violation of "nothing-but-the-truth") and incompleteness or narrowness (violation of "the whole truth"). These are separate notions, but F53 fails to keep them separate – and so does much of other commentary on the realisticness issue. In particular, the violation of the whole truth does not imply the violation of nothing but the truth about some part of the whole. Here we come across with one major limitation of the logical accounts: they miss the distinction between the whole truth and nothing but the truth, focusing just on the latter and dealing with the former as if it were reducible to the latter.

Consider an example. One of the targets that F53 seeks to rebut consists of the criticisms of the maximization assumption in the "marginalist controversies" launched by Hall and Hitch in the UK and Lester in the USA. Friedman invites the reader to consider "the recent criticisms of the maximization-of-returns hypothesis on the grounds that businessmen do not and indeed cannot behave as the theory 'assumes' they do" (31). F53 here formulates the message of the criticism as the charge that the maximization assumption violates nothing but the truth about business behavior: businessmen do not, perhaps cannot, behave the way they are assumed to behave.

Right after this, F53 sketches "a completely 'realistic' theory of the wheat market" that would have to mention the color of the traders' and farmers' eyes and hair, antecedents and education, the physical and chemical characteristics of the soil on which the wheat was grown, the weather prevailing during the growing season, etc., etc. (32). Another notion of realisticness is implied by such a "completely realistic theory": deviations from such a "theory" by leaving out various details would be a matter of violating "the whole truth" about a certain subject. One can easily imagine any number of further details that would have to be mentioned in such a "theory" of the wheat market, including the detailed career of the causal and constitutive ancestors of each farmer, trader, parcel of land, and seed of wheat during the process of cosmological, geological, biological, and cultural evolution over the course of billions of years.

F53 implies a close connection or sameness between these two notions of truth when suggesting that to criticize the maximization assumption is as ridiculous as to insist on building such a completely realistic theory. The reasoning is not sound: it is trivial that nobody will insist on having such a "theory" – but it also should be trivial that this has nothing to do with the insistence that it is no recommendation for the maximization of returns assumption as such that it violates nothing but the truth. The violation of the whole truth (which is unavoidable) implies nothing about the violation of nothing but the truth (which is avoidable).[4] Only a small fraction of all facts (even of the causally efficacious ones) are mentioned by any theory, hence the violation of the whole truth; but statements about those facts – such as whether actors in the wheat market are maximizers – are not necessarily false. One cannot justify false assumptions by citing the trivial fact that all theories are necessarily incomplete.

F53 thus conflates the whole truth with nothing but the truth. This conflation may be seen to serve a rhetorical function: just like every sensible person, my dear reader, you surely agree that the insistence on a "completely realistic theory" is undesirable, therefore you are naturally reasonable enough also to agree that to criticize the maximization assumption for falsehood is misguided.

Why is it important to resist this conflation? Keeping the two notions distinct has implications for the assessment of the basic thesis of F53. One may argue that good theories violate the whole (or comprehensive) truth in that they isolate just narrow slices of the world and leave out most of it – such as most of the things listed in the "completely realistic theory" of the wheat market. One may go further and argue that, subject to further (perhaps ontological and pragmatic) constraints, the more a theory leaves out the better it is. One may also point out that such theoretical isolations are often accomplished by way of false idealizing assumptions (such as those of a vacuum or homogeneous goods) that help exclude factors (such as actual air pressure or product differentiation) that are viewed as

---

[4] Many qualifications would have to be added to the two claims about avoidability.

irrelevant for a problem at hand. These are some of the ways in which good theories may be unrealistic. More about this in a moment.

7   Assumptions and their roles: vacuum and maximization

Here is another limitation of the logical accounts: they miss a relevant and sufficiently rich idea of sentence role. In the logical accounts, the only conceivable roles of sentences are those of premises and conclusions in logical arguments. In order to understand economic theorizing, we need to have a more qualified notion of role.

One of F53's famous examples is Galileo's law of freely falling bodies. In the formulation used, the law states that $s = 1/2 \, gt^2$. One of the assumptions behind the law is that of a vacuum:

[1] Air pressure = 0

F53 argues that for many purposes (such as predicting the fall of a cannon ball) it does not matter even if the vacuum assumption is false. It then uses this as an analogy in its defense of the maximization assumption:

[2] Producers and traders pursue maximum expected returns.

F53 argues that just as, in many cases, it does not matter if the vacuum assumption is false, it does not matter even if the maximization assumption is false. This argument exploits a mistaken analogy, based on ignoring the roles that these two assumptions [1] and [2] are supposed to play within their home theories.

The purpose that assumption [1] serves is similar to that of [3]:

[3] All forces other than gravitation = 0

Assumptions [1] and [3] are idealizations. They idealize by assuming that certain forces or causes are powerless, they have zero strength: no air pressure, no magnetic forces, no winds, no other kinds of pushes and pulls such as the pull of the Moon. The assumptions are "unrealistic" in that, in the presently actual world, [3] is always false (for example, the pull of the Moon, the Sun, and other planets are always there), while [1] is mostly false but may sometimes be true if made true (vacuum conditions can be artificially created). By means of such falsehoods, a model is constructed in which all causes of the behavior of a falling body except for one are neutralized. The one cause that remains non-neutralized is the gravity of the Earth. The idealizing assumptions play the important role of helping to isolate the impact of gravitation from other causal influences.

What about the profit maximization assumption? Is it also an idealization that helps isolate one cause while neutralizing the influence of other causes? One manifest difference between [2] and [1]&[3] is this: while [1]&[3] explicitly refer to the factors that they serve to eliminate or neutralize, [2] does not seek to neutralize what it is about, namely profit maximization. Indeed, rather than removing the impact of profit maximization, it establishes profit maximization as a major motive of economically relevant behavior. Instead of saying agents do not maximize, it says they do. The analogy between maximization and vacuum seems to collapse.

If one were to formulate an analogue of assumptions [1] and [3] in Galileo's law, it would not be [2] as F53 suggests, but rather something like

[4] All other motives except the maximization motive have zero strength.

This is an idealization that helps isolate the motive of the maximization of expected returns from all other possible motives (such as moral deliberations, sense of security, fairness, reputation, maximization of sales and/ or market share, etc.) in order to make it possible to examine the impact of profit maximization on market phenomena in the absence of such other motives. Maximization would be isolated as *the* motive rather than just *a* motive among others. Now one may argue that this indeed is intended already by assumption [2]: by assuming that firms are motivated by expected maximum returns one thereby assumes that they are motivated by nothing but expected maximum returns. In other words, assumption [2] is intended to have assumption [4] as its implicit component. But this does not save the suggested analogy from my rebuttal. In our more literal moods, we might want to say that the profit maximization assumption is a combination of [2] and [4]. This will help us retain the claim that there is an analogy between [1] and [4] but not between [1] and [2].

The analogue of component [2] of the maximization assumption in Galileo's law is not the vacuum assumption but instead something like

[5] The gravitational field of the Earth pulls physical objects by force g.

It is the gravitation of the Earth that is being isolated by means of idealizing assumptions [1] and [3]. Likewise, it is the drive to maximize that is being isolated by means of idealization [4]. Insofar as truth and falsehood are concerned, it is an entirely different matter for "assumptions" [2] and [5] to be true or false, and for assumptions [4] and [1]&[3] to be true or false. Moreover, the truth or falsehood of assumptions [1] and [3] does not imply anything about the truth of [5]. Statement [5] may be true even though [1] and [3] are false, and even if they are false to the extent that Galileo's law were to yield radically incorrect predictions, such as in the case of a falling feather in the weekend market of my hometown plaza.

The difference between the two is striking and has important philosophical implications. Of the two, (a) is in the spirit of realism, while (b) invites a fictionalist and instrumentalist reading. Formulation (a) says that the behavior of certain phenomena is shaped by a real force isolated by the theory, and that it is to be treated without considering the role of other factors, suggesting that those phenomena behave as if the theoretical isolation were materialized also in the real world. This is what F53 is effectively saying in one of its general passages:

> A meaningful scientific hypothesis or theory typically asserts that certain forces are, and other forces are not, important in understanding a particular class of phenomena. It is frequently convenient to present such a hypothesis by stating that the phenomena it is desired to predict behave in the world of observation *as if* they occurred in a hypothetical and highly simplified world containing only the forces that the hypothesis asserts to be important. (40)

That this is in line with (a) should be evident. There are a number of causally relevant forces in the world. But they are not equally relevant, thus the economist proceeds by assuming that it is just the most powerful forces that shape the explanandum phenomenon, that they function in isolation from all other forces: the phenomenon occurs *as if* nothing but those powerful forces were in operation. The reality of none of these forces is denied. If one wants to identify a fiction here, it is the isolation that is a fiction, not the isolated forces (Mäki 1992, 2004).

In its concrete illustrations, on the other hand, F53 is closer to formulation (b). The imaginative hypothesis of the leaves of a tree is the most striking of its examples. F53 suggests the "hypothesis that the leaves [around a tree] are positioned as if each leaf deliberately sought to maximize the amount of sunlight it receives, given the position of its neighbors, as if it knew the physical laws determining the amount of sunlight that would be received in various positions and could move rapidly or instantaneously from any one position to any other desired and unoccupied position" (19). However, "so far as we know, leaves do not 'deliberate' or consciously 'seek,' have not been at school and learned the relevant laws of science or the mathematics required to calculate the 'optimum' position, and cannot move from position to position" (20). In contrast to the general statement cited above, this suggests that the forces cited after "as if" are not real: we are fully aware of the fictionality of the forces postulated, and this awareness is expressed in terms of the "as if." This represents a fictionalist use of "as if." Our realist rereading of F53 will ignore this passage.

Note that the fictionalist use of the "as if" rules out yet another way of using the "as if," namely its epistemological use in expressing uncertainty. In this case, what follows an "as if" is a hypothesis describing one possible causal trajectory, and it is taken to be the task of further research to establish whether what seems possible is also actually the case. This is not an option for the fictionalist use of the "as if" but can (and should) be accommodated in a realist account. (Mäki 1998)

11   Theoretical isolation and explanatory unification

In line with the realist use of the "as if," F53 contains passages suggesting that theory construction is a matter of theoretical isolation whereby economists "abstract essential features of complex reality" (7). This is a widely endorsed idea in economics and elsewhere: the real world is complex, therefore we need to build simple models that theoretically isolate causally significant aspects of the world. This general idea also provides justification for the employment of false assumptions in such models. The simplest version of Galileo's law isolates the significant impact of gravity on the falling body. It excludes the impact of other forces by false idealizations such as those of vacuum, absence of magnetic forces, flatness of the earth. On this picture, it is the task of false assumptions to help isolate major causal factors.

F53's remarks about these matters seem to be ontologically motivated. The economist is supposed to theoretically isolate "essential features of complex reality" – which suggests that it is a (higher-order) feature of reality itself that some of its features are essential. The same idea is conveyed by another important passage in F53. This one introduces the realist notions of deceptive appearances and ontologically grounded explanatory unification:

A fundamental hypothesis of science is that appearances are deceptive and that there is a way of looking at or interpreting or organizing the evidence that will reveal superficially disconnected and diverse phenomena to be manifestations of a more fundamental and relatively simple structure. (33)

One is invited to read this roughly as follows. The world is, really, not as it appears to be: appearances are deceptive manifestations of more fundamental structures. Scientific theories are required to capture those fundamental structures. This suggests a distinction between reality and appearance. To this the passage adds the notion of explanatory unification, the idea of theoretically describing what appears diverse as really constituting a unity. A theory unifies apparently disconnected phenomena by showing them to be manifestations of the same fundamental structure. Unification amounts to showing that those phenomena are really connected and only apparently disconnected, and this is accomplished by successfully representing how things are related in the way the world works. This is a matter of ontological unification (Mäki 2001), and is only attainable by using a theory that truthfully manages to isolate the key causes and relations underlying such apparently disparate phenomena. This gives us a realist notion of explanatory unification.

Once again, the leaves-of-a-tree example offers a different story. It, too, appeals to the virtue of unification. Indeed, in F53 the hypothesis that the leaves of a tree actively and deliberately seek some goals emerges, after all, as inferior precisely because it does not exhibit the virtue of unifying power. The alternative hypothesis – according to which the leaves only passively adapt to external circumstances – is presented as superior because it unifies, because "it is part of a more general theory that applies to a wider variety of phenomena, of which the position of leaves around a tree is a special case, has more implications capable of being contradicted, and has failed to be contradicted under a wider variety of circumstances" (20). This passage, taken alone, would be compatible with the realist notion of ontological unification. But the account given by F53 about this example departs from the realist view after all: even though F53 is explicit that the power to unify constitutes a significant criterion of theory choice, realist hopes are undermined as no role is supposed to be played by what is justifiably believed to be the case in the real-world causation of leaves' behavior. The argument here in F53 ignores the fact that the core assumptions of the "activist" hypothesis are false and those of the "passivist" hypothesis are more realistic in isolating the key lines of that causation (20). What is claimed to be decisive is not related to what causal processes are actually believed to take place in nature, but rather to the range of conclusions that can be derived from the two hypotheses and the range of theoretic connections they exhibit. What the argument appeals to is derivational unification (Mäki 2001): the power of theories to generate large sets of logical conclusions. The power of theories to describe what is really going on – and what real unity there might be in the world – is viewed as irrelevant, thus this argument is a non-realist one.[6] In our realist rereading of F53 we simply put its treatment of this example aside.

12   Underdetermination and theoretical virtues

One of the troubling logical features of theorizing is that theory choice is underdetermined by empirical evidence. No body of evidence is sufficient for determining a unique choice of theory. Yet another reason for reading F53 as an up-to-date statement of methodology is that it indicates

---

[6] In the philosophy of science, the current interest in explanatory unification started evolving after Michael Friedman's 1974 article and Philip Kitcher's articles in 1976 and 1981.

admirable awareness of the underdetermination issue:[7] predictive success of a theory "is not by itself a sufficient criterion for choosing among alternative hypotheses" (9). F53 then explains why this is so:

> Observed facts are necessarily finite in number; possible hypotheses infinite. If there is one hypothesis that is consistent with the available evidence, there are always an infinite number that are. For example, suppose a specific excise tax on a particular commodity produces a rise in price equal to the amount of the tax. This is consistent with competitive conditions, a stable demand curve, and a horizontal and stable supply curve. But it is also consistent with competitive conditions and a positively or negatively sloping supply curve with the required compensating shift in the demand curve or the supply curve; with monopolistic conditions, constant marginal costs, and stable demand curve, of the particular shape required to produce this result; and so on indefinitely. (9)

This is to say that the observational implications of an infinite number of alternative hypotheses are identical; in the example, they all imply a rise in price equal to the tax. F53 thus subscribes to what is generally recognized as the thesis of *observational equivalence* between theoretical hypotheses. This thesis has opened up a strategic opportunity for anti-realists to undermine realist hopes for rationally believing scientific theories to be true. Such anti-realists have used the opportunity by inferring from the thesis of observational equivalence to the thesis of *epistemic equivalence*: all the observationally equivalent theoretical hypotheses are also equally believable. Given any number of observationally equivalent hypotheses, there is no rational way of believing one of them to be true or closer to the truth than the others (or even the stronger thesis that none of them actually is true or closer to the truth). The choice between epistemically equivalent hypotheses is epistemically arbitrary and must be based on non-epistemic factors. Theory choice is not only empirically undecidable but also epistemically undecidable.

F53 goes some way toward conceding epistemic equivalence and arbitrariness as an implication of observational equivalence: "The choice among alternative hypotheses equally consistent with the available evidence must to some extent be arbitrary..." (10). Immediately after this F53 invokes extra-empirical virtues as criteria of making non-arbitrary (or at least less arbitrary) choices between observationally equivalent theories: "...there is general agreement that relevant considerations are suggested by the criteria 'simplicity' and 'fruitfulness,' themselves notions that defy

---

[7] The two classical statements of the underdetermination issue were published at about the same time as F53. Quine's "Two dogmas of empiricism" had appeared in 1951, while the English translation of Duhem's book was to be published in 1954 (the French original appeared in 1904).

completely objective specification … Logical completeness and consistency are relevant but play a subsidiary role…" (10) Note that the list of favorite theoretical virtues includes, foremost, simplicity and fruitfulness (F53's name for unifying power). The "Walrasian" virtues of logical completeness and consistency are ranked lower, while mathematical elegance, another popular theoretical virtue, is not mentioned at all.

F53 thus conforms to the popular solution to the underdetermination conundrum: it cites theoretical virtues as the remedy. Because empirical evidence is insufficient for deciding which theories to accept and reject, we need to supplement empirical virtues with theoretical virtues. When choosing between empirically equivalent theories, we choose the one that is theoretically more virtuous. Arbitrariness becomes eliminated or at least reduced.

This invites two observations. First, the argument from theoretical virtues is a standard move amongst realists against those anti-realists who infer from observational equivalence to epistemic equivalence and arbitrariness. F53 would hence seem to stand in the realist camp on this issue, the point being that of all the observationally equivalent theories, we are to believe the one that is simplest and has maximum unifying power. On the other hand, an instrumentalist may argue that such theoretical virtues are epistemically irrelevant and thus fail to be of help in guiding the allocation of belief, in driving theory choice towards the most truthlike theory. It might therefore seem that in matters of underdetermination, F53 holds an indeterminate position between realism and instrumentalism. I can think of one insight in F53 that might be used for making the position more determinate: we have seen that F53 contains the realist idea of ontological unification (in contrast to the instrumentalist idea of mere derivational unification). Since F53 cites unification (or fruitfulness) as a major theoretical virtue, we may conclude that it might be, after all, inclined toward a realist solution to the underdetermination challenge.

The second observation about the position taken by F53 is this: even though the conundrum of underdetermination can be alleviated by means of an appeal to theoretical virtues, theory appraisal will not thereby turn into a fully objective rule-governed affair. As we saw, simplicity and fruitfulness are "notions that defy completely objective specification" and cannot therefore completely eliminate all arbitrariness involved in theory choice. As we will see next, this is a prominent theme in F53 even though it has been overlooked by most readers.

13   Subjective and social dimensions of theory appraisal

Those who have read F53 as a positivist or falsificationist statement of economics as a strictly rule-governed and evidence-constrained endeavor will be disappointed upon being pointed out a few passages, completely ignored by most commentators. If one takes the methodology of positive economics to amount to a set of fixed and explicit rules for reasoning from given evidence (or evidence fixed by convention or agreement), one should be frustrated by the statements in F53 that emphasize the role of subjective judgment, of the background of economists, of tradition and disciplinary institutions, and of consensus amongst them. These statements in F53 further fortify the concession that strict predictivist tests are unavailable in economics. These statements do not appeal just to theoretical virtues such as simplicity and unifying power but rather to the social nature of scientific work, its embeddedness in academic and other institutions.

Here is a representative passage, making reference to something like the methodological culture of economics in comparison to that of sociology:

> Of course, neither the evidence of the economist nor that of the sociologist is conclusive. The decisive test is whether the hypothesis works for the phenomena it purports to explain. But a *judgment* may be required before any satisfactory test of this kind has been made, and, perhaps, when it cannot be made in the near future, in which case, the judgment will have to be based on the inadequate evidence available. In addition, even when a test can be made, *the background of the scientists* is not irrelevant to the judgments they reach. There is never certainty in science, and the weight of evidence for or against a hypothesis *can never be assessed completely "objectively."* The economist will be *more tolerant* than the sociologist in judging conformity of the implications of the hypothesis with experience, and he will be *persuaded* to accept the hypothesis tentatively by fewer instances of "conformity." (30; emphases added)

"Complete objectivity" in testing a theory is thus unattainable: *judgment* and *persuasion* are involved, and they are directed by the *background* of the scientist and the degree of *tolerance* characteristic of the disciplinary culture. In passing, F53 uses falsificationist jargon by referring to the "repeated failure to be contradicted" as evidence for a theory, but it simultaneously acknowledges the role of social factors in shaping the fate of a hypothesis. It recognizes the *tenacity* with which hypotheses are held against negative evidence and the powerful role of *tradition* and *continued use* in creating the image of an acceptable hypothesis: the discipline has its own epistemically forceful *folklore* that supports a theory but is irreducible to an explicit list of successful empirical tests. Here goes another key passage:

> [The evidence for the maximization-of-returns hypothesis] is extremely hard to document: it is scattered in numerous memorandums, articles, and monographs concerned primarily with specific concrete problems *rather than with submitting the hypothesis to test.* Yet the *continued use and acceptance* of the hypothesis over a long period, and the failure of any coherent, self-consistent alternative *to be developed*

and be widely accepted, is strong indirect testimony to its worth. The evidence for a hypothesis always consists of its repeated failure to be contradicted, continues to accumulate so long as the hypothesis is used, and by its very nature is difficult to document at all comprehensively. It tends to become part of *the tradition and folklore of a science* revealed in the *tenacity* with which hypotheses are held rather than in any textbook list of instances in which the hypothesis has failed to be contradicted. (22–3; emphases added)

What F53 suggests here is that the *social performance* (embeddedness in disciplinary institutions and culture, continued use, collective acceptance, tenacious grip) of a theory provides *indirect evidence* in its support. The core idea is that acceptances and rejections of theories are not strictly rule-governed responses to direct empirical evidence, they rather depend on the subjective judgments of economists whose behavior is shaped by their background and social context. Part of the reason for this can be traced to the character of the rules of application that are described as concrete and incomplete: "The rules of using the model ... cannot possibly be abstract and complete. They must be concrete and in consequence incomplete ..." (25). It is this incompleteness that creates room for judgment and social shaping: no matter how explicitly we succeed in formulating the rules "there inevitably will remain room for judgment in applying the rules ... It is something that cannot be taught; it can be learned but only by experience and exposure in the 'right' scientific atmosphere, not by rote" (25). The set of rules is embedded in concrete examples and it escapes explicit formulation: it is "mostly implicit and suggested by example" (35–6).[8]

It is then only natural to wonder whether the acknowledgment of the social shaping of theory appraisal is in tension with the optimism about the prospects of "positive economics" expressed in the opening pages of F53. The suspicion is that once you let the social influences in, the values characteristic of "normative economics" are included in the package and will play a role in undermining hopes of empirically grounded consensus. Whatever consensus there is among economists may emerge as a mixture of empirical, institutional, and ideological influences. The empirical

---

[8] These are ideas that would be made more widely known by Thomas Kuhn in his 1962 book, *The Structure of Scientific Revolutions*. On rules of application, F53 anticipates Kuhn's idea: the rules of application are socially shaped, linguistically inexplicable, and embedded in previous archetypical concrete examples of scientific practice. The orthodox positivist idea of correspondence rules as explicit components of a theory governing its use is replaced by Kuhn by the notion of a concrete exemplar whose implicit guidance of theory application is brought into scientists' awareness only through the socialization process of scientific education. I first pointed out the Kuhnian features of the account given by F53 in Mäki 1986 (of which an earlier version was published as a discussion paper in 1981).

control of belief turns out to be regrettably weak, because of which theories exhibit remarkable capacities of survival.

The denial to economics of the dramatic and direct evidence of the "crucial" experiment does hinder the adequate testing of hypotheses; but this is much less significant than the difficulty it places in the way of achieving a reasonably prompt and wide consensus on the conclusions justified by the available evidence. It renders the weeding-out of unsuccessful hypotheses slow and difficult. They are seldom downed for good and are always cropping up again. (11)

Whatever label one may wish to use for these ideas – pragmatism, collective conventionalism, or social constructivism – it is obvious that they reflect, and resonate with, the practitioner's actual experience that cannot be easily corrupted by positivist or falsificationist textbook teachings about the scientific method. These statements convey highly agreeable insights into the "imperfect" – yet perfectly human – reality of scientific work. But this has a price: tensions emerge with some other ingredients of the image of economics argued by F53. In my rereading, the above valuable observations about the social and institutional nature of economic inquiry will be given precedence.

14   How to rewrite F53

I keep admiring F53 for its insightfulness and its capacity to give rise to intriguing questions and to suggest challenging answers. F53 is a rich source of issues and observations that may help us understand important aspects of the intellectual endeavor of economics in its institutional setting. As I have indicated in the footnotes, F53 was ahead of its time in regard to many issues: falsification, comparative testing, unification, underdetermination, pragmatics of theorizing, social shaping of scientific reasoning.[9] At the same time, it appears to share the old methodological wisdom in economics: theories seek to isolate what are believed to be causally significant aspects of social reality.

If we take the F-mix to be based on ambiguities, inconsistencies and confusions in F53, and if we have a taste for a coherent and defensible account of economic methodology, then the task will be to remove such flaws in F53 and to develop its more promising ingredients into a coherent methodology of economics. This is a project of elimination, reinterpretation,

---

[9] Based on this observation, I would take partial departure from the conventional claim that F53 is an example of amateur philosophy of science. My qualified judgment is that F53 contains a set of amazingly sophisticated philosophical insights about scientific theorizing, while at the same time failing to put them together in the form of a coherent system. Rewriting is required precisely in order to remedy this failure.

and amendment: one of rereading and rewriting F53. I believe a solid and sensible methodology will emerge as a result of such an exercise. A rewritten F53 will also create new common ground for many participants in the controversies over F53 itself and over economics and its methodology more generally. Within such a shared framework, the remaining disagreements can then be debated in a more focused manner.

I have reread F53 by focusing on a selected set of ambiguities that open up opportunities for reinterpretation. I have exploited these opportunities by highlighting the partly hidden realism in F53's conception of economic science. On this basis, F53 could be rewritten as an unambiguous and consistent realist manifesto. It conveys a methodology of economics that conforms to the tradition of viewing theories or models as partial but potentially true descriptions of causally significant mechanisms. Their primary service is to convey explanatory understanding (answers to why- and how-questions) and only secondarily to yield predictions (answers to what-, when-, and where-questions). The tradition runs from Senior, Mill, and Cairnes to Menger, Marshall, and Robbins up to present-day economics. In regard to this matter, the often-heard claim about a radical rupture from the Robbinsian to the Friedmanian regime in mainline economic methodology seems exaggerated. What does change is the sophistication with which it is now possible to put some of the key ideas such as the following.

For the purposes of pursuing significant truths by theory, many of its assumptions are allowed to be false. More strongly, false assumptions are required for true theories. The best theories are simple – thus violate comprehensive truth – and unify large classes of apparently diverse phenomena. Such phenomena are ontologically unified by explaining them as manifestations of the same simple causal structures. So much for the ontological underpinnings and veristic ambitions of economic theorizing. Another set of sophistications pertains to epistemological concerns, the issues related to assessing theory candidates. One is supposed to test theory candidates by their comparative predictive and explanatory performance, but this will never yield conclusive results. Theory choices are underdetermined by evidence, and they are shaped but not fully determined by theoretical virtues, thus room is created for various subjective judgments as well as social constraints that reflect the institutional structure of economic inquiry. The recognition of this requires a social epistemology involving a strong fallibilism. Of these, fallibilism recommends modesty and awareness of the possibility of being mistaken, while social epistemology recommends critically assessing and redesigning the institutions of economic inquiry so as to improve their capacity in facilitating the acquisition of significant truths about economic reality.

The outcome of this exercise in brief is this: the rewritten F53 = realism + fallibilism + social epistemology. According to this methodology, excellent economists are *epistemically ambitious* in seeking deep truths about underlying causal structures, and at the same time *epistemically modest* in acknowledging the possibility of error and the shaping of inquiry by academic and other institutions – and again *epistemically ambitious* in demanding the design and implementation of institutions that are adequate for enhancing the acquisition of significant truths. This combination is not easy to keep in balance. For perfectly sound reasons, therefore, F53 claims: "More than other scientists, social scientists need to be self-conscious about their methodology" (40).

15   From reception to the author's intentions?

Even though the foregoing has been an exercise in reception methodology, a final speculation may be permitted about how all this might relate to the intentions and beliefs of the author of F53. I have argued that F53 fails to unambiguously express any coherent set of beliefs and intentions about economic methodology. The unavailability of a single coherent methodology in F53 is consistent with two possibilities concerning Milton Friedman's beliefs and intentions. The first possibility is that Friedman did not have a coherent methodology in mind and that F53 reflects this fact accurately (for a rhetorical account of this option, see Mäki 1986). The second possibility is that Friedman had a coherent methodology in mind but just failed to convey it in F53 due to flaws in textual production.

Whatever the case, the ambiguities and inconsistencies in F53 have enabled multiple receptions and mutually incompatible interpretations in the long series of commentaries. In a special sense, we might say that any such interpretation is underdetermined by textual evidence: the textual evidence does not fix any of the interpretations as the correct one. However, this is not a situation of underdetermination in precisely the same sense that was recognized by F53 itself as discussed above: namely that an infinite number of theories are consistent with the same set of data. Here, various interpretations of F53 rely on reading selected passages rather than the textual data in its entirety: the selected sets of evidence overlap but are not identical (for example, most of the instrumentalist interpretations of F53 have neglected those passages that are crucial for my realist and social constructivist readings). This is bound to be so as no interpretation is possibly consistent with the textual data as a whole. What I am envisaging here is not exactly the same idea as the standard argument from underdetermination – but it may have interesting affinities with actual situations in economics and elsewhere in science!

In a sense, then, the economic methodology possibly intended by the author of F53 is underdetermined by F53 itself and is therefore open for multiple interpretations. There is just one way I can think of that might help reduce this multiplicity: analyze Friedman's other statements on methodology, and analyze Friedman's work in economics for its implicit methodology. This is a task for historians of economic methodology interested in one Nobel laureate's views – not a task for reception methodology in the sense pursued here. Yet, were these two perspectives combined, I would not be surprised if it turned out to be the case that F53 as rewritten along the lines suggested above is the methodological statement that the author of F53 intended to write.

References

Boland, Lawrence A. (1979). A critique of Friedman's critics. *Journal of Economic Literature*, 17, 503–22

Caldwell, Bruce J. (1992). Friedman's methodological instrumentalism: a modification. *Research in the History of Economic Thought and Methodology* 10, 119–28

Duhem, Pierre (1954). *The Structure of Physical Theory*. Princeton: Princeton University Press

Friedman, Michael (1974). Explanation and scientific understanding. *Journal of Philosophy*, 71, 5–19

Friedman, Milton (1953). The methodology of positive economics. In *Essays in Positive Economics*. Chicago: Chicago University Press, 3–43

Hands, D. Wade (2003). Did Milton Friedman's methodology license the formalist revolution? *Journal of Economic Methodology*, 10, 507–20

Hindriks, Frank (2005). Unobservability, tractability, and the battle of assumptions. *Journal of Economic Methodology*, 12, 383–406

Hirsch, Abraham. and Neil De Marchi (1990). *Milton Friedman: Economics in Theory and Practice*. Hertfordshire: Harvester Wheatsheaf

Kitcher, Philip (1976). Explanation, conjunction, and unification. *Journal of Philosophy* 73, 207–12

(1981). Explanatory unification. *Philosophy of Science*, 48, 507–31

Kuhn, Thomas S. (1970/1962). *The Structure of Scientific Revolutions*. Chicago: University of Chicago Press

Lakatos, Imre (1970). Falsification and the methodology of scientific research programmes. In I. Lakatos and A. Musgrave (eds.), *Criticism and the Growth of Knowledge*. Cambridge: Cambridge University Press, 91–196

Mäki, Uskali (1986). Rhetoric at the expense of coherence: a reinterpretation of Milton Friedman's methodology, *Research in the History of Economic Thought and Methodology*, 4, 127–43

(1992). Friedman and realism. *Research in the History of Economic Thought and Methodology* 10, 171–95

(1998)."As if." In J. Davis, W. Hands and U. Mäki, (eds.) *The Handbook of Economic Methodology*. Edward Elgar 1998, 25–7

(2000). Kinds of assumptions and their truth: shaking an untwisted F-twist. *Kyklos*, 53, 303–22

(2001). Explanatory unification: double and doubtful. *Philosophy of the Social Sciences*. 31, 488–506

(2003). "The methodology of positive economics" (1953) does not give us *the* methodology of positive economics. *Journal of Economic Methodology*, 10, 495–505

(2004). Realism and the nature of theory: a lesson from J. H. von Thünen for economists and geographers. *Environment and Planning A*, 36, 1719–36

Mayer, Thomas (1993). Friedman's methodology of positive economics: a soft reading. *Economic Inquiry* 31, 213–23

Musgrave, Alan (1981). "Unreal assumptions" in economic theory: the F-twist untwisted. *Kyklos* 34, 377–87

Popper, Karl (1959). *The Logic of Scientific Discovery*. London: Unwin Hyman

Rotwein, Eugene (1959). On the methodology of positive economics. *Quarterly Journal of Economics*, 73, 554–75

Samuelson, Paul (1963). Problems of methodology – discussion. *American Economic Review, Papers and Proceedings*, 53, 231–36

Wong, Stanley (1973). The F-twist and the methodology of Paul Samuelson. *American Economic Review*, 63, 312–25

Part 3

Models, assumptions, predictions, evidence

4 The influence of Friedman's methodological essay

Thomas Mayer

Many leading methodologists have described the central role that Milton Friedman's 1953 essay (henceforth referred to as F53) has played in methodological discussions. (See, for instance, Hammond 1998; Hoover 2001; Backhouse 2002.) Yet Friedman himself did not intend his essay to be a contribution to methodology – about which he did not claim any expertise – but only a description of the approach he found useful in his practice. However, it does not necessarily follow from Friedman's intention that his essay has had a great influence on the practice of economics. Practicing economists pay little attention to free-standing discussions of methodology. At best they learn their method-ology by seeing it put to work on substantive problems.[1] Arguably, Friedman and Schwartz's (1963) *A Monetary History of the United States* has had more influence on the methodology of practicing economists than did F53. The most pervasive methodological influence in macroeconom-ics in the last thirty years has been the insistence of new classical econo-mists on reducing macroeconomics to microeconomics, and in this they paid no attention to the debate about reductionism among philosophers of science. All the same, I will go along with Friedman's intention, and deal only with F53's effect on its intended audience, practicing economists. And here I will look almost only at mainstream economists. Heterodox economists have been highly critical of F53, so that it is unlikely to have had much influence on them. I also omit its influence on econometrics (for that see Hoover, 2004) and on government and business economists, since their work is almost invisible to other economists. Several other essays in the book containing F53 also discuss methodology. If these discussions relate to ideas discussed in F53 I treat them as part of it, but refer only occasionally to methodological claims that Friedman made in other publications.

---

[1] Partha Dasgupta (2002, 57) remarked that he knows "no contemporary practicing econo-mist whose investigations have been aided by the writings of professional methodologists."

Before seeing how F53 has influenced economics we need to look at its message (section I), at some difficulties in evaluating its influence (section II), and at the reviews it initially received (section III). Due to limitations of space – and knowledge – I limit the discussion to a survey of (a) three general trends in economics: formal modeling, game theory, and econometric testing (section IV); (b) Nobel lectures (section V); and (c) certain topics in macroeconomics (section VI). This emphasis on macroeconomics is not based on any deep principle, but only on my greater familiarity with it. I end the discussion of macroeconomics with the new classical counter-revolution, because the further one goes beyond 1953, the greater is the probability that a change advocated in F53 is due to some other influence. But I discuss Nobel prizes up to 2002 because of the lag until work is recognized by the Nobel committee.[2]

1   Friedman's themes

F53 has one general and six specific themes. The former is the desirability of combining theoretical and empirical work, and thus to heal the split between theorists and institutionalists, to whom Friedman is closer than is often appreciated (see Friedman 1949, 1950). He was, of course, not the only one who attempted this. It was a general trend that would eventually have prevailed even in his absence. In any case, what has dominated the discussion is F53's specific theme that hypotheses should be not be tested by the realisticness of their assumptions. A second theme of F53 is the superiority of Marshallian over what Friedman calls "Walrasian" economics. This creates a terminological problem. As Hutchison (1954) pointed out, the latter does not represent Walras's own views on methodology. Nor does it necessarily represent the methodology of those using a general equilibrium approach; we now have computable general equilibrium models. But Friedman's terminology has caught on, so rather than

---

[2] I do not consider the number of citations to F53 in the *Social Science Citation Index* (*SSCI*). On the one hand, a citation count may understate a paper's influence, since its influence may be indirect via another paper that is cited instead of the original one. Indeed, once an idea becomes well known, it no longer requires citation. Moreover, a paper may exert a strong negating influence that does not generate a single citation: no citation appears if F53 prevented an economist from writing a paper criticizing a theory for its unrealistic assumptions. It is even possible for a paper's influence to be inversely related to the frequency of its citations. If it criticizes a research program convincingly, it may terminate work on that topic and therefore not be cited. Another problem is that the *SSCI* ignores citations in books. On the other hand, a citation count may overstate a paper's influence. Many citations are just hat-tipping references, made to show that the author is familiar with the paper, or they may be from a paper that criticizes the cited paper. Moreover, an economist may cite F53 as a justification for an unrealistic assumption he or she would have made in any case.

use the more appropriate term "formalistic" I will use Friedman's term, but with a lower-case "W" to mark the misuse of Walras's name. The third theme is the rejection of introspection and other forms of casual empiricism, and the fourth is the distinction between normative and positive economics. A fifth theme, relating to the context of discovery, is the benefit of a continual interplay of attention to data and to theory construction. A final theme is the need for modesty about what economic theory can accomplish. This theme (which deserves a paper of its own, since it underlies most of Friedman's other themes and some of his substantive work) is not well articulated and usually ignored, so, I, too, will ignore it.[3]

1.1   Realisticness of assumptions

Friedman's claim that hypotheses should not be judged by the realisticness of their assumptions but by the predictive success of their implications does not seem so startling once one recognizes that F53 still allowed testing by the realisticness of *critical* assumptions, since these can be rephrased as implications (see Baumol 1954; Mayer 1995, ch. 7).[4] If Friedman's objection to testing hypotheses by the realisticness of their assumptions is so much less startling than it appears at first glance why did it almost monopolize the discussion? Likely reasons include the fact that he stated it with much elan and at much greater length than his other themes, its wide scope, and its seeming conflict with intuition. Moreover, it was seen as a massive salvo in the ongoing battle about neoclassical theory. And, while practicing economists might applaud Friedman's deep insight into how economists work, for methodologists Friedman's

---

[3] Hirsch and De Marchi (1990, 154–9) in discussing both Friedman's methodological writings and his practices categorize his themes somewhat differently as: (1) "adopt an outside view," that is, reject arguments from introspection; (2) begin with observations; (3) continually test the implications of hypotheses, though not in a falsificationist mode; (4) base empirical tests on the framework of the most reliable available knowledge; and (5) focus on concrete problems. Perhaps because I deal with F53 and not with Friedman's own methodological practice, I am using a different framework.

[4] Not all the stated assumptions of a theory are necessary assumptions, some are expository assumptions, or domain-defining assumptions, etc. (see Musgrave 1981). Moreover, the necessary assumptions may be stated more broadly than required. A way to determine whether an assumption is a necessary one and is stated no more broadly than required, is to see if it can also be stated as an implication. But what about a theory's power to explain? Friedman surely considered explanation in the sense of subsuming an observation (or a narrow theory) into a (broader) theory to be important – his reference to generality, and his substantive work both before and after 1953 bear witness to that – as does the fact that he taught price theory. To Friedman, generality, and thus explanation, is important, but the acid test is prediction.

philosophically amateurish exposition, combined with his high status in the profession, made F53 a tempting target, and the assumptions issue seemed a weak spot.

1.2   *Marshallian intuition vs. walrasian rigor*

Many economists have (wrongly) read Friedman's objection to testing by the realisticness of assumption, not as an argument for testing by predictive success, but as enhancing the importance of three other criteria for theory choice, elegance, generality, and rigor, and hence as supporting their insistence on formal derivation of hypotheses from explicitly stated assumptions. So, assumptions again play a key role. But what matters now is not their realisticness, but their congruity with the canonical assumption of rational profit maximization, as well as their parsimony. But that is not Friedman's criterion for theory choice.

The only relevant test of the *validity* of a hypothesis is comparison of its predictions with experience ... Logical completeness and consistency are relevant, but play a subsidiary role; their function is to ensure that the hypothesis says what it is intended to say ... One of the effects of the difficulty of testing substantive economic hypotheses has been to foster a retreat into purely formal or tautological analysis ... [T]autologies have an extremely important role in economic analysis ... But economic theory must be more than a structure of tautologies ... if it is to be something different from disguised mathematics. (Friedman 1953, 8–12; italics in original)

Friedman paid much attention to the shortcomings of such "disguised mathematics" masquerading as economics. In F53 he referred readers to another chapter of *Essays on Positive Economics*, a review of Oscar Lange's *Price Flexibility and Employment*, where he wrote:

Here is a brilliant display of formal logic, abstract thinking, complicated chains of deductions, yet the analysis seems more nearly a rationalization of policy conclusions previously reached than a basis for them. What is there about the type of theorizing employed that makes it sterile ... ? The basic sources of the defects ... are the emphasis on formal structure, the attempt to generalize without first specifying in detail the facts to be generalized, and failure to recognize that the ultimate test of the validity of a theory is not conformity to the canons of formal logic but the ability to deduce facts that have not yet been observed, that are capable of being contradicted by observation, and that subsequent observations do not contradict. (Friedman [1946] 1953, 277, 300)

Elsewhere in *Essays* Friedman (1953, 112–13) wrote that: "formal analysis can seldom if ever give easy answers to hard problems. Its role is quite different: to suggest the considerations relevant to an answer and to provide a useful means of organizing the analysis." And in his discussion of the Marshallian demand curve Friedman (1953, 91) told us that:

The test of the theory is its value in explaining facts, in predicting the consequences of changes in the economic environment. Abstractness, generality, mathematical elegance – these are all secondary, ... Doubtless, most modern economic theorists would accept these general statements ... But our work belies our professions. Abstractness, generality and mathematic elegance have in some measure become ends in themselves, criteria by which to judge economic theory.[5]

Hammond (1990) considers Friedman's rejection of formalism a more important component of F53 than rejection of testing by the realisticness of assumptions, and calls "Marshallianism" the "hallmark of Friedman's methodology" (Hammond 1996, 43).

1.3   Casual empiricism and introspection

Friedman's belief that appearances may be misleading, and his resulting criticism of casual empiricism and introspection, is set out in more detail in his review of Lange than in F53.[6] There he showed that Lange's analysis is a deductive system based on certain assumptions that are just unverified conjectures. To Friedman such casual empiricism is insufficient. And though he did not mention this, this theme supports his insistence on testing implications rather than assumptions since many assumptions can only be tested casually.[7] Along with rejecting casual empiricism he also rejected reliance on the responses of firms to questions about what they do and why.

1.4   Normative and positive economics

F53 claimed that the normative/positive distinction has received inadequate attention, and conjectured that disagreements on economic policy among disinterested people in the West are primarily disagreements about positive issues. In stressing the positive–normative distinction Friedman

---

[5] Friedman, like many economists of his generation, became an economist because of the suffering he saw during the Great Depression (see Snowdon and Vane 1999, 124–5). That may explain his emphasis on practicality.

[6] Hirsch and De Marchi (1990, 19) argue that it is Friedman's rejection of introspection that distinguishes his methodology from the traditional one. They also call confidence in introspection "undoubtedly a major reason that methodologists argue on the basis of 'realistic' assumptions" (1990, 56).

[7] Some assumptions, such as rational behavior, are hard to formulate as testable hypotheses, and many others, such as a closed economy, are obviously not intended to be realistic, and hence not something anyone would want to test.

furthered the unfortunate tendency to ignore a third category of economics, J. N. Keynes's (1891) *art* of economics, that is the knowledge required to apply positive and normative economics in a way that results in successful policies. (See Colander 1991.) This is surprising since in his chapter reviewing Abba Lerner's *Economics of Control* Friedman castigated Lerner for ignoring problems pertaining to the art of economics. Also, Friedman lacked the postmodernists' nose for any whiff of normative elements.

1.5   *Interplay of theory and observation*

Friedman's fifth theme concerns the process of discovery. He advised against developing theory from a merely casual acquaintance with the data. He also advised against just concentrating on the data, and either being satisfied with mere description, or else expecting theory to spring from the data like Athena from the head of Zeus. This "interplay" theme characterizes Friedman's own research. In writing *A Theory of the Consumption Function* (1957) he started with a thorough knowledge of the data. In his monetary theory he carefully combined theory with his empirical evidence. The primary reason *A Monetary History of the United States* (1963) has been so influential is the masterly way it combines detailed knowledge of historical facts with an overarching theory.

2   Some difficulties in estimating the influence of F53

Several major difficulties arise in gauging the influence of F53. First, suppose that in its absence some other methodology, such as operationalism, had taken over. If so, then F53 had a great, but hidden, influence. Second, what economists write might not accurately reflect how they act or what motivates them.[8] Thus, F53 may prevent an economist from writing a paper criticizing a model for its assumptions, and yet he or she may still not accept it because of these assumptions. Third, in the absence of F53 someone else might have written a similar and just as influential paper. There is nothing that can be said about this, except that a similar thing is true of Darwin. So, I will ignore it.

Fourth, the influence of a methodological paper is often subtle and more difficult to detect than the influence of other papers. Suppose an economist who in 1935 analyzed inflation in terms of the money supply and its velocity, analyzed it in 1937 in terms of the marginal efficiency of

---

[8] An example of this is the treatment of Gurley and Shaw's *Money in a Theory of Finance* (1960). It was savaged when it appeared, but over the years some of its ideas became influential without acknowledgments.

Table 4.1 *Effect of changes in economics on the acceptance of F53*

	Mathematization	Computers, econometrics, data	Increased resources	Greater policy role	Prestige of Chicago	Quality of economists
Assumptions vs. predictions	+[a]	+	+	+	+	?
Marshallian vs. walrasian	−	+	?	+	+	?
Casual empiricism, introspection	−[?]	+	+	?	+	?
Theory/data interaction	−[?]	?	?	+	+	?

Note: + denotes influence in the direction of F53, − denotes influence in the opposite direction, ? denotes direction unknown, and a superscripted [?] some doubt about the direction.
[a] Likely but not certain direction.

capital. The influence of Keynes is obvious. And when economists use unit root tests Granger's influence is clear. But the influence of F53 may be less obvious; Marshallian or walrasian outlooks are a matter of emphasis, and since F53 allows testing by assumptions that are also implications, not every test by the realisticness of assumption shows a lack of influence of F53. Nor is every instance of unconcern about the realisticness of assumptions due to F53.

Another difficulty is inferring causation from correlation. Economics may have evolved in ways advocated in F53, but primarily for other reasons. These include (a) economists' increased mathematical skills; (b) the revolution in data analysis due to computers, new econometric techniques and greater availability of data; (c) an increase in the funding and volume of academic research; and (d) the increased role of economists in policy-making; (e) the greater prestige of Chicago economics (which is, in part, endogenous to F53), and (f) an apparent improvement in the intellectual quality of economists, probably due largely to improved academic salaries. Table 4.1 summarizes the likely effects of these factors for all of Friedman's themes, except the confounding of positive and normative economics, a point at which economics has not changed much.

The increased use of mathematics (apart from its effect through econometrics) has had conflicting effects for F53. It increased formal modeling which often requires tolerance for many unrealistic assumptions. But it also encouraged a shift away from the empiricism and from the emphasis on predictive success that underlies Marshallian economics. This decreased emphasis on genuine empiricism may perhaps also have resulted in an increase in casual empiricism, and by emphasizing theory might have reduced the interplay of theory and data.

The revolution in data analysis obviously stimulated Marshallian empirical work. It also made it much easier to evaluate predictive success, but had less effect on the ability to test the realisticness of assumptions, so that it shifted emphasis toward the former.[9] It also reduced the reliance on casual empiricism and introspection. Its effect on the interaction between theorizing and data analysis is ambiguous. There is an obvious positive effect, but the ease with which one can now test a hypothesis, and, if the data reject it, quickly formulate and test another version, has reduced the pressure to rethink one's theories when the data do not oblige, and this reduces the effectiveness of theory and data interaction.

The resources devoted to economic research have increased dramatically. By 1953 in the USA the shift in the self-image of faculty members from that of learned gentlemen enjoying considerable leisure to that of harried researchers had not yet run its full course, resources, such as research assistants, were scare and universities were fewer and smaller. With increased resources and numbers came an increased professionalization, and thus a greater belief that economics is an autonomous subject and not just one of the social sciences. Hence, economists no longer had to be so concerned if their assumptions seemed bizarre to other social scientists and to the public, or even to themselves – there is safety in numbers. While Irving Fisher may have worried about how the assumptions he made in his books would strike the general reader, this is of no concern to someone publishing in *Econometrica*. Increased professionalization also favored walrasian economics as economists focused more on acclaim from fellow economists rather than from the general public. Walrasian economics with its claims of rigor and elegance has relatively more appeal to a self-absorbed profession that claims to be "scientific," while Marshallian economics has more appeal to those who address the concerns of a broader public. On the other hand, it is quite possible that with the expansion of the profession the opportunity for any particular economists to make an even arguably worthwhile contribution to abstract theory has declined, and hence Marshallian empirical work has filled the gap. A rise in the ratio of research assistants to faculty researchers could also shift research in an empirical direction, but with falling teaching loads

---

[9] It did, however, also facilitate the use of questionnaires, but probably not by as much as time-series data, particularly since it did not reduce the cost of interviewing, or mailing, and editing surveys.

and increased pressure to publish, it is not clear that this ratio has risen. The net effect on Marshallian versus walrasian economics is therefore unclear.

Increased resources have reduced the need for casual empiricism and introspection. But their effect on the interplay of theorizing and data analysis is unclear. On the one hand, they have facilitated the use of statistical data, but on the other, increased professionalization has reduced the use of observations in the form of the reality checks provided by personal every-day experience, which could now be dismissed as "mere anecdotes."

The greater role that economists now play in policy-making may perhaps have led them to stress predictive success more than realisticness of assumptions, and it surely led them to prefer Marshallian to walrasian theory. But, given the lack of information required for many policy issues, and the pressure to come up with answers (and sometimes with answers pleasing to policy-makers), it may have increased reliance on casual empiricism. Also, it has probably increased the interplay of data and theory since that is helpful in dealing with applied problems. In the period following Friedman's paper the prestige of the Chicago economics department rose as its members gathered a disproportionate share of Clark medals and Nobel prizes (see Reder 1982), and as more of their substantive work appeared. That economists tended to view markets more favorably also helped. This probably enhanced the standing of all of Friedman's work, including F53. This leaves the higher intellectual caliber of entrants into the profession. Supporters of Friedman's themes surely believe that this facilitated their acceptance, while their opponents believe the opposite.

Table 4.1 summarizes these influences. Only on the assumptions/predictions issue (and perhaps on the casual empiricism issue) did all the changes, with the possible exception of the increased quality of economists, favor F53. On the other issues it is unclear whether the prevailing winds favored or hindered the acceptance of F53. Hence, it is possible that its apparent success was due less to its persuasive power than to good luck. But one also cannot just dismiss the opposite idea that, except on the issue of realisticness of assumptions, its successes were won in the face of strong headwinds. This is an unsatisfactory conclusion, but when dealing with causality unsatisfactory conclusions are hardly rare.

A final issue on causality is overdetermination. Were Friedman's themes "in the air" at the time? There is no evidence for this, neither in the reviews of F53 nor in the initial responses of methodologists. While Terence Hutchison and Fritz Machlup shared some of Friedman's ideas, that is not the same as these ideas being "in the air," particularly since Hutchison and Machlup lacked Friedman's persuasive power.

3   Reviews of F53

Essays in Positive Economics was reviewed in *The American Economic Review*, *The Economic Journal*, *The Economic Record*, *Economica*, *The Review of Economics and Statistics*, *The Southern Economic Journal*, and the *Weltwirtschaftliches Archiv*. Surprisingly, the *Journal of Political Economy* did not review it. Nor did *The Canadian Journal of Economics and Politics*, *The Indian Journal of Economics*, *The Journal of the American Statistical Association*, *Kyklos*, *Revu Economique* or the *Zeitschrift für Nationalökonomie*, even though Friedman was at that time already well known, having won the Clark medal two years earlier.[10]

William Vickrey (1954) commented extensively on the book's macroeconomic chapters, while not mentioning F53 at all, and dismissed the chapter criticizing Lange in one sentence. But William Baumol (1954, 465) called the book: "certainly one of the most engrossing volumes that has appeared recently in economic theory," and devoted about one-fifth of his review to F53. (It accounts for 13 percent of the book.) He called it "highly stimulating" (1954, 464), even though "it rides hard on a single point", and fails to present Friedman's viewpoint systematically (1954, 463). In particular, while it *seems* to suggest that economists should seek only correlations, even if they are spurious, he believed that Friedman said something much more acceptable that "badly needs saying" (1954, 465), because he permitted testing by assumptions – if these assumptions can be reformulated as implications. While agreeing with the essence of Friedman's argument he nonetheless objected to accepting a hypothesis that has ridiculous assumptions, because we should ask whether it abstracts in a way that omits aspects important for the problem at hand.

Peter Newman (1954) called the book "an enjoyable feast, though perhaps some readers should be warned to take it *cum grano salis*, … stimulating, provocative, often infuriating, but well worth reading" (1954, 259 and 260; italics in original). Only two and a half sentences of his one-and-a-quarter page review dealt with F53. He referred to Friedman's principle of testing hypotheses by predictive success instead of realisticness of assumptions as "salutary and rewarding … [if] temperately used" (1954, 206), but warned about taking this too far.

[10] At the time both the *Journal of Political Economy* and the *American Economic Review* reviewed books, *The Journal of Economic Literature* not yet having appeared. The *Journal of the American Statistical Association* reviewed some economics books, but not this one.

Hutchison (1954) described the book as containing so "much that is acute, independent and stimulating", that though "there is much to disagree with ... this collection of essays should be widely and warmly welcomed" (1954, 799). Almost half his review dealt with Friedman's methodology, both in F53 and in other chapters. He did not mention Friedman's strictures against testing by the realisticness of assumptions, though he did discuss his insistence on testing by predictive success. Unlike most reviewers, he also dealt with other aspects of Friedman's methodology, such as Friedman's emphasis on the distinction between normative and positive economics and his criticism of the prevailing overemphasis on elegance, generality, and taxonomy.

Allen Clark (1954) called it "a collection of remarkable essays" (1954, 394) that refutes claims that neoclassical theory is of no use to policymakers. And "what is profoundly more significant" (1954, 394), it shows that in some areas where we thought we had unequivocal knowledge, we do not. In discussing F53, Allen summarized Friedman's criticism of testing by the realisticness of assumptions, but did not go beyond that. C. S. Soper (1954) devoted about a third of his review to F53, summarizing Friedman's belief that most disputes among economists concern positive issues, and to his rejection of testing by the realisticness of assumptions. While he mostly just summarized F53, he also argued that Friedman, by stressing that a theory's predictions can only be tested for the phenomena it seeks to explain, fails to tell us how to enlarge its sphere of validity. In his two-paragraph review Erich Schneider (1955) dispatched F53 in two sentences, saying that Max Weber and Joseph Schumpeter will already have familiarized German readers with its contents, but even so, that the clarity of Friedman's presentation makes it enjoyable reading.[11]

In summary then, four of the seven reviews of F53 were laudatory, one can at best be described as mixed, another was dismissive, and one made little attempt at evaluation. None predicted its future importance. Nor did the decision of many journals not to review Friedman's book suggest a brilliant future for it. And only one reviewer, Hutchison, was able to see sufficiently beyond the realisticness-of-assumptions issue to discuss at some length Friedman's criticisms of empirically inapplicable formalism, perhaps because that resembled Hutchison's own position. But the reviews did have a commendable characteristic; while casual observation

---

[11] Such a short review was unusual for this journal, but in the same issue Schneider also reviewed in just two paragraphs the second edition of Michael Kalecki's *Theory of Economic Dynamics*.

suggests that many economists treated F53 as an apologetic for neoclassical price theory, none of the reviewers took that line.

4   An overview

Friedman's underlying theme – combine theoretical and empirical work by focusing on predictive success – carried the day and the relative importance of empirical work has increased (see Figlio 1994; Hoover 2004). By no means all of the credit here belongs to Friedman. Thus, James Duesenberry (1949) had previously published an outstanding example of such work, which, I was told, had much influence on Harvard students. From outside economics there was the influence of Popper and of positivism in general. Other social sciences moved in the same direction. But surely Friedman deserves some of the credit, if only because he furnished neoclassical economists with a defense against their institutionalist critics, thus giving economic theory some breathing room, while commending the use of data to test theories rather than just to compile facts.

But the subsequent decline of old-line institutionalism should not be entirely (or even largely?) attributed to Friedman. The rise of econometrics also played a part. One could now be an empiricist in a more glamorous way than by just gathering data – if one could manage the required math. And since many institutionalists could not, they had to relinquish their claim to be the shining example of the empirical and hence "scientific" approach to economics. The increased professionalization of economics with its tendency to draw sharp disciplinary lines also played a role since it meant that the preoccupation of some institutionalists with sociological and historical problems tended to place them outside the limits of economics. All the same, it seems plausible that Friedman's essay significantly and perhaps even substantially contributed to the decline of institutionalism; perhaps – given his tribute to Mitchell (Friedman 1950) – by more than he wished.

Contemporary academic economics consists primarily of modeling exercises, particularly in game theory and in exploring the implications of asymmetric information. Some of these models try to earn their keep by eliminating assumptions made in previous models. But they do this to generalize them, and not to criticize them for unrealisticness. That "all models are false, but some are useful," has become a familiar cliché. Granted that occasionally economists criticize a paper for its unrealistic assumptions (see, for instance, Waldman 2003), this is consistent with F53 if these assumptions are also relevant implications. But Friedman's victory is incomplete. While most economists no longer explicitly reject some model for its unrealistic assumptions, they may still (perhaps uncon-sciously) be unwilling to accept it for that reason. And much more seriously, Friedman's stricture that the implications of models need tough-minded testing is often ignored. Tests of implications are often perfunctory, "playing tennis with the net down" (Blaug 1980, 256; Mayer 2001).

Friedman has been much less persuasive on the superiority of Marshallian economics. While most empirical work is Marshallian, within theory the walrasian approach has become more common since 1953. But only a small proportion of papers are purely theoretical, so that the vaunted victory of walrasian economics is more a matter of Sunday dress than workday dress. But it is to the profession's Sunday dress that many (most?) economists point with pride.

Casual empiricism is a pejorative term and, *in principle*, few economists would now explicitly defend it, but few would have done so in 1953 either. Whether the indifference curve between using casual empiricism and admitting ignorance has changed is hard to say. What has changed mas-sively is the budget constraint due to increased research funding and the computer revolution. Friedman has, however, been more successful in combating the Robbinsian emphasis on introspection, though it probably still plays a significant implicit role by excluding certain models that do not make intuitive sense. It is hard to say whether the surveys of motives and beliefs that Friedman criticized are less frequent now than before 1953.[12]

While postmodernism has had virtually no influence on mainstream practicing economists, so that Friedman's dictum to separate normative from positive statements still holds sway, there is little reason to think that it is obeyed any better or worse now than before 1953. It is, however, likely that in theory construction there is now more interplay of theorizing and data analysis than before 1953.

5   Nobel Prize lectures

Two considerations justify using Nobel lectures to characterize the way economics has changed. First, in economics Nobels are given, not for establishing indubitable results, but for initiating, or carrying to fruition, a

---

[12] F53's discussion of surveys is perfunctory, but in a paper cited in F53 Friedman (1949) had already set out his criticisms of surveys that ask agents to reveal their motives or thinking. In that paper he did not criticize surveys of factual information, indeed he himself (Friedman and Kuznets 1945) had used such evidence. As Boulier and Goldfarb (1998) show, survey information now pervades empirical economics, but most of it comes from objective questions, not questions about opinions and motives.

particular sub-literature. They therefore highlight the growth points of economics. Second, the Nobel committee largely represents the judgment of the profession. My sample consists of all Nobel lectures up to 2002 with the following exceptions: when several recipients split the prize I used the lecture of only one of them, chosen somewhat arbitrarily. I also excluded Klein, Tobin, and Modigliani because I cover their work in the next section. Laureates have considerable latitude in their lectures. Most focus on their own work, or work that derives directly from it, but six did not, and are therefore excluded from the sample.[13] Table 4.2 categorizes the remaining 22 lectures by four characteristics of F53. A plus denotes consistency with the characteristic, a minus inconsistency, and a zero the irrelevance of this characteristic.[14] Such a classification is inevitably subjective and sometimes somewhat arbitrary – but then tracing the influence of a paper is more like doing literary criticism than like doing physics. (Appendix B of Mayer 2004, provides summary information on the included Nobel lectures.) While the minuses in table 4.2 have a straightforward interpretation, the pluses do not. They show only that the lecture conforms to a certain recommendation of F53, and not necessarily that F53 influenced it. For example, someone who tests a hypothesis by its implications may do so only because in this case it is quicker than testing it by the realisticness of assumptions.

What is remarkable in table 4.2 is the paucity of minuses. If the Nobel committee's judgment is correct, few of the outstanding breakthroughs have come from those employing a methodology contrary to F53. On the issue of assumptions versus predictions there are 11 pluses, and only 4 minuses, while on the Marshallian/walrasian dichotomy there are 16 pluses and 4 minuses. On the rejection of casual empiricism there are 15 pluses and 1 minus. And on the interplay of data and theories 12 pluses confront 2 minuses.

Such a tabulation is subject to the criticism that I followed the naive empiricist's bad advice of: "go measure something, never mind what it is." In depicting the thrust of mainstream economics, some prizes (e.g. Samuelson's) may deserve more weight than others. Indeed, it seems obvious that the frequencies in table 4.2 shortchange the formalist trend in economics. With only 4 of the 23 prizes going to formalists (Samuelson, Arrow, Debreu, and Harsanyi) the influence of formalism is surely understated.

---

[13] These six are: Kantorovich, Kuznets, Meade, Miller, Stigler, and Stone.
[14] I exclude the normative/positive distinction because economics has changed little in that respect.

Table 4.2 *The Nobel Prize lectures and Friedman's criteria*[a]

Author and date	Assumptions vs. predictions	Marshallian/ walrasian	Casual empiricism	Interplay of theory and data
Tinbergen, 1969	+	+	+	+
Samuelson, 1970	−[b]	0	0	0
Arrow, 1972	−[c]	−	0	0
Leontief, 1973	+	+[d]	+	+
Hayek, 1974	−	−	−[e]	−
Simon, 1978	?[f]	+	+	+
Shultz, 1979	+[g]	+	+	+
Debreu, 1983	0	−	0	−
Buchanan, 1986	0	+	+[h]	?[i]
Solow, 1987	+	+	+	+
Allais, 1988	+	+	+	0
Haavelmo, 1989	+	+	+	0
Coase, 1991	−[j]	+	+	+
Becker, 1992	+	+	+	+
North, 1993	+[k]	+	+	+
Harsanyi, 1994	0	+	0	0
Mirrlees, 1996	0	−	0[l]	0
Scholes, 1997	+	+	+	+
Sen, 1998	0	0	0	0
McFadden, 2000	+	+	+	+
Akerlof, 2001	?	+	+	+
Smith, 2002	+[m]	+	+	+

Note: + denotes consistent with F53, − denotes inconsistent with F53, 0 unrelated to F53 with respect to that criterion, and ? hard to say.

[a] This table does not cover all Nobel lectures; for the reasons some were excluded see the text.

[b] Samuelson does not discuss this issue in his lecture, but has elsewhere strongly rejected Friedman's stricture against testing by the realism of assumption.

[c] Arrow's advocacy of minimizing assumptions is in principle consistent with F53, but points in a different direction.

[d] Leontief uses a general equilibrium model, but is Marshallian in paying attention to the details of specific industries.

[e] This is not explicit in Hayek's lecture, but is inherent in his general position.

[f] In his lecture Simon strongly criticizes Friedman's essay, but the substance of his lecture is consistent with it, at least if it is given a soft reading.

[g] Based on the general tenor of Schultz's lecture rather than on an explicit statement.

[h] There is little empiricism in Buchanan's lecture, but it plays a large role in the work of his school.

[i] No data are discussed in Buchanan's lecture, but in the work of his school there may well be an interplay of theory and data.

[j] Coase does not criticize Friedman on this score on this lecture, but does so elsewhere.

[k] Applicability of assumptions determines domain of theory.

[l] There is casual empiricism, but at this stage of the development of the model one cannot expect anything more.

[m] By implication.

6   Macroeconomics

This sections deals with the three major macro research programs, Keynesian, monetarist, and new classical. It omits the Austrian and post-Keynesian programs because they are heterodox, and new Keynesian theory, and endogenous growth theory, because they came too late.

6.1   *The Keynesian program*

The major components of the traditional Keynesian program are the consumption function, the investment function, a general equilibrium version of monetary theory, econometric models, and growth theory. All are positive theories that do not introduce normative elements to a greater extent than is usual in economics.

The consumption function   Here the most important breakthrough was the permanent income theory (PIT) of Friedman (1957) and the closely related life-cycle hypothesis (LCH) of Modigliani and associates, followed by Hall's reformulation of these theories in a rational-expectations framework. All three followed F53 in judging their hypotheses by their predictive successes and not by the realisticness of their assumptions. Specifically, they assumed intertemporal utility maximization even over long horizons. Friedman and (though more tentatively) also Modigliani assumed that the savings/income ratio is uncorrelated with permanent income. They did not justify these assumptions as realistic, but instead tried to show that their theories predicted consumption accurately and resolved some puzzling anomalies.

These theories are Marshallian in treating income as exogenous. A more walrasian approach would use as the budget constraint, not permanent income, but the household's potential labor supply multiplied by the wage rate, plus non-human wealth. They also avoid the casual empiricism and introspection on which Keynes relied when he grounded his consumption function in: "The fundamental psychological law upon which we are entitled to depend with great confidence, both *a priori* from our knowledge of human nature and from the detailed facts of experience" (Keynes 1936, 96; italics in original). Friedman (1957, ix), who stated that he developed his theory from a close study of the data, gives the strong impression of an interplay of data and theory. This is less so for Modigliani.[15]

---

[15] Modigliani and Ando developed the theory initially like a "ray of light" while on a car trip. Although Modigliani in developing the relative income theory had previously analyzed consumption data, he had then "neglected the problem" until his conversation with Ando (Modigliani 2001, 59).

Investment   In the two decades after 1953 the two most notable developments here were Dale Jorgenson's neoclassical theory and James Tobin's q theory. The former is based on two insights: that earlier work on investment had confounded the capital stock and investment (its first derivative), and on the need to pay attention to the institutional details of the tax treatment of investment. The latter is based on the gap between the market price of new capital and its costs of production. Neither is easy to trace to F53. Jorgenson's theory appeared fourteen years after F53. Its attention to the distinction between capital and investment is a clarification of the internal logic of the theory, and hence unrelated to F53. The inclusion of tax variables may seem to show concern about the realisticness of assumptions. But Friedman did not object to adding realistic details if they improve predictive success. Tobin's q theory, too, appeared only long after F53. Since it does not attempt to explain the firm's equity price, it is more a tool for predicting investment than an explanatory theory. An instrumentalist reading of F53 would therefore make it seem Friedmanian, but, as the chapters by Mäki and Hoover in this volume show, such a reading is mistaken. Both theories are Marshallian in that they focus on a concrete problem rather than on elegant formulations. Developing them may well have involved a close interplay of theory and data; no information on this is available.

Monetary and portfolio theories   The most influential Keynesian monetary theory is that of Tobin and his Yale school. It takes account of the complexity of the financial system, with money being just one asset in a continuum of liquid assets. Such an approach rejects F53. It seeks to give a realistic picture of the financial system, and does not stress prediction. It is also walrasian. And Tobin gives the impression that he relied on broadly based observations (akin to casual empiricism), such as Treasury bills having characteristics similar to money, rather than on a close interplay of theory and data.

Econometric models of the economy   Although F53 was not published until three years after Lawrence Klein's (1950) model it could have influenced subsequent models. Or, if these models follow the methodology recommended in F53, that could account for their popularity, and hence document the influence of F53.

Predictive success, not the realisticness of their assumptions, is the main criterion by which these models ask to be judged.[16] But that does

---

[16] Predictive success is, however, not the only important criterion. Even if it predicts accurately, we would reject a theory that explains the US price level by the league standing of Manchester United. Friedman himself rejects large econometric models because he believes that they require much more knowledge than we have.

not bear testimony to the influence of F53, because prediction is clearly their main purpose, even if one believes that scientific hypotheses should be judged by their assumptions. Although they are general equilibrium models in Friedman's terminology, they are actually Marshallian, because they seek to provide empirical and practical knowledge and make no claim to elegance. Casual empiricism may play a role in choosing their individual equations, but primarily they are chosen to accord with substantive empirical results. Their development relies on a constant interplay of observation and theory. Indeed, one of the criticisms of these models is that they are overfitted.

Growth models   In the early 1960s the first wave of growth theory accounted for a substantial part of the work in macroeconomics. Much of it consisted of varying some previously made assumptions. It essentially stopped after a critical survey by Frank Hahn and Robbin Matthews (1964), who wrote:

> The variety of growth models is very great and with ingenuity can evidently be almost indefinitely enlarged. This is very largely due to the rather extreme level of abstraction employed and the very artificial nature of the problems considered ... We want theories that can be used as plumbers use a spanner – not simply abstract systems ... It would be difficult to claim that any of the models we have discussed goes far towards explaining ... [the observed differences in growth rates of countries and periods]. (Hahn and Matthews 1964, 888–90)

Clearly, these models are contrary to F53. Whether Hahn and Matthews were influenced by F53 (which they did not cite) is hard to say, as is whether the apparently widespread acceptance of their conclusion owes much to F53.

6.2   Monetarism

F53 provided monetarists with a battering ram for their assault on the prevailing Keynesian orthodoxy. At that time the wealth effect of falling interest rates on consumption was little known, and with exchange rates being more or less fixed, the claim that changes in the money supply could substantially affect income appeared to require an (at that time) seemingly implausibly high interest elasticity of investment. Friedman responded that while it would be desirable to trace the channels by which money affects income, this is not necessary. Instead, one can document numerous cases in which changes in nominal income have followed exogenous changes in money, and combine this fact with the general explanation from price theory, that when there is an exogenous increase in the supply of one asset (money) the demand for the other asset (goods) increases. The other leading variant of US monetarism, the work of Brunner and Meltzer, too, emphasized testing by implications, even though they provided a fairly elaborate theoretical discussion.[17]

Without the focus on prediction that F53 advocated monetarism would not have achieved its popularity. Most economists would then have agreed with Frank Hahn's (1971, 61) objection that: "Friedman neither has nor claims to have a monetary theory. His strong and influential views are not founded on an understanding of 'how money works,' but on what his empirical studies have led him to believe to have been the course of monetary history." In principle, it is obvious that the demand for money, and hence its velocity, depends upon the expected yields of all competing assets. Yet, unlike the Yale school, Friedman disregarded them because he believed that including them did little to improve the theory's predictions.

The monetarists' case is also bound up with their rejection of the mixture of introspection and casual empiricism that was a prominent part of then prevailing Keynesian thinking. Examples are Keynes's consumption function, his intuition that the main factors generating changes in GDP are changing expenditure motives rather than changes in the money supply, and the empirical significance of the speculative demand for money. To successfully challenge Keynesian theory monetarists had to show that what seemed commonsensical and intuitively obvious was an insufficient basis for macroeconomics.[18]

The need to distinguish sharply between normative and positive elements played little role in the debate. Although normative issues permeated policy discussions, both sides failed to draw sufficiently clear distinctions between normative and positive issues. Still another Friedmanian theme, the need for interplay between theoretical and empirical work, may have played a substantial role in the rise of monetarism, since it was well suited to

---

[17] Brunner's (1969) view on the role of assumptions was similar to Friedman's.

[18] That expenditures depend more on the incentives to spend than on money holdings seems obvious to middle-class people (such as most economists) who think of expenditures primarily as consumption. It may not be so obvious to the rich who are busy with asset reallocation, or to the poor who are severely cash constrained. From the late 1930s to the early 1950s Keynesians attached much importance to speculative liquidity preference without any evidence that it is empirically significant. The issue of plausibility of assumptions vs. accuracy of predictions also plays an important role in disputes about monetary policy. Until the application of time-inconsistency theory one of the two central points in this debate was the Keynesian argument that one can infer from the plausible assumption that central bankers are well intentioned and intelligent, that they will pursue reasonable policies. Monetarists responded by citing instances of perverse policy, that is instances where the Keynesian theory predicted badly.

what monetarists were doing. Moreover, the monetarists' interplay of theory and empirical work may have made monetarism more popular by providing a welcome contrast to the bifurcation of much of the Keynesian research effort between theorists who did not test their theories, and applied economists who focused on forecasting.

6.3   New classical theory

The substantive message of new classical theory, rapid market clearing and real business cycles, has won a foothold in macroeconomics, but not a victory. But its methodological message, that is, its reductionist dogma, has. Despite Friedman's own rejection of new classical theory, some economists credit (or blame) F53 for it, since it justifies the use of unrealistic assumptions, such as highly flexible wages. As Wade Hands's chapter in this volume shows, within the science-studies dimension this is so, and the victory of new classical methodology documents the influence of F53. But this is more a defeat than a victory for Friedman, because the new classicals misuse F53. By insisting that discussions of macroeconomic phenomena make no assumptions that are not firmly grounded in microeconomics they treat assumptions as an integral and crucial part of the analysis, while to Friedman, assumptions are background scenery that can be varied, depending upon the play currently on stage. Moreover, when Friedman objected to testing by the realisticness of assumptions, he did not do so in favor of a priorism, but in favor of predictive testing. And, although the new classicals often present predictive tests, they give the impression that these tests are tagged on more for the sake of decoration than for the heavy lifting: "Theory ahead of observation" is their slogan. I conjecture that no economist has ever accepted rational-expectations theory primarily because he or she found the empirical evidence convincing.

On the issue of Marshallian versus walrasian economics, new classical economists are obviously not Friedmanian. It is unclear to what extent they adhere to his rejection of casual empiricism, in part, because using elaborate econometrics is no talisman against casual empiricism, and in part because it is unclear whether the estimates inserted into calibrated models are derived from an objective survey of the literature or selected because they happen to give results consistent with new classical theory. Friedman's insistence on distinguishing positive from normative elements is again not relevant. But the interplay between theory development and intimate knowledge of the data that Friedman recommended is relevant and, it seems missing in new classical theory.

7   Sources of influence

Although, as previously discussed, several factors independently impelled economics in the directions advocated in F53, I believe (though I certainly cannot prove it) that F53 played a significant role in changing economics. One reason for this belief is the merit of its thesis. Methodologists are right in calling it philosophically naive and confused, and yet it is a much better guide for practicing economists than its two main rivals at the time, a priorism and naive empiricism. A second reason is its persuasive style which presents seemingly audacious, and hence stimulating, statements with an air of sweet reasonableness. Third, we have Friedman's achievements in substantive economics, often grounded in a methodology which, if not exactly that of F53, bears a reasonably close relation to it. Whether the association of F53 with the marginalist controversy helped or hindered is hard to say. Marginalists had a strong incentive to welcome F53. But institutionalists could dismiss it as "enemy propaganda," without appreciating the large olive branch Friedman extended to them by his opposition to walrasian economics. Friedman's political views may also have induced some economists to oppose F53. But I suspect that this was only a minor factor. Finally, Friedman's personality for some reason, seems to provoke either ardent admiration or sharp opposition; the net effect of that is hard to gauge.

8   Conclusion

Since 1953 economics has changed along the lines F53 recommended. However, other factors could also have accounted for these changes, particularly for the shift away from testing by the realisticness of assumptions. At the same time, some of these factors could also explain why Friedman seems to have failed in his opposition to walrasian economics. But it is certainly possible that without F53 the walrasian tide might have been stronger, so that even on this issue F53 may have been influential.

How much of the observed changes in economics one attributes to F53 and how much to these other factors depends, in part, on one's acceptance of the Stiglerian and postmodernist view that economists' theory choice is governed by their self-interest. But even if it is, F53 could still have been influential by providing a convenient rationalization for, and thus accelerating, the changes that occurred. To what extent it did so is a matter of intuitive appraisal rather than of solid evidence, and I feel qualified to make such an appraisal only with respect to macroeconomics.

Although the immediate inspiration for, and the examples given in, F53 are microeconomic, F53 seems to have been more influential in macroeconomics since so much of modern microeconomics consists of building models that explore the implications of various assumptions (see also Williamson's chapter in this volume). Perhaps F53's greater influence on macroeconomics is due, in part, to Friedman's own shift of emphasis towards macroeconomics, or to macroeconomics being traditionally more policy oriented, and hence more aware of the need for a Marshallian approach and for correct predictions.

Within macroeconomics F53 probably played an important – perhaps a *very* important – role in the ready acceptance of the LCH, PIT, and the rational-expectations consumption function. And it did play a major role in the monetarist counter-revolution, and in that way in the synthesis of monetarism and new Keynesianism that underlies the currently prevailing macroeconomics. Eventually the hard facts of experience would have prevailed over the Keynesianism of the 1960s and 1970s even without F53, but it would have taken them longer. And perhaps new classical theory, too, would not have made the big time were it not for F53's warnings against testing by the realisticness of assumptions, and against reliance on casual empiricism. It is even possible that this was the most important influence of F53. That would be ironic.

In microeconomics I suspect, but that may just reflect my lack of familiarity with it, that F53 did influence primarily Chicago economists, and perhaps work on public choice theory. But by its stress on the explanation of specific phenomena it may also (probably indirectly) have influenced work on asymmetric information.

References

Allen, Clark (1954). Review of Milton Friedman *Essays in Positive Economics*. *Southern Economic Journal*, 10, January, 394–9

Backhouse, Roger (2002). Economic models and the role of informal scientific methods. In Uskali Mäki (ed.), *Fact and Fiction in Economics*. New York: Cambridge University Press, 202–13

Baumol, William (1954). Review of Milton Friedman *Essays in Positive Economics*. *Review of Economics and Statistics*, 36, November, 462–5

Blaug, Mark (1980). *The Methodology of Economics*. Cambridge: Cambridge University Press

Boulier, Brian and Robert Goldfarb (1998). On the use and nonuse of surveys in economics. *Journal of Economic Methodology*, 5, June, 1–22

Brunner, Karl (1969). "Assumptions" and the cognitive quality of theories. *Synthese*, 20, 501–25

Colander, David (1991). The lost art of economics. *Journal of Economic Perspectives*, 6, Summer, 191–8

Dasgupta, Partha (2002). Modern economics and its critics. In Uskali Mäki (ed.), *Fact and Fiction in Economics*. Cambridge: Cambridge University Press, 57–89

Duesenberry, James (1949). *Income, Saving and the Theory of Consumer Behavior.* Cambridge, MA: Harvard University Press

Figlio, David (1994). Trends in the publication of empirical economics. *Journal of Economic Perspectives*, 4, Summer, 179–87

Friedman, Milton (1949). Discussion. *American Economic Review*, 39, May, 196–9
  (1950). Wesley C. Mitchell as an economic theorist. *Journal of Political Economy*, 58, December, 463–95
  (1953). *Essays in Positive Economics.* Chicago: University of Chicago Press
  (1957). *A Theory of the Consumption Function.* Princeton: Princeton University Press

Friedman, Milton and Simon Kuznets (1945). *Income from Independent Professional Practices.* New York: National Bureau of Economic Research

Friedman, Milton and Anna Schwartz (1963). *A Monetary History of the United States.* Princeton: Princeton University Press

Gurley, Jack and Edward Shaw (1960). *Money in a Theory of Finance.* Washington, DC: Brookings

Hahn, Frank (1971). Professor Friedman's views on money. *Economica* n.s., 39, February, 61–80

Hahn, Frank and Robin Matthews (1964). The theory of economic growth: a survey. *Economic Journal*, 74, December , 779–902

Hammond, J. Daniel (1990). McCloskey's modernism and Friedman's methodology: A case study with new evidence. *Review of Social Economy*, 48, Summer, 158–71
  (1996). *Theory and Measurement.* Cambridge: Cambridge University Press
  (1998). Friedman, Milton. In J. Davis, D. W. Hands and U. Mäki (eds.), *Handbook of Economic Methodology.* Cheltenham: Edward Elgar

Harsanyi, John (1995). Games with incomplete information. *American Economic Review*, 85, June, 291–393

Hayek, Friedrich von (1992). The pretence of knowledge. In Assar Lindbeck (ed.), *Nobel Lectures, Economic Sciences, 1969–1980.* Singapore: World Scientific

Hirsch, Abraham and Neil De Marchi (1990). *Milton Friedman.* New York: Harvester Wheatsheaf

Hoover, Kevin (2001). *The Methodology of Empirical Macroeconomics.* Cambridge: Cambridge University Press
  (2004). Lost causes. *Journal of the History of Economic Thought*, 26(2), 149–64

Hutchison, Terence (1954). Review of Milton Friedman *Essays in Positive Economics. Economic Journal*, 64, December, 796–9

Keynes, John M. (1936). *The General Theory of Employment, Interest and Money.* New York: Prentice Hall

Keynes, John N. (1963). *The Scope and Method of Political Economy.* New York: Augustus Kelly

Klein, Lawrence (1950). *Economic Fluctuations in the United States, 1921–1941.* New York: Wiley

Leontief, Wassily (1992). Structure of the world economy. In Assar Lindbeck (ed.), *Nobel Lectures, Economic Sciences, 1969–1980.* Singapore: World Scientific

Lerner, Abba (1944). *The Economics of Control.* London: Macmillan

Mayer, Thomas (1993). Friedman's methodology of positive economics: a soft reading. *Economic Inquiry* 31, 213–223

(1995). *Doing Economics*, Cheltenham: Edward Elgar

(2001). Misinterpreting a failure to confirm as confirmation: a recurrent misreading of significance tests., Working paper, www.econ.ucdavis.edu

(2004). *The influence of Friedman's methodological essay*. University of California, Davis, Working paper no. 04–1

Modigliani, Franco (2001). *Adventures of an Economist*. New York: Texere

Musgrave, Alan (1981). Unrealistic assumptions in economic theory. *Kyklos*, 34, (3), 377–87

Newman, Peter (1954). Review of Milton Friedman *Essays in Positive Economics*. *Economica*, 21, August, 259–60

Reder, Melvin (1982). Chicago economics: permanence and change. *Journal of Economic Literature*, 20, March, 1–38

Schneider, Erich (1955). Review of Milton Friedman *Essays in Positive Economics*. *Weltwirtschaftliches Archiv*

Snowdon, Brian and Howard Vane (1999). *Conversations with Leading Economists*. Cheltenham: Edward Elgar

Soper, C. S. (1954). Review of Milton Friedman *Essays in Positive Economics*. *Economic Record*, 30, November, 323–6

Sugden, Robert (2002). Credible worlds: the status of theoretical models. In Uskali Mäki (ed.), *Fact and Fiction in Economics*. Cambridge: Cambridge University Press

Tinbergen, Jan (1992).The use of models: experience and prospects. In Assar Lindbeck (ed.), *Nobel Lectures, Economic Sciences, 1969–1980*. Singapore, World Scientific

Vickrey, William (1954). Review of Milton Friedman *Essays in Positive Economics*. *American Economic Review*, 44, June, 397–400

Waldman, Michael (2003). Durable goods theory for real world markets. *Journal of Economic Perspectives*, 17, Winter 2003, 131–54

5 Did Milton Friedman's positive methodology license the formalist revolution?

D. Wade Hands

> A man who has a burning interest in pressing issues of public policy, who has a strong desire to learn how the economic system really works in order that that knowledge may be used, is not likely to stay within the bounds of a method of analysis that denies him the knowledge he seeks. He will escape the shackles of formalism, ... A far better way is to try to derive theoretical generalizations to fit as full and comprehensive set of related facts about the real world as it is possible to get.
>
> (Friedman 1946, 631)

1 Introduction

Milton Friedman's 1953 paper "The methodology of positive economics" (hereafter F53) is clearly the best-known and most cited work in twentieth-century economic methodology. F53 often exhausts the practicing econo-mist's exposure to the methodological literature. As the philosopher Daniel Hausman put it: "It is the only essay on methodology that a large number, perhaps a majority, of economists have ever read" (Hausman 1992, 162).

There is a vast methodological literature surrounding F53, but this chapter will not approach the essay from the perspective of any of these familiar methodological positions. For example, what follows will not: (1) summarize Friedman's argument in any detail;[1] (2) try to situate Friedman's essay within the existing philosophical, particularly

* Earlier versions of this paper were presented in "Milton Friedman's Methodology Paper after 50 Years" at the ASSA meetings in Washington, DC, January 2003 and in the Philosophy Department Colloquium at the University of Quebec at Montreal, April 2003, as well as at the EIPE conference "Positive Economics: Milton Friedman's Essay at 50" in Rotterdam, December 2003. A shortened version, with the title "Did Milton Friedman's methodology license the formalist revolution?" was published in *Journal of Economic Methodology*, 10 (2003), 507–20. I would like to thank Roger Backhouse, Robert Leonard, Uskali Mäki, Tom Mayer, Robert Nadeau, and numerous other attendees of the above presentations for helpful comments. Errors and omissions are of course solely my responsibility.
1 There are numerous summaries available in the secondary literature, including Blaug 1980/1992, Caldwell 1982/1994, Hands 2001, and Hausman 1992.

philosophy of science, literature;[2] (3) make the case for a particular interpretation of key words like "assumptions," "realism," "prediction," etc;[3] (4)
try to reconcile (or critique) the relationship between Friedman's methodological advice and his actual scientific practice;[4] (5) evaluate the adequacy
of Friedman's stated methodology as an economic methodology. What
follows is broadly concerned with F53, but it will not address any of the
traditional methodological questions associated with Friedman's famous
essay.

What I will do is summarize and evaluate two conflicting interpretations
of F53 that have emerged within the recent methodological literature;
in particular, I will address a disagreement regarding the relationship
between the advice contained in Friedman's essay and the ascent of
formalism in economics. I will not take any substantive (new or existing)
position on Friedman's essay, but I will take a position on the role that F53
played in "licensing" the so-called formalist revolution. I will leave the
debate over whether one "ought" to do economics in the way suggested by
Friedman's essay, as well as various questions about the true essence of
Friedman's position, to methodologists with greater expertise in such
subjects. I will focus on the more naturalistically inclined question of the
role that Friedman's ideas played in the ascendancy of a particular set of
socially held beliefs about the (only) acceptable way to do research within
the science of economics.

I will focus my discussion on three influential contributors to this
ongoing debate: Mark Blaug, Terence Hutchison, and Thomas Mayer.
Blaug and Hutchison have argued repeatedly that F53 *did in fact license*
the formalist revolution, while Mayer has argued precisely the opposite;
the formalist revolution was (at least in part) a result of *not* following
Friedman's methodological advice. Juxtaposition of the views of these
two sets of authors on the question of Friedman's essay raises important
questions about the relationship between how one interprets F53 and how
one views its impact on the profession. For as we will see, all three parties
agree about essentially every methodological issue surrounding the
famous essay – they have fundamentally the same conception of "formalism"; they all agree that it became the dominant approach to economic

---

[2] Although Boland's (1979) instrumentalist reading is the most popular of such philosophical reconstructions, Mäki (1989, 1992, 2000, this volume) and Hoover (2004 this
volume) offer persuasive realist interpretations. A realist reading is also supported by
Friedman's emphasis on the importance of novel facts.

[3] Although I consider Mäki's (1989, 1992) suggestion that we replace Friedman's "realism"
with "realisticness" to be a good one.

[4] Although I would admit that I find the most detailed of such efforts – Hirsch and De
Marchi (1990) – to be relatively unpersuasive.

theorizing in the post-World War II era and that it was generally a bad thing; they agree in principle that the right way to do economics involves less mathematical abstraction, more and more serious empirical testing, increased focus on the real facts of economic life, and a greater emphasis on economic policy – and yet they disagree sharply about the impact of Friedman's essay on the rise of formalism.

2   On the formalist revolution

The "formalist revolution" has received increasing attention from those working in the history and philosophy of economics during the last few years. While debate rages about the causes and many of the specific characteristics of the formalist revolution, there does appear to be a consensus regarding the broad general features and approximate timing of this fundamental change in the dominant form of economic theorizing.[5] There was an identifiable difference between the representative research paper appearing in the most prestigious economics journals in the 1930s versus the 1970s; and it is equally clear that the later work was more *formal* – more mathematical, more analytical, less historical, less institutional, more standardized, and more narrow regarding admissible priors – than the economic theorizing of an earlier period.

Although I agree with Roy Weintraub and others[6] that a serious "archeology of formalism" (Weintraub 1998, 1844) would require a careful, and deeply textured, historical investigation – involving a sensitivity to the subtle variations among the different versions of formalism that have existed within the history and philosophy of mathematics; attention to the evolving and overlapping epistemic visions at work in science, social science, and mathematics; as well as an examination of the socially constructed character of all of the relevant disciplinarities – I do not believe that such an historical archeology is required here. The current project is simply to investigate two different, rather starkly conflicting, answers to the question of whether Friedman's methodology licensed the formalist revolution: Blaug and Hutchison claiming that it did, and Mayer claiming that it did not (and could actually have prevented it). If these three authors had substantially different views of the essential features of the "formalist revolution," then it would be necessary to ferret out those differences in

---

[5] Hutchison (2000, 16) seems to give Benjamin Ward (1972) credit for initially discussing formalism in economics, but the Friedman quote at the beginning of this chapter shows that it goes back far beyond the early 1970s.

[6] This literature includes Backhouse (1998), Golland (1996), Mirowski (1986, 2002), Punzo (1991), Weintraub and Mirowski (1994), and Weintraub (2002).

order to determine if their different interpretations of formalism were responsible for their different views of the role of F53. But there are no such differences. All three authors are concerned with roughly the same features of postwar economic theorizing and they define, and date, formalism in basically the same way. Since all three authors share the same notion of formalism, the variation in their views about Friedman cannot be explained by the variation in their views about formalism, and thus the only characterization of formalism relevant to the current investigation is their (shared) view. The question of a serious archeology of formalism can wait for another context.

Blaug, Hutchison, and Mayer all essentially agree about *what* formalism is/was, roughly *when* it hit economics, *which* subfields within economics are the best exemplars of the formalist influence, and *whether* formalism was a good thing for the discipline or not (it was not). They also seem to agree, though perhaps less strongly, about the essential methodological features of a better, less-formalist, approach to economic theorizing, and which economists come closest to living up to these quite different standards. The most relevant texts on these issues are Blaug (1994, 1997, 1998, 2002, 2003), Hutchison (1992, 2000), and Mayer (1993, 1995). It is useful to note that while the arguments of these three authors will be the main subject in what follows, they are certainly not alone in their agreement about the what, when, which, and whether of formalism; recent commentators as disparate as Tony Lawson (2003) and Deirdre McCloskey (1994) also agree on these same basic issues.

According to the three authors mentioned above the formalist turn clearly involved the increased use of mathematics, abstraction, and deductive modes of reasoning. Theorems and proofs replaced systematic argumentation; success came to be measured almost exclusively in terms of the development and application of new techniques; and the form of a theoretical argument came to take precedence over its economic content. According to Blaug, formalism involves "the *worship* of technique" (Blaug 2002, 36) and "giving absolute priority to the form of economic theories rather than their content" (2002, 34); for Hutchison it is the "method of rigorous, logical deduction from (what have been claimed to be) a small number of self-evident 'principles'" (Hutchison 2000, 17) and the substitution of "fantasy content for realistic, or relevant, content" (2000, 18). For Mayer formalism is "abstract theory that is concerned with high-level generalizations, and looks toward axiomization" (Mayer 1993, 7) and the criteria by which formalists "judge economic research are, to a large extent, those of mathematicians" (Mayer 1993, 25). Formalism transformed economics "from an informal field, mainly using a natural language and relatively simple techniques, to a more formal field that converses much of the time in the language of mathematics, and puts a great stress on the use of the latest techniques" (Mayer 1995, 73).

While formalism is clearly linked to mathematics, all three authors recognize that the formalist mode of argumentation does not actually require the use of mathematical analysis. All three cite Ricardo as an example of a proto-formalist (Blaug 2002, 36; Hutchison 2000, pp. 3, 17; Mayer 1993, 7). It is also clear that none of the three are against the general idea of using mathematics as a tool in economic analysis; mathematical symbolism and/or an occasional derivative are not the problem.

Now "formalism" is not the same thing as "formalization" or "mathematization" because it is possible to express a theory mathematically and even axiomatically without necessarily degenerating into "formalism," which simply means giving top priority to the formal structure of modelling irrespective of its content; it is to prefer rigour and precision to relevance, and elegance and logical coherence of analysis to practical implications; it is to make a fetish of theory and to deride a vulgar appeal to the real world. (Blaug 1994, 131)

Even though mathematics is neither necessary nor sufficient for formalism, the rise of mathematical economics, and particularly Arrow–Debreu general equilibrium theory, during the 1950s and 1960s clearly represented the high-water mark for formalism in economics and it set the tone for the most prestigious economic theorizing during the latter half of the twentieth century. All three authors have very negative things to say about the impact of Walrasian general equilibrium theory; Mayer is not quite as harsh as Blaug and Hutchison, but he still considers it an example of formalism rather than his preferred "empirical-science" economics. They all agree that economics took a seriously wrong turn and Arrow and Debreu (1954) pointed the way. A few of their remarks are worth quoting in detail.

If we can date the onset of the illness at all, it is the publication in 1954 of the famous paper by Nobel laureates Kenneth Arrow and Gerard Debreu; it is this paper that marks the beginning of what has since become a cancerous growth in the very centre of microeconomics. (Blaug, 1997, 3)

If there is such a thing as "original sin" in economic methodology, it is the worship of the idol of mathematical rigour, more or less invented by Arrow and Debreu (1954) and then canonized by Debreu (1959) in his *Theory of Value* five years later, probably the most arid and pointless book in the entire literature of economics. (Blaug 2002, 27)

In the 1950s and 1960s the formalist revolution met with very little critical resistance. In fact, the high confidence of leading mathematical abstractionists and formalizers in the impregnability of their achievements continued unabated through the 1970s and much of the 1980s, especially with regard to their flagship, the new ultra-abstract and extremely refined version of "general equilibrium" analysis ... (Hutchison 2000, 20)

Not only do they agree about the pernicious effect of Arrow–Debreu general equilibrium theory, they also agree about the succeeding theorizing that most clearly followed in its formalist footsteps. There are many formalist successors, but new classical macroeconomics and rational expectations theory are perhaps the clearest examples. Given Mayer's interest in policy-driven macroeconomics, it is not surprising that he argues that the "new classical coup d'état is a striking attempt to impose a formalist regime on what was previously largely an empirical science domain" (Mayer 1993, 80) and that the goal of new classical theory is "to develop, not theories, but theorems" (1993, 90). But the other authors also echo his remarks: "Unfortunately, macroeconomics in recent years has fallen prey to empty formalism in which the principal goal of theorizing seems to be analytical elegance and not a better grasp of practical problems and hence greater control of economic events" (Blaug 2002, 30). It is important to note that such criticism is not restricted to economic theorizing with the same political-economic slant as rational expectations theory. Blaug (2002, 27–8) blasts Sraffa; Hutchison blames his old teacher Joan Robinson (ostensibly a formalist "even in her Keynesian and Marxian periods" [Hutchison 2000, 25n13]); and, as we will see below, Mayer actually defends the methodological practice of mid-century Keynesians. Formalism seems to be scattered all over the political-economic landscape, and for these three authors it is equally bad wherever it appears.[7]

In addition to agreement about the methodological disease and those most responsible for the contamination, there also seems to be a consensus about a better economic methodology – what economists should do instead of practicing formalism – as well as the economic exemplars for this proper methodological practice. Blaug and Hutchison have long argued that economics should be a real SCIENCE, and that the proper way to do that is to follow the strict falsificationist rules associated with the philosophy of Karl Popper. Blaug, of course, has often veered off the falsificationist path in the direction of Lakatos, but even there his methodological focus has remained fixed on "empirical progress," the aspect of Lakatos's work that emphasized empirical testing almost as much as

---

[7] Backhouse (1998) lists three types of formalism in economics – axiomatization, mathematization, and methodological. The formalism that concerns these authors undoubtedly involves all three of Backhouse's categories, but the first, axiomatization, is clearly the main culprit.

Popper's bold conjectures and severe tests.[8] Mayer endorses a similar position that he calls "empirical science economics," a methodology that is less concerned with the philosophy of Karl Popper, but is quite similar in its emphasis on empirical testing and the necessity of confronting economic theories with economic reality.

> In contrast to formalist economists, there are the empirical science economists, who take as their model the natural sciences; not only physics, but also the less highly developed sciences, such as geology and biology. These fields, too, use mathematics, but only as a convenient tool. They are much less concerned with mathematical virtues, and more concerned with empirical testability, and with the extent to which a theory enhances our understanding of what we actually observe. (Mayer 1993, 25)

In addition to these similar views about the proper scientific method, there also seems to be agreement about which economists best characterize this good empirical practice. They all point to Alfred Marshall as an exemplar of the right, non-formalist, way to do economics. Hutchison claims that Marshall "had very subtle but incisive methodological views" (Hutchison 2000, 4) and doubts that "any other leading economist has ever had quite such broad and penetrating insights on fundamental methodological issues as the nature of economic theorizing" (2000, 290), while Mayer argues that his distinction between formalist and empirical science economics is quite similar to the "distinction between Marshallian and Walrasian economics, since Marshallians are much more in the empirical science camp than are Walrasians" (Mayer 1993, 35). They also consider Keynes and a few others to be methodological exemplars, but the Marshallian focus on economics as a practical tool for solving policy problems in the "ordinary business of life" makes his approach the paradigm case of non-formalist economic theorizing. It is useful to note that Friedman has also consistently cited Marshall as an (perhaps the best) example of the proper methodological approach, and that Friedman's Marshallianism is supported by many later methodological commentators (Hoover, this volume, for example).

Finally, there is the fact that all three of these authors praise the other two for their methodological insights. While this is not surprising for Blaug and Hutchison who have, and agree that they have, essentially the same methodological position, it also seems to be true for Mayer as well. Mayer praises both Blaug and Hutchison (1992, 39–43) for their analysis of formalism and general equilibrium theory, and Hutchison (2000, 21) returns the favor. Blaug even goes so far as to say that his view and Mayer's

---

[8] I will not summarize the well-known positions of Hutchison and Blaug. The interested reader can examine Hutchison (1938, 1992, 2000) and Blaug (1980/1992) or the summaries in secondary sources such as Caldwell (1982/1994) or Hands (2001).

are essentially the same; Mayer relies less on the philosophical literature, but the final result seems to be the same.

> Thomas Mayer (1993) has recently published a study of *Truth versus Precision in Economics*. He eschews all discussion of formal methodology but he also denies that an invisible hand always impels economists to develop the best kind of economics; in general, he argues for an empirically oriented economics against a formalistic one. As far as I am concerned, he is on the side of the angels and his book is full of illuminating illustrations of how many modern economists have sacrificed relevance for rigour, technique for substance. (Blaug 1994, 131)

3   Friedmanic license

It is clear that Blaug, Hutchison, and Mayer fundamentally agree about economic methodology; they agree about what is wrong, who does/did it most wrong, how to do it right, who does/did it most right, and they even praise each other's views. Given this agreement, they should have similar views regarding key contributions to the field such as Friedman's essay, right? Well actually, no; as suggested above, they disagree substantively about the question of Milton Friedman's methodology, in particular the question of whether F53 was responsible for – whether it "licensed" – the formalist revolution.

Since they agree about so much, one might suspect that they disagree about Friedman because they have different interpretations of what Friedman said in his famous essay, but that is not the case. Although the methodological literature is rife with various "interpretations" of Friedman's methodology, these three economists essentially agree about the content of Friedman's essay: the only test of an economic theory is the accuracy of its predictions, and the realism of its assumptions does not matter.[9] The disagreement is not about Friedman's main methodological message, but rather about the impact of that message on the profession.

According to Blaug and Hutchison, the formalist revolution was based on turning away from the "facts," the "real facts," of economic life and focusing instead on abstract modeling deduced from empirically ungrounded assumptions. Their position is that by asserting that the truth, or the realism, of the assumptions is not important, Friedman's methodology openly licensed the anti-empirical practice of formalist economics. Friedman of course also emphasized prediction and the importance of verifiable empirical implications, but they argue that once the "assumptions do not matter"

---

[9] There is of course much more to Friedman's essay than this one simple sentence, but it is the key, and generally agreed upon, message. See Friedman (1953) or the secondary sources cited in note 1 for more details.

cat was out of the methodological bag, the profession was free to go speeding down the formalist road.

> The tendency with regard to abstraction towards "anything goes" was further encouraged by the doctrine, none to clearly expounded in Milton Friedman's famous essay "The methodology of positive economics," according to which the unrealism of "assumptions" need, and should, not be questioned, provided the conclusions or predictions were tested. (Hutchison 2000, 193)

> What runs through all this is the licence that Friedman's "methodology of positive economics" gave economists to make any and all unrealistic assumptions, provided only that their theories yielded verifiable implications. But even if one grants for the sake of argument that assumptions do not need to be descriptively accurate, Friedman failed to insist that they do need to be robust, that is, capable of being relaxed without fatal damage to the model they underpin. (Blaug 2002, 30)

Although Blaug and Hutchison both cite a number of other, primarily sociological and profession-specific factors that helped to bring about the formalist revolution – such as the Americanization of academic economics and the rise of publish-or-perish – Friedman's methodological message is clearly one of the most important forces.

Mayer's reading of the impact of Friedman's positive methodology is of course quite different. Mayer supports not only Friedman's methodology, but also most aspects of his monetarist economics. In fact Mayer has spent much of his life furthering the Friedman macroeconomic program; including vigorously defending it against later developments in rational expectations and new classical macroeconomics that others consider to be the offspring of Chicago monetarism. One way to interpret Mayer's writings on economic methodology during the last decade or so is to view this work as the explicit defense and further elaboration of Friedman's methodological position that Friedman himself never provided.

According to Mayer, the profession started its path down the formalist road when economists *turned away* from the methodological injunctions in Friedman's essay. Although Mayer often sides with monetarism on questions of macroeconomic theory and policy, he considers the methodological behavior of both sides of the "Keynesianism versus monetarism" debate to be fundamentally sound. The two sides of the debate clearly differed about theory (the elasticity of money demand, for example), the empirical evidence (the stability of the consumption function, for example), and policy (monetary versus fiscal policy, for example), but they did not differ fundamentally about the grounds on which one should conduct a scientific debate about theory, evidence, and policy. Both sides were doing "empirical science economics" – they were using the best available empirical evidence in an effort to identify general macroeconomic principles and regularities that could be used as the basis for effective policy. This "positivistic" methodology followed Friedman's prescriptions, and found an exemplar in his monetarist practice, but it was not unique to the monetarist side, since "Keynesian methodology is more or less similar to monetarist methodology" (Mayer 1995, 76). Both sides shared a common, and for Mayer a proper methodological stance, a stance that was best described and defended in Friedman's essay. Mayer argues that while there were many sociological and professional factors that contributed to the transformation of the dominant style of theorizing within economics, the mistake could have been prevented by listening to, and following, Friedman's methodological advise. F53 did not license the formalist revolution; in fact it could have prevented it.

> ... the rise of monetarism was fostered by the spread of the then new positivistic methodology among economists. This methodology combined the insistence of traditional theory on the rational behavior of maximizing agents with the insistence of institutionalists, such as Wesley C. Mitchell, on explaining observed phenomena. It was largely, but by no means entirely, the work of Milton Friedman. (Mayer 1995, 74)

4   License? We don't need no stinking license!

If these differing views about whether F53 licensed the formalist revolution do not stem from different interpretations of Friedman's essay, the formalist revolution, or even the proper way to do scientific economics, then what is the source of the disagreement? I would like to suggest the difference stems from fundamentally different views regarding the function and role of methodological inquiry. Crudely put, Blaug and Hutchison approach economic methodology more from the viewpoint of, and with the values of, professional philosophers of science; while Mayer approaches it more from the perspective of a practicing economist. Since this is a relatively strong statement that conflicts with how the authors themselves view the situation, it will require some elaboration. Let me begin with Mayer's case since it is not quite as controversial, and then move on to Blaug and Hutchison where my interpretation is diametrically opposed to the way the authors view their own positions.

Mayer grounds his interpretation of the rise of formalism, and the corresponding demise of good policy-driven economics, in what is essentially an economic analysis of the behavior of those within the economics profession during the post-World War II period. Mayer's most explicit statement of the causes of the formalist turn are contained in chapter 2 of Mayer (1993); the chapter is titled "Economists as economic agents: towards a positive theory of methodology." In this chapter he does not offer the type of epistemic advice that characterizes most philosophy of science, but rather provides an economic analysis, specifically a public choice analysis, of the relevant episode in the history of economic thought. His argument is simply that what happened in economics was a market failure in the market for economic knowledge. Various institutional changes during the immediate postwar period led the economics profession to look inward, rather than outward, for both inspiration and praise. The professionalization of academic economics; the standardization of graduate education; and the consolidation of an "invisible college" of editors, referees, and grant-funding agencies, all contributed to the establishment of a market for academic research in economics that had, and still has, "much in common with the market for government services" (Mayer 1993, 11). The result is a situation where academic economists "by and large, write for each other" and thus "the usual market discipline does not exist" (1993, 10). The people responsible for determining and enforcing the standards are the same people that must work within the confines of those standards.

The market for economic research is therefore self-referential; we write papers to please ourselves and each other. This would be consistent with maximizing the public's welfare if we evaluated papers entirely objectively by their social utility, without being biased by our self-interest. But the assumption that producers disregard their self-interest is one that we would be loath to make about others. (1993, 12)

Although one might criticize the details of Mayer's public choice story, my purpose here is neither to challenge the adequacy of his narrative nor to speculate about how the story would be different if it were told from a different explanatory perspective within the social sciences. The issue here is not the details of Mayer's particular story, but the general *tack* or *style* to methodological questions his approach exhibits. His style is grounded in a particular social science – public choice theory – and for that reason it is far less likely to blame an observed set of methodological practices on bad, or easily misinterpreted, methodological rules. The behavior of the profession, the choices that were made rather than others that were not made, can be *explained*, but from Mayer's point of view they are to be explained in essentially the same way that one would try to explain any other set of social behaviors/choices. Looked at from the perspective of public choice theory, a social organization that is based on the self-interested behavior of individual agents is very likely to be inefficient (epistemically or economically) when those choices are not constrained by the forces of a competitive market. In particular, if there is imperfect competition in the market and suppliers determine demand, then inefficiency will be the (perfectly understandable) consequence. The profession had other available choices – they could have listened to what Friedman had to say about methodology – but they chose not to for good (good in the sense of being able to be explained by social science) reasons. The onus of the inquiry is to explain the path that was taken, explain the observed social behavior, rather than fret about finding the perfect set of rules. This is not to say that social scientists are never interested in what appears on a particular tablet of rules; it is just not one of the first explanatory issues that come to mind. The more obvious issues requiring social explanation seem to be why the rules were or were not accepted by the crowd, and what were the social consequences of those actions. Friedman's essay does not provide a very good explanation in this sense: that is, it does not provide a very good social explanation of the causes and consequences of the social phenomenon of the formalist revolution.[10]

My claim is that neither Blaug nor Hutchison would be particularly troubled by the fact that Friedman's essay is not a very good social explanation for the rise of formalism, because they are not really interested in social explanations – the explanation of why, or how, or for what interests, certain methodological rules came to be accepted – they are more interested in the philosophical question of whether the rules are true or right. The priority is on the content of the tablet, not on the social explanation of its acceptance, rejection, or revision. The implicit presumption is that if it is true, if the methodological tablet contains the correct rules, then they *will* be accepted. This is essentially a philosopher's approach to questions of either epistemology or ethics. Let the philosophers write the rules correctly – what exactly is the true, the good, and the beautiful? – and the really important job is done. The rest is mere mundane social explanation; leave it to the pocket-protector crowd.

It is important to emphasize that *neither* Blaug nor Hutchison would endorse such an attitude if the issue were *economic* policy. For good

---

[10] It is useful to note that social explanation-based approaches are increasingly becoming the norm, rather than the exception, in the methodological literature on formalism in economics. This is true of Weintraub (2002), but there are many others as well. For example, both Tony Lawson and Deirdre McCloskey, two economists who hold quite different views about both methodology and economics, have recently examined the question of the formalist revolution: Lawson (2003, ch. 10) and McCloskey (1994, chs. 10 and 11). Both of them offer social explanations of the phenomenon (rather than philosophical homilies) and both couch their explanations in the same type of explanatory framework they would employ in the explanation of any other social phenomenon. In this sense – in their general approach to the question of formalism (not the answers they provide) – both Lawson and McCloskey approach formalism more like Mayer than like Blaug and Hutchison.

economic policy they both argue that one should take into consideration the behavior of those conducting the policy, the response of the agents that will react to it, and the fact that such responses can never be worked out in formalist-inspired detail; actual economic science should be situation-sensitive and will generally not produce universal results. There is no "good" policy independent of the context of its intended, perhaps messy, economic application. This is the local, small-scale, applied, Marshallian focus that Blaug and Hutchison both advocate in economics: the "empirical, case-by-case method of the leading authorities from Adam Smith onwards" (Hutchison 2000, 333). Positing abstract and universal economic theories that are not based on the real economic context is precisely the problem with Walrasian formalism. Hutchison, in particular, argues that effective policy can never be based on pristine "optimization," but will always be imprecise, rule-of-thumb, and conditional. Such policy-driven economics is still serious science; even though "it is obviously remote from the Utopian, fantasy levels, traditionally assumed to obtain throughout the economy by 'pure' theorists in their blackboard exercises about optimal or maximizing equilibria (which have provided such a seriously misleading basis for the discussion of real-world policy making)" (Hutchison, 2000, 215–16). So when one is doing economics, the notion of the "right" rules is not independent of context, agency, and collective response; in fact the whole idea of a "right" rule does not even make sense independently of the relevant social context. On the other hand, when Blaug and Hutchison are doing methodology the emphasis is entirely reversed. No longer are things messy, rule-of-thumb, and context-sensitive; in the domain of methodology, the only worthwhile results are abstract, universal, and context-transcendent rules for differentiating legitimate science from illegitimate non-science/nonsense; context-specific rules are necessary for economic policy, but epistemic policy requires exceptionless universal norms.

This attitude, the attitude that methodology is about finding universal, epistemically correct, rules for scientific inquiry, and not about the more social science-based questions of how rules in fact become socially operative epistemic norms or how the norms change from one research site to another is precisely (or at least has been until recently) the dominant attitude of mainstream philosophers of natural science. According to this view, there exists a special philosophical method, not grounded in the social science or science generally, that can evaluate and pass judgment on the epistemic virtues or cognitive significance of various domains of scientific knowledge. Once the rules for the epistemically proper scientific method had been found – they were not of course, but that is a separate story – then proper/good scientists would follow them and bad/non-scientists would not. The only role for social explanation in this view of science is negative. If scientists did not follow the proper scientific method, their failure could be explained by social forces. So the Lysenko-inspired period in Soviet biology is to be explained solely by social forces, while Watson and Crick were just following the proper scientific method. The Blaug–Hutchison way of "doing" methodology is a page right out of the philosophy of science textbook.

It is important to emphasize that this philosopher's-way characterization of the Blaug–Hutchison position is not at all how they would characterize their own view. In fact they characterize it in just the opposite way. According to their interpretation of their own view, they are taking a position that is closer to economics, and those who focus on more descriptive or explanatory methodological issues are letting the philosophical piper play the tune. Although they would not put Mayer in this camp, they spend a lot of time criticizing methodologists who take a more contextual or sociological approach – as opposed to searching for universally correct rules – for being under the spell of "avant-garde" philosophy. In Hutchison's words: "With no respect for the history and objectives of economics, valuable and vital distinctions are rejected by comprehensive academic-philosophical *decree*, regardless of the special characteristics and problems of economics and political economy, and of 'the job' which economists 'want to get done'" (Hutchison 2000, 205). As Blaug and Hutchison see it, those who want to describe and/or explain how methodological rules become dominant, get reinforced, or emerge from the self-interested actions of scientific agents are acting like philosophers, while those (such as themselves) who want to proscribe abstract universal rules of the one true scientific method are respecting "the history and objectives of economics." Frankly, I just do not get it; I just do not see how they could possibly believe this to be the case. It seems so obvious that philosophers have generally sought abstract universal truths, while economists (at least non-formalist economists) have acted like dutiful social scientists and sought the best available answers to context-specific social questions. While Marshall would undoubtedly agree with what Blaug and Hutchison have to say about economics, he is surely spinning violently in his grave when they talk about methodology.

Both Blaug and Hutchison are very critical of the argument – offered by Arrow, Debreu, Hahn, and others – that abstract general equilibrium theory, particularly the first and second fundamental theorems of welfare economics, provides a "formalization," and thus a defense, of the free market and/or Adam Smith's invisible hand. They both poke fun at the notion that somehow no one understood, or could defend, the free market until Arrow and Debreu offered us their formal theorems based on "blatantly and even scandalously unrepresentative of any recognizable economic system" (Blaug 2002, 26). Historically persuasive arguments for the free market – for example those of Smith, Mill, and Marshall – have been based on the "'wishly-washy,' case-by-case approach" (Hutchison 2000, 319) and in no way come from, or are even enhanced by, the formal "rigorous" results of Arrow–Debreu theory. The real defense of competitive markets has not come from abstract universal characterization of efficiency and perfect competition, but from case-by-case investigation of real situations in actually occurring market economies; "what GE analysis has done to Smith's conjecture is to eviscerate it of real-world content, and transform it into a piece of 'rigorous,' empirically vacuous, hyper-abstract analysis, based on a range of fantastic, science-fictional assumptions" (Hutchison 2000, 314).

What Blaug and Hutchison do not seem to notice is that their approach to *methodology* is exactly like the Arrow–Debreu approach to the invisible hand. Arrow and Debreu are arguing that the only way to settle real-world controversies about the efficiency of actual markets is first to obtain formal theorems regarding the relationship between a universal concept of efficiency and abstract competitive equilibrium prices. Blaug and Hutchison are entirely correct that the latter is neither necessary nor sufficient for the former. What they do not seem to recognize *is that they are saying essentially the same thing about methodology*; we cannot settle real-world controversies about the efficiency of actual practices within the context of specific economic research programs, until we first obtain a general characterization of the relationship between universal scientific laws and the abstract empirical basis. As Blaug and Hutchison would say when the same problem is presented in the economic (as opposed to epistemic) context: pshaw. It is not the case that no serious science got, or gets, done until the abstract questions of formalist philosophy of science get answered. The only way that such purely philosophical questions have ever been answered is within the context of a very abstract model of the relationship between statements in the theoretical language and those in the observation language involving formal correspondence rules, and these formal answers (as Thomas Kuhn and an array of others have shown) have absolutely nothing to do with the far messier activities of real successful science. Such positivist-inspired models of epistemic efficiency bear exactly the same relationship to actual decision-making in real science as Arrow–Debreu proofs of existence of competitive equilibrium prices bear to actual decision-making in real market economies: that is none. We don't need no stinking formalist license, in either economic or in epistemic policy.

5   A short answer, a long answer, and conclusions

The previous section made the case that Mayer's methodological approach is grounded in social science; he employs just one particular social science – public choice theory – but his mode of thinking and argumentation comes from social science, not philosophy. Blaug and Hutchison on the other hand, approach questions in economic methodology from a traditional philosophy of science point of view. While one might criticize the details of Mayer's argument, or his selection of public choice theory, there is a consistency between his approach to methodology and his approach to understanding other aspects of social life. Relative to Mayer, the approach of Blaug and Hutchison seems almost schizophrenic. They engage in armchair philosophizing about universals and absolutes when addressing methodological questions, and yet endorse a brand of economics that claims to be empirical, case-by-case, and context-specific. Worse yet, the same kind of formalized abstract intellectual exercises they dislike most in economics (exemplified by Arrow–Debreu general equilibrium theory) are just fine when the subject matter is philosophy of science (exemplified by logical empiricism and Popperian falsificationism); for them formalism is a bad way to approach questions of economic efficiency, but a good way to address questions of epistemic efficiency.

Even if one accepts my analysis of the differences between these two approaches, it is still not clear how this bears on the question of whether Friedman's methodology licensed the formalist revolution. So did Friedman's economic methodology license the formalist revolution or not? Is Mayer right, or Blaug and Hutchison? I have a relatively short answer and then a longer answer that I will attempt to connect up to the whole issue of the two different approaches I have elaborated.

The short answer is that Mayer is right; there does not seem to be a convincing argument that Friedman's essay on economic methodology in any way caused, or even substantially contributed to, the formalist revolution. Neither Debreu (1959), the canonical Arrow and Hahn (1971), nor any other major work in Walrasian general equilibrium theory even cite Friedman. More importantly, the leaders of the formalist revolution were generally not sympathetic to either Friedman's brand of economic theory or his political economy; as Philip Mirowski (2002) and others have argued, Walrasian formalism germinated at Cowles by economists who were generally left-leaning, Keynesians, and less than happy about their relationship with the Chicago economics department in general and Friedman in particular. Recall the Friedman quote at the beginning of this chapter; it came from his 1946 review of Oskar Lange's *Price Flexibility and*

Employment. Friedman's attack on Lange, like his ongoing criticism of the Cowles approach in general, was based primarily on their commitment to formalism in economic modeling: "the theory provides formal models of imaginary worlds, not generalizations about the real world" (Friedman 1946, 618). He clearly disagreed with their support for Keynesian macroeconomic policies, but, as Mayer argued, the conflict between Friedman's monetarism and Keynesian macroeconomics was more of a disagreement about the significance of certain empirical relationships than about the methodological question of whether the behavior of empirical aggregates should play a role in macroeconomic theorizing. The whole idea that Friedman's essay, with its emphasis on empirical prediction and practical application, licensed people to write, and professional journals to accept, papers whose main results were theorems deduced from the assumption that an economy is defined by:

for each i = 1, ..., m a non-empty subset X_i of $\mathfrak{R}'$ completely preordered by $\underset{i}{\leq}$ for each j = 1, ..., n a non-empty subset Y_j or $\mathfrak{R}'$ a point of $\mathfrak{R}'$ (Debreu 1959, 75)

does seem to be, on the face of it, a bit ludicrous.

Clearly as Mayer (this volume), Hirsch and De Marchi (1990), and many others have argued, Friedman's own work, particularly Friedman and Schwartz (1963), is about as far from formalism as any research in economics could possibly be. Of course one could always argue that even though his own work was not formalist, his methodological essay still might have licensed the formalism of others. But even if one only reads the "assumptions don't matter" part of Friedman's essay and skips the "only successful empirical predictions do matter" part, there still doesn't seem to be any reason to believe that Friedman's essay was any more likely to "license" formalism than the other popular methodological positions of the period.

In particular, Samuelson's "operationalism" seems prima facie to be far more amenable to the kind of licensing role that Blaug and Hutchison assign to F53. Samuelson's "weak axiom of revealed preference" (1938, 1948) ostensibly rendered all of demand theory "operationally meaningful," thus qualifying it as legitimate empirical science and licensing it to be used as the cornerstone for the next four decades of formalist exercises in excess demand-based Walrasian economics. In order to see how Samuelson's methodology played such an important role it is necessary to go back to the period 1930–50 when the current textbook "theory of demand" was being stabilized. Although everyone working on demand theory during this period agreed that the theory should be grounded in the empirical evidence, there was substantive disagreement about exactly how/where that empirical evidence should make its presence felt. The

most obvious approach, taking one's cues from philosophical interpretations of the natural sciences, would be to empirically "test" the theory that
appears at the end of the theoretical process. That is, start with a theory of
demand based on some version of individual optimization, aggregate over
the relevant individual agents, deduce various empirical implications of
the theory, and then finally test those implications against accepted empirical evidence. The problem was that this straightforward approach to
the empirical grounding of demand theory proved to be extremely problematic (see Hands and Mirowski 1998; Mirowski and Hands 1998).
An alternative approach – and one that proved to be less problematic –
involved putting "the empirical" in at the very front of the process. By
using Samuelson's weak axiom of revealed preference to empirically
ground the individual preferences that constituted the primitives of the
theory, the "theorizing" could go on happily without ever needing to test
the results at the end of the theoretical process. Once the empiricism
was "in" at the beginning, one was entirely free to deduce whatever
formal results one desired, never again confront these deduced results
with the evidence, and yet still remain on perfectly firm epistemic ground.
Samuelson's operationalism thus conveniently provided just the empirical
licensing that the formalist revolution needed. Friedman's methodology
does not work so neatly; Friedman would keep asking those pesky questions
about testing the theory at the end of the process. Is it any wonder that
Arrow and Hahn (1971) and other key formalist texts *did* repeatedly cite
Samuelson's theory of revealed preference and never cited Friedman's
essay. It should also be noted that the weak axiom played a key role in
many of the most important theorems about the uniqueness and stability of
Walrasian competitive equilibrium. Taken as an ensemble, Samuelson's
methodology and his revealed preference theory neatly solved (or at least
seemed to solve at the time) a myriad of problems associated with Walrasian
formalism. Clearly if any methodology provided a license for formalism, it
was Samuelson's, not Friedman's.

I would also note that similar remarks can be made about other methodological positions in the literature at the time. While it is hard to make the
case that a strict falsificationist reading of Karl Popper's philosophy of
science would license formalist theorizing in economics (falsificationism
has its own problems, but turning economics into existence theorems is not
one of them), it is important to recognize that the most self-consciously
Popperian authors of the day were Klappholz and Aggasi (1959) and their
critical rationalist and non-falsificationist brand of Popperian methodology
would allow for various types of non-empirical, including perhaps purely
mathematical, criticism. I believe the case for Samuelson's operationalist
methodology is much stronger, but the point is simply that there were any

number of methodological positions that could have licensed the formalist revolution a whole lot more effectively than F53.

Well, so much for the short answer. What does this short answer have to do with my long story about the differences between the methodological approaches of Mayer on the one hand and Blaug and Hutchison on the other? Perhaps the key point in the long answer can be stated rather briefly. I have tried to make the case in Hands (2001) and elsewhere that philosophical ideas about the character of scientific knowledge in economics (or other sciences) is not independent of how one thinks about social activity, including economic activity, more generally. Sometimes this relationship is recognized and explicit, but more often it is not. In fact there are good reasons to try to separate, and thereby purify, the two. It may well be that how a particular culture X characterizes their deity super-X reflects, among other things, the social relations within culture X; and yet drawing attention to this fact would hardly be a good career strategy for a prospective spiritual leader. The word is most powerful and persuasive when it comes from elsewhere (preferably above), and keeping them (the gods) and us (social life) separate is often key to the whole normative endeavor. The point is that this is as true for the epistemically normative (how one ought to do science) as for the ethically normative (how one ought to act toward others). The approach of Blaug and Hutchison, and for that matter most of traditional philosophy-of-science-inspired economic methodology, has been to use philosophy as the "them" from which the rules come. This is what I have called the "shelf of scientific philosophy" view of economic methodology. Now (and finally getting to the point about Friedman's essay) this type of methodology is much more likely to find undesirable behavior to be grounded in bad methodological teachings. Since good economics follows the rules set down by philosophers of scientific knowledge, theoretical behavior that seems to be bad must be because practitioners were given the wrong rules. On this scenario, methodology really matters and bad practice must be because of bad methodology. Hence if economics took what seemed to be a wrong turn, then some methodology must have licensed it. F53 is the most famous paper in economic methodology, therefore it must be responsible for the wrong turn.

Mayer's approach is more willing to admit that how one views economic and social life can have an impact on how one views scientific knowledge. If one comes from a discipline where competitive markets produce efficiency, and one observes inefficiency, then it seems natural to start looking for the market imperfections that caused it. If one can explain how certain social beliefs (such as formalism is the way to do economic research) emerged as an equilibrium solution from the self-interested behavior of rational agents under reasonable external constraints, then one has an explanation for the belief. This answer will undoubtedly be less persuasive among those outside the community of economists, those who explain the emergence of socially held beliefs in other ways, but down here on the ground in day-to-day professional life that is not really a problem. Such a vision, or any vision grounded in social science, will be far less likely to blame the licenser. Methodological rules matter if they are grounded in the disciplinary form of life, but such rules are only one small piece of any explanation of why the particular social result occurred. For Mayer, Friedman's methodological ideas were grounded in his activities as an economist and those that engaged in formalist economics did so for reasons, but those reasons had much more to do with the social conditions and constraints the relevant economic theorists faced than with any of the particular words in Friedman's methodological essay. Thus Mayer is less likely to view F53 (or for that matter any other essay on methodology) as licensing formalism than Blaug and Hutchison's more philosophy-driven view.

I would like to close by admitting that I have probably overstated my case: both the case that Blaug and Hutchison are examples of methodology-as-viewed-from-philosophy, and also that Mayer has a naturalistic and context-specific approach to methodological questions. Blaug and Hutchison do discuss various sociological, and even economic, forces that contributed to the profession's change in theoretical style; and Mayer does defend Friedman's methodology philosophically as a properly scientific way of doing economics. But while there are certain ways in which both views leak a bit in the opposite direction, I contend that the main point remains; even with their occasional nod to social forces, Blaug and Hutchison are doing methodology in the spirit of the philosophy of science; and Mayer, while retaining the philosophical high ground for Friedman's methodology, is conducting his methodological inquiry primarily as applied social science. And I claim these differences provide the best explanation for their difference of opinion about whether Friedman's methodology did or did not license the formalist revolution.

References

Arrow, Kenneth J. and Gerard Debreu (1954). Existence of an equilibrium for a competitive economy. *Econometrica*, 22, 265–90

Arrow, Kenneth J. and Frank H. Hahn (1971). *General Competitive Analysis*. San Francisco: Holden-Day

Backhouse, Roger (1998). If mathematics is informal, then perhaps we should accept that economics must be informal too. *The Economic Journal*, 108, 1848–58

Blaug, Mark (1980). *The Methodology of Economics: Or How Economists Explain*. Cambridge: Cambridge University Press

(1992). *The Methodology of Economics: Or How Economists Explain*, 2nd edition. Cambridge: Cambridge University Press

(1994). Why I am not a constructivist: confessions of an unrepentant popperian. In R. E. Backhouse (ed.), *New Directions in Economic Methodology*. London: Routledge, 109–36

(1997). Ugly currents in modern economics. *Policy Options*, 3–8

(1998). Disturbing currents in modern economics. *Challenge*, 41, 11–34

(2002). Is there really progress in economics? In S. Boehm, C. Gehrke, H. D. Kurz, and R. Sturn (eds.), *Is There Progress in Economics?*. Cheltenham: Edward Elgar, 21–41

(2003). The formalist revolution of the 1950s. *Journal of the History of Economic Thought*, 25(2), 145–56

Boland, Lawrence A. (1979). A critique of Friedman's critics. *Journal of Economic Literature*, 17, 503–22 [reprinted with minor revisions as chapter 2 of Boland 1997]

(1997). Critical Economic Methodology: *A Personal Odyssey*. London: Routledge

Caldwell, Bruce J. (1982), *Beyond Positivism: Economic Methodology in the Twentieth Century*, 1st edition. London: George Allen and Unwin

(1994). *Beyond Positivism: Economic Methodology in the Twentieth Century*, 2nd edition. London: Routledge

Debreu, Gerard (1959). *Theory of Value*. New Haven: Yale University Press

Friedman, Milton (1946). Lange on price flexibility and employment: a methodological criticism. *American Economic Review*, 36, 613–31

(1953). The methodology of positive economics. In *Essays in Positive Economics*. Chicago: University of Chicago Press, 3–43

Friedman, Milton and Anna Schwartz (1963). *A Monetary History of the United States 1867–1960*. Princeton: Princeton University Press

Golland, Louise Ahrndt (1996). Formalism in economics. *Journal of the History of Economic Thought*, 18, 1–12

Hands, D. Wade (2001). *Reflection Without Rules: Economic Methodology and Contemporary Science Theory*. Cambridge: Cambridge University Press

Hands, D. Wade and Philip Mirowski (1998). Harold Hotelling and the neoclassical dream. In R. Backhouse, D. Hausman, U. Mäki, and A. Salanti (eds.), *Economics and Methodology: Crossing Boundaries*. London: Macmillan, 322–97

Hausman, Daniel M. (1992). *The Inexact and Separate Science of Economics*. Cambridge: Cambridge University Press

Hirsch, Abraham and Neil De Marchi (1990). *Milton Friedman: Economics in Theory and Practice*. Ann Arbor, MI: University of Michigan Press

Hoover, Kevin (2009). Friedman's methodological stance: causal realism (this volume)

Hutchison, Terence (1938). *The Significance and Basic Postulates of Economic Theory*. London: Macmillan

(1992). *Changing Aims in Economics*. Oxford: Blackwell

(2000). *On the Methodology of Economics and the Formalist Revolution*. Cheltenham: Edward Elgar

Klappholz, Kurt and Joseph Agassi (1959). Methodological prescriptions in economics. *Economica*, 26, 60–74

Lange, Oskar (1944). *Price Flexibility and Employment*. Bloomington, IN: Principia Press

Lawson, Tony (2003). *Reorienting Economics*. London: Routledge

Mäki, Uskali (1989). On the problem of realism in economics. *Ricerche Economiche*, 43, 176–97

(1992). Friedman and realism. *Research in the History of Economic Thought and Methodology*, 10, 171–195

(2000) Kinds of assumptions and their truth: shaking an untwisted F-twist. *Kyklos*, 53, 303–22

(2009). Unrealistic assumptions and unnecessary confusions: rereading and rewriting F53 as a realist statement. This volume

Mayer, Thomas (1993). *Truth versus Precision in Economics*. Aldershot: Edward Elgar

(1995). *Doing Economic Research: Essays on the Applied Methodology of Economics*. Aldershot: Edward Elgar

(2009). The influence of Friedman's methodological essay. This volume

McCloskey, D. N. (1994). *Knowledge and Persuasion in Economics*. Cambridge: Cambridge University Press

Mirowski, Philip (1986). Mathematical formalism and economic explanation. In P. Mirowski (ed.), *The Reconstruction of Economics*. Boston: Kluwer-Nijhoff, 179–240

(2002). *Machine Dreams. Economics Becomes a Cyborg Science*. Cambridge: Cambridge University Press

Mirowski, Philip and D. Wade Hands (1998). A paradox of budgets: the postwar stabilization of American neoclassical demand theory. In M. S. Morgan and M. Rutherford (eds.), *From Interwar Pluralism to Postwar Neoclassicism* [supplement to *HOPE* vol. 30]. Durham, NC: Duke University Press, 269–92

Punzo, Lionello F. (1991). The school of mathematical formalism and the Viennese circle of mathematical economists. *Journal of the History of Economic Thought*, 13, 1–18

Samuelson, Paul A. (1938). A note on the pure theory of consumer's behaviour. *Economica*, 5, 61–71

(1948). Consumption theory in terms of revealed preference. *Economica*, 15, 243–53

(1947). *Foundations of Economic Analysis*. Cambridge, MA: Harvard University Press

Ward, Benjamin (1972). *What's Wrong with Economics?* New York: Basic Books

Weintraub, E. Roy (1998). Controversy: Axiomatisches Mißverständnis. *The Economic Journal*, 108, 1837–47

(2002). *How Economics Became a Mathematical Science*. Durham, NC: Duke University Press

Weintraub, E. Roy and Philip Mirowski (1994). The pure and the applied: Bourbakism comes to mathematical economics. *Science in Context*, 7, 245–72

6 Appraisal of evidence in economic methodology

Melvin W. Reder

Though not the only topic of Milton Friedman's "Methodology of positive economics" (F53) the subject of this chapter is a very important theme of that essay. To understand the influence of that essay it is necessary to view it as a section of a major thread in the history of economic thought. The thread is more easily identified than characterized precisely: starting with Adam Smith's *The Wealth of Nations* and after making juncture with Utilitarianism, the thread emerged in the late nineteenth century as neo-classical economics and after much further elaboration has become (in the late twentieth century) strongly associated with new classical economics. The thread identifies with what Schumpeter (1954) called a preanalytic vision or, alternatively, a particular frame for perceiving the functioning of an economy. Let us call this frame "The Invisible Hand."

Two dominant characteristics of the frame are an emphasis upon (i) the advantages of specialization and division of labor and (ii) the role of voluntary exchange in facilitating their achievement. Following the thread and the associated frame is one way of organizing a history of economic thought and it is in this context that I interpret F53. In short, I consider F53 to be an important part of a long intellectual tradition that has undergone intermittent and continuing change without losing its essential character.

Notoriously F53 has been subject to differing interpretations. The one offered here has been partly anticipated in the literature, though it may contain some new wrinkles. However, I am not sure on the latter point and make no claims to originality. As I interpret it, F53 constitutes an (important) link between the earlier neoclassical literature, notably Marshall's *Principles*, and the post-1960 new classical writings that feature an insistence on explicit "microfoundations" as a condition of acceptability for any piece of economic theory. As will be seen, what constitutes a

Although this chapter has benefited greatly from the comments of David Colander, Kevin Hoover, Uskali Maki, and Thomas Mayer, the author retains sole responsibility for whatever errors of substance or infelicities of expression remain.

165

proper microfoundation of a theory is intimately related to what would constitute acceptable evidence in appraising its validity.

Section I locates F53 in the thread of economic thought associated with the Invisible Hand with special attention to the criteria for appraising the validity of an economic theory. Section II considers the relation of the criteria discussed in section I to some other criteria that have been proposed. Section III instantiates the criteria discussed in the preceding sections by reference to a recent attempt to obtain empirical information bearing (adversely) on the neoclassical theory of wage behavior. The final section summarizes the preceding argument and discusses the reasons for the survival of the Invisible Hand frame and its relation to the positive-normative distinction upon which F53 places heavy emphasis.

I

Persisting methodological dispute(s) between neoclassical economists and their new classical successors on one side and various opponents (Keynesians, Institutionalists, devotees of Behavioral Finance, etc.) on the other have been a facet of a disagreement about how economic problems should be *framed*.[1] For the first group (for brevity, neoclassicals) an economic problem is framed as a situation in which each of a set of resource-constrained but interacting individuals attempts to maximize his or her utility. The level of utility attainable by any individual is limited both by his or her resource endowment and a (publicly known) technology that specifies the set of attainable outputs that the resource endowment can generate. For most problems output is taken to include exchanges at market-determined prices which are exogenous to any given individual: these prices function as additional resource constraints to each individual.

A major topic of the history of economic thought from 1776 to about 1920 was refinement of this frame to make it consistent with the theory of market price. A major application of this (latter) theory was the competitive industry, the output of which was treated as a homogeneous product produced by a large number of independent firms, each firm identified with an individual owner assumed to be a constrained maximizer of (his or her own) utility of which profit was taken as an indicator. The firm was assumed to be a price taker with the prices of the output and of each input generated by (competitive) markets. The output quantity of the industry and the utilization quantity of each of its inputs were assumed to be equal to the sum of the analogous quantities of its constituent firms.

---

[1] The concept of a frame is used in the sense of Tversky and Kahneman (1974) from whom the concept has been borrowed.

While this is a roughly accurate, albeit oversimplified, description of the theory of the competitive industry as of (say) 1920, no competent economist believed that any real-world industry satisfied the assumptions specified. However, varying from one writer to another, they would argue – especially in applications – as though they believed the departures of "reality" from this theory were not sufficiently important to warrant abandonment of the Invisible Hand frame. While occasionally the incongruity of the theory of the competitive industry with the characteristics of real-world industries was recognized in economic literature, prior to 1920 the difficulties were papered over rather than confronted. The main attempt at reconciling the theory of the competitive industry with some theory of the firm was made in Marshall's *Principles* where the conceptual Representative Firm was introduced.[2]

The difficulties associated with the notion and use of the Representative Firm served as a major point of departure for the efforts of the 1920s to rectify the seeming incompatibility of the price-taking, profit-maximizing firm with the theory of the competitive industry. These efforts culminated in the emergence of an explicit neoclassical concept of a competitive firm that was a price-taking, profit maximizing entity. But the development of this theory clearly revealed the descriptive inadequacy of such a firm as a representative of the constituents of observable competitive industries. As a result, the neoclassical concept of a competitive firm was widely rejected as "unrealistic" (i.e. descriptively inaccurate) almost at first sight, with the result that in the early 1930s alternative concepts (e.g. Monopolistic Competition and Imperfect Competition) were developed in which the firm was portrayed as a *price-setting*, quantity- and quality-choosing entity although (usually) still considered to be focused on profit making. Such concepts allowed for the possibility that firms might exploit tradeoffs among posted selling prices, quantities sold, product characteristics (qualities), terms of payment and delivery, etc., to enhance profits, with the neoclassical competitive firm nesting within any of them as a special case where all such tradeoffs were limited to zero. Because they permitted consideration of such tradeoffs, which were obviously of very frequent occurrence, it was claimed that such concepts were more "realistic" than the neoclassical competitive firm.

The economic history and intellectual spirit of the times (1930–mid 1950s) allowed the claim to greater realism of non-competitive theories to prevail against the weak arguments offered in support of the neoclassical

---

[2] The term "industry" refers generally to aggregates of independent decision entities whose productive activity reflects the impact of common forces (e.g. geographic areas, use of common inputs) and is not restricted to producers of a common product.

competitive theory. For a time – roughly two decades – the failure of the competitive theory to allow for the possibility that observed behavior might reflect exploitation of the aforementioned tradeoffs was sufficient to make it generally unacceptable. It was as an attempt to buttress this rejection that testimony of economic actors (e.g. business managers) was introduced as support for the claim of unrealism of the assumptions of the competitive theory. In large part, F53's attack on the relevance of such testimony to appraisal of the competitive theory was in the nature of a rebuttal.

Briefly to review F53's attack, consider an economic analyst attempting to choose between two explanations of price setting and output determination among a group of firms assumed to be competitors in the sale of output and the purchase, hire or rent of inputs. Let one of these explanations be the competitive theory and the alternative any member of a class of theories whose common characteristic is that they permit tradeoffs among prices, quantities, qualities, and contract terms. The competitive theory is similar to, though not identical with, the theory of an idealized competitive industry as presented in contemporary textbooks.

In the idealized competitive industry inputs and outputs are homogeneous: this is consilient with the notion that as of any given time all units are bought or sold at a single price with the identity of the transacting parties a matter of indifference to all concerned. Moreover, the characteristics of the constituent firms are irrelevant to the analysis of their price–quantity behavior so that the "firm" is a convenience of speech; a redundant notion without independent function. However, for real-world application it is necessary to recognize that both firms and competitive industries have differentiating characteristics that somehow must be taken into account. Organized exchanges aside, the output of a real-world competitive industry is a congeries of differing products, sold on a variety of contract terms, delivered in various ways, etc. An analogous remark applies to each of its constituent firms.

To apply the conceptual structure of an idealized competitive industry to measurement of such a collection of heterogeneous products and contract terms requires decisions of classification and weighting as discussed below. Deferring discussion of details, the result of such statistical editing is the production of price and quantity numbers referring to an entity called an industry that are designed to reflect the impact of the forces – usually operating through costs – that bear similarly upon (most of) the constituent firms.

The argument of F53 was designed to focus attention upon the operation of these common forces: i.e. the intent was to apply the competitive model of the idealized industry to the analysis of (real-world) relations among stylized prices and quantities of stylized industries, ignoring (abstracting from) variations in these relations among constituent firms. The focus of theories of imperfect and/or monopolistic competition was the opposite: i.e. these theories highlighted the options of individual firms in the setting of sale prices, product characteristics, and terms of transaction. Implicitly, Friedman argued that when the empirical counterparts of the price and quantity variables of the idealized industry were properly defined and measured, usually the relations among them would be found similar to those alleged by earlier neoclassical economists and robust to whatever additional information could be gained from detailed study of interfirm differences in the relation of price to marginal cost resulting from differences in selection of product characteristics, contract terms, etc. From this it followed that a sound research strategy would abstract from such differences (without denying their existence) and concentrate upon the relations among industry variables. This contention was denied by devotees of Imperfect/Monopolistic Competition.

Industry variables and reports of firms

As already indicated, the "facts" of industry prices and quantities are obtained from reports furnished – in one way or another – from constituent firms and aggregated to obtain numbers referring to the industry. Consequently, whatever information about prices and quantities might be obtained from managers of individual firms would also be contained in the reports from which the industry facts were derived. Thus, when consistent with what is reported about industries, statements of managers about prices and quantities made in interviews with researchers is redundant. When not consistent such statements are false.

Let me amplify: published reports of industry prices and quantities refer to the behavior of an industry, but they are constructed from reports of individual firms. Of necessity the reports of firms to a survey involve various sorts of editing, some by the reporting firm and very often by the compiler of the aggregate as well. Editing by the compiler is required by the need to combine interfirm differences in qualities of outputs and inputs, technology, business practices reflected in the manner of price quotation, etc. Moreover, because reporting firms must fit the particulars of their activities into categories prescribed by the compiler of industry data, the reporting process inevitably does violence to the concepts for which the categories were designed. Still further, often the compiler must adjust the reports so as to avoid letting "weight shifts" among firms generate results that do not reflect industry-wide movements in variables of theoretical interest. Added to these editing effects there are reporting errors, simple mistakes, and, occasionally, deliberate falsifications.

I can think of no basis for a general statement of the comparative reliability of a firm's report that is encapsulated in a number purporting to reflect the state of an industry-wide variable, and what its manager would report, one-on-one, to a researcher. However, depending on its format, an individually tailored inquiry (e.g. an interview) might elicit information about the details of a firm's business practices, especially about its rules of thumb and overall strategy, that generally could not be obtained from a standard-form questionnaire administered to a number of firms.

Obviously, the quality of the information that can be elicited through an interview is heavily dependent upon the knowledge and understanding of the individual(s) that speak for the firm in communicating with the investigator. At one extreme the spokesperson may not grasp the purpose of the interrogation and furnish virtually no information, while at the other he or she may become an active participant in the study, formulating original questions and criticizing proposed interpretations of the responses.[3] But while the information obtainable from "in-depth" interviews and/or questionnaires designed for specific firms may serve as the basis for "case studies" of individual firms, they will not help in analyzing the behavior of industries.

This is because the analysis of the price–quantity relations of a competitive industry focuses upon changes in conditions of demand or supply that impact similarly upon all firms in the industry, while the focus of a case study is upon changes that alter the position of a studied firm (e.g. its market share) relative to that of competing firms.

In providing information to an investigator, typically the spokesperson of a firm highlights material that bears upon the firm's relative position, leaving in the background determinants of the firm's response to developments common to all firms in the industry. While an increment to information about a particular firm may be relevant to an economic history of that firm, or of value to a prospective investor, it is not relevant to an appraisal of the application of the theory of a competitive industry to the firm's (real-world) industry.

In short, if a report emerging from an interview with a firm's manager is consistent with the theory of a competitive industry it may be accepted as credible albeit redundant; but if not consistent it should be judged either as false or, if not false, as reflective of behavior idiosyncratic to the firm

---

[3] A classic example of collaboration between an analyst and a "manager" is furnished by Herbert Simon and Chester I. Barnard. See Simon (1947).

and/or to a particular time period (i.e. as a disturbance). This is not the place to defend or attack such a procedural rule, but to identify it and describe its methodological function, which is to separate propositions that are compatible with the Invisible Hand frame from those that are not. Accordingly, the rule advises one to treat reports of price-setting or wage-setting behavior that are indicative of failure to maximize profits, or of alteration in the relation of price to marginal cost (or of the price of an input to the value of its marginal product), as meriting zero weight in appraising the validity of propositions of price theory. This is not to say that Friedman denied that such departures from pure competition might occur, but that F53 recommended that such statements should be ignored (abstracted from) in formulating and testing theories about market behavior, except where there are "genuine" monopolies.

The underlying rationale for recommending such a procedure is that it provides a better guide to the formulation of successful theories about economic phenomena – as judged by the criteria advocated in F53 – than some alternative procedural rule that allowed a significant role for variations in the relation of price to marginal cost among firms. The procedure is recommended with a caveat against applying it where a monopoly is present. Without going into details, let me assert that acceptance of the Invisible Hand frame is associated with belief that in a given situation it is (i) almost always possible for properly trained economists to make commonsense judgments on which model (competition or monopoly) is to be applied and (ii) that such judgments will cluster sufficiently well as to suggest the existence of a consensus.

F53 and the theory of the firm

In F53, idiosyncratic behavior of a firm that cannot be reconciled with price-taking/profit-maximization was considered to be the reflection of a transitory stochastic disturbance to any price–quantity relationship in which the record of such behavior might be incorporated. Thus, inter alia, F53 was an attack on the then current fashion of hedging the application of propositions about price–quantity relations among industry variables with qualifications stemming from the effects of idiosyncratic variations in the relation of price to marginal revenue among its constituent firms. The intention was to reduce concern of economic theorists with the details of individual firm behavior, in effect expelling its study to Business History and/or other disciplines. One consequence of this was to diminish the value of information about the idiosyncratic characteristics of particular firms and its main source, individualized reports from their managers.

However, this effort has been only partially successful. The success is reflected in the continuing search for relations among aggregate variables, with observations on individual entities (e.g. firms) serving as data points. Often empirical workers engaged in such search are disdainful of detailed accounts of the behavior and intentions of particular individuals. Nevertheless the theory of the firm, an imperiled embryo in 1953, has since become a vigorous and independent branch of economics.

Although always present among reflective businessmen, interest in explaining the behavior of firms had long been repressed among economic theorists by the unchallenged assumption that competitors must be price-takers. While the Monopolistic Competition Revolution freed them of their inhibitions on this point, it offered little guidance beyond the insight that the implications of pure competition were "unrealistic" and entailed drastic oversimplifications of the problems faced by the management of a competitive firm.

While theoretical analysis of such problems begins with Coase's (1937) seminal paper, "The nature of the firm", the subject did not take hold among economists until the 1970s with the development of theories about transaction costs, incentive payments, etc. As these ideas were symbiotic with new developments in game theory they had the effect of marginalizing the theory of monopolistic competition among students of firm behavior. Another, and more important effect, was greatly to increase the interest of (many) economists in obtaining detailed information about individual firms.

The best – often the only possible – source of such information is the manager(s) of these firms. The most important – and difficult – questions concern not so much the details of behavior as the strategies, intentions and objectives that motivate the behavior. Managers can and do discourse at length on these subjective matters, sometimes persuasively. Notoriously, the problem of accepting their statements at face value is that they reflect the preconceptions of the speakers and the effects that the speakers desire their statements to have upon auditors. Nevertheless, because of the paucity of alternative sources, such statements (often embellished with self-serving accounts of pertinent events) get factored into the histories of firms.

To the sceptical suggestion "ignore the talk, just look at the record of behavior" (aka "the facts"), the answer lies in the need for consilience as discussed in section II. The importance of consilience, especially between accounts of the behavior of aggregates and the alleged intentions of component individuals, is rooted in the immanent objective of all economics to relate the intentions of individual actors to their (often unintended) consequences.

II

Although not the only criterion of theoretical merit that it recognizes, F53 places great stress upon capability of making correct predictions (including retrodictions). This view is consilient with its argument that the validity of an economic theory depends upon the conformity of its implications with the observed behavior of prices and quantities to which the realism (descriptive accuracy) of its assumptions is irrelevant. But while it is generally accepted that predictive capability is an important criterion for judging the merit of any theory, there has been considerable dissent as to its importance relative to other criteria. As the reader may surmise, opinions about how the evidence offered in support of a theory should be appraised is closely related to the criteria by which the merit of the theory is to be judged.

While I shall not attempt a general discussion of the criteria to use in appraising theories, our topic requires that we consider some criteria other than predictive capability. Though logical consistency is an obvious candidate, I have little to say about it beyond pointing to its obvious importance. The criterion that I shall stress is, I think, underemphasized in F53: consilience of a theory with other beliefs, especially those associated with other theories, that have wide acceptance. ("Other beliefs" include the oft-mentioned beliefs that arise from intuition and/or introspection.) In "Consilience", E. O. Wilson (1998) argues strongly for contribution to the "unity of knowledge" as an evaluative criterion for theories in any subject.

Wilson is especially critical of the failure of economics, especially the theory of individual choice, to establish proper connections with theories in psychology covering the same subject. However, after some strong though not altogether accurate criticism of its procedures, Wilson concedes that "We are better off if the economists speak than if they remain silent ..." (1998, 197). While it is obvious that the implied subject of such allegedly beneficial speech is public policy, Wilson does not offer any explicit rationale for this concession.

I submit that the implicit rationale for the concession is belief that general knowledge of relevant facts about the behavior of economies and of the ideas – present and past – about their functioning, together with their visible efforts to advance this knowledge, makes economists a source of valuable information. However, Wilson's concession is weak: i.e. economists should be invited to speak but in competition with other speakers, and not necessarily to be believed.

An important reason for the weakness of the concession, though surely not the only one, is lack of consilience of what economists say about choice behavior with the dicta of psychology and, indirectly, with biology and so forth. This lack of consilience is a major reason, though perhaps not the only one, for Friedman's desire to make prediction about the behavior of aggregate variables – prices and quantities – the primary criterion of theoretical validity, despite the non-realism – non-realisticness pace Uskali Mäki – of the associated theory of individual choice. All that Friedman, and neoclassicals generally, require of a theory of individual choice is that it be logically compatible with the implications of theoretical propositions about the behavior of prices and related (aggregate) quantities.

Consequently, the testimony of individual economic actors about their preferences and motivations is to be given zero weight in appraising propositions of price theory: i.e. considered redundant where it is compatible with the theory, and irrelevant where it is not. But if consilience with psychology is also to be considered a criterion of theoretical merit, such summary rejection will not do. In 1953 experimental economics had hardly commenced, so it is not surprising that its embryonic activities escaped Friedman's attention. But a half century later Nobel awards and a growing stream of books and articles, both by economists and psychologists, have made it impossible to avoid considering experimental evidence bearing upon the choice behavior of individuals. By no means has all of this evidence been adverse to the viewpoint of F53, but because some of it has been – or could be interpreted so as to make it seem – adverse it would be well to remark on the problems facing economists and psychologists concerned with the apparent lack of consilience with this burgeoning field.

As this is beyond the purview of the present chapter, I shall limit discussion to one salient example: the effect on choice behavior of framing a given prospect as a gain or a loss. As usually interpreted, the conventional definition of rationality implies that an individual's choice among a set of alternative sources of utility will depend upon (inter alia) the contents of the various sources and not upon the manner in which the sources are presented. While it is often recognized that incompleteness of information may lead individuals to make "wrong" choices (i.e. choices incompatible with the assumption of rationality), the general neoclassical view is that such errors will be transient and/or will cancel out so that their net impact upon the observed relations of price–quantity aggregates will be negligible.

However, the experiments of (psychologists) Tversky and Kahnemann (1974) showed that by framing an *identical* utility prospect as the result of a gain or a loss, laboratory subjects could be induced systematically to choose the former in preference to the latter. While it is not to the present purpose to appraise these findings, it may be noted that they have received wide acceptance among psychologists and experimental economists and were cited in the Nobel Prize awarded to Kahneman (2003). Therefore for the sake of the argument I shall assume the findings to be valid, and focus upon the problem(s) of integrating them with neoclassical theory. A convenient point of departure for discussing the framing effect of shocks to the determinants of individual choice and the effect of such shocks (or lack of it) upon the relation between prices and aggregate quantities is the cluster of issues associated with money illusion.

In Keynes's *General Theory of Employment* (1936) it was asserted that individual workers would accept reductions in real wages provided that their money wages were not reduced (framed as a non-loss), but would resist reductions in money wages even if they were offset by decreases in consumer prices (framed as a loss): i.e. aggregate labor supply was alleged to be influenced by money illusion. Whether true or false, such an allegation of asymmetry in the reaction of labor supply to inflation and deflation is incompatible with the tenets of neoclassical price theory. Its occurrence forces economists to choose between accepting as valid the reported outcome of experiments about the effects of framing on individual behavior on the one hand and maintaining adherence to the neoclassical theory of labor supply on the other.

Let us consider the making of such a choice as an exercise in Bayesian decision-making. Allow the neoclassical theory of labor supply to be the hypothesis and experimental results about the effect of framing on choices among utility source bundles to be the sample. Whether the hypothesis should be altered by the results of the experiment will depend upon the characteristics of the sample, and upon the confidence reposed in the validity of the hypothesis. For the application at hand assume the sample characteristics to be such as to warrant rejection of the hypothesis, or at least to require amendment of it. However, assume that confidence in the validity of the hypothesis together with the difficulty of finding an acceptable alternative (including amended versions as alternatives) make rejection unacceptable.

To a non-human seeker of "truth," this dilemma is not critical: "it" would simply accept its inability to reach a decision as transitory and continue research. However, most economists, along with many non-economists, would join Wilson in saying that it is better that economists speak out (decide on the hypothesis) in an agenda-determined time frame rather than remain silent. But to speak out – to accept the hypothesis despite its lack of consilience with the findings of other sciences – requires that economists must reject the relevance and/or the validity of (some of) what the other sciences say – and men of affairs believe – about price-setting and resource allocation. Though not stated explicitly, F53 contains a powerful exhortation to minimize concern about (lack of) consilience of the propositions of neoclassical economic theory with the opinions of outsiders.

Without pursuing the matter I would suggest that, for any science, appraisal of theories should involve balancing the desirability of consilience with the results obtained in neighboring fields against the urgency of applying the findings in its own. But while this suggestion expresses little more than common sense, it is often forgotten in discussions of methodology.

III

In the multifaceted controversies surrounding F53, it is easy to identify and label the doctrines of one major party: neoclassical economics. But while the opposing ideas are more diffuse, they are unified on one point: the frame of the economy associated with neoclassical economics – the Invisible Hand – is misleading. The various opponents of the neoclassical frame include partisans from other disciplines and, among economists, Keynesians, institutionalists, etc., with each category covering a considerable diversity of opinion.

However, one point on which all Keynesians concur is that an economy may vary in the degree to which it utilizes available resources, and that the unutilized resources respresent waste. Basically, neoclassicals deny this and have offered a variety of subtle arguments to "explain away" the appearance of waste due to unemployment that is alleged to be involuntary. For better than half a century the validity of such arguments has been strongly contested, with a critical issue being the involuntariness of the undisputed fact of *non*-employment. As will be seen, the issue turns upon whether, and (if so) how, involuntariness can be identified and the associated quantity measured.

Is the notion of an involuntary decision – about anything – an oxymoron, or can it be interpreted so as to make sense? If the latter, can testimony of decision-makers be considered as a source of evidence and, if so, how should it be weighed against (potentially) conflicting evidence inferred from observable behavior? As some potential answers to such questions are obviously incompatible with adherence to the Invisible Hand, adherents of that frame have good reason to reject them as an acceptable source of information.

But if unemployment – on some basis – is judged to be involuntary, a further question arises: why don't employers offer unemployed workers lower wages than they are paying their current employees? For the moment, I shall merely remark that the only possible source from which answers to such a counterfactual question could come must be statements of individuals who have the capability of setting wages: it is impossible to draw inferences from behavior in which they did not engage. Bewley (1999) gives an extensive report on an effort to elicit statements from employers on this matter. But before discussing the methodological implications of this report, we need to discuss the troublesome concept of involuntary unemployment and its correlative, sticky nominal wages.[4]

Involuntary unemployment and sticky wages

From the publication of *The General Theory* to the present, the concept of involuntary unemployment has been a source of confusion rooted in the dual purpose of the book. Keynes wanted both to displace the neoclassical vision of the economy which precludes involuntary unemployment, and to persuade neoclassical economists that his alternative vision was superior.

Had he been concerned only with the first objective, the difficulty with "involuntariness" could have been avoided easily. Given technology, the stock of capital goods and the real wage rate, the level of aggregate output could have been assumed plausibly to depend solely upon the level of effective demand. Then, given a fixed number of job seekers, finding the quantity of unemployment would have been a matter of arithmetic.

The analogy with a game of musical chairs is striking: assuming there are more players than chairs when the music stops, some participants will have no seats, with the number unseated determined in advance as the difference between the number of seats and the number of players. Clearly, being without a seat would be involuntary. While the identity of the players who were to be unseated would not be explained, neither did *The General Theory* purport to identify which workers were to be unemployed, but only their quantity.

While something like this musical chair analogy had popular currency during the second quarter of the last century, and even now is not extinct, it is far too crude to appeal to most economists, among whom Keynes was no exception. Both to convince others, and probably himself, he had to devise a story that would reconcile an economy being in a state of equilibrium although there were desirous sellers of labor services who were unable to transact at the "going wage." The main story presented in *The General Theory* (there were several) ran in terms of workers being resistant

---

[4] Another interesting and painstaking effort to obtain information from economic actors about thought processes relevant to their price-making behavior is reported in Blinder *et al.* (1998). Although the findings in the report are germane to the argument of this chapter, they raise so many collateral issues that (reluctantly) I have decided not to comment upon it.

to reductions in money wages even though real wages remained unchanged: i.e. the explanation suggested the presence of money illusion and was at least first cousin to a Tversky–Kahneman framing effect. I pass over the details of the explanation because it never really caught on even among Keynesians, and Keynes's own attachment to it is uncertain.

For roughly a quarter of a century the labor market side of *The General Theory* was left in a kind of limbo, with the process of wage determination obscured by treating both money wages and labor supply as exogenous. However, this state of affairs was highly unsatisfactory to a new generation of economists, including adherents of both the Keynesian and the neoclassical traditions, who demanded (as a condition of acceptability) that economic theories should have sound microfoundations.

There has been a plurality of candidates for the role of microfoundation provider. One of these is a development and extension of the neoclassical frame, frequently identified as new classical.[5] The distinguishing characteristic of new classicalism is insistence on the fulfillment of all implications of the assumption that (in equilibrium) markets clear with resource owners optimizing: neoclassicals sometimes fudged this requirement. As I see it, the principal difference between new classicals and neoclassicals is rooted in the problem of discussing the behavior of individuals in a situation of market disequilibrium, while continuing to assume they are always optimizing. Without going into details, new classicals proposed to solve this problem by assuming that individuals always maximized expected utility on the maintained assumption that expectations were rational. Although the problem of establishing microfoundations arises in all markets, a major point of reference has been the labor market and the interpretation of the concept of involuntary unemployment.

What the various approaches to microfoundations other than the new classical share is rejection of the neoclassical frame. Two papers having much in common, in addition to salience and merit, are the Nobel lectures of Akerlof (2002) and Stiglitz (2002) which I shall use as exemplars of the "other than new classical" approach to involuntary unemployment and labor market behavior. While the new classical approach to microfoundations of labor markets and involuntary unemployment has been presented in various ways, for convenience I shall focus upon one of the earliest – and still one of the best – Lucas and Rapping (1969). Leaving aside other aspects of labor supply I shall concentrate upon the effects of intertemporal planning by individuals and households.

---

[5] An excellent summary and critique of this development is Hoover (1988).

In essence, *The General Theory* sought to frame fluctuations in employment as resulting from fluctuations in effective demand with above normal non-employment identified as involuntary unemployment: possible fluctuations in labor supply were ignored. In contrast, Lucas and Rapping sought to frame fluctuations in employment as the result of fluctuations in labor supply, sometimes (but not always) caused by fluctuations in aggregate effective demand. While the Keynesian conception of unemployment is single period with no attention paid to intertemporal relations of labor supply, Lucas and Rapping consider individuals to be multiperiod utility maximizers, whose plans allow for the possibility of interperiod substitution of labor supply.

In any given period decisions about labor supply are conditional upon the state of current employment opportunities (real wage rate).[6] Should current employment opportunities be less favorable than an individual had anticipated, he or she might find it advantageous to substitute further education, a vacation, engaging in home repair, etc., for current gainful employment. Such intertemporal substitution of employment would be coordinated with intertemporal deviations from an asset accumulation plan: e.g. drawing down of savings, increased borrowing, reduction of current consumption. Conversely, regardless of the current state of employment opportunities, previous periods in which labor market states had been more favorable than anticipated would lead an individual to work less and/or reduce his or her rate of asset accumulation in order to increase his or her rate of consumption. Still further, in multiperson households, shock-induced deviations from an intertemporal household plan might induce crossperson as well as intertemporal substitutions of time. However, because the costs of exercising options to alter intertemporal plans of labor supply may appear excessive, some workers may avoid them by accepting lower wages and/or inferior jobs.

Implicit in the Lucas–Rapping story is the assumption that shock-caused deviations from intertemporal plans may be anticipated and planned for. Indeed, the implicit self-insurance that such plans envisage might conceivably be supplemented by purchased insurance as proposed by Robert Shiller (2003). But the uncertainty associated with intertemporal plans cannot be insured against. Occurrence of a shock always raises questions as to whether the regime upon whose continuation such plans

---

[6] Lucas and Rapping use real wage rate as a synonym for "net advantages of employment." So defined, the real wage rate covers fringes of all kinds, especially the prospect of an increased probability of future employment as a result of present employment. While this definition presents problems, a discussion of them would take us far afield.

were based might have undergone an adverse change, and if so what the new regime might be and what reformulation of such plans it would entail.

The psychic cost of the entailed uncertainty is greatly enhanced by the fact that because an individual's life cycle is finite and affected by hysteresis it is often infeasible to defer study or adventures of one kind or another for later realization. To this should be added the high cost of overcoming the moral hazard associated with lending to an impecunious loan seeker. Together, these obstacles to intertemporal substitution of labor supply can provide a rationale for rejecting the new classical viewpoint as a frame for viewing involuntary unemployment.[7]

But *The General Theory* nowhere invokes such psychic costs as a rationale for deploring involuntary unemployment. Left implicit, although clearly present, is the claim that involuntary unemployment is the obverse side of unused productive capacity and that the potential output of such capacity (valued at market prices) can serve as a measure of the resulting loss. For the sake of argument, assume that while this claim might hold for a short period window (say six months), as the window lengthens to two years the effect of intertemporal substitution of employment would begin to affect the level of potential output: i.e. initial subnormal employment would be (at least partially) offset by later supernormal employment. Thus, viewed through a sufficiently long window, lost output due to a major depression might be offset – more or less – by the effects of a supernormal supply of labor from workers struggling to make up for the potential earnings previously lost. Conversely, an unusually large or prolonged boom might lead to earlier retirements, longer vacations, etc. by workers who had already earned and saved enough to satisfy the aspirations embedded in their multiperiod supply plans.

I conjecture that in viewing the economic history of the past century most economists would agree that during particular short periods where aggregate output and employment fell below their respective potentials the shortfalls were partly (or even wholly) offset by unusually large supplies of productive services, earlier or later. Moreover, they would also agree that because measuring the relevant magnitudes is very difficult, summary characterizations should be tentative. However, in choosing a frame for viewing the normal state of a capitalist economy, many of them would desert the ranks of the tentative and become more or less committed adherents to either the Invisible Hand frame or the frame of the Keynesians.

---

[7] The reader will note the relation of the above remarks to Frank Knight's (1921) distinction between risk and uncertainty.

For reasons to be given, adherence to the Invisible Hand frame is congenial to framing fluctuations in employment as the result of fluctuations of labor supply rather than of labor demand. This does not imply that neoclassicals deny that adverse shocks to aggregate labor demand ever occur. What the framing preference reflects is belief that the response of individuals to shocks to labor demand – favorable or adverse – is to vary the current quantity of labor supplied with offsetting variations occurring subsequently. Individuals who are unusually averse to such intertemporal substitution, or to whom it would be unusually costly, can avoid it by accepting reductions in their current real wage including acceptance of less attractive jobs. Such a view of non-employment precludes the possibility of using it as a basis for inferring a loss of potential output over any substantial period of time.

By contrast, the Keynesian frame enables one to consider employment levels that are less than some exogenously given labor supply as an indicator of wasted potential output. That is, the Keynesian framework provides a rationalization for neglecting the possibility that current under-employment might cause an increase in future output by increasing future labor supply. Such neglect makes it possible to sum (across periods) the losses of potential output inferred from allegedly involuntary unemployment.

The policy implications of preferring one of these frames to the other are obvious: the Keynesian frame highlights current gains in aggregate output due to "Full(er) Employment" while the Invisible Hand implies that such gains are illusory and reflect intertemporal shifts of resources. Similarly, the Keynesian frame facilitates pointing to the benefits of policies that accelerate industrialization, while the Invisible Hand highlights the costs of going faster than market forces would (seem to) warrant.

While not explicitly adopting the Keynesian frame, the view of the functioning of a capitalist economy and the attitude toward public policy associated with that frame are reflected clearly in the Nobel lectures of George Akerlof (2002) and Joseph Stiglitz (2002). In revealing a shared aversion to the Invisible Hand, both lectures cite trivialization or outright denial of the occurrence of involuntary unemployment as a source of complaint. However, they do not cling to Keynes's concept of involuntary unemployment, but introduce a quite different – though now widely accepted – definition. As stated by Akerlof:

The existence of good jobs and bad jobs makes the concept of involuntary unemployment meaningful: unemployed workers are willing to accept, but cannot obtain, jobs identical to those currently held by workers with identical ability. At the same time, involuntarily unemployed workers may eschew the lower paying or lower-skilled jobs that are available … A meaningful concept of involuntary unemployment constitutes an important first step forward in rebuilding the foundations of Keynesian economics. (2002, 415).[8]

While this statement is congenial to commonsense, it has the effect of seriously changing the meaning of "involuntary unemployment". What is a "good job"? I suggest that the term has reference to a consensus view (in a given society) of what would be appropriate for one of its members of given characteristics (age, education, job experience, geographical location, etc.) to accept. On the Akerlof definition the amount of involuntary unemployment depends critically upon a society's consensus definition of the kinds of job offers that individuals may not refuse on pain of sanctions being invoked. In judgmental societies a given level of effective aggregate demand might generate much less involuntary unemployment than in more tolerant societies. Indeed, if it were required that in order to escape the stigma of being voluntarily unemployed an individual was required to accept job offers where compensation was solely by results without a guarantee of minimum payment, involuntary unemployment would cease to exist on the Akerlof definition.

As his lecture indicates, Akerlof's concept of involuntary unemployment dovetails with the notion of "efficiency wages." This notion presents the employer as a price (wage) setter and not as the taker of a market- (or sometimes a union-) determined wage rate. In the context of this notion the presence of involuntary unemployment raises the question of why employers don't reduce the wages that they set. Answering this question is the subject of a monograph by Truman Bewley (1999). (Bewley's wage concept is the commonsense nominal wage and not the Lucas–Rapping real wage which would be quite likely to fall in the presence of excess labor supply.) Bewley's concern is with the nominal wages of employees who retained their jobs in the presence of excess labor supply without experiencing a wage cut.

Bewley did not study the recorded history of what such workers were paid (as F53 would recommend), but instead asked employers (or their representatives in charge of compensation decisions) about why they had not reduced the wages they did offer, or why they had failed to reduce them more than they had, contrary to the recommendation of F53. In the early 1990s Bewley interviewed over 300 "wage setters" in the New England region adjacent to Yale University where there had been a severe recession. Because of the conditions prevailing in the local labor market, a maintained (though unspoken) assumption in most of the interviews was

---

[8] The idea of a job applicant having identical ability with a current job holder raises methodological problems about the notion of specific human capital. While such problems are not always trivial, I shall refrain from discussing them here.

that the proposal of a (temporary) wage cut would not have provoked an immediate quit. Yet such cuts were rarely proposed when circumstances required a reduction in payroll: the typical response was to lay off workers, or dismiss them, but only rarely to reduce their rates of pay and even less frequently to give workers an option of some combination of shorter hours and reduced rates of pay.

The striking feature of the interviews was the failure of most managers to invoke labor market considerations as an explanation of their wage-setting behavior. While the reasons given for their behavior included a variety of considerations (e.g. fairness to the employees, avoidance of worker resentment that might cause future shirking or quits when labor market conditions became more favorable to employees, maintenance of a pleasant atmosphere in the workplace). Only rarely did the expressed sentiments make reference to conditions in the labor market. As Bewley points out, the reasons for wage decisions given by managers run strongly parallel to the views expressed by personnel experts, social psychologists, sociologists, and other academic non-economists.[9]

Bewley summarizes the reasons given for not reducing wages under the rubric of employer desire to maintain morale: i.e. wages don't fall during recessions because employers don't wish to damage employee morale. Worker and/or trade union resistance is not invoked as a causal factor in explaining the failure of employers to exploit excess labor supply to reduce wages. This implies that in a recession most employed workers cannot reduce their probability of being laid off or dismissed by accepting a wage cut because their employers do not wish to lower wages for fear of adversely affecting morale. For the same reason, employers would not respond to offers by unemployed workers to accept lower wages than those paid to current job holders of equal productivity. In short, unemployed workers cannot use the tools of a competitive market – accepting lower wages – to increase their probability of finding (or retaining) a job and therefore their unemployment should be considered involuntary.

This state of affairs would seem to be inconsistent with the idea that employers seek to maximize expected profits and Bewley so interprets it, constructing a theory alternative to profit maximization in which employer wage-setting behavior is made subject to a morale-maintenance constraint. (While the details of this theory are of substantive interest, they have no direct bearing on the present discussion so I shall refrain from

---

[9] While Bewley does not stress the point, his interviews reveal a tendency (frequently remarked elsewhere) toward enhanced employer willingness to exploit excess labor supply to reduce wages when pressed to improve cash flow (e.g. threatened action by creditors), as well as lessened resistance of workers to such exploitation.

comment.) Nevertheless, it is possible to interpret employer concern for maintenance of morale in a manner consistent with pursuit of maximum expected profits.

To make such an interpretation it is necessary for the concept of *specific* human capital to be accorded greater salience than Bewley – or most other authors – give it. Specific human capital (pace Gary Becker) reflects skill and/or knowledge embodied in a worker, but useful only to a specific employer: hence it can be destroyed by a job separation, to the loss of both worker and employer. Typically, specific human capital is created by investments (of time and resources) by both parties implying the expectation of both to a multiperiod return. Consequently, a disgruntled employee might (rationally) retain a job despite dissatisfaction with his or her employer's behavior and respond by withholding some effort (accordingly reducing productivity), but not enough to provoke the employer to dismiss him or her and thereby lose that employee's share of the joint investment.

Being aware of this possibility a rational employer might, subject to the constraint of expected present value maximization, forego potential gains of current quasi-rent made possible by transitory excess labor supply and refrain from reducing nominal wages. However, he or she might also (à la Lucas–Rapping) seek out other components of the real wage that could be reduced without causing as much loss of morale as would result from a reduction in nominal wages. Perceptive readers will note that concern for maintaining morale could serve as a rationalization of the reported reluctance to engage in temporary layoffs as well as an impediment to temporary reductions of nominal wages. (While the morale constant tradeoff of layoffs against wage cuts is an interesting topic, it is not relevant to the argument of this chapter.)

In considering the concern of employers with maintenance of morale, it helps to remember that a rational employer considers an investment in specific human capital as similar (in many respects) to an investment in plant or equipment. Customarily such investments may be maintained in depressed periods despite the considerable cost of doing so. For specific human capital such cost takes the form of higher wages than an imaginary spot labor market for workers of equivalent human capital would require.[10]

What new classicals might term "maintenance of specific human capital," Akerlof, Bewley *et al.*, along with many others (business persons, personnel specialists, psychologists, and sociologists) would describe as concern with fairness, honoring implicit promises and other praiseworthy objectives that are incompatible with the profit maximization entailed by

---

[10] A critical reader might object to the concept of a market for *specific* human capital. While I believe that I could defend use of the concept, I recognize the difficulty but eschew the lengthy diversion that such a defence would entail.

the Invisible Hand. This difference in perceptions of long-term employer objectives is one consequence of using the Invisible Hand frame rather than some alternative. A second consequence is the interpretation of non-employment as involuntary unemployment and a waste of resources rather than a realization of a stochastic process affecting the intertemporal allocation of time and output. Yet a third consequence is refusal to accept explanations for counterfactual behavior (why possible courses of action not taken by economic actors) are rejected as rationalizations of behavior seeming to violate economic laws associated with the Invisible Hand. This chapter argues that concern for about the first two of these consequences is a major reason for the methodological decision reflected in the third.

IV

In seeking to influence the views of other people, economists and other social scientists attempt to induce them to think in a particular way about whole classes of problems, many of which cannot be specified in advance. Many of the most important problems concern public policy. Although far from the whole of the matter, the frame that one uses is an important element of one's "method of thinking" about a particular class of problems. In addition to the frame (or frames) that an individual uses, he or she usually has one or more theories and/or prejudices.

Neoclassical economics is associated with a variety of theories and (possibly) a plurality of frames. However, in this article I have been concerned with one particular neoclassical frame, the Invisible Hand, which is embedded in F53 and exhibited in most of Friedman's other writings as well. As reiterated here, and innumerable times in the literature for well over half a century, that frame presents economic problems as involving choices or decisions made by individuals who are subject to constraints of endowed resources and seek to maximize some objective function which (loosely) can be identified as expected utility. In the process of maximization, individuals engage in mutually agreeable transactions with others in which the terms of trade (prices) are determined by competitive markets and are accepted as givens by all parties concerned.

The competitive market and the associated method of price determination are very important characteristics of this frame: it is these properties that lead to the identification of market-determined prices with alternative marginal costs. This identification generates many of the non-intuitive implications of neoclassical theories that make the Invisible Hand frame intellectually appealing, and motivates efforts to encourage its adoption and utilization.

As stated in section I, Friedman is noted (inter alia) for his insistence that a major determinant of the quality of a theory is the extent to which it facilitates useful predictions. But what he urges (in F53 and elsewhere) is not the collection of unrelated theories, each possessing great power to make useful predictions, but adoption of a specific frame for a set of theories that share certain important characteristics. In effect he is telling economists that (in non-monopoly situations) the best way to find successful theories is to restrict search to theories that are compatible with the Invisible Hand frame. By implication Friedman holds that it is members of this class of theories that have the best chance of yielding useful predictions.

As already indicated, economics has no salient criterion for theory selection that is alternative to what is proposed in F53. However, during the past half century there has been increasing emphasis on the importance of achieving consilience between the implications of theories accepted in economics and those accepted in psychology and/or sociology that purport to explain the actions of individuals and firms by allowing for the possibility of non-rational behavior.

But to achieve consilience with such theories entails abandonment, or at least drastic alteration, of the Invisible Hand frame. A striking example of attempts to compel such alteration is provided by the Nobel lectures of Akerlof and Stiglitz, discussed in section III. The arguments of these lectures dovetail nicely with the findings of Bewley's interviews with wage setters in the 1990s, which are strikingly similar both in style and results to the empirical research that F53 sought to discredit.

At first blush, the combined effect of the arguments of Akerlof and Stiglitz and the reports of Bewley's interviews with wage setters would seem to limit the applicability of the Invisible Hand framework. However, as argued in section III, the contrast between that framework and the opposing Keynesian vision is very much blurred when intertemporal substitution of labor is considered. Indeed, the issues involved in interpreting a given spell of aggregate unemployment as an irreparable loss of potential output rather than an intertemporal substitution of labor involve so much conjecture on both sides that it is hard to understand the intensity with which this, and similar disputes, are pursued.

The explanation lies in the importance attached to maintaining the intellectual viability of the alternative frames for viewing a competitive economy that are associated with alternative interpretations of unemployment. The importance attached to maintaining the viability of a frame is due to the influence that its acceptance is believed to exercise on the views that individuals take of the propriety of governmental intervention in the functioning of an economy. Over the decades Friedman has many times insisted upon the separation of his views on positive economics (as in the title of F53) from those on normative economics, especially on public policy. And this posture is shared widely among economists: not only among his many disciples, but also among his opponents.

To some extent I also share it. Nevertheless, I suggest that it is no accident that the overlap between adherence to the Invisible Hand frame and advocacy of laissez-faire – though not complete – should be very substantial. Acceptance of the Invisible Hand leads one to look for amelioration of shortages – either of supply or demand – to the workings of markets rather than to quantity adjustments directed by a communal authority. It also sensitizes one to hitherto unexploited opportunities for using the instrumentalities of the market, thereby reducing the scope for governmental actions, and the seeming need for its regulative activity.

Conversely, rejection of the Invisible Hand is likely to arise from perception of instances where it appears to have failed. Such perceptions often are not deduced from widely applicable theories but are inspired by observation of particular cases, either personally or through reports of affected persons, and often are associated with ad hoc remedies. When such remedies conflict with one or another implication of neoclassical economic "laws," as they often do, their intellectual support must come from testimony of affected parties often based on (what they believe to be) their first-hand experience.

The history of economic thought, especially in the last half century, strongly suggests that the best obtainable empirical evidence manipulated by the best available econometric techniques is inadequate to persuade adherents of a particular frame to support a policy that is uncongenial to that frame. Hence the importance attached to the selling of a conceptual frame that is conducive to acceptance of policies that one thinks one will find congenial.[11]

References

Akerlof, George A. (2002). Behavioral macroeconomics and macroeconomic behavior. *American Economic Review*, 92, 411–33
Bewley, Truman (1999). *Why Wages Don't Fall During a Recession*. Cambridge, MA: Harvard University Press

---

[11] While I do not say that economists typically choose theories, frames, etc. to rationalize preconceived policy conclusions, I believe that, varying from one economist to another, theory may inspire policy, and vice versa. Careful sorting out of the positive from the normative comes at the stage of presentation – sometimes consciously, sometimes not – but after the stage of inspiration.

Blinder, Alan S. *et al.* (1998). *Asking About Prices*. New York: Russell Sage Foundation

Coase, Ronald H. (1937). The nature of the firm. *Economica*, 4, 386–405

Hoover, Kevin D. (1988). *The New Classical Macroeconomics: A Sceptical Inquiry*. Oxford: Blackwell

Kahneman, Daniel (2002). Maps of bounded rationality: psychology for behavioral economics. *American Economic Review*, 93, 1449–75

Keynes, John Maynard (1936). *The General Theory of Employment, Interest and Money*. New York: Harcourt, Brace and Company

Lucas, Robert E. and Leonard A. Rapping (1969). Real wages, employment and inflation. *Journal of Political Economy*, 77, 721–54

Schumpeter, Joseph A. (1954). *History of Economic Analysis*. New York: Oxford University Press

Shiller, Robert J. (2003). *The New Financial Order*. Princeton, NJ: Princeton University Press

Simon, Herbert A. (1947). *Administrative Behavior*. New York: Macmillan

Stiglitz, Joseph E. (2002). *Globalization and its Discontents*. New York: W. W. Norton

Tversky, Amos and Daniel Kahneman (1974). Judgment under uncertainty: heuristics and biases. *Science*, 185, 1124–30.

Wilson, Edward O. (1998). *Consilience*. New York: Alfred A. Knopf

7   The politics of positivism: disinterested predictions from interested agents

David Teira Serrano and Jesús Zamora Bonilla

1   Politics in "The methodology"

Of the six sections composing "The methodology of positive economics" (F53), the first ("The relation between positive and normative economics") is apparently the least discussed in the F53 literature, probably as a result of it being not only the shortest section, but also the least relevant for the issue of realism. In view of Milton Friedman's subsequent career as a political preacher, one wonders whether this first section ruled it in the way the other five directed Friedman's scientific performance. After all, the role of prediction in defining positive economics was already advanced therein: when an economist predicts, his or her results are "independent of any particular ethical position or normative judgments." This is also why positive economics is a politically relevant discipline: as long as the differences about economic policy – *among disinterested citizens* – derive only from different predictions about the economic consequences of taking action, these differences could be eliminated by the progress of positive economics. Our plan in this chapter is to present, in the first place, the role of *political motivations* in the development of Friedman's methodological stance. As we will discuss in section 2, Friedman was involved in the policy-making process right from the beginning of his professional career, and was able to experience at first hand the relevance of economic predictions in generating a consensus not only among politicians or the public opinion, but among the profession itself. Conversely, Friedman could also appreciate how difficult it was to reach a consensus on a particular policy when the economists disagreed on its practical consequences. In this respect, as we will see, F53 attempted to guarantee the political efficiency of economic research. However, the sociological turn in science studies raises the question on what basis can we deem a prediction *neutral*? Is it simply that economists produce these positive

Our joint research was funded by the Urrutia Elejalde Foundation and by the grant BF2003-04372.

predictions *disinterestedly*, even while deeply engaged in political debates? In section 3, we analyze how Friedman himself produced predictions immediately before F53 was drafted, and how this procedure lies at the core of his Marshallian approach, which he contrasted to the Walrasian strategy on the grounds of its higher political relevance. Yet, from a sociological viewpoint, it is precisely this Marshallian strategy that seems most objectionable: the way Friedman deals with theoretical concepts in economics in order to obtain predictions makes them particularly susceptible to manipulation by a not so disinterested economist. We will see that F53 does not provide any defense whatsoever to counteract this.

Finally, we argue that the "knowledge" produced by economists can only gain the trust of lay audiences if the latter know that the activity of the former is constrained by an appropriate *methodological contract* (Zamora Bonilla 2002), and we suggest that F53 can be best understood as an attempt to persuade the economics profession to adopt a certain methodological contract, an agreement which ensures that supporting economic research is a rational choice for citizens and politicians (section 4). Nevertheless, our own case will not be long, as a brief article we add by way of conclusion makes it much better than we did (section 5).

2   Predicting for the policy-makers

Whereas only a minor section of F53 was devoted to normative issues, a significant part of Friedman's professional experience between 1935 and 1945 took place in Washington, DC, quite close to the political arena. We are going to examine the various contexts in which Friedman came to experience the connection between prediction and politics, which, in our opinion, provide the drive behind F53's first section. We discuss Friedman's first stay in Washington in the New Deal years, also paying attention to the debate on the political relevance of statistical economics in the early 1930s. We will also consider how Friedman developed a position of his own early in the 1940s, while appointed at the Treasury. By the end of the decade, it had become a standard view among the profession – if we are to judge by an American Economic Association (AEA) report that Friedman coauthored in 1947. Finally, we exemplify the role Friedman assigned to prediction as a consensus-generating tool by means of an analysis of two of the papers included in his *Essays in Positive Economics*.

Let us then start in 1935. A growing demand for young economists sustained by New Deal policies gave the young Friedman an opportunity to enter a depressed labor market (Friedman and Friedman 1998, 60). Paradoxical though it may seem now, he was appointed at an agency intended to promote economic planning at the highest levels of government, the National Resources Committee (NRC) (Brinkley 1995, 245–50). Under the supervision of Hildegarde Kneeland, Friedman joined an NRC task force assigned to coordinate the Study of Consumer Purchases (SCP), a wide-ranging statistical survey intended to quantify consumer incomes and expenditure in the United States in the period 1935–6 (NRC 1938, 1939). Or, in other words, to provide a statistical answer to the debate over the causes of the Great Depression which heated up the 1932 presidential campaign. At its roots – Roosevelt had argued then – lay the maladjustment between industrial production and the purchasing power of would-be consumers, and the way out consisted simply in raising the latter (Brinkley 1995, 69–72; Balisciano 1998,160–5). Six years after Roosevelt's election, the NRC income report was printed. It still addressed the underconsumption issue in its preamble (NRC 1938,1), even if the policies so far implemented had worked to the detriment of consumers (Brinkley 1995, 71). Though credited among the contributors, Friedman's memoirs skip the political implications of the SCP, focusing instead on the statistical challenges involved therein (Friedman and Friedman 1998, 61–6).

New Deal policies required government intervention in the American economy on a scale never seen before. In need of figures (Duncan and Shelton 1992, 322), the American administration multiplied its statistical production, and most economists were appointed with a view to conducting empirical research, their lack of technical qualification notwithstanding (Hotelling 1940, 458). As a result of the year he spent in Columbia with Harold Hotelling, Friedman was certainly familiar with the subtleties of the methods introduced by Ronald Fisher in the 1920s, but sampling design was a newborn discipline, almost unknown to most federal agencies.[1] The SCP thus gave him the opportunity to face the challenges of applying theoretical statistics to the design and implementation of a large-scale survey (Kneeland et al. 1936; Schoenberg and Parten 1937). Indeed, the SCP gave none other than Jerzy Neyman the opportunity to devise a double sampling procedure to correct the one applied by the NRC team, to which he was exposed during his stay at the Department of Agriculture Graduate School in 1937. Friedman himself posed the problem during one of Neyman's lectures.[2] In sum, New Deal planning fostered the completion

---

[1] On the introduction of mathematical statistics in the USA in 1933, see Stigler (1996). The use of mathematical statistics by Federal agencies in that same year is discussed in Duncan and Shelton (1992, 321). For an overview of the development of sampling techniques, see Seng (1951) and Desrosieres et al. (2001). For an extended discussion of the methodological challenges herein involved as Friedman could have met them, see Teira (2007).

[2] Cf. Neyman (1938, 328). On the context, see Reid (1998, 137–8) – Friedman's contribution is mentioned in p. 148. For an extended discussion, see Teira (2007).

of Friedman's statistical training, both on a practical and theoretical level. It is quite plausible that he had then become aware of the political relevance of statistical economics. However, it is also possible that he already knew that statistical economics could also make economists differ.

In 1932, Roosevelt recruited three Columbia professors as campaign advisers. Among the members of this *Brain Trust*, as they came to be known, was an economist, Rexford Tugwell, who had proclaimed the year before in the AEA meeting the end of the laissez-faire era (Tugwell 1932). According to Tugwell, it was federal government responsibility to adjust production and consumption through price control, securing the purchasing power of salaries. Moderate voices demanded a mere *indicative* planning, an ineffective solution for Tugwell since it did not eliminate *uncertainty* (Tugwell 1932, 85).

It was certainly the end of free entrepreneurial activity, as Frank Knight – Milton Friedman's "revered teacher" – had conceived in his 1921 classic *Risk, Uncertainty and Profit.*[3] Economic planning required *perfect information*, which was, for Knight, unattainable: the decision of each economic agent is essentially unique and thus unpredictable. Individual freedom was at stake if the planners were to reach their goals (Knight 1932, 448).

In response to those who viewed economics as a mere technique of prediction and control, Knight warned that only the short-term view of the price problem, as contained in static economics, is to be deemed scientific. Unfortunately, static economics did not allow for far-reaching predictions as required by planners, whereas those derived from institutional approaches to economics amounted to nothing more than sheer "philosophy of history" (Knight 1924, 146). This was hardly good news to announce in the times of the Great Depression: still an undergraduate student in Chicago, Friedman could attest to the reactions it aroused in 1932 when Knight delivered his tongue-in-cheek lectures on "The Case for Communism" before an over-reactive audience (Friedman and Friedman 1998, 37).

By the end of the 1930s, in sum, Friedman had already experienced how predictions were requested by economists with a normative purpose (namely, state intervention) and the objections raised against economics assuming such a role. As for his own position concerning statistics and economic planning, little is known; but even in 1938 Aaron Director could make jokes about Friedman's "very strong New Deal leanings – authoritarian to use an abusive term" (*apud* Friedman and Friedman 1998, 81).

In the 1940s, Friedman's stance began to take shape. By 1942, he was a self-proclaimed "thorough Keynesian": the terms *money* or *monetary policy*

---

[3] On this particular point, see Pradier and Teira (2000, 2002).

seldom appeared in his writings (Friedman and Friedman 1998, 113). The year before, he had been summoned again to Washington, this time appointed as the *Principal economist* at the Treasury's division of tax research (Friedman and Friedman 1998, 105–25). Having completed the draft of his dissertation at the NBER that same year, Friedman was an accomplished expert in both income and consumption studies, a profile highly demanded again by the Federal Government. Hitler's Germany had already proven how menacing state intervention could be if economic planning were taken to its furthest consequences. Roosevelt's liberals were now inclined to intervene through more *compensatory* tools, in Alan Brinkley's words: i.e. a combination of Keynesian fiscal measures and enhanced welfare-state mechanisms (Brinkley 1995, 154–64). In a crude war context, stabilizing consumption required active taxing policies that prevented inflation. Friedman's role at the Treasury obliged him to take part in the real policy-making debate, which involved frequent congressional testifying, providing consulting services to many a senator, speech drafting, and so forth. Friedman argued for a demand-oriented approach to income analysis, which conferred theoretical significance to the available statistical data (e.g. Shoup *et al.* 1943, 111–53) – an approach already exemplified in his own dissertation: see below section 3.

By the end of the 1940s, the two main theses later stated in F53's first section were already explicit in Friedman's texts: statistical economics was affirmed as a politically relevant discipline, not only for being instrumental in the policy-making process, but also for its virtue as a consensus-generating device. We should take into account that this was not a minority view among the profession by then, as may be noticed in a report delivered by the AEA Committee on Public Issues in 1950. Friedman and three coauthors[4] were assigned to present to a general audience the state of the art concerning the problem of economic instability. One of the first topics they addressed was the relevance of economics in dealing with inflations and recessions, *its forecasting limitations notwithstanding.* Taking sides against Knight's indictment on institutional economists, the AEA committee proclaimed:

A second misconception is contained in the proposition that effective stabilization policies can be designed only if we understand fully all the causes of fluctuations. Partial knowledge can be very useful for deciding how to act. (Despres *et al.* 1950, 512)

Even if the calculations involved in planning were out of the reach of any statistical economist, the policy-maker could still benefit from concrete

---

[4] Together with Emile Despres, Albert Hart, and Paul Samuelson. The committee had been appointed in 1947.

forecasts of the evolution of certain economic variables. On the basis of this partial knowledge, the profession could reach a consensus on which policies were most convenient to the country (Despres *et al.* 1950, 505). That is, they deserved to be trusted by the public opinion, their usual discrepancies notwithstanding (511).

The connection between partial knowledge, predictions and consensus among the profession was even more explicit in another paper, by Friedman alone, on the issue of stability – published the year after the committee formed. In "A monetary and fiscal framework for economic stability" (Friedman [1948] 1953a) he argued for an economic agenda which would lead to the attainment of a number of consensual values such as *freedom, efficiency,* and *economic equality* (Friedman [1948] 1953a, 134), on which not many *disinterested citizens* would disagree. If the profession could be persuaded first of the convenience of the agenda – "the greatest common denominator of many different proposals" –, it may be presented as a "minimum program for which economists of the less extreme shades can make common cause" (Friedman [1948] 1953a, 135). Friedman's agenda consisted of the following four core points:

The essence of this fourfold proposal is that it uses automatic adaptations in the government contribution to the current income stream to offset, at least in part, changes in other segments of aggregate demand and to change appropriately the supply of money. (Friedman [1948] 1953a, 139)

The case for this proposal was thoroughly presented two years later in "The effects of a full-employment policy on economic stability: a formal analysis" (Friedman 1951). Full-employment policies were usually analyzed on the basis of a four-variable model: consumption (C), income (Y), investment (I), and government expense (G).

$$Y = C + I + G$$
$$C = f(Y)$$

The income level Y_0 that will bring about full employment depends directly on government expense, which must counterbalance I. Stability is therefore the stability of income Y. The discussion of the effects of discretional government action proceeds in a way inspired by "the theory of statistics rather than economic theory" (Friedman [1948] 1953a, 121), more precisely by the statistical analysis of variance.[5] Income at t $Z(t)$ is decomposed into two variables, the first one $X(t)$ measuring the level

---

[5] Friedman (1949, 951), from which the idea evolved (Friedman [1948] 1953a, 121n.)

attained without a full-employment policy, the effects of which are measured by the second one $Y(t)$. The analysis of income stability would thus
work analogously to that of variance:

> For X or Z the variance measures the fluctuations in income in the absence or
> presence of a countercyclical policy. For Y the variance may be regarded as
> measuring the magnitude of the countercyclical action taken. (Friedman [1948]
> 1953a, 123)

In this way, it would be possible to analyze in which conditions the
variance of Z is less than the variance of X, obtaining Y's optimal value.

Therefore, Friedman concludes, the variance of Y and its coefficient of
correlation with X allow us to classify any full-employment policy according to its effects on economic stability. Yet, statistics would not allow any
planner to control the cyclical variations at will. Quite the opposite: only
automatizing the response, Friedman argues, would minimize the delay
between the variation to counteract and the action which would counteract it – or, in statistical terms, to approximate the value of the correlation
between X and Y to the desired -1. Therein lies, according to Friedman,
the *positive* superiority of a monetary and fiscal program based on automatic reactions over discretional policies, beyond their normative convenience to each particular citizen.

These two papers thus exemplify the role that F53's first section
assigned to prediction in the generation of public consensus about particular policies: as long as the divergence lies in the policy to be chosen, it
may be resolved on a purely consequentialist basis through statistical
analysis. Given that positive economic predictions are independent of
any normative commitment on the part of their authors, they deserve to
be trusted by any *disinterested citizen* when a decision on the policy to adopt
is at stake.[6] In spite of its brevity, F53's first section reflects thus a
significant part of Friedman's professional experience, a real methodological concern about the role an economist could play in promoting
public policies without losing his scientific integrity. The question we
are going to address in the next section is how F53 contributes to such a
goal.

---

[6] Yet, although unmentioned in F53, attention should also be paid to the fact that *professional
consensus among economists on the most convenient policies* is required for any general consensus to be reached (Friedman [1948] 1953a; Despres *et al.* 1950). Or conversely, as Rose
Friedman put it: "It is not difficult to see why different layman might have different
predictions about the economic consequences of certain actions when the experts disagree" (Friedman and Friedman 1998, 217). For laymen and experts alike, the way to
attain consensus is the same one: predicting. This topic will be taken up again in section 4.

3   How to disagree on predictions

Between meeting Hotelling in Columbia (1933) and returning to Chicago (1946), Friedman's statistical qualification grew incessantly: on the practical side, he extended his training first at the NRC (1935–7) and later at the NBER (1937–40), where he collaborated with Simon Kuznets while completing his dissertation; on the theoretical side, he was also able to benefit from his two-year appointment at the Statistical Research Group (1943–5).[7] Friedman also engaged in a collective effort to renew the teaching of statistics in American higher education, a task he undertook first during his brief stay in Wisconsin and later on in Chicago, where he contributed to the creation of a separate Department of statistics (Olkin 1991, 125–7). Friedman was therefore extremely well qualified not only to advocate predictive theories, as he did in F53, but to settle a methodological standard on what should count as a good prediction. He did not do this, however, either in his 1953 paper or afterwards. The methodological dilemma that arises therein may be stated as follows: can we really base a consensus, both public and professional, on predictions without any criterion to assess them? F53 proves to be extremely effective in discriminating politically relevant vs. irrelevant economic theories, once we assume that a predictively empty theory is *eo ipso* politically useless. However, lacking such a criterion, the particular predictive procedure that Friedman had in sight seems to be particularly capable of manipulation today, suspicious as we have become after the sociological turn in the study of science. In order to show it, let us examine first how Friedman achieved predictions.

By way of example, let us focus on a NBER joint monograph, part of which was also submitted to Columbia as a doctoral dissertation by Friedman. Friedman and Simon Kuznets finally published it under the title *Income from Independent Professional Practice* in 1946. Its methodological relevance was emphasized by Friedman himself, who declared to E. B. Wilson in 1946 that its chapters 3 and 4 were his most successful pieces (Stigler 1994, 1200): the balance between demand theory and statistical analysis exemplified a particular combination of the approaches to economics developed in Chicago and Columbia which were to distinguish Friedman's own style. Besides, the study was explicitly aimed at reaching "conclusions relevant for public policy," educational in this case (Friedman and Kuznets 1945, v). Friedman's expertise in income analysis was now applied to discern whether professional workers "constitute a 'noncompeting' group"; i.e. whether their number (and hence their

---

[7] For further details, see Friedman and Friedman (1998, 67–76, 125–47).

income) was exclusively determined by the "relative attractiveness of professional and nonprofessional work," or rather by the number of prospective students who count on the particular resources required to pursue the career in question (Friedman and Kuznets 1945, 93).

Among the five professions considered, medicine and dentistry provide particularly suitable data. Given that both professions require similar abilities and training, we should expect the prospective practitioners to choose between them mainly on the basis of their respective "level of return" (Friedman and Kuznets 1945, 123). Did the differences in average income between doctors and dentists correspond thus to the equilibrium level, or do they rather point to an entry restriction – such as the licenses imposed by the American Medical Association?

In our opinion, the most salient methodological feature in these two chapters lies in the way demand categories are redefined so that predictions can be derived therefrom. Instead of searching for an empirical counterpart that corresponds to its theoretical definition, Friedman restates demand theory so that it corresponds with the statistical variables at hand: e.g. careers would be chosen according to the average expected income as reflected in the arithmetic mean (Friedman and Kuznets 1945, 65, 145); prices and expected income would approximate the commodities offered by doctors and dentists, in the absence of a definite unit to measure them (155); regression analyses performed separately on the 1934 and 1936 data for per capita income of both professions, their number per 10.000 population and general per capita income (161–73) would do as proxy to discern whether the difference between their average incomes lies at the equilibrium level. Though admitting that none of these variables would account for the behavior of any particular individual, Friedman and Kuznets argue that they may nevertheless explain the behavior of the group of prospective entrants as a whole (96). In short, even if there is not a perfect correspondence between theoretical concepts and the data, it is preferable to relax our definition of the former so that predictions may be derived.

Indeed, the alternative at hand (rigorous definitions without an empirical counterpart) seemed to Friedman methodologically undesirable. Friedman opted for avoiding "schizoid concepts," i.e. those "thoroughly competent in the field of deductive analysis but utterly incompetent for quantitative analysis" – as he claimed in a joint paper with Allen Wallis from the same period (Wallis and Friedman 1942, 176). The more mathematical constraints are imposed by the definition of a theoretical concept, the less value it will have for the organization of empirical data (Wallis and Friedman 1942, 186). This sort of "taxonomic theorizing" was precisely the mark of the Walrasian approach, which was canonically criticized in Friedman's 1946 review of Lange: no empirical counterpart will correspond to those abstract taxonomies in the data (Friedman [1946] 1953a, 286–9).

The core of the dichotomy between Walrasian and Marshallian approaches seems to lie in the way theoretical concepts are defined: Walrasian *taxonomies* are opposed to Marshallian *filing cases*. Whereas theoretical concepts in the former were defined by purely logical means, producing entirely abstract taxonomies without correspondence in the data, in the latter they were redefined with a view to obtaining a classification of the data. We may better understand what this classification issue had to do with predictions if we take into account Friedman's predictive technique of choice: linear regression enhanced by the analysis of variance.

It was probably Hotelling who introduced Friedman to this technique in Columbia, given that he counted among the few in the USA who were then abreast of Ronald Fisher's recent breakthrough in statistical inference (Friedman 1992, 2131; Stigler 1996). According to the teaching of Fisher,[8] for a regression curve to be traced the first step consisted in classifying data in a *contingency table*, so that every observed figure was *filed* under a given variable. On the basis of this classification, contingency correlations – and eventually regression – may be calculated. Therefore very strict definition of the variables would make unfeasible the classification of the data, thus preventing predictions from being obtained. Handling variables in a more Marshallian spirit would allow the economist to render a theory predictively more fruitful.

Let us return now to the opening question of this section: in view of all this, why did Friedman not set up a standard in order to assess predictions? Part of the answer may be that such a standard could have affected the very definition of the variables involved, restricting its predictive capacity. On the other hand, it seems as if F53 was aimed more at discriminating between predictive and non-predictive approaches than at characterizing good predictions. For Friedman, choosing between "Marshall" and "Walras" was not an entirely methodological issue: it depended also on "the purpose for which the theory is constructed and used" (Friedman 1953b, 90).

Part of Friedman's purposes was to derive politically relevant predictions, as we saw in section 2. In this respect, a rough prediction is better than none: even if the theoretical relevance of the variables analyzed by

---

[8] In this respect, an extension of Galton and Pearson's approach, also adopted by Hotelling later on. Allen Wallis still used it in his 1956 manual (Wallis and Roberts 1956). For a superb analysis of this intellectual tradition, see Armatte (1995).

Friedman and Kuznets was at most conjectural, they did not hesitate in blaming the difference observed in the average income between medicine and dentistry on the medical licenses.[9] Conversely, if policy conclusions were always to rest on a prediction, Walrasian approaches were inherently useless for the policy-maker, as Friedman often pointed out.[10] Irrespective of its purported precision as a demarcation criterion, prediction proves to be extremely discriminating when it comes to the political efficiency of an economic theory.

However, in the aftermath of the science wars, the mere claim that such a criterion may pick out theories being at once positive and politically useful is clearly suspicious. Friedman's definitional strategy called into question a central claim in our methodological received view: *theoreticity*. In order to guarantee that each theoretical term had a clear empirical (*positive*) counterpart, rigorous definitions were called for. From this point of view, it is not strange that Walrasian axiomatizations have been so often appreciated by philosophers of science. However, when rigor in definitions is relinquished with a view to facilitating predictions, the sociological challenge to the neutrality of scientific classifications seems most threatening. According to a tradition dating back to Durkheim and Mauss,[11] our most basic classifications of sense-data are inescapably biased by social interests, since the concepts we use to this effect are rooted in our daily practice. There is no disinterested ground on which to base scientific concepts. Now, in our opinion, even those who disagree with David Bloor should concede that Friedman's methodology does not provide such a disinterested ground. Quite the contrary: for those economists whose daily practice consists in obtaining predictions with a political view, it is essential that the definition of theoretical concepts is loosened so that the data they are provided with can be classified and predictions follow. Yet, once the rigor of the definition is relaxed, who could guarantee that it will not be manipulated in order to obtain interested predictions?

By way of example, let us recall that the conclusions of Friedman and Kuznets's analysis were called into question by the American Medical Association. Apart from a few years' delay, it took a "Director's

---

[9] "The analysis is necessarily conjectural and our quantitative results are only a rough approximation. But the problem is real, and a rough approximation seems better than none" (Friedman and Kuznets 1945, viii).

[10] E.g. Friedman ([1946] 1953a, 300; [1947] 1953a, 316)

[11] After all, *categorization* is a central concern in many a sociological approach to science: the starting point was E. Durkheim and Marcel Mauss's 1903 essay "Primitive classification". Bloor (1982) vindicated its relevance for the *Strong program*. Philip Mirowski introduced this tradition in the sociology of economic knowledge in his *More Heat than Light* (1989, 412).

comment" by Carl Noyes (Friedman and Kuznets 1945, 405–10) to be added before the NBER accepted the publication. The note's major concern was to state certain "reservations" over the scientific validity of the results obtained in chapters 3 and 4. More precisely, to argue that it could have been different, had the authors introduced additional distinctions (e.g. specialists vs. general practitioners) in their analysis of the data: i.e. *different classifications*. In this respect, Friedman's methodological theses on prediction as the real mark of value-free science fail to provide an adequate defense against objections over the possibility of manipulating the classification of the data according to the particular predictions you want to derive therefrom. How much *precision and conformity with our experience* should a prediction render to rule out any possible bias?

Friedman was obviously not unaware of this particular bias – Ronald Fisher himself had the occasion to warn him when the Friedmans visited him in Cambridge, just a year after the publication of F53 (Friedman and Friedman 1998, 244). We may wonder why he left this objection unanswered. For the moment, the only available clue is the one provided by Rose Director Friedman:

> I have always been impressed by the ability to predict an economist's positive views from my knowledge of his political orientation, and I have never been able to persuade myself that the political orientation was the consequence of the positive views. My husband continues to resist this conclusion, no doubt because of his unwillingness to believe that his own positive views can be so explained and his characteristic generosity in being unwilling to attribute different motives to others than to himself. (Friedman and Friedman 1998, 218–19)

That is to say, a principle of mutual methodological trust, which "like most ideals" is "often honored in the breach" (Friedman 1967, 5). In the end, the production of positive predictions of political use would require a sort of tacit normative commitment on the part of the economist: "to serve the public interest," albeit self-interestedly (Friedman 1986, 9). The obvious question is *why*? A tacit consensus may have still existed early in the 1950s among a cohort of American economists who had been attracted to the profession in the lower reaches of a big depression, to be subsequently recruited by the government to fight it (Friedman and Friedman 1998, 34). However, it is dubious whether this consensus still exists today. As we pointed out in section 2, Friedman's claim was quite the opposite: consensus on the best economic policy available, both among professionals and general audiences, was to be grounded on predictions, so that its normative neutrality should be guaranteed right from the beginning. If we still expect economics to play such a consensual role in our public sphere, we should somehow restate this previous tacit consensus among the profession.[12] A reexamination of F53 in a contractarian light might provide several clues to achieving it.

4   Making the contract explicit

Let us then reason *as if*. What if we reread Friedman's methodological case as if it were a plea addressed to his fellow economists in order to gain the trust of the public opinion on the results attained by the profession? The problem would then center around how economists can signal to their lay fellow citizens that the advice provided by the former is scientifically sound. Stated in terms of the economics of information, Friedman's plea may be thus restated as the economists' part in *a contract* (as "agents") with the *consumers* of their science (the "principals"). The parties to the contract find themselves in an *asymmetrical* situation: those who produce knowledge can better judge the true quality of their output (or their own capabilities as producers) than those who consume it. Therefore, the demanders' desideratum would be that the contract be designed in such a way as to oblige the suppliers to work efficiently in the production of items (of knowledge) having the highest possible utility for them.

The principals' main difficulty is that they are often incapable of controlling by themselves whether the contract is being complied with by the agents or not, or to what extent it is. Even more, they are unable to design by their own means something like an "optimum" contract: ironically, the principals would perhaps need to hire an economist to design an optimum contract for them. Due to the inability of the scientists to gain the trust of the principals, the former would be forced to set up the contract as an agreement *among themselves*, which would serve as the *constitution* of their discipline. Under its rule, the consensus they reach and/or their past technical success would do as *signals* of epistemic quality. However, this also opens the door for *moral hazard* problems: since the consensus among experts is the only signal that users may often have of the quality of researchers or of the "knowledge" produced by them, the losers in the race for a discovery could simply deny that real knowledge has been attained by other colleagues, preventing as a result the constitution of that consensus.

As we saw in section 2, throughout the 1930s and the 1940s, Friedman often found himself acting as an agent for many different principals: first as a member of the NRC task force researching consumer incomes and expenditures for the Roosevelt administration and later as the *Principal*

---

[12] For further details about our discussion of Friedman's methodology, see Teira 2004.

economist at the Treasury's division of tax research. It may be said that in this case the principal's trust in the use of statistical economics had already been gained at least a decade before Friedman came to Washington – for example, during the Hoover administration (cf. Barber 1985, 8–9). However, as we pointed out before, different views on the political use of statistical economics were in dispute among the profession in the early 1930s, a debate which was not completely closed by the time the AEA commission addressed the problem of economic instability late in the 1940s. The fact that Roosevelt could have initially ignored Keynes himself may indicate that choosing the *right* economist was still difficult, and the disagreement among the profession certainly did not contribute to simplify the choice. Both the AEA report and Friedman's parallel paper coincided in the need for a professional consensus that ensured that the best policy could be implemented. Furthermore, Friedman was arguing for a particular procedure to reach it, i.e. judging each alternative according to its predictive reliability. His 1953 proposal of a *methodological constitution* for the economic profession took this rule as its cornerstone. Once this rule was adopted, economics would turn into a positive endeavor – in our terms, a trustworthy alternative for every principal.

A contractarian assessment of Friedman's proposal requires further refinements of our notion of a "social scientific contract." Basically, the aim of such a contract is to render compatible, on the one hand, the incentives of the people supporting scientific research (i.e. the desire for *useful* knowledge), and, on the other, the incentives of researchers themselves. These are generally considered to be seeking recognition in return for their discoveries, as well as for other sorts of privileges that may result therefrom. There are two possible sources of divergence between the researchers' interests and those of their "customers": first, it may be that the opportunity arises for the scientist to obtain recognition without producing real discoveries; second, their research domains may be really worthless for the customers. But the incentives of the researchers themselves may also be in mutual conflict, not only because of the competition to attain better results, but also because scientists may simply opt for denying public recognition to their *rivals* even when they believe that they really deserve it. A well-designed social scientific contract is, then, a set of *norms* that make researchers behave in an "honest" way toward those who support the production of science (producing useful knowledge) and toward their colleagues (e.g. acknowledging their discoveries when appropriate). Though different scientific communities or schools may have different "social contracts," their essential and common elements should be the following ones:

(a) A set of *methodological rules*, determining which actions (in particular, which assertions) a researcher is entitled or committed to perform; these norms are of an *inferential* nature, since they connect the previous entitlements and commitments of a researcher with a specific action which can be seen as their "consequence." Needless to say, this type of norms has been the main traditional topic of the philosophy of science.

(b) A set of *scoring rules*, which, formally understood, is a function transforming the entitlements and commitments acquired by a researcher into *publicly expressed "scientific merit"* (or his/her "score"); these norms serve basically to define the *significance* of a scientific item as well as the *competence* of a researcher.

(c) Lastly, a set of *resource allocation rules*, which determine what and how many scientific resources are to be apportioned to a researcher according to his or her absolute or relative merit; violations of these rules can also modify a researcher's score if he or she is considered responsible for the misallocation.

Traditional views of the "social contract" of science initially had an almost absolutely naive conception of the second and third types of rules. As to the former, it was assumed that scientists could be relied on to assess the score of their colleagues; concerning the latter, the deference of the public toward the scientists' decision about what projects deserved to be funded was simply presupposed. Friedman was probably not far from sharing this "positivist" view (cf. Friedman 1986, 8). However, after the social turn in science studies, trust in science seems to require an explicit commitment to scoring and allocation rules, if scientists and non-scientists are to reach a reasonably efficient and self-supporting equilibrium in the game of science.

In this respect, the conclusions of section 2 seem devastating. It may happen, for instance, that a *quack* succeeded in deceiving public opinion by producing apparently good, yet theoretically irrelevant predictions (Friedman 1991, 36). If scoring rules existed, scientific economists would penalize the deceiver, but that would require in turn that a clear standard to assess predictions were settled. After our discussion in section 2, we know that there is no such standard. Friedman seems rather to opt for relying exclusively on the personal integrity of each economist in producing predictions, on a purely reciprocal basis. As for the orientation of lay audiences in funding economic research, Friedman seems to doubt its very possibility,[13] his previous methodological plea notwithstanding.

---

[13] E.g.: "There is no satisfactory solution to the dilemma posed by the propositions: (1) there is a body of 'positive' economics that can yield reliable predictions of the consequences of change; (2) there are 'experts' in positive economics; (3) differences about the desirability

5   Friedman rewritten?

Fortunately, other methodologists are now facing this challenge. By way of example and conclusion, we would like to transcribe here a singular piece we came across while surfing the internet some time ago. The article, signed by a certain Pierre Menard, was posted on an old site on Friedman, no longer active – as a matter of fact, the domain was canceled soon afterwards, and replaced by the following: www.coldbacon.com/writing/borges-quixote.html. However, it deserves attention from a contractarian viewpoint, as it rewrites a substantial part of Friedman's 1953 paper in precisely the spirit of our reconstruction. *Stat rosa pristina nomine…*

The economics of a positivist methodology

1.   The relation between positive and normative economics   Confusion between positive and normative economics is to some extent inevitable. The subject matter of economics is regarded by almost everyone as vitally important to himself and within the range of his own experience and competence; it is the source of continuous and extensive controversy and the occasion for frequent legislation. Self-proclaimed "experts" speak with many voices and can hardly all be regarded as disinterested. The conclusions of positive economics seem to be, and are, immediately relevant to important normative problems, to questions of what ought to be done and how any given goal can be attained. Laymen and experts alike are inevitably tempted to shape positive conclusions to fit strongly held normative preconceptions and to reject positive conclusions if their normative implications – or what are said to be their normative implications – are unpalatable.

It seems that positive economics should in principle be independent of any particular ethical position or normative judgments, for it deals with "what is," not with "what ought to be." Its task, it has been sometimes argued, is to provide a system of generalizations that can be used to make correct predictions about the consequences of any change in circumstances, and so, its performance should be judged by the precision, scope, and conformity with experience of the predictions it yields. In short, positive economics should be an "objective" science, in precisely the same sense as the physical sciences are assumed to be. Of course, the

of governmental policies often reflect different beliefs about the consequences of the policies – conclusions of positive economics – rather than different values; (4) there is no simple litmus test by which a citizen can decide who is an 'expert' and who is a 'quack'; yet (5) even though the patient is incompetent to choose the physician, there is no alternative in a free society." (Friedman 1975, p. x).

fact that economics deals with the interrelations of human beings, and that the investigator is himself part of the subject matter being investigated in a more intimate sense than in the physical sciences, raises special difficulties in achieving objectivity at the same time that it provides the social scientist with a class of data not available to the physical scientist. But, after all, surely neither the one nor the other makes a fundamental distinction between the goals and methods of the two groups of sciences.

More importantly, normative economics cannot be independent of positive economics. Any policy conclusion necessarily rests on a prediction about the consequences of doing one thing rather than another, a prediction that must be based on positive economics. Governments wanting to improve the living conditions of their citizens, or wanting at least to maximize the chances of being re-elected by favoring a majority of their constituency, need to be confident about the likely consequences of the policies that "experts" are recommending. It is then both in the interest of the economist and of the politician to have a corpus of substantive hypotheses that are successful when judged by its predictive power. On this basis, the judgment has been ventured that currently in the Western world differences about economic policy among citizens who try to be disinterested derive predominantly from different predictions about the economic consequences of taking action – differences that could perhaps be eliminated by the progress of positive economics – rather than from fundamental differences in basic values, differences about which individuals ultimately face a choice between fighting or showing tolerance. For example, in the debate about the so called "basic income," no one seems to deny that the ultimate goal is to attain an acceptable standard of living for all, but strong differences arise when predictions on whether this goal would be attained or not with the application of that policy, and at what costs, begin to be drawn. The same takes place in numerous other examples. Hence, the argument follows, achieving consensus about the relevant consequences of each economic policy would reduce to a high extent the dissensus existing about alternative courses of political action.

This is, of course, a "positive" statement to be accepted or rejected just on the basis of empirical evidence, but this evidence could only be achieved if positive economics "advanced" as much as to generate a degree of consensus on empirical predictions much higher than what has been attained until now. On the other hand, an apparent consensus about economic predictions can derive either from an "appropriate" scientific methodology, or from any political strategy to silence those making different predictions, and the same dilemma arises regarding a possible consensus about the normative implications of those predictions. If this judgment is valid, it means that the normative relevance of positive economics (i.e. the usefulness of its empirical predictions for the fostering of our social values) can only be assessed through an analysis of the conditions under which economic "knowledge" is generated, discussed, and applied, in order to understand whether the *actual* conditions can be expected to generate a corpus of predictively useful generalizations about economic phenomena, or whether some amendments of those conditions are both desirable and feasible.

2.　　　*Positivist economics*　Any normative judgment presupposes some particular values, for there is no such thing as an absolutely impartial evaluation. When we describe someone as "disinterested," we simply mean that, in the assessment of positive as well as of normative propositions, he is adopting a *moral* perspective which does not only take into account his own private interest and opinions, but also the welfare and the opinions of other people. However, since different individuals may obviously have different moral values, the judgments of "disinterested" evaluators need not coincide, although a higher degree of agreement can be expected than in the case of "interested" agents. The first essential point in making any normative pronouncement as "experts" is, then, to openly declare the moral values which underlie that judgment. In the argument elaborated here, these values reduce to the following: *the point of view that must be adopted in order to evaluate the methodological practices of economists is essentially the point of view of the citizens.* After all, policy-makers have to use the best available economic knowledge in order to promote the welfare of the members of the political community. Under a democratic regime, this demand transforms easily into a necessity, for those parties most capable of putting into use the "right" economic knowledge will tend to be the winners in the political competition. The task left for us, economists, is then that of "supplying" those theories, models or hypotheses which can be most efficient in the formulation of "right" economic policies, i.e. policies that *actually* promote the interests of the citizens of a democratic society.

As a methodological ideal, the positivist conception of science is certainly more appropriate for orienting the practice of economics toward that goal than the methods which, according to a common interpretation, are customarily employed in our discipline. Committing surely a blatant oversimplification, current economics is usually described as divided into two camps: on the one hand, "mainstream" economics would basically be organized as a kind of disguised mathematics, in which the production of *theorems* is seen as a much more important and praiseworthy job than the discovery of *regularities* about the empirical world. Of course, the formal models those theorems are about are usually devised as abstract representations of possible economic circumstances, but not much effort is put – the criticism follows – into discussing how one can know whether a concrete empirical situation is better represented by means of a specific formal model or by a different one. So, the practical usefulness of this model-building activity is in general rather low, save perhaps in producing Nobel Prize winners. On the other hand, a heterogeneous bunch of "heterodox" approaches would permanently complain about the lack of "realism" of the models produced by mainstream economists; unfortunately, the positive contributions of these critical schools consist either in mere descriptive explorations of the "ontology" to which the orthodox models fail to respond, or in the development of formal models presumably more "realistic" but in the end no more efficient in the discovery of true empirical regularities.

From a positivist point of view, the common mistake of these two approaches, at least in their unadulterated forms, would be the presumption that *truth* is the basic value of scientific research, instead of *predictive capacity*. Mathematical economists glorify theorems because, as purely formal statements, these are necessarily true, whereas heterodox economists criticize the models from which those theorems are derived because their assumptions are clamorously false. But, clearly, what makes a theorem an interesting one is not just its truth, for all of them are equally true but not equally relevant, and likewise, the practical relevance of a model does not depend on the realism of its assumptions, but only on the accuracy of its empirical predictions.

In general, economists, lacking the capacity to experiment with most of the parcels of reality they study, have traditionally developed a method which is based on introspection and casual observation for guaranteeing the truth of the *premises* from which their argument starts, and on logico-mathematical deduction for guaranteeing that those arguments are truth-preserving, and hence, that their *conclusions* are also true. But we may doubt that, from the point of view of practical relevance, this strategy is optimal. For, in order to successfully apply economic knowledge to reality, the empirical accuracy of the conclusions is much more important than the descriptive truth of the premises, and hence, a theory with false assumptions (such as simplifications and idealizations) but from which many accurate conclusions follow is much more useful than a theory with only true axioms but from which just a couple of trivialities can be derived, even if the first theory has a few false empirical implications as well.

Truly important and significant hypotheses will be found to have "assumptions" that are wildly inaccurate descriptive representations of reality, for a hypothesis is significant if it "explains" much by little, that is, if it abstracts the common and crucial elements from the mass of complex and detailed circumstances around the phenomena to be explained and permits valid predictions on the basis of them alone. In general, both the process of abstraction (for constructing hypotheses) and the process of prediction (for testing their validity) demand that the theory is mathematically well organized. Mathematization is just an economical tool for achieving a great deductive power with a tractable set of premises; it must not be pursued for its own sake, and less still has it to be hoisted as the dominant criterion for judging the validity of an economic theory. In the end, predictive success must be the ultimate criterion, if economics wants to become a socially relevant discipline.

Of course, all this does not mean that political pressures must be the exclusive, or even the most important guide of economic research. As in any other field of science, sheer curiosity is often the most powerful stimulus toward discovery. The truly significant point is that the method employed for selecting the "best" theories or models, even if this selection is carried out with no interference from politics, should favor those hypotheses with the highest predictive success. Only if economists follow this "positivist" method will they advance toward the ultimate *practical* goal of their science, which is the development of a theory that yields valid and meaningful (i.e. not truistic) predictions about phenomena not yet observed, and will they also satisfy their *intellectual* desire of revealing how superficially disconnected and diverse phenomena are manifestations of a more fundamental and relatively simple structure.

3.   *Some implications for an economics of economics*   The abstract methodological issues we have been discussing in the past section serve to describe the ideal form economic knowledge should have, "ideal" from the point of view of the common citizens, who, in a sense or another, are supporting economic research. We have referred in passing to some ways economics is usually practiced, which, all our gross simplifications considered, do not seem to correspond to this ideal. We have not examined to what extent the spread of these "wrong" economic methods depend on the specific academic organization of inquiry within the field of economics. Perhaps all intellectual practices have some kind of "internal life" which makes some ideas grow no matter what the institutional setting where they disseminate is. Indeed, past proponents of a positivist method for economics have put the question as if all that mattered were the *logical persuasiveness* of their proposals, and not so much the *interests* of the people which the proposals affect. In this sense, they have actually preached with the voice of the methodologist, rather than from the attitude of a "positivist economist" like the one they pretended to be.

However, the assumption of single-minded pursuit of self-interest by individuals in competitive "industries" (and the academia can be taken to be such an "industry") has worked very well in a wide variety of hypotheses, and it is therefore likely to seem reasonable to us, economists, that it may work in this case as well. The epistemologist or methodologist, on the other hand, is accustomed to a very different kind of model for explaining the spread and the working of scientific ideas, in part because he uses a different body of indirect evidence (the "logical connections" between ideas, rather than the phenomena of interdependent choice economics is usually about), but of course, neither the evidence of the economist nor that of the epistemologist is conclusive: the decisive test of any hypothesis is just whether it works for the phenomena it purports to explain. So, I propose to analyze the question about the means to establish an "optimum" economic method from the point of view of economic theory itself.

Seen from this economic viewpoint, a fundamental problem for the instauration of an appropriate economic method is that of *asymmetric information*: the people for whom the "right" method is appropriate (the citizens) are not those who can better appreciate what the power of each alternative method is (the economists). The desideratum for the demanders of economic knowledge (the citizens/principals) would be that of designing a contract so that the suppliers (the economists/agents) worked efficiently in the production of items of knowledge having the highest possible utility for the former. The principals' main difficulty, however, is that they often cannot control by themselves whether the contract is being obeyed by the agents or not, and usually they even ignore the issue of how to design something like an "optimum" contract; they have trusted some economists to design it, and this clearly leads to a vicious circle, for how are we to know who are the "good" economists in the first place?

We also need to take into account the fact that the citizens/principals do not form a homogeneous group: a few of them have much more political power than the rest, and all have interests, values, and beliefs that are in conflict with those of many others. Therefore, *collective action* problems arise as well. For example, perhaps the people who had the capacity to enforce an "optimal" contract in economics would prefer that no real empirical progress were made in this field, in order to keep using the aura of mathematical certainty of some branches of economics to justify before the public some policies designed to favor the most privileged. This possibility – well documented in the history of our discipline – and in general the plurality of interests existing within our societies, suggests that this plurality should be somehow reflected within the "optimal" contract.

In this situation, the economists/agents are forced, if they want to gain the principals' trust, to establish the contract as an agreement among themselves, as a *"disciplinary contract,"* so to speak, and to use this consensus as a "signal" of the quality of their "output." Unfortunately, this also opens the door for "moral hazard" problems: since the consensus among experts is often the only signal that users may have of the quality of a researcher or of the "knowledge" produced by her, the losers in the race for a discovery could simply deny that real knowledge has been attained by other colleagues, preventing as a result the constitution of that consensus. The possibility also exists that a majority of the agents "sign" a contract which is efficient for them, but not for the citizens. In principle, the interests of the economists may be incompatible with those of the citizens for two reasons at least: first, scientists may sometimes have an opportunity to attain their goals without producing real discoveries (for example, by inventing their data), and second, they can devote their effort to fields or problems which are of no obvious value for the people supporting science (for example, by looking just for "elegant" equilibrium solutions). The "disciplinary contract" of scientific research has to be seen, then, as a set of *norms* which would ideally make researchers behave in an "honest" way toward the citizens (producing useful knowledge) and toward their colleagues (e.g. acknowledging their discoveries when it is "due").

I want to suggest that a good task for future economists will be to devise some alternative, hypothetical "disciplinary contracts" for the practice of economics, exploring their properties both analytically (by way of game theory, economics of information, social and public choice, etc.) and, as far as possible, empirically (by way of institutional and experimental economics, as well as history of economics), and subjecting these proposals to serious discussion and criticism not only by the economists themselves, but also by political or civilian organizations. To some extent, the result of this discussion would count as an empirical test of the *positive* predictions of those hypothetical contracts about the *normative* judgments they would induce. Many economists will certainly doubt that this task is necessary at all, for they are persuaded that, in the long run, academic competition leads by itself to the adoption of a "right" disciplinary contract, as much as political competition tends to select those parties who choose the "right" economic advisers. But the progress experienced during the last fifty years in our knowledge of how to efficiently solve people's main economic problems has been so tiny, and the reasons are so clear – namely that, realistically, both academic and political competition can lead to stagnation rather than to progress – that it would be worth the effort to devise a new disciplinary contract for economics.

P. Menard

References

Armatte, M. (1995). Histoire du modèle linéaire. Formes et usages en statistique et économétrie jusqu'en 1945. Unpublished doctoral dissertation, EHESS

Balisciano, Márcia L. (1998). Hope for America: American notions of economic planning between pluralism and neoclassicism, 1930–1950. In Mary S. Morgan and Malcolm Rutherford (eds.), *From Interwar Pluralism to Postwar Neoclassicism*, annual supplement to *History of Political Economy*, 30. Durham, NC: Duke University Press

Barber, W. J. (1985). *From New Era to New Deal. Herbert Hoover, the Economists, and American Economic Policy, 1921–1933*. New York: Cambridge University Press

Bloor, D. (1982). Durkheim and Mauss revisited: classifications and the sociology of knowledge. *Studies in History and Philosophy of Science*, 13(4), 267–97

Brinkley, A. (1995). *The End of Reform: New Deal Liberalism in Recession and War*. New York: Vintage Books

Despres, E., M. Friedman, A. Hart, P. Samuelson, and D. Wallace (1950). The problem of economic instability. *American Economic Review*, 40, 505–38

Desrosières, A., E. Lie, M. Mespoullet, and E. Didier (2001). *Sampling Humans*. Berlin, Max-Planck-Institut für Wissenschaftsgeschichte

Duncan, J. and W. Shelton (1992). US government contributions to probability sampling and statistical analysis. *Statistical Science*, 7(3), 320–38

Friedman, Milton (1946). Lange on price flexibility and employment. *American Economic Review*, 36, 613–31. Reprinted in *Essays in Positive Economics* (1953a)

   (1947). Lerner on the economics of control, *Journal of Political Economy*, 55, 405–16. Reprinted in *Essays in Positive Economics* (1953a)

   (1948). A monetary and fiscal framework for economic stability. *American Economic Review*, 38, 245–64. Reprinted in *Essays in Positive Economics* (1953a)

   (1949). "Rejoinder" to "Professor Friedman's proposal": comment. *American Economic Review*, 39, 949–55

   (1951). The effects of a full-employment policy on economic stability: a formal analysis. Reprinted in *Essays in Positive Economics* (1953a)

   (1953a). *Essays in Positive Economics*. Chicago: University of Chicago Press

   (1953b). The methodology of positive economics. In *Essays in Positive Economics*. Chicago: University of Chicago Press, 3–43

   (1975). *There's No Such Thing as a Free Lunch*. LaSalle, IL: Open Court Publishing Co.

   (1967). Value judgments in economics. In S. Hook, *Human Values and Economic Policy*. New York: New York University Press, 85–93. Reprinted in K. Leube (ed.), *The Essential Friedman*. Stanford: Hoover Institution, 3–8

   (1986). Economists and economic policy. *Economic Inquiry*, 24(1), 1–10

   (1991). Old wine in new bottles. *The Economic Journal*, 101, 33–40

   (1992). Do old fallacies ever die? *Journal of Economic Literature*, 30, 2129–32

Friedman, Milton and Rose Friedman (1998). *Two Lucky People. Memoirs*. Chicago: University of Chicago Press

Friedman, Milton and Simon Kuznets (1945). *Income from Independent Professional Practice*. New York: National Bureau of Economic Research

Hammond, J. Daniel (1993). An interview with Milton Friedman on methodology. In Bruce C. Caldwell (ed.), *The Philosophy and Methodology of Economics*, vol. 1. Aldershot: Edward Elgar, 216–38

Hotelling, H. (1940). The teaching of statistics. *Annals of Mathematical Statistics*. 11, 457–71

Hotelling, H., W. Bartky, W. E. Deming, M. Friedman, and P. Hoel (1948). The teaching of statistics [a report of the Institute of Mathematical Statistics committee on the teaching of statistics]. *Annals of Mathematical Statistics*, 19, 95–115

Kneeland, H., E. Schoenberg, and M. Friedman (1936). Plans for a study of the consumption of goods and services by American families. *Journal of the American Statistical Association*, 31, 135–40

Knight, F. H. (1924). The limitations of scientific method in economics. In R. Tugwell, (ed.), *The Trend in Economics*. New York: Alfred A. Knopf, 229–67. Reprinted in F. Knight (1935), *The Ethics of Competition and Other Essays*. New York and London: Harper & Brothers, 105–47

 (1932). The newer economics and the control of economic activity. *Journal of Political Economy*, 40(4), 433–76

 (1991). The case for communism: from the standpoint of an ex-liberal. In W. J. Samuels, (ed.), *Research in the History of Economic Thought and Methodology [Archival Supplement]*. Greenwich, CT: JAI Press, 57–108

Mirowski, Philip (1989). *More Heat Than Light: Economics as Social Physics*. New York: Cambridge University Press

National Resources Committee (1938). *Consumer Incomes in the United States*. Washington, DC: United States Government Printing Office

 (1939). *Consumer Expenditures in the United States*. Washington, DC: United States Government Printing Office

Neyman, J. (1938). Contribution to the theory of sampling human populations. *Journal of the American Statistical Association*, 33, 101–16. Reprinted in *A Selection of Early Statistical Papers of J. Neyman*. Cambridge: Cambridge University Press, 1967

Olkin, I. (1991). A conversation with W. Allen Wallis. *Statistical Science*, 6(2), 121–40

Pradier, P. C. and D. Teira (2000). Frank Knight: le risque comme critique de l'économie politique. *Revue de Synthèse*, 121(4), 79–116

 (2002). Frank Knight y los positivistas. In Wenceslao González *et al.* (eds.), *Enfoques filosófico-metodológicos en economía*. Madrid: FCE, 107–41

Reid, Constance (1998). *Neyman – from Life*. New York: Springer Verlag

Schoenberg, E. and M. Parten (1937). Methods and problems of sampling presented by the urban study of consumer purchases. *Journal of the American Statistical Association*, 32, 311–22

Seng, Y. P. (1951). Historical survey of the development of sampling theory and practice. *Journal of the Royal Statistical Society*, 114, 214–31

Shoup, C. S., M. Friedman, and R. P. Mack (1943). *Taxing to prevent inflation; techniques for estimating revenue requirements*. New York: Columbia University Press

Stigler, S. (1994). Some correspondence on methodology between Milton Friedman and Edwin B. Wilson. *Journal of Economic Literature*. 32, 1197–203

(1996). The history of statistics in 1933. *Statistical Science*, 11(3), 244–52

Teira, David (2004). Azar, economía y política en Milton Friedman. *Biblioteca Virtual Miguel de Cervantes*, Alicante

(2007). Milton Friedman, the statistical methodologist. *History of Political Economy*, 39(3), 511–28

Tugewell, R. (1932). The principle of planning and the institution of laissez faire. *American Economic Review*, 22(1), 75–92

Wallis, W. A. and M. Friedman (1942). The empirical derivation of indifference functions. In O. Lange *et al.* (eds.), *Studies in Mathematical Economics and Econometrics*. Chicago: University of Chicago Press, 175–8

Wallis, W. A. and H. V. Roberts (1956) *Statistics – a New Approach*. New York: Free Press

Zamora Bonilla, J. (2002). Scientific inference and the pursuit of fame: a contractarian approach. *Philosophy of Science*, 69, 300–3

Part 4

Theoretical context: firm, money, expected utility,
Walras and Marshall

Roger E. Backhouse

1 Introduction

The marginalist controversy of the 1940s was arguably one of the debates through which modern microeconomic theory – that underlying Paul Samuelson's "neoclassical synthesis" – was established (Backhouse 2003). Milton Friedman's "The methodology of positive economics" (1953)[1] played a major role in the resolution of that controversy and many of the ideas on which the essay was based arose out of it. The marginalist controversy, narrowly defined, took place in 1946–7, sparked by the challenge to marginal theory made by Richard Lester, a labor economist. Section 2 outlines this controversy, picking out aspects that are relevant to understanding Friedman's essay. However, this controversy formed part of a much broader, more complicated debate over price theory and the theory of the firm, drawing on and responding to the "full-cost pricing" debates of the 1930s (see Lee 1984; Lee and Irving-Lessman 1992; Mongin 1992; Hausman and Mongin 1997). It also fed into further debates on the theory of the firm that took place in the first half of the 1950s. These are discussed in sections 3 to 5. Section 6 then considers the way in which Friedman responded to the challenge posed by this controversy, drawing on his correspondence with Don Patinkin over the period 1948 to 1950. This leads, in section 7, into a discussion of F53 in relation to these controversies.

2 The marginalist controversy of 1946–7

Lester (1946) approached the subject of marginalism as a labor economist aware of a large gap between the way the labor market was treated in price theory and in macroeconomics.[2] In the former, labor demand depended on the wage rate and the marginal product of labor but in the latter it was

---

[1] Referred to simply as F53 from now on.
[2] It has been argued that labor economics remains a more empirical field than many others in economics. See Oswald and Trostel (2000).

determined by the level of aggregate demand. Lester sought to bridge this gap by drawing together a wide variety of evidence on the way the labor market worked. He started his article by drawing attention to question-naire evidence that businessmen saw output as more important than wage rates in their employment decisions. However, this was arguably the least important amongst the pieces of evidence that he cited. (1) He cited a wide variety of evidence showing that average variable cost decreased up to full capacity, after which it rose very sharply. (2) The Oxford econo-mists had established that businessmen were ignorant of the elasticity of demand. (3) Because wage rates differed across regions in the USA, the imposition of minimum wages after 1939 had caused wages to rise diffe-rently in different industries. Lester found that, where wages had risen most, so too had employment. Minimum wages had not had the effect on employment that marginalist theory predicted. (4) He asked businessmen how they would respond to rises in wages (a phenomenon of which they had recent experience), finding that employment would not be reduced: instead, firms would improve efficiency, introduce labor-saving machi-nery, and increase their sales effort. His conclusion was that, for a wide variety of reasons, businessmen did not adjust employment in relation to wages and productivity in the way that marginal theory required.

The challenge to marginalist theory was taken up by Machlup (1946), the source of some of the arguments in F53. However, Machlup's article was much more than a response to Lester: it was a wide-ranging defense of marginalism and an attack on the empirical research that had been undertaken to refute it. He sought to clarify the meaning of marginalist theory, which he claimed was much misunderstood, and he criticized both Lester's questionnaire evidence and his statistics. Differences between economists' and accountants' language meant that detailed interviews were needed to back up questionnaires and to probe the possibility that ethical beliefs or the law influenced the way in which businessmen rationalized their output decisions. Statistical work on the relationship between wage rates and employment was "nearly useless" because "we have no way of eliminating the simultaneous effects of several other significant variables, especially those of a psychological nature" (Machlup 1946, 548).

Lester (1947) chose to reply to Machlup and to Stigler (1947), on minimum wage rates, eliciting rejoinders from both of them. Beyond this, Lester did not respond, though his position was defended against Machlup and Stigler by Oliver (1947). One of the things revealed by Lester's reply is the extent to which he believed that theory should be empirically based.

At the heart of economic theory should be an adequate analysis and understanding of the psychology, policies and practices of business management in modern industry. (Lester 1947, 146)

Awareness of institutional differences led him to criticize marginalists for treating all markets as though they were the same.

Reasoning about labor markets as though they were commodity markets seems to be an important explanation for erroneous conclusions on such matters as minimum wages. (Lester 1947, 146)

This was in complete contrast to the view expressed by Machlup (1947, 519).

Economics in a narrow sense is confined to such aspects of conduct as can be explained with reference to the principles of maximizing satisfaction, income, or profit. Under definitions of this sort any deviations from the marginal principle would be extra-economic.

It is impossible to imagine Lester making such a remark. For Machlup, it clearly established the presumption that maximizing behavior should be assumed unless there were overwhelming evidence that a phenomenon could not be explained in this way. In contrast, Oliver (1947, 379), supporting Lester, suggested that normal rules of debate implied that,

if business men *say* that they think in average-cost terms, then, if the burden of proof rests on anyone at all (and it should not in economic discussion), it rests on the marginalists who do not believe the business man, rather than on the economic iconoclasts who (with modifications of varying importance) take him at his word.

Oliver provided a list of phenomena that, he claimed, were inconsistent with marginalism and argued that the onus was on marginalists to provide evidence that was consistent with their theory and not with any other. Lester emphasized the quality of his evidence: he claimed that his questionnaire results were replicable, that results could be cross-checked and that they could be tested against other studies. Machlup, he contended, argued for a subjective interpretation of profit maximization (maximization given perceptions of costs and revenues) but when it was shown that businessmen did not think this way, he disputed the evidence as inconsistent with his prior beliefs.

Lester's empiricism also emerged in his exchange with Stigler. His main criticism of Stigler's analysis was that he did not understand how wages were determined, how labor markets operated, or how business decisions were made (Lester 1947, 142). Stigler had ignored the "wealth of experience with minimum-wage laws" over thirty or forty years, giving his paper "a pre-World War I flavor" (Lester 1947, 143). Lester, supported by Oliver, was thus arguing that theories should, somehow, be testable and that they should be tested. Their contention was that Machlup was defending marginalism by interpreting it so broadly that it was irrefutable, and that Stigler was simply ignoring evidence.

Stigler (1947, 154–5) accused Lester of being confused about what he meant by marginal analysis. Did he mean that the logical structure of "formal theory" was invalid, or did he just question the theory's empirical content? Use of the phrase "marginal analysis," he contended, suggested the former. More serious (given that any reader of Lester would know he was criticizing the empirical relevance of marginalism) was a confusion over whether or not perfect competition was being assumed. Stigler (1947, 155) took Lester to task for claiming that marginal productivity theory depended on the assumptions that agents were price-takers and that monopoly power was absent. Yet, rather than citing Robinson (1933) or Chamberlin (1933), surely standard works by that time, to draw attention to the issue of imperfect competition, he poured scorn on Lester for criticizing the "stupid assumption," that no economist had ever held, that an employer in an imperfect market would reduce his price to increase his sales if it increased his short-run profit. The result was that the issues of profit maximization and perfect competition were not clearly distinguished.

This exchange provides the immediate background to F53, which later took up several of Machlup's arguments. Though it concerned the relevance of profit maximization, many other issues were involved, such as attitudes toward imperfect competition and the criteria by which theories should be appraised. These can be understood only by considering earlier debates. Because of their variety, they have to be considered separately, though there were, of course overlaps.

3   The Cambridge and Harvard responses to Marshall

To understand developments in the theory of the firm and market structure from the 1920s to the 1950s, it is essential to start with Alfred Marshall's theory, as developed in his *Principles of Economics* ([1890] 1920) and *Industry and Trade* (1919).[3] The most important feature of his theory was that it was *not* an equilibrium theory: it was an attempt to analyze a world in which technical progress led to continuous change; in which knowledge was limited and organizational forms were changing (see Raffaelli 2003, 2004). He criticized the use of static mechanical analogies, preferring the use of biological ones, such as that of the trees

---

[3] O'Brien (1984) provides the best discussion of this. See also O'Brien (1983 and 1990).

in the forest. Every tree in a forest was changing, but the forest might remain the same (cf. Marshall [1898] 1925).

Confusion has arisen because although Marshall used mathematical arguments, he did not confine himself to things that he could express using mathematics. "Exact but limited knowledge" needed to be "combined with broader estimates that rest on uncertain foundations" (Marshall 1919, 676). He drew an analogy with navigating a ship in waters with uncertain currents: knowing the ship's precise location was impossible, but it was important to ensure that further errors were not introduced. In his theory of the firm and the market, profit maximization provided the exact theory of the firm, and competitive supply and demand provided the theory of price. However, these did not constitute his theory, for they were merely the skeleton around which he hung a more realistic theory that encompassed many factors that were not covered by the mathematics. On the demand side, these factors included changes in human character; on the supply side, the effects of time, imperfect knowledge, technical change, and pricing policy.

Marshall's firms were unable to sell as much as they wished at the prevailing market price (competition was not perfect) but neither did they face a given demand curve: they engaged in marketing, which might account for a large proportion of total costs and of capital, and they might use temporary price cuts as a way to shift the demand curve outwards. Increasing returns to scale were widespread and were hard to distinguish from technical progress: returns to scale might not be reversible, with the result that cost curves depended on time as well as on output. In addition, firms were continuously evolving, changing the way they were organized and the shape of their cost curves. Even if the industry were in equilibrium (in the sense that its price and output were not changing) individual firms would typically not be in equilibrium: they would be entering, exiting, and changing the scale of their operations. The representative firm was not the average firm but the firm that was relevant in a particular context. Supply and demand were used as conceptual tools even though Marshall did not confine himself to competitive equilibrium analysis. For Marshall (1919, 512), "general propositions in regard to either competition or monopoly are full of snares": the most extreme forms of competition aimed to undermine competition and had to be restrained.

Faced with Marshall's industrial analysis, economists moved, during the 1920s and 1930s, in different directions. Though the labels are an oversimplification, the main ones that need to be considered can be called the Cambridge, Harvard, institutionalist, and Oxford approaches. There were also many other writers whose work fits into none of these categories, such as Friedrich Hayek, John Hicks, or Fritz Machlup.[4] In brief, the Cambridge approach was to develop a static equilibrium theory that eliminated the inconsistencies that Marshall's theory was perceived to contain. The Harvard approach was also to develop equilibrium theory, though in a more Marshallian way, taking account of industrial developments that were less important when Marshall wrote his *Principles*. The institutionalist and Oxford approaches involved collecting evidence on short-run price-setting behavior and building theories that might account for this behavior. Though it is the non-marginalist theories developed by the last two groups that formed the immediate background to the Lester–Machlup–Stigler exchange, to understand the controversy and Friedman's response to it, it is important to realize that at least four approaches to the firm and market structure were being debated.

The Cambridge approach was rooted in the so-called "cost controversy" of the 1920s during which a number of criticisms were raised concerning Marshall's price theory. John Clapham (1922) accused Marshall's categories of increasing and decreasing returns industries of being "empty boxes": no one had established which industries fell into which category. More important, Piero Sraffa (1926) raised two objections to Marshallian theory. The first was Marshall's failure to solve the problem of making increasing returns to scale compatible with perfect competition. Assuming economies of scale that were external to the firm but internal to the industry might be theoretically acceptable but they were the class of returns "most seldom to be met with" (Sraffa 1926, 540).[5] His second objection was the incompatibility of partial equilibrium analysis with decreasing returns to scale. In the long run, costs could rise with output only if factor prices rose, violating the *ceteris paribus* assumption needed for partial equilibrium analysis. Sraffa suggested that these problems be solved by moving toward a theory of monopoly. Alongside this were criticisms of the Marshallian theory of the firm – in particular of the "representative firm." Marshall's representative firm was a way to handle the problems arising from having many types of firm in an evolutionary context. If markets were viewed in terms of static equilibrium it was, not surprisingly, taken to be the average firm and was arguably redundant. Lionel Robbins (1928) and Pigou (1928) both attacked Marshall's concept, paving the way for the replacement of Marshall's realistic, evolutionary theory with a theory of static equilibrium.

---

[4] For discussion of other approaches see O'Brien (1983, 1984).
[5] He was clearly not convinced by Marshall's extensive work on industrial districts, where he found extensive evidence for such returns.

The marginal revenue curve (e.g. Harrod 1930) and the theory of imperfect competition (Robinson 1932, 1933) emerged out of this destruction of Marshallian price theory. Marginal revenue was implicit in Marshall's (and Cournot's) first-order conditions for equilibrium under monopoly, but around 1930, economists introduced the label, enabling it to be placed against marginal cost. They also noted the point (known to Cournot) that if the demand curve were not horizontal, there would be no supply curve: supply would depend on the elasticity of demand as well as on price. The geometry of marginal revenue, marginal cost, average revenue, and average cost was provided by Robinson, establishing the theory of the firm found in modern introductory textbooks. She labeled the general case, encompassing both monopoly and competition, "imperfect" competition. Firms faced downward-sloping demand curves and faced a large number of competitors, but freedom of entry and exit eliminated monopoly profits, pushing the firm to a point where its demand curve was tangential to the downward-sloping portion of its average cost curve. On the assumption that downward-sloping demand curves were the result of advertising, not substantive differences between products, she drew conclusions about the waste and inefficiency caused by having output lower than that at which average cost was minimized, and about the exploitation of labor caused by the real wage being less than labor's marginal product. In this sense she was working in the Pigovian welfare economics tradition.

The central figure in the Harvard approach to the theory of the market structure is Edward Chamberlin. Though his work has often been bracketed with Robinson's, its content and background were very different. Frank Knight's *Risk, Uncertainty and Profit* (1921) had provided a very strict definition of perfect competition, involving perfect information. John Maurice Clark's *The Economics of Overhead Costs* (1923) had explored the implications of overhead costs for business decision-making. There was also the influence of Allyn Young, his PhD supervisor at Harvard. Chamberlin, in the thesis that became *The Economics of Monopolistic Competition* (1933), was concerned not to repair or replace Marshallian theory but to extend it to encompass features of business life that were barely developed when Marshall wrote his *Principles* in the 1880s, notably advertising and product differentiation. His firms chose not just price and output, but also advertising (selling costs) and the degree of product differentiation. He also devoted considerable attention to oligopoly.

Chamberlin did not think, like Robinson, in terms of monopoly versus competition. His operated with a far richer menu of market structures, classifying them in at least three dimensions: product differentiation; advertising expenditure; and the number of firms. Monopolistic competition was simply one of many market structures in a range that included different types of oligopoly. Taking account of the fact that knowledge might not be perfect, he distinguished between "pure" and "perfect" competition, a distinction that did not appear in Robinson's work. He developed a theory with two demand curves for each firm, one which applied if other firms matched a price change, the other if they did not. Using these two curves he was able to explain how price might be determined under oligopoly, and the processes whereby markets adjusted to changes in the underlying conditions. In these processes, firms would adjust not just price and output but also selling costs and product differentiation.

The Harvard approach to the theory of the firm and market structure may have touched the Cambridge one with the theory of imperfect/monopolistic competition but just as it had different origins it led in different directions. The most important was the project of extending Chamberlin's theory into a general theory of industrial structure (Mason 1939; Bain 1942, 1956). The number of dimensions to industrial structure was increased to include durability of the product, the degree of vertical integration, and other aspects of market structure. This was assumed to influence firms' conduct, and hence economic performance. This established an empirical research agenda looking at relations between industrial structure and measures of performance across industries. Though rooted in Chamberlin's work, Mason and Bain laid the foundations for a thoroughly empirical analysis of industrial organization that was capable of a range of theoretical interpretations.

4   Institutionalism and Oxford

During the 1930s, in response to the Great Depression, economists questioned whether prices were in practice more rigid than conventional theory would suggest. In the United States, Gardner Means (1935) drew a sharp distinction between market prices (as in the market for wheat or cotton) and what he called "administered prices." These were set by firms and maintained for considerable periods of time. They might occur in either competitive or monopolistic markets. He found evidence that goods could be divided into two clear categories: in one prices changed frequently (nine times or more every year) and in the other very infrequently (less than three times a year). A quarter of all prices changed less than once every ten months. This was far more stability than could be expected if all prices were subject to the vagaries of supply and demand. Its relevance for the depression was that output fell most rapidly in markets with stable prices, and held up in markets where prices were flexible. The ratio of flexible to rigid prices was highly correlated with the index of industrial production in the late 1920s and early 1930s (Means 1936, 27). His policy conclusion was not that businesses should be broken up to make prices more flexible (this would drastically reduce wealth), but that monetary policy should be used to keep (flexible) market prices in line with those prices that were more stable.

Means's work was part of a much broader interest in pricing policies in the United States. The National Recovery Act (1933) led to the production of much statistical data, generating a wide range of responses to what was discovered.[6] Inflexibility of prices was believed to be important and Roosevelt established a Cabinet committee on price policy in 1934. Walter Hamilton undertook a series of investigations on prices, and Means continued his work after 1935 as Director of the National Resources Committee. Price policy was very much "in the air" in the 1930s. Most of the empirical work was very much in the institutionalist tradition, which spurned thinking about abstract individuals in favor of grounding theory firmly in empirical data (cf. Rutherford 1999).

In Britain, parallel work was done by the Oxford Economists Research Group (OERG). Harrod (1939, 1–2) introduced this by pointing out that the theory of the firm presumed full knowledge, an assumption that was formally incorrect. There was thus scope for empirical work to establish whether or not firms' short-run behavior deviated systematically from short-run profit maximization. He wanted to establish the principle that there was scope for "the method of direct question" (1939, 3). The OERG set out to question businessmen about their knowledge of costs and demand, and the methods by which they set prices in the short run.

The results of these surveys, described by Hall and Hitch (1939, 18) was that businessmen overwhelmingly followed what they called "full-cost" pricing.

An overwhelming majority of the entrepreneurs thought that a price based on full average cost (including a conventional allowance for profit) was the "right" price, the one which "ought" to be charged.

The reasons why Hall and Hitch believed that firms followed this policy were that they did not have the information needed to maximize short-run profits and, more important, that many markets were oligopolistic. In such markets, understandings about prices might have evolved (some trade bodies published price lists that could be followed) or they might involve basing prices on the full-costs of a dominant firm. Firms feared to lower price below full-cost because they feared competitors would cut their prices too, or because they believed demand to be very inelastic.

[6] See Lee (1984, 1109ff) for a discussion of this evidence and responses to it.

They did not raise prices because they expected competitors would take business away from them. They formalized these beliefs in the kinked demand curve, the origins of which can be found in the work of Chamberlin and Robinson.

Full-cost pricing, as presented by Harrod, Hall, and Hitch, presented only a limited challenge to conventional theory, taken to be the Chamberlin model of monopolistic competition. They were aware that full-cost pricing was consistent with profit maximization if the mark-up bore the appropriate relationship to firms' perceived elasticities of demand. More important, they did not question that profit maximization was an appropriate assumption for the long run. Harrod (1939, 3) wrote that the profit motive was "securely grounded": "Any one seeking seriously to challenge this would be regarded as a hopeless sentimentalist."[7] Phrases such as "taking goodwill into account" when setting prices implied concern for longer-run profits (Hall and Hitch 1939, 18). Moreover, even in the short-run, they were very circumspect in their treatment of theoretical results derived from profit maximization and seeing themselves, to some extent, as filling the gaps. For example, under oligopoly, all theory could say was that price would be somewhere between the pure polypoly price (taking no account of other firms' responses) and maximization of joint profits (Hall and Hitch 1939, 30). Empirical work was needed to establish whether the assumption of perfect knowledge, known to be incorrect, led to results that were systematically wrong.

5   From controversy over markets to controversy over marginalism

In response to these concerns, there was, in the early 1940s, an explosion of empirical work on cost curves and firms' pricing policies. Because there were so many approaches to the problem, we find several different debates going on. For example, exponents of the Harvard approach, which sought to relate price policy to variables describing industrial structure, were skeptical about the value of Means's correlations of price-stickiness with fluctuations in output. Thus Mason (1939, 65–6) criticized the measures of price used by Means, claiming that they failed to take account of discounts and quality changes. At the other extreme, he criticized Walton Hamilton (1938) for going too far in relating business decisions to specific circumstances: it required knowing "what Messrs Ford and Firestone dreamed in the night before the morning of their big tire deal"

---

[7] So much for Marshall's "economic chivalry"!

(Mason 1939, 61). The Harvard approach, which sought to relate price policies to specific indicators of market structure, lay in between these approaches.

On Harvard's second front, Mason (1939, 62) was critical of theorists in what I have called the Cambridge approach: "The extent to which the monopoly theorists ... refrain from an empirical application of their formulae is rather striking."[8] In a footnote to this sentence, he added, presumably alluding to Robinson (1933, 1),

Some theorists, pursuing their analysis on a high plane, refer to their work as "tool making" rather than "tool using." A "toolmaker," however, who constructs tools which no "tool user" can use is making a contribution of limited significance. Some knowledge of the use of tools is probably indispensable to their effective fabrication.

(This is a remark that one could easily imagine coming from Marshall's pen.[9]) When confronted with theory, he looks with favor towards institutionalism.

The theory of oligopoly has been aptly described as a ticket of admission to institutional economics. It is to be regretted that more theorists have not availed themselves of this privilege. (Mason 1939, 64–5)

Harrod's remarks, cited above, fit into this same general category, of economists seeking to establish the legitimacy of empirical research to augment the results of theoretical inquiry.

After the near simultaneous publication of *The Economics of Imperfect Competition* and *The Economics of Monopolistic Competition*, there were debates over definitions of concepts and how monopoly power might be measured. Machlup (1937, 1939) was a contributor to these, seeking to establish consistent terminology. He supported neither the Cambridge nor the Harvard approaches; citing John Hicks in support, he argued that monopolistic competition was less important than was generally thought. However, he defended the theory against empirical attack. He dismissed the value of questionnaire evidence, citing his own experience in business (Machlup 1939, 233–4). He argued that his partners, who were ignorant of economic theory, did not reach conclusions that were significantly different from his. His partners, he contended, behaved "as sensible economists suppose them to act" even though they often "rationalized their decisions in a misleading way." The result was that an investigator using questionnaires would have reached mistaken conclusions. He went so far as to refer to an "average-cost superstition," explicitly leaving it

---

[8] His examples were Richard Kahn and Abba Lerner.   [9] Cf. Pigou (1925, 427, 437).

open whether this referred to non-profit-maximizing businessmen, or to economists who believed that businessmen behaved in this way. However, unlike in his later work, he defended aspects of the Harvard approach. Examining the many dimensions of market structure would no doubt show that many of these were irrelevant, but it was worth knowing that. He went on (1939, 236) to provide a long list of things that government could learn from the monopolistic competition literature.

In his 1939 paper, Machlup made some of the criticisms of empirical and questionnaire research that were later to emerge in the marginalist controversy proper. However, in 1939 they were side issues. The validity of marginalist methods was but one amongst many issues in a debate that was primarily about market structure and price determination. Similar remarks could be made about the contributions of the OERG: Harrod explicitly endorsed profit maximization and saw empirical research as establishing the theory's applicability. Hall and Hitch presented full-cost pricing as supplementary to standard theory, and were ambiguous about whether it conflicted with profit maximization. It was only after Lester's challenge in 1946 that the main issue came to be seen as marginalism *versus* a non-marginalist alternative. After the marginalist controversy of 1946–7, the debate over the theory of the firm took on a different character. Debate over markets was transformed into debate over marginalism. This was precisely the time when Friedman began working on F53.

The outcome of the debate, to which F53 contributed in no small measure, was to marginalize the full-cost approach. Several economists took up the task of developing the idea of full-cost pricing from a decision rule that described firms' pricing policies into an alternative to marginal analysis. For example, in the United States, Wilford Eiteman (1945, 1947, 1948; cf. Lee 1984, 1116–18) put forward a critique of marginalist theory based on the structure of firms' costs. In multi-product firms, marginal costs of individual products were not identifiable. Even when they were, the typical pattern was for costs to fall up to full-capacity, meaning that for a wide range of revenue functions there would be no point below full capacity at which marginal cost and marginal revenue would be equal. There would be a discontinuity in the marginal cost curve at full capacity, and firms would produce at this point. Eiteman and Guthrie (1952) used a questionnaire to ask businessmen about their costs, finding that the overwhelming majority of the 366 firms that responded believed that costs declined, reaching a minimum either at or shortly before full capacity output, a result they thought inconsistent with marginal analysis.

In Britain, the OERG, after being disbanded during the war, continued its work. The key figure was Philip Andrews. He moved from the surveys used by Hall and Hitch to detailed studies of individual industries: rayon, dominated by Courtaulds, and the boot and shoe industry. On the basis of this work, he developed a theoretical alternative to Chamberlinian monopolistic competition theory (1949a, b; see Lee and Earl 1993, 1–34; Lee and Irving-Lessman 1992). He saw himself as moving away from Chamberlin's theory back to a Marshallian conception of the "equilibrium" of the industry. Industries typically comprised firms of different size, with different cost conditions, and a major factor behind pricing decisions was *potential* entry from firms that produced in related markets. His studies of technology in both synthetic fabrics and footwear persuaded him that capital and labor had to be used in relatively fixed proportions, causing costs to be constant up to full capacity. Firms typically aimed to produce at less than full capacity, not because of falling marginal revenue but because they designed plant so as to allow some spare capacity beyond their expected level of output (machinery might break down, and over time they would hope for an increase in sales). Prices would be set in terms of "normal costs," similar in conception to full costs. Because firms were concerned with the long run, they attached great value to goodwill, and did not maximize short-run profits. Though Andrews never fully developed his theory (Lee and Earl 1993, 22–3), he was, unlike Hall and Hitch, clearly offering an alternative to marginalism. Andrews had several supporters amongst more traditional Marshallians, but the predominant reaction was one of hostility (Lee and Irving-Lessman 1992).

However, whilst the case against marginalist theory was being developed in several directions, the evidence in favor of full-cost pricing was also being reinterpreted in such a way as to defuse controversy and to rally support round more orthodox, Chamberlinian theory. The major contributor here was Richard Heflebower (1955). This paper was presented at a conference at Princeton University in June 1952 and offered a careful survey of much of the literature, both American and British (Stigler, Machlup, and Bain were present, but the main critics of marginalism were not). He was considered by most economists to take the full-cost arguments very seriously, but came down on the side of arguing that the evidence was consistent with marginalist theory.[10] He was skeptical about the questionnaire evidence and argued that industry studies did not support full-cost conclusions. He concluded that profit margins were in practice much less rigid than they appeared at first sight to be and that firms deviated from their normal margins when they faced a competitive

[10] The paper is useful as a source of references to the earlier literature.

reason to do so (1955, 383–5). This suggested that there was no inconsistency between full-cost pricing and marginalism.

Heflebower saw merit in full-cost pricing under some circumstances.
Under oligopoly, where rationality did not define a unique price, full-cost
pricing was persuasive and there was evidence that firms had followed
such policies during the 1930s. Full-cost pricing also made sense in
industries where price decisions had to be made very frequently, as in
industries such as metal casting, metal stamping and forging. In these, it
was important to have a formula that could be used to calculate prices that
might vary from one order to the next. Similar considerations applied in
retailing, though here he noted that the same retailer might charge very
different margins on different products. Margins on products were not the
same as overall margins. He accepted Harrod's point that full-cost pricing
might be a way to achieve long-term profit maximization.

However, despite accepting many of the full-costers' claims, in the last
resort he came down against full-cost pricing being important. In the
tradition of Chamberlin, Mason, and Bain, he emphasized the need to
take account of the peculiar circumstances of individual markets, expressing skepticism about any general rule. Good theories, he believed, had to
be historically situated and they needed to be dynamic. But rather than
seeing full-cost theories as a way of dealing with dynamics, he emphasized
the need to explain pricing in terms of the evolution of market structures.

A satisfactory theory must go beyond explaining the cost-price output relations for
a given product and must be prepared to appraise the conditions of choice among
other variables and the economic results of that choice. This requirement, like the
others set forth here, is not introduced for the sake of descriptive realism but
because it is essential for better prediction. (1954, 122)

This was the "Harvard" structure–conduct–performance approach,
expressed using different language. "Conditions of choice" meant market
structure and other aspects of the situation in which firms operated; "economic results" meant performance. Against the full-costers he argued the
need for a theory of why firms behaved as they did, going beneath observed
behavior to its causes; against Chicago (and presumably Friedman), he
argued that market structure had to be considered because it affected
predictions, not simply for the sake of being realistic.

6   Friedman's early reactions to the Lester–Machlup–Stigler exchanges

These controversies form the background to F53, which Friedman started
writing soon after the Lester–Machlup–Stigler exchanges. Don Patinkin

had been a PhD student at Chicago, but left in 1948 to take a position at the University of Illinois, after which he moved to Jerusalem. Their correspondence, therefore, begins in 1948.[11] In this correspondence, Patinkin repeatedly criticizes Friedman for not following his own empiricist methodology and Friedman responded to Patinkin in much more detail than he responded to Lester. This means that Friedman's letters to Patinkin show clearly how he responded to empiricist claims such as Lester and others were making.[12]

In the first letter, after some paragraphs on debt and Friedman's political philosophy, Patinkin turned to methodology.

Now too, some questions on your insistence that our theory should consist only of statements that people act "as if." You once used this argument to explain to me that you felt the criticism made of the Chamberlin analysis of imperfect competition (viz. that the business man does not know the shape of the curves postulated by the theory) was invalid, since all that has to be shown is that the business man acts as if he knows these curves. On this I agree with you insofar as you restrict yourself to the implication of the "as if" hypothesis which can be checked up without referring to the assumption. For example, one such implication of the theory is that profits are zero. This can be checked. But what about the implication that the businessman will operate at the point where marginal costs and revenues are equal? I see no way of checking up on this implication. The same problem holds also for the position which substitutes "subjective" curves for "objective" ones. (Patinkin to Friedman, October 25, 1948).[13]

Patinkin is here making the point that theoretical implications must be testable, reminiscent of the Lester–Oliver objection that Machlup broadened marginalism to the point of tautology. However, it is worth noting that Patinkin recalls having heard Friedman use the "as if" argument against Chamberlin, not the full-costers. Friedman's reply refers to the article that he was trying to write and which later became F53.

I have been trying to write some kind of an article on the general methodological problem you raise, and maybe I ought to neglect that. I don't regard the statement that marginal costs and revenues are equal as in any way an empirical implication of an economic hypothesis. It is simply a restatement of the hypothesis or, if you will, a mathematical deduction from it. It seems to me the kinds of implications that one needs to check are of a different order. Thus, from the hypothesis that an

---

[11] For a broader perspective on this correspondence, see Leeson (1998) and Backhouse (2002). See also Hammond (1996) and Hirsch and De Marchi (1990).

[12] Lester is rarely mentioned by name, but there is no doubt that they are discussing this controversy. In one letter, Patinkin even offered Friedman a specimen examination question, based on data on motives for saving, that *exactly* parallels Lester's questionnaire on what determined employment.

[13] All quotations from the Friedman–Patinkin correspondence are taken from the Don Patinkin Papers, held in the Economists' Papers Project, Duke University.

entrepreneur will operate at the point at which marginal costs and revenues are equal, one can infer that a change which is known to have increased his costs but not to have increased his revenues will tend to reduce output. That's an empirical implication that one can check, and so on. Again, by substituting subjective curves for objective ones, it is possible to take all the content out of a hypothesis and make it not a hypothesis at all but a pure tautology. For example, if one says that he behaves in such a way as to equate marginal costs and marginal revenue for subjective curves which are subject to change at any time, then of course no observable phenomena would be inconsistent with that hypothesis, hence the hypothesis has no content and is of no interest. (Friedman to Patinkin, November 8, 1948)

Friedman saw MR=MC as *equivalent to* profit maximization. He ruled out the idea of MR=MC as a means of making decisions: he implies that applying it to decision-making would mean adopting a subjective interpretation of revenue and cost, rendering the theory untestable. In his next letter, Patinkin pursued this point, asking whether it would constitute a test of the theory to ask whether businessmen undertook projects only when the extra profit they believed they would generate exceeded the extra costs they expected to incur (Patinkin to Friedman, December 13, 1948). A month later (January 11, 1949) he switched to the issue of firms giving to charity: enlarging the concept of profit maximization to encompass public esteem and prestige, he suggested, rendered the concept of "profit" meaningless. He drew the conclusion that in social science, we deal with subjects who can express themselves in subjective ways. "You run into the whole problem of whether we can believe what a person says. This is the problem that is obviously absent from the physical sciences." He thus objected to Friedman's extending physical-science methodology to social science.

This letter elicited a clear statement from Friedman on two points: that a theory is designed to explain only a certain class of problems, and the role of introspection. Given the importance of these points they are worth quoting in full.

I don't think there is any essential difference between us on the experiment about testing the theory of maximizing profit. The point you make is, as I see it, that maximizing profit cannot appropriately be considered the sole or exclusive concern of corporations. That is, not all observable behavior of corporations can be rationalized as a consequence of strict single-minded profit maximization. This is undoubtedly correct. I have no quarrel with you. The point is that the profit maximization theorem or hypothesis does not say this. What it does say is that there exists an important class of phenomena (not all phenomena) which can be rationalized in terms of a single-minded profit-maximizing entrepreneur. Your experiment does not provide any test of this. Thus, to use my favorite example, the fact that a feather did not fall a particular distance in the time that would be predicted by the vacuum formula is not universally applicable. It does not tell you that the formula may not be applicable over a wide range of circumstances.

Similarly with respect to your point about physical sciences and social sciences. It seems to me that the two are fundamentally essential so far as methodology is concerned. The existence of human beings does not change any of the fundamental methodological principles. It has two rather different effects. The first of these is that it provides a new source of information namely, introspective observation. This information is extremely important and relevant and is the one important advantage we get out of the fact that our science deals with human beings. It seems to me the role this additional information can play is in suggesting fruitful hypotheses, that is, it enters at the stage of deriving hypotheses. The second way that the existence of human beings affects our science is that it introduces a fundamental element of indeterminateness. This is a point that Knight has always made and I think quite correctly. In the physical sciences the observer and the thing observed are separable and distinct. In the social sciences they are the same. Thus in the social sciences the enunciation of a result or a law for predicting the stock market perfectly may make that law invalid. For example, if one were to state a technique for predicting the stock market perfectly, you know that if that technique were believed in it would then become wrong. That's the real difficulty raised by human beings. (Friedman to Patinkin, January 18, 1949)

Introspection comes in as a source of hypotheses: it is not relevant for testing them. Patinkin (January 22, 1949) took up the point about marginalist theory referring only to "an important class of problems." He argued that it was important "to specify exactly what properties that class of problems will have. Otherwise you are getting into a tautology." Unfortunately for us, Patinkin then visited Chicago where, presumably, their discussion continued face-to-face.

A year later (February 4, 1950), Patinkin returned to his concerns about the conclusions reached by Machlup and Stigler.

I've also reread the 1946–7 *AER* Lester–Machlup–Stigler controversy on marginal productivity. It has left me with mixed reactions, On the one hand, Lester had made some definite empirical investigations. Admittedly, his technics were crude. But I definitely do think that Machlup and Stigler dispense with his finding much too glibly. There's something else that's worrying me: I'm afraid Machlup proves too much. For him marginal productivity can explain everything, and hence (does this sound familiar?) it can explain no thing. In particular, I should like to ask Machlup your question: under what circumstances would you reject the marginal productivity theory. I don't know if he could produce any (can you?); but even if he did, I would be willing to bet that faced with such circumstances he would plead "special factors." The dammed thing is that it's almost impossible to set up a critical experiment in economics.

March 5, 1950
My God! Is that how long this letter has been lying here unfinished? In the interim many things have happened. But before I get on to them, I'd like to finish up the previous discussion.

What I was going to say is that one thing Stigler said in that marginal productivity argument sent shudders through me. That was his statement on the bottom of p. 156 (*AER*, March 1947) that even he would not accept a certain result "even if Lester obtains it from 6,000 metal working firms." A similar statement is at the bottom of p. 99, first column, in Stigler's review of Survey of Contemporary Economics (*JPE*, April, 1949) where Stigler summarily dismisses an observation of Reynolds on wage differentials. I don't know who's right or wrong on this; but it does seem to me that Stigler must present some empirical evidence before sounding off like that. And in this respect I completely agree with Lester; we have had some experience already on minimum wage legislation. Isn't it a sad reflection on the sad state of economics that Stigler can write a straight textbook analysis of minimum wage legislation without even feeling himself obligated to make any empirical surveys. Stigler is just an example of what everyone does – including yours truly. I am merely bemoaning the type of training we receive that doesn't make us horrified at "casual empiricism." That's all for the moment, though I'd like to get your reaction.

Here we find Patinkin putting to Friedman precisely the points made by Lester, by way of criticism of Machlup and Stigler: that Machlup rendered the theory tautological and that Stigler turned his back on evidence.[14] Friedman (March 21, 1950) agreed with Patinkin, clearly differentiating his position from those of Machlup and Stigler.

P. S. (2) Re Lester–Machlup–Stigler controversy – I agree thoroughly with you. I say, a plague on both their houses. Lester *et al*'s criticism is beside the point, and Machlup's and Stigler's replies are beside point. Lester asks: Do businessmen behave the way theorists say they do; M and S answer yes – or if not, we'll change our statement so as to empty it of content. Right point is: economic theorists do not (or should not) say anything about how businessmen behave or how they make their decisions. They should say: the consequences of such and such a ch[an]ge can be predicted by treating bus. men *as if* they did such and such. Test of that theory is whether predictions are correct, not what bus. men say they do. So Lester is asking foolish question and M and S giving foolish answer. My best example [word illegible] to illustrate point is to say that Lester's method of investigation is

---

[14] In a letter to Martin Bronfenbrenner (February 4, 1950), Patinkin expressed himself even more strongly. Referring to Lester's "empirical attempt," he wrote: "One cannot merely wave it away with the hand, as do Machlup and Stigler. Furthermore, I think these gentlemen – especially former – prove too much. According to their formulation, the marginal productivity theory proves everything, and hence nothing. In particular, I should like to ask Machlup what empirical findings he would take as evidence that the marginal productivity was incorrect. I am sure that what would happen is that he would not be able to cite a case, and even if he did, if he were ever confronted with empirical evidence that this case had actually happened, he would find some reasons for calling it 'special circumstances' and hence not refuting the theory. Stigler is even more doctrinaire. His statement that certain of Lester's empirical findings he would not accept even if presented with '6,000 cases' sends shudders down my spine. Is that the way a supposedly empirical science is supposed to be presented?" [Some spellings have been corrected.]

like trying to figure out causes of longevity by asking old people to what factors they attribute their longevity. (Friedman to Patinkin, March 31, 1950, handwritten)

Friedman thought Lester's questions were misconceived because they reflected a misconception about the way theory should be used; and Machlup and Stigler were wrong to dismiss evidence so completely.

This exchange clarifies Friedman's rejection of any idea that theory should be trying to explain business decisions. Such decisions depended on subjective factors and were therefore untestable. His reference (January 18) to Knight's principle of indeterminacy suggests that he thought this a fundamental problem, which helps account for his consistently held view that the attempts of Lester and others to answer this involved asking foolish questions.[15] Friedman's comment that there was a class of problems for which marginalist theory provided the answer was completely beside the point: few of the full-costers would have disagreed. Their aim was to find a way to solve problems that it could not answer.

7   F53 as a response to the marginalist controversy

Friedman (F53, 16) used the 1946–7 marginalist controversy as the motivation for what he described as "a more extensive discussion of methodological principles involved than might otherwise seem appropriate." In his brief discussion of the controversy, as in his letter to Patinkin, he criticized both sides, Machlup and Stigler as much as Lester.

The articles on *both sides* of the controversy largely neglect what seems to me clearly the main issue – the conformity to experience of the implications of marginal analysis – and concentrate on the largely irrelevant question of whether businessmen do or do not reach their decisions by consulting schedules, or curves, or multivariable functions showing marginal cost and marginal revenue (F53, 15; emphasis added).

Friedman is here criticizing both those (Lester) who questioned the relevance of marginal analysis and those (Machlup and Stigler) who supported it. By focusing on the 1946–7 marginalist controversy, in which Machlup and Stigler ignored these issues, Friedman was led to focus on one among many issues involved in the controversy over full-cost pricing.

Friedman's explicit criticisms of anti-marginalist writings came later in his essay (F53, 31–3). He echoed Machlup's dismissal of questionnaire

---

[15] If fundamental uncertainty played such an important role in Friedman's thinking, it is worth noting the parallel with Keynes.

evidence but his main focus was on the desire for a "realistic" theory rather than one that predicted better than an alternative theory for as wide a range of phenomena. One would not guess from this dismissal of this work that behind the controversy lay the goal of explaining the large amount of evidence on the behavior of prices during the 1930s and 1940s. In this literature was much work that could be construed as finding a theory that could predict firms' price policies (understood to refer to the prices set by firms in relation to relevant circumstances). Full-costers claimed that full-cost pricing had predictive power, whereas their opponents claimed it had not. Friedman is not explicitly dismissing full-cost so much as rejecting one (but only one) of the arguments used to support it.

However, although Friedman motivated F53 in this way, it was both more and less than an attack on the full-cost pricing literature. It was more in that he had other targets; it was less in that he addressed only a few full-cost arguments. Another important target, arguably his main one, was the theory of monopolistic competition. He objected to the claim made by Chamberlin (1957) and Triffin (1940)[16] that monopolistic competition might prove the basis for a more general theory of value. The theory, he claimed, "possesses none of the attributes that would make it a truly useful general theory" (F53, 38). It was useful in that it refined Marshall's theory, thereby "enrich[ing] the vocabulary available for describing industrial experience." His most substantial criticism was that whilst it might be useful in analyzing firms or even the economy as a whole, it could not offer any analysis of the industry. Once one admitted product differentiation, every firm produced a unique product.

> The theory of monopolistic competition offers no tolls for the analysis of an industry and so no stopping place between the firm at one extreme and general equilibrium at the other. It is therefore incompetent to contribute to the analysis of a host of important problems: the one extreme is too narrow to be of great interest; the other, too broad to permit meaningful generalizations. (F53, 39)

The solution, he contended, was to adopt Marshall's practice of dividing firms into industries, "such that the similarities among the firms in each group were more important than the differences among them" (F53, 35). Here, it is important to him that Marshall did not assume perfect competition, even when using supply and demand to analyze a competitive market.

> Marshall, it is said, assumed "perfect competition"; perhaps there once was such a thing. But clearly there is no longer, and we must therefore discard his theories. The reader will search long and hard – and I predict unsuccessfully – to find in Marshall any explicit assumption about perfect competition or any assertion that

---

[16] And to some extent Robinson (1933) in her last chapter, "A world of monopolies."

in a descriptive sense the world is composed of atomistic firms engaged in perfect competition ... Marshall took the world as it is; he sought to construct an "engine" to analyze it, not a photographic reproduction of it. (F53, 34)

Thus he judges the Cambridge and Harvard approaches both to be misconceived. The Cambridge economists were wrong to suggest that in exposing logical inconsistencies in the theory of competitive equilibrium, they were exposing problems with Marshall's theory, for he did not assume perfect competition. The Harvard economists were wrong to assume that because product differentiation, advertising expenditure, and so on were more "realistic," their theories were better than Marshall's theory. Thus Friedman was rejecting both branches of the "new establishment" in value theory, without claiming that the world was perfectly competitive.[17]

Hausman and Mongin (1997, 266) suggest that full-cost theories aroused controversy because "the exact interpretation of fundamental theory was not yet settled." This is correct, though arguably it understates the variety of theoretical and empirical approaches that existed. From the 1920s and 1940s, economists engaged in wide-ranging discussions about the theory of the firm and market structure, approaching the problem from different angles. Some developments were theoretically driven, resolving apparent inconsistencies in Marshall's theory. Others were driven by observations about business practices and institutional details, supplemented very extensively by statistical investigations. The result was a complex variety of approaches, with debates across many of these. Imperfect/monopolistic competition was seen very differently in Cambridge and Harvard. Full-cost ideas and price stickiness were discussed by exponents of this new establishment in value theory, who saw it as filling a gap in the theory of oligopoly, as well as by institutionalists (Means and Hamilton), and by Marshallians (Andrews). The distinction between Marshallian theory and perfect competition was rarely spelled out.[18]

Against this mixture of approaches, some compatible with each other and others not, Friedman was defending an almost unique position. He did not accept either the Cambridge or the Harvard version on imperfect/monopolistic competition (though he accepted that their formal analysis of monopoly was useful for certain problems) or the theoretical arguments used to defend full-cost pricing. On the empirical front, he was skeptical about the relevance of most of the evidence being accumulated for administered and full-cost pricing, and about the Harvard economists'

---

[17] He also rejected Walrasian general equilibrium theory as represented by the Cowles Commission, but that is a different story.

[18] An exception was Shove (1933).

attempt to explain prices in terms of industrial and market structure. However, he also rejected the anti-empirical stance of the Austrians, Machlup and Stigler. Ironically, he was in some ways closest to Andrews, who shared his commitment to a Marshallian approach (and his sympathy towards free enterprise). His argument about "as if" reasoning was particularly important because it enabled him to attack on several sides simultaneously. Much of the marginalist controversy and the debates out of which it arose had been concerned with explaining how economic outcomes were actually reached. Dismissing this entire problem made much of this literature irrelevant, greatly narrowing the scope of economic theory.[19] Though he remained Marshallian in many ways, in this respect Friedman was moving theory further away from Marshall.

References

Andrews, P. W. S. (1949a). *Manufacturing Business*. London: Macmillan
  (1949b). A reconsideration of the theory of the individual business. *Oxford Economic Papers* 1, 54–89
Backhouse, Roger E. (2002). Don Patinkin: interpreter of the Keynesian revolution. *European Journal of the History of Economic Thought*, 9(2), 186–204
  (2003). The stabilization of price theory, 1920–55. In Warren J. Samuels, Jeff E. Biddle, and John B. Davis (eds.), *A Companion to The History of Economic Thought*. Oxford: Blackwell
Backhouse, Roger E. and David Laidler (2004). What was lost with IS–LM. *History of Political Economy* 36, annual supplement, *The History of IS–LM*, ed. M. de Vroey and K. D. Hoover, 25–56
Bain, Joe S. (1942). Market classification in modern price theory. *Quarterly Journal of Economics*, 56, 560–74
  (1956). *Barriers to New Competition*. Cambridge, MA: Harvard University Press
Chamberlin, Edward (1933). *The Theory of Monopolistic Competition*. Cambridge, MA: Harvard University Press
  (1957). *Toward a More General Theory of Value*. New York
Clark, John Maurice (1923). *The Economics of Overhead Costs*. Chicago: University of Chicago Press
Clapham, J. H. (1922). Of empty economic boxes. *Economic Journal*, 32(127), 305–14
Eiteman, Wilford J. (1945). The equilibrium of the firm in multi-process industries. *Quarterly Journal of Economics*, 59(2), 280–6
  (1947). Factors determining the location of the least-cost point. *American Economic Review*, 37(5), 910–18
  (1948). The least-cost point, capacity and marginal analysis: rejoinder. *American Economic Review*, 38(5), 899–904

---

[19] A similar narrowing took place in macroeconomics. See Backhouse and Laidler (2004).

Eiteman, Wilford J. and Glenn E. Guthrie (1952). The shape of the average cost curve. *American Economic Review*, 42(5), 832–8

Friedman, Milton (1953). The methodology of positive economics. In *Essays on Positive Economics*. Chicago: University of Chicago Press, 3–43

Hamilton, Walton (1938). *Price and Price Policies*. New York: McGraw Hill

Hammond J. Daniel (1996). *Theory and Measurement: Causality Issues in Milton Friedman's Monetary Economics*. Cambridge: Cambridge University Press

Harrod, Roy (1930). Notes on supply. *Economic Journal*, 40, 232–41
    (1939). Price and cost in entrepreneurs' policy. *Oxford Economic Papers* 2 (old series), 1–11

Hausman, Daniel M. and Phillippe Mongin (1997). Economists' responses to anomalies: full-cost pricing versus preference reversals. *History of Political Economy*, 29 (annual supplement), 255–72

Heflebower, Richard B. (1954). Toward a theory of industrial markets and prices *American Economic Review, Papers and Proceedings*, 44(2), 121–39
    (1955). Full cost, cost changes and prices. In G. J. Stigler (ed.), *Business Concentration and Price Policy*. Princeton: Princeton University Press

Hirsch, Abraham and Neil De Marchi (1990). *Milton Friedman: Economics in Theory and Practice*. Brighton: Harvester Wheatsheaf

Knight, Frank Hyndman (1921). *Risk, Uncertainty and Profit*. Boston: Houghton Mifflin

Lee, Frederic S. (1984). The marginalist controversy and the demise of full-cost pricing. *Journal of Economic Issues*, 18(4), 1107–32

Lee, Frederic S. and Peter Earl (eds.) (1993). *The Economics of Competitive Enterprise: Selected Essays of P. W. S. Andrews*. Cheltenham: Edward Elgar

Lee, Frederic S. and J. Irving-Lessman (1992). The fate of an errant hypothesis: the doctrine of normal-cost prices. *History of Political Economy*, 24(2), 273–309

Leeson, Robert (1998). The early Patinkin–Friedman correspondence. *Journal of the History of Economic Thought*, 20(4), 433–48

Lester, Richard A. (1946). Shortcomings of marginal analysis for wage-emplyment problems. *American Economic Review*, 36, 63–82
    (1947). Marginalism, minimum wages, and labor markets. *American Economic Review*, 37(1), 135–48

Machlup, Fritz (1937). Monopoly and competition: a classification of market positions. *American Economic Review*, 27(3), 445–51
    (1939). Evaluation of the practical significance of the theory of monopolistic competition. *American Economic Review*, 29(2), 227–36
    (1946). Marginal analysis and empirical research. *American Economic Review*, 36(4), 519–54
    (1947). Rejoinder to an antimarginalist. *American Economic Review*, 37(1), 137–54

Marshall, Alfred ([1890] 1920). *Principles of Economics*, 8th edition. London: Macmillan
    (1925). Mechanical and biological analogies in economics. In A. C. Pigou (ed.), *Memorials of Alfred Marshall*. London: Macmillan. Originally published in Distribution and exchange. *Economic Journal*, 8 (1898), 37–59
    (1919). *Industry and Trade*. London: Macmillan

Mason, E. (1939). Price and production policies of large-scale enterprise. *American Economic Review*, Papers and Proceedings, 29(1), 61–74

Means, Gardiner C. (1935). Price inflexibility and the requirement of a stabilizing monetary policy. *Journal of the American Statistical Association*, 30(90), 410–13 (1936). Notes on inflexible prices. *American Economic Review*, 26(1), 23–35

Mongin, Phillippe (1992). The 'full-cost' controversy of the 1940s and 1950s: a methodological assessment. *History of Political Economy* 24(2), 311–56

O'Brien, D. P. (1983). Research programmes in competitive structure. *Journal of Economic Studies* 10(4), 29–51. Reprinted in O'Brien 1994

    (1984). The evolution of the theory of the firm. In Frank H. Stephen (ed.), *Firms, Organization and Labour*. London: Macmillan. Reprinted in O'Brien 1994

    (1990). Marshall's industrial analysis. *Scottish Journal of Political Economy*, 37(1), 61–84. Reprinted in O'Brien 1994

    (1994). *Methodology, Money and the Firm: The Collected Essays of D. P. O'Brien, vol. I*. Cheltenham: Edward Elgar

Oliver, Henry M. (1947). Marginal theory and business behavior. *American Economic Review*, 37(3), 375–83

Oswald, Andrew and Philip Trostel (2000). What can recent labour research teach us about macroeconomics? In Roger E. Backhouse and Andrea Salanti (eds.), *Macroeconomics and the Real World*, vol. 2: *Keynesian Economics, Unemployment and Policy*. Oxford: Oxford University Press, 113–44

Pigou, A. C. (ed.) (1925). *Memorials of Alfred Marshall*. London: Macmillan (1928). An analysis of supply. *Economic Journal*, 38, 238–57

Raffaelli, Tiziano (2003). *Marshall's Evolutionary Economics*. London: Routledge (2004). Whatever happened to Marshall's industrial economics? *European Journal of the History of Economic Thought*, 11(2), 209–29

Robbins, Lionel (1928). The representative firm. *Economic Journal*, 38, 387–404

Robinson, Joan (1932). Imperfect competition and falling supply price. *Economic Journal*, 42, 544–54

    (1933). *The Economics of Imperfect Competition*. London: Macmillan

Rutherford, Malcolm. (1999). Institutionalism as 'scientific' economics. In Roger E. Backhouse and John Creedy (eds.), *From Classical Economics to the Theory of the Firm: Essays in Honour of D. P. O'Brien*. Cheltenham: Edward Elgar, 223–42

Shove, Gerald F. (1933). The imperfection of the market: a note. *Economic Journal*, 43, 113–24

Sraffa, Piero (1926). The laws of returns under competitive conditions. *Economic Journal*, 36, 535–50

Stigler, George J. (1946). The economics of minimum wage legislation. *American Economic Review*, 36(3), 358–65

    (1947). Professor Lester and the marginalists. *American Economic Review*, 37(1), 154–7

Triffin, Robert (1940). *Monopolistic Competition and General Equilibrium Theory*. Cambridge, MA: Harvard University Press

Whitaker, John K. (1996). *The Correspondence of Alfred Marshall, Economist*. 3 vols. Cambridge: Cambridge University Press

9   Friedman (1953) and the theory of the firm

Oliver E. Williamson

Inasmuch as "all theories, not just the neoclassical, start with the existence of firms" (Arrow 1999, vi), since the theory of the firm figures prominently in both Milton Friedman's essay on "The methodology of positive economics" (F53) and my own research agenda, and since we are all closet methodologists, I responded with alacrity to the invitation to prepare a paper on F53 as it relates to the theory of the firm. My remarks are organized in four parts.

I begin with what I take to be the main message of the essay: most economists are and should be engaged in the study of positive economics. What I regard as overreaching parts of the essay are discussed in section 2. Post-1953 developments in the theory of the firm are sketched in section 3. Concluding remarks follow.

1   The main message

The first ten pages of the F53 contain the main message. Specifically, the task of positive economics "is to provide a system of generalizations that can be used to make correct predictions about the consequences of any change in circumstances. Its performance is to be judged by the precision, scope, and conformity with experience of the predictions it yields" (F53, 4). Additionally, simplicity and fruitfulness are important criteria in evaluating alternative theories (F53, 10). As Friedman subsequently remarks, "Most phenomena are driven by a very few central forces. What a good theory does is to simplify, it pulls out the central forces and gets rid of the rest" (Snowdon and Vane 1997, 196). Indeed, "a fundamental hypothesis of science is that appearances are deceptive and that there is a way of looking at or interpreting or organizing the evidence that will reveal superficially disconnected and diverse phenomena to be manifestations of

Comments on earlier versions by Jack Letiche and Robert Solow, by participants at the Friedman (1953) conference in Rotterdam, and by Claude Menard are gratefully acknowledged.

a more fundamental and relatively simple structure" (F53, 33). But whereas Friedman puts it in the singular – "a way" and "a...simple structure" – I would put it in the plural: there are "ways" and "simple structures" (on more of which later).

His argument that a theory "is more 'fruitful' the more precise the resulting prediction, the wider the area within which the theory yields predictions, and the more additional lines for further research it suggests" (F53, 10) is instructive, recognizing that there may be tradeoffs among these three. Also, although all would-be theories must expect to come under criticism, you don't beat something with nothing but must offer something in its stead (Kuhn 1970, 77). Awaiting a rival theory, "the continuous use and acceptance of [a] hypothesis over a long period, and the failure of any coherent, self-consistent alternative to be developed and to be widely accepted, is strong indirect testimony to its worth" (F53, 23).

As between normative and positive theory, F53 tells us that (1) more economists should concern themselves with real phenomena rather than idealizations and (2) all would-be positive theories should stand up and be counted – by making predictions and submitting these to empirical testing. This last is the way by which to sort the sheep (hard-headed theories) from the goats (fanciful constructions).

2   Overreaching

F53 is unarguably controversial – witness that we are still debating the merits fifty years later. Partly this may be because rhetorical purpose is often served by exaggeration, but there is also reason to believe that the author revels in controversy. (The latter interpretation is suggested by Friedman's remark that "If you want to get controversy about one of your articles, write something which will be attacked and then don't answer the attackers because it opens a field day" (Snowdon and Vane 1997, 203).) The merits of the central message notwithstanding, Friedman is also given to overreaching.

2.1   *Assumptions*

Truly important and significant hypotheses will be found to have "assumptions" that are *wildly inaccurate* descriptions of reality, and, in general, the more significant the theory, the *more unrealistic* the assumptions. (F53, 14; emphasis added).

Wildly inaccurate? Unrealism is a virtue? To be sure, Friedman subsequently observes that "the relevant question to ask about the 'assumptions' of a theory is not whether they are descriptively 'realistic,' for they never are, but whether they are sufficiently good approximations for the purpose at hand" (F53, 15), with which few would disagree. And he further admits to a tradeoff if confronted with "a theory that is known to yield better predictions but only at a greater cost" (F53, 17). If, for example, the more fine-grained predictions of a theory that works out of less extreme assumptions imposes added data collection costs, the gains may be "worthwhile" for only a subset of circumstances. Indeed, one of the challenges to extreme assumptions – such as perfect gas laws or zero transaction costs – is to specify the circumstances under which these can be presumed to work (F53, 18). Who could disagree? But if that is the argument, why the bombastic introduction?

2.2   *Alternative theories*

Friedman observes that

> The abstract methodological issues we have been discussing have a direct bearing on the perennial criticism of "orthodox" economic theory as being "unrealistic" as well as on the attempts that have been made to reformulate theory to meet this charge … [C]riticism of this type is largely beside the point unless supplemented by evidence that a hypothesis differing in one or another of these respects from [orthodoxy]…yields better predictions for *as wide a range of phenomena.* (F53, 30–1; emphasis added)[1]

But why the insistence on wide range? What if a rival theory provides better predictions only for some phenomena? What if it calls our attention to new phenomena? As posed by Friedman, the contest between textbook orthodoxy, which is the product of many years of development, and upstart contenders, which have not had the benefit of successive extensions, applications, and refinements, is needlessly protective of the former. (As Thomas Kuhn observes, the "early versions of most new paradigms are crude" [1970, 156], often heuristic models [1970, 184]. *"Clumsiness [is] inevitable in a first venture"* [1970, 33]. Successive refinements thereafter take shape, sometimes with the benefit of a new mathematics.)

Thus although Friedman subsequently takes the position that "Science in general advances primarily by unsuccessful experiments that clear the ground" (Snowdon and Vane 1997, 296), F53 has a much narrower view of the enterprise. As previously remarked, he speaks of *a* way and *a* simple structure, both in the singular (F53, 33).

---

[1] Even more restrictive would be an insistence that rival theories yield better predictions for the same range of phenomena.

2.3   Theories of the firm (singular)

The 1930s witnessed the appearance of Chamberlin's theory of monopolistic competition, which aspired to close a gap between Marshall's polar cases of monopoly and perfect competition. On Melvin Reder's reading of F53, monopolistic competition theory, with its emphasis on descriptive realism, posed a serious threat to the neoclassical theory of firm and markets. Rather than defend neoclassical theory by "affirming the descriptive accuracy of the perfect competition model, Friedman argued that ... the primary criterion for judging the merit of any model is its capacity for generating correct and substantively important predictions" (Reder 2003, 528). Restoring "confidence in the validity of neoclassical theory ... [was] high among Friedman's objectives" (Reder 2003, 528).

Friedman took the position that not only was monopolistic competition theory lacking in tools (F53, 39), but Marshallian theory – which worked out of "two 'ideal' types of firms: atomistically competitive firms, grouped into industries, and monopolistic firms" (F53, 35) – was altogether adequate.[2] "Everything depends on the problem; there is no inconsistency in regarding the same firm as if it were a perfect competitor for one problem, and a monopolist for another" (F53, 36). Earlier he explains that "Each occurrence has some features peculiarly its own ... The capacity to judge that these are or are not to be disregarded ... can be learned but only by experience and exposure in the 'right' scientific atmosphere, not by rote" (F53, 25). Again, by referring to *the* right scientific atmosphere, Friedman appears to scant the possible benefits of pluralism.

Friedman's efforts to buttress the neoclassical theory of the firm by invoking economic natural selection are also instructive. His famous "as if" arguments – on the positioning of leaves on trees "*as if* each leaf sought to maximize the amount of sunlight it receives" (p. 19); and that an expert billiard player makes shots "*as if* he knew the complicated mathematical formulas that would give the optimum" (F53, 21; emphasis in original) – are introduced to support the hypothesis that "under a wide range of circumstances individual firms behave *as if* they were seeking rationally to maximize their expected returns" (F53, 21; emphasis in original), since otherwise they will not be viable (F53, 22).

Correct as far as it goes. But why not name the circumstances under which the maximization of expected returns hypothesis is problematic, as recommended by Tjalling Koopmans (1957, 141):

---

[2] "Chamberlin versus Chicago" issues have been addressed at length elsewhere. See George C. Archibald (1961, 1987), Robert Kuenne (1967), and Richard Lipsey (2001).

Such a change in the basis of economic analysis would seem to represent a gain in realism attributable to a concern with the directly perceived descriptive accuracy of the postulates. It would lead us to expect profit maximization to be most clearly exhibited in industries where entry is easiest and where the struggle for survival is keenest, and would present us with the further challenge to analyze what circumstances give to an industry that character. It would also prevent us, for purposes of explanatory theory, from getting bogged down in those refinements of profit maximization theory which endow the decision makers with analytical and computational abilities and assume them to have information-gathering opportunities such as are unlikely to exist or be applied in current practice. It seems that nothing is lost, and much may be gained, in thus broadening the postulational basis of economic theory.

To delimit the adequacy of the profit maximization hypothesis along these lines is not apostasy, but progress.

3   Theories of the firm (plural)

3.1   The atmospherics

F53 makes no reference to the heady atmospherics of the 1950s, which was a decade during which the social sciences were rushing toward rigor. Paul Samuelson's *Foundations of Economic Analysis* had been published in 1947. John von Neumann and Oskar Morgenstern's *Theory of Games and Economic Behavior*, first published in 1944, went into its third edition in 1953. Kenneth Arrow's *Social Choice and Individual Values* was published in 1951. And exciting new general equilibrium treatments of welfare economics were taking shape (Arrow 1951b; Debreu 1954). The Cowles Commission (then at the University of Chicago, but soon to leave for Yale) had become the mecca of mathematical economies.

The contiguous social sciences also had mathematical ambitions. As Herbert Simon put it,

Mathematics has become the dominant language of the natural sciences not because it is quantitative – a common delusion – but primarily because it permits clear and rigorous reasoning about phenomena too complex to be handled in words. This advantage of mathematics over cruder languages should prove to be of even greater significance in the social sciences, which deal with phenomena of the greatest complexity. (1957, 89).

The idea that success in the social sciences would be realized by the "mathematization of everything" was in the air.[3]

---

[3] Interestingly, Simon subsequently revised his views and recommended that the economics profession be more attentive to the needs of the many students who view "mathematical tools with distrust and deplore the necessity of devoting their research time to formalisms

As between positive and normative, much of the research during this era was predominantly normative. As discussed below, needless errors of public policy have normative origins. Possibly Friedman's 1953 essay was intended (in part) to forestall these developments. Be that as it may, the view that rival theories do not coexist but collide and that there is one "right way" discourage a plurality of instructive constructions.

In fact, the self-imposed limits of the theory of the firm as production function to which a profit maximization purpose was ascribed were highly restrictive. Faced with the anomalies posed by non-standard and unfamiliar contracting practices and organizational structures, industrial organization economists from both Harvard (barriers to entry) and Chicago (price discrimination) appealed to monopoly purpose to explain these phenomena.

A problem with such explanations is that the requisite market power preconditions to exercise monopoly purpose were often missing. More generally, the one-string banjo of monopoly reasoning was often humbug (Coase 1972, 67):

> ... if an economist finds something – a business practice of one sort or another – that he does not understand, he looks for a monopoly explanation. And as in this field we are very ignorant, the number of ununderstandable practices tends to be very large, and the reliance on a monopoly explanation, frequent.

Absent an alternative lens, monopoly reasoning ran amok. As Justice Stewart put it in his dissenting opinion in *Von's Grocery* (1966), the "sole consistency that I can find in [merger] litigation under Section 7 [is that] the Government always wins." An antitrust steam roller had been loosed. Public policy toward business was careening out of control (Williamson 1985, ch. 14).

Insistence on a single, all-purpose theory of the firm was at the heart of the problem. As would subsequently become apparent, it is "a mistake to confuse the firm of [orthodox] economic theory with its real-world namesake. The chief mission of neoclassical economics is to understand how the price system coordinates the use of resources, not the inner workings of real firms" (Demsetz 1983, 377). Theories of the firm that regard the inner workings of real firms as consequential have since moved beyond technology (production functions) to make provision for organization. Prior preoccupation with monopoly purpose has given way to a larger set of purposes, to include efficiency, in the process.

---

that they regard as mainly sterile" (Simon 1997, 90). Assar Lindbeck puts it somewhat differently: university teachers and researchers of economics should "assume a greater responsibility for transmitting knowledge and understanding of real-world problems, including common sense" rather than dwell on "simple classroom exercises, with over-simplified and often unrealistic assumptions" (2001, 32).

The argument is not that the orthodoxy lens of choice is wrong but that it is not all-purpose. There are other instructive perspectives. As Avinash Dixit has recently put it (1996, 9):

... the neoclassical theory of production and supply viewed the firm as a profit-maximizing black box. While some useful insights follow from this, it leaves some very important gaps in our understanding and gives us some very misleading ideas about the possibilities of beneficial policy intervention. Economists studying business and industrial organization have long recognized the inadequacy of the neoclassical view of the firm and have developed richer paradigms and models based on the concepts of various kinds of transaction costs. Policy analysis ... stands to benefit from ... opening the black box and examining the actual workings of the mechanism inside.

3.2   Managerial and behavior theories

The large size of modern firms has often resulted in diffuse ownership. Is it reasonable under such circumstances to assume that the managers of a modern corporation will "choose to operate it in the interests of the owners" (Berle and Means 1932, 121)? Or might the management operate such corporations in a fashion that sometimes compromised ownership interests?

The "obvious" way to respond to this possibility was to take exception with the assumption of profit maximization. If managers had the latitude to tilt the operations of the firm in pursuit of managerial purposes, then restate the objective function of the firm to reflect these added purposes. That simple change aside, the firm would still be described as a production function and the same marginal apparatus could be employed. Upon postulating a different (more realistic) objective function to which managerial purposes were ascribed, the ramifications of managerialism could be derived and contrasted with those of profit maximization.

Albeit a topic of ongoing discussion, models of managerial discretion did not appear until almost thirty years after Berle and Means highlighted the separation of ownership from control issue in 1932. The first of these was William Baumol's model (1959) postulating that large firms maximize revenues subject to a minimum profit constraint. Robin Marris (1964) shortly thereafter advanced a growth maximization hypothesis. And I expressed the objective function of the firm as a utility function in which managerial staff and emoluments as well as profits appeared (Williamson 1964).

Because all three of these models described the firm as a production function, all remained within the resource allocation tradition. Greater realism – for size preference (Baumol), growth preference (Marris), and expense preference (Williamson) – notwithstanding, few novel ramifications for public policy emerged. To be sure, competition in product and capital markets were both viewed as "good," in that these served as a check upon managerial discretion, but such competition was also desired for standard resource allocation reasons. Also, although lump-sum taxes induced changes in factor proportions in the expense preference model that differed from neoclassical predictions and it could further be shown that the intertemporal management of "slack" had business cycle ramifications (Williamson 1968), qualitative responses by firms to changes in "tax rates, interest rates, wages, investment subsidies and the like ... [turned out to be] pretty much the same, regardless of what firms are assumed to maximize" (Solow 1971, 319). Thus even though "firms with different objectives [will differ quantitatively], if their qualitative response is more or less insensitive within limits," then objective function differences do not much affect the research agenda (Solow 1971, 319).

Put differently, so long as the firm is described as a production function, it does not matter much, at least qualitatively, which of several plausible objective functions is chosen. In that event, considerations of parsimony support continued use of the profit maximization setup.

The "behavioral theory of the firm" (Cyert and March 1963) took a different tack. Rather than emphasize realism in motivation (as in the managerial theories), behavioral theory focused on realism in process. The purpose was to explain (predict) price and output decisions of the firm with process-oriented models in which internal decision rules and routines were featured. Albeit successful at a very microanalytic level of analysis (e.g. predicting department store pricing "to the penny" (Cyert and March 1963, ch. 7)), the theory did not engage issues of resource allocation more generally. Also, although the behavioral theory of the firm devotes two pages (295–6) to antitrust policy, the discussion focuses entirely on "uncertainty avoidance," is wholly devoid of specific applications, and has had no discernible impact on antitrust enforcement. Evolutionary economic theory aside, which also adopted the routine as the unit of analysis (Nelson and Winter 1982), the main influence of behavioral theory has been in the field of organization theory – where it has been massive – rather than economics.

3.3   The lens of contract

What I refer to as the lens of contract approach to economic organization breaks away from the resource allocation paradigm (prices and output; supply and demand) to examine economic organization from a different – partly rival but mainly complementary – perspective. To be sure, contractual approaches to economic organization had been under discussion for a long time (Condillac 1776). It was not, however, until the 1970s that operationalization got under way in a concerted fashion.

The lens of contract approach to economic organization was prefigured by John R. Commons, who had long contested the all-purpose reliance on the efficient resource allocation paradigm. But there was more than mere criticism in Commons. As against simple market exchange between "faceless buyers and sellers who meet for an instant to exchange standardized goods and services at equilibrium prices" (Ben-Porath 1980, 4), Commons had an abiding interest in "going concerns" and reformulated the problem of economic organization as follows: "the ultimate unit of activity ... must contain in itself the three principles of conflict, mutuality, and order. This unit is a transaction" (1932, 4). Not only does Commons move to a more microanalytic unit of analysis (the transaction), but his three principles prefigure the concept of governance – in that governance is the means by which to infuse *order*, thereby to mitigate *conflict* and realize *mutual gain*. This latter turns out to be a recurrent theme in the evolving contractual account of the purposes served by complex contract and organization.

Coase's classic paper, "On the nature of the firm" (1937), also raised related concerns. Three lapses in the orthodox theory of firm and market organization are especially noteworthy: (1) the distribution of transactions between firm and market were taken as given, whereas these should be derived; (2) going beyond production costs, there was a need to recognize that transaction cost differences were often responsible for the choice of one mode rather than another; and (3) orthodoxy had no good answers for the puzzle of what is responsible for limits to firm size.

Coase's subsequent critique of the market failure literature in his equally famous paper on "The problem of social cost" (1960) identified additional lapses of logic. Upon reformulating the tort problem (or, more generally, the externality problem) as a problem of contract, he showed that externalities vanished when the logic of zero transaction costs is pushed to completion. As Coase put it in his Nobel Prize lecture (1992, 717; emphasis added):

Pigou's conclusion and that of most economists using standard economic theory was ... that some kind of government action (usually the imposition of taxes) was required to restrain those whose actions had harmful effects on others (often termed negative externalities). What I showed ... was that *in a regime of zero transaction costs, an assumption of standard economic theory*, negotiations between the parties would lead to those arrangements being made which would maximize wealth and this irrespective of the initial assignment of property rights.

Kenneth Arrow's examination of "The organization of economic activity: issues pertinent to the choice of market versus nonmarket allocation"

(1969) likewise made a prominent place for transaction costs, both in general and with reference to vertical integration. The general argument is this (Arrow 1969, 48; emphasis added):

> I contend that market failure is a more general condition than externality; and both differ from increasing returns in a basic sense, since market failures in general and externalities in particular are relative to the mode of economic organization, while increasing returns are essentially a technological phenomenon.
>
> Current writing has helped to bring out the point that market failure is not absolute; it is *better to consider a broader category, that of transaction costs,* which in general impede and in particular cases completely block the formation of markets ... [T]ransaction costs are the costs of running the economic system.

Organizational considerations now take their place alongside technology, which had previously been treated as determinative. Upon recognizing that organization matters, transaction cost differences, as between internal organization and market exchange (where both are now regarded as alternative modes of contracting), have obvious ramifications for vertical integration: "An incentive for vertical integration is replacement of the costs of buying and selling on the market by the costs of intrafirm transfers; the existence of vertical integration may suggest that *the costs of operating competitive markets are not zero, as is usually assumed by our theoretical analysis*" (Arrow 1969, 48; emphasis added).

The need to place the study of positive transaction costs onto the agenda was clearly posed. Adding a perfunctory transaction cost term to production cost or utility function expressions would not, moreover, suffice. If, as James Buchanan puts it, *"mutuality of advantage from voluntary exchange is ... the most fundamental of all understandings in economics"* (2001, 28), and if the purposes of complex exchange are frequently misconstrued by orthodoxy, then a "science of exchanges" approach (Buchanan 2001, 28) to economic organization is awaiting development.

As perceived by Buchanan, the principal needs for a science of exchange were in the field of public finance and took the form of *public ordering*: "Politics is a structure of complex exchange among individuals, a structure within which persons seek to secure collectively their own privately defined objectives that cannot be efficiently secured through *simple market exchanges*" (1987, 246; emphasis added). Inasmuch as the preconditions for simple market exchanges are not satisfied when problems of collective choice are posed, a new "calculus of consent," so to speak, was needed (Buchanan and Tullock 1962; Brennan and Buchanan 1985). The field of public choice took shape in response to the perceived needs.

Public ordering is not, however, the only or even the predominant way of dealing with complex market exchange. On the contrary, huge numbers

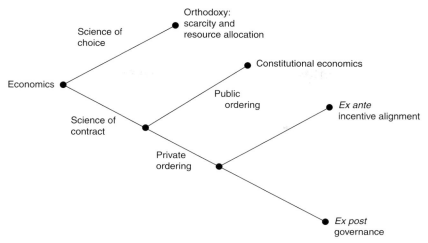

Figure 9.1 The sciences of choice and contract

of private-sector transactions do not qualify to be described as simple market transactions between "faceless buyers and sellers." Given that anti-competitive interpretations for non-standard and unfamiliar contracting practices and organizational structures are frequently bankrupt, and since mutuality of advantage is the fundamental purpose of exchange, why not interpret the governance of contractual relations as an effort to implement the Commons Triple of conflict, mutuality, and order?

Complex contracting and organization would thus be construed mainly (but not exclusively) as self-help efforts by the immediate parties to a transaction to align incentives and craft governance structures that are better attuned to their exchange needs. The study of private ordering (with reference to industrial organization and microeconomics more generally) thus takes its place alongside public ordering.

Figure 9.1 sets out the main distinctions. The initial divide is between the science of choice (orthodoxy) and the science of contract. The former corresponds to the ideal transaction in both law and economics – namely, simple market exchange to which the resource allocation paradigm applies and competition prevails. The science of contract, by contrast, applies to complex exchanges for which non-market supports are required. As discussed above, complex contracting then divides into public (constitutional economics) and private ordering parts, where the second is split into two related branches. One branch deals with *ex ante* incentive alignment (mechanism design, agency theory, the formal property rights literature), often with reference to efficient risk bearing. The second features the *ex post* governance of contractual relations (contract implementation, with emphasis on the mitigation of contractual hazards).

Interestingly, Chester Barnard's book on *The Functions of the Executive* (1938) is prominently featured in both the *ex ante* incentive alignment and *ex post* governance approaches to economic organization. Thus the recent book by Jean-Jacques Laffont and David Martimort on *The Theory of Incentives* credits Barnard with being "the first [to] attempt to define a general theory of incentives in management" (2002, 11). Even more important, in my judgment, is Barnard's insistence that adaptation is the central problem of economic organization, where the adaptations to which Barnard had reference were those of a "conscious, deliberate, purposeful" kind (1938, 4) accomplished through administration. Taken together with the autonomous adaptations to changes in relative prices to which Friedrich Hayek (1945) gave prominence, the stage was set, as it were, for the combined study of markets (autonomous adaptations) and hierarchies (cooperative adaptations).

The incentive branch has been principally concerned with the employment relation whereas the paradigm problem for the governance branch is vertical integration. The latter is the make-or-buy decision in intermediate product markets. The manner in which this is decided has obvious ramifications for the boundary of the firm. More generally, a large number of contractual phenomena turn out to be variations on the very same transaction-cost economizing themes that surface when vertical integration is examined in comparative contracting terms. Vertical market restrictions (customer, territorial, and franchise restrictions), hybrid modes of organization, the organization of labor, the choice between debt and equity, the assessment of regulation/deregulation, the use of public bureaus, and the like are all matters to which the logic of transaction-cost economizing has been usefully applied. Not only do many of the predictions of transaction-cost economics differ from orthodoxy, but the data have been broadly corroborative.

Whereas the conceptual framework out of which transaction-cost economics works differs from orthodoxy (in that it is a contractual construction with emphasis on *ex post* governance), it is nevertheless in agreement with F53 that predictions attended by empirical testing are the cutting edge. The key message of the methodology of positive economics thus reaches beyond orthodoxy. Yet the methodology to which transaction-cost economics subscribes is even closer to that of Robert Solow (2001). Describing himself as a native informant rather than as a methodologist, Solow's "terse description of what one economist thinks he is doing" (2001, 111) takes the form of three injunctions: keep it simple; get it right; make it plausible.

He observes with reference to the first that "the very complexity of real life ... [is what] makes simple models so necessary" (2001, 111). Keeping it simple entails stripping away the inessentials and going for the jugular. The object is not to explain everything but to narrow the focus to central features and key regularities (some of which may previously have been scanted). Getting it right "includes translating economic concepts into accurate mathematics (or diagrams, or words) and making sure that further logical operations are correctly performed and verified" (Solow 2001, 112). But there is more to it than that. A model can be right mechanically yet be unenlightening because it is "imperfectly suited to the subject matter. It can *obscure the key interactions*, instead of spotlighting them" (Solow 2001, 112; emphasis added). If maintaining meaningful contact with the key phenomena of interest (contractual or otherwise) is valued, then rigor that sacrifices meaningful contact poses a tradeoff, especially if more veridical models yield refutable implications that are congruent with the data.

This last brings me to a fourth injunction: derive refutable implications to which the relevant (often microanalytic) data are brought to bear. Nicholas Georgescu-Roegen had a felicitous way of putting it: "The purpose of science in general is not prediction, but knowledge for its own sake," yet prediction is "the touchstone of scientific knowledge" (1971, 37). There is a need to sort the sheep from the goats when rival theories are at an impasse.[4]

Inasmuch, however, as the immediate prospect for a unified, all-purpose theory of the firm is very doubtful, there may be several sheep from which to choose – depending on the specific problems for which good answers are wanting. In the event, pluralism has much to recommend it. As Simon puts it, "I am a great believer in pluralism in science. Any direction you go has a very high *a priori* probability of being wrong, so it is good if other people are exploring in other directions – perhaps one of them will be on the right track" (1992, 21) – to which I would add that *several* investigators might be on rights tracks (plural).

5   Conclusions

Very few books, and even fewer papers, are celebrated on their fiftieth anniversary. There is no question but that F53 was and remains influential – mainly because the central message, at least among pragmatically oriented economists, is fundamentally correct. Would-be theories, in

[4] The fruitfulness to which F53 (33) refers is also pertinent in comparing theories: theories that have wide application, in that many phenomena turn out to be variations on a theme, are to be preferred to theories of narrow scope, *ceteris paribus*.

economics and throughout social sciences, need to stand up and be counted – by making predictions and inviting empirical tests.

Interestingly, although the theory of the firm was once criticized for the paucity of empirical work (Holmstrom and Tirole 1989, 126), I would argue that the critics have the empirical cart before the theoretical horse. What is sorely needed in the theory of the firm literature are interesting and testable predictions. As such predictions began to appear, empirical research mushroomed.[5] I am persuaded that Melvin Reder's advice that economists "focus on the construction of relatively simple theories that have some prospect of accounting for the gross facts" (1999, 298) is apposite.

References

Archibald, George C. (1961). Chamberlin versus Chicago. *Review of Economic Studies*, 29(1), 2–28

(1987). Monopolistic competition. In J. Eatwell *et al.* (eds.), *The New Palgrave Dictionary of Economics*, vol.3. London: Macmillan, 531–4

Arrow, Kenneth J. (1951a). *Social Choice and Individual Values*. New York: John Wiley

(1951b). An extension of the basic theorems of classical welfare economics. In Jersey Neyman (ed.), *Proceedings of the Second Berkeley Symposium on Mathematical Statistics and Probability*. Berkeley, CA: University of California Press, 507–32

(1969). The organization of economic activity: issues pertinent to the choice of market versus nonmarket allocation. In *The Analysis and Evaluation of Public Expenditure: The PPB System*, vol. 1. US Joint Economic Committee, 91st Congress, 1st Session. Washington, DC: US Government Printing Office, 39–73

(1999). Forward. In Glenn Carroll and David Teece (eds.), *Firms, Markets, and Hierarchies*. New York: Oxford University Press, vii–viii

Bain, Joe (1956). *Barriers to New Competition*. Cambridge, MA: Harvard University Press

Barnard, Chester (1938). *The Functions of the Executive*. Cambridge: Harvard University Press (fifteenth printing, 1962)

Baumol, W. J. (1959). *Business Behavior, Value and Growth*. New York: Macmillan

Ben-Porath, Yoram (1980). The F-connection: families, friends, and firms and the organization of exchange. *Population and Development Review*, 6 (March), 1–30

Berle, Adolph A. and Gardner C. Means, Jr. (1932). *The Modern Corporation and Private Property*. New York: Macmillan

---

[5] To be sure there were lags. By the year 2000, however, there were over 600 published empirical papers in transaction-cost economics alone (Boerner and Macher 2001).

Boerner, Christopher and J. Macher (2001). Transaction cost economics: a review and assessment of the empirical literature. Unpublished manuscript, Haas School of Business, University of California–Berkeley

Brennan, Geoffrey and James Buchanan (1985). *The Reason of Rules*. Cambridge: Cambridge University Press

Buchanan, James (1987). The constitution of economic policy. *American Economic Review*, 77 (June), 243–50

   (2001). Game theory, mathematics, and economics. *Journal of Economic Methodology*, 8 (March), 27–32

Buchanan, James and Gordon Tullock (1962). *The Calculus of Consent*. Ann Arbor, MI: University of Michigan Press

Condillac, Etienne Bonnot ([1776] 1821). Le commerce et le gouvernement. In *Oeuvres completes de Condillac*, vol. 4, Paris: Briere

Coase, Ronald H. (1937). The nature of the firm. *Economica* n.s., 4, 386–405

   (1960). The problem of social cost, *Journal of Law and Economics*, 3 (October), 1–44

   (1972). Industrial organization: a proposal for research. In V. R. Fuchs (ed.), *Policy Issues and Research Opportunities in Industrial Organization*. New York: National Bureau of Economic Research, 59–73

   (1992). The institutional structure of production. *American Economic Review*, 82 (September), 713–19

Commons, John R. (1932). The problem of correlating law, economics, and ethics. *Wisconsin Law Review*, 8, 3–26

Cyert, Richard M. and James G. March (1963). *A Behavioral Theory of the Firm*. Englewood Cliffs, NJ: Prentice-Hall

Debreu, Gerard (1954). Valuation equilibrium and Pareto optimum. *Proceedings of the National Academy of Social Sciences*, 40, 588–92

Demsetz, Harold (1983). The structure of ownership and the theory of the firm. *Journal of Law and Economics*, 26 (June), 375–90

Dixit, Avinash (1996). *The Making of Economic Policy: A Transaction Cost Politics Perspective*. Cambridge, MA: MIT Press

Friedman, M. (1953). The methodology of positive economics. In *Essays in Positive Economics*. Chicago: Chicago University Press

   (1997) [in Snowdon and Vane (1997)]

Georgescu-Roegen, Nicholas (1971). *The Entropy Law and Economic Process*. Cambridge, MA: Harvard University Press

Hayek, Friedrich (1945). The use of knowledge in society. *American Economic Review*, 35 (September), 519–30

Holmstrom, Bengt and Jean Tirole (1989). The theory of the firm. In Richard Schmalensee and Robert Willig (eds.), *Handbook of Industrial Organization*. New York: North Holland, 61–133

Koopmans, Tjalling C. (1957) *Three Essays on the State of Economic Science*. New York: McGraw-Hill

Kuenne, Robert E. (ed.) (1967). *Monopolistic Competition Theory: Studies in Impact : Essays in Honor of Edward H. Chamberlin*. New York: John Wiley

Kuhn, Thomas S. (1970). *The Structure of Scientific Revolutions*, 2nd edition. Chicago: University of Chicago Press

Laffont, Jean-Jaques and David Martimort (2002). *The Theory of Incentives.* Princeton: Princeton University Press

Assar Lindbeck (2001). Economics in Europe. CESifo Forum, Spring, 31–3

Lipsey, Richard (2001). Successes and failures in the transformation of economics. *Journal of Economic Methodology,* 8(2), 169–201

Marris, Robin (1964). *The Economic Theory of Managerial Capitalism.* New York: Free Press.

Nelson, Richard R. and Sidney G. Winter (1982). *An Evolutionary Theory of Economic Change.* Cambridge, MA: Harvard University Press

Reder, Melvin W. (1999). *Economics: The Culture of a Controversial Science.* Chicago: University of Chicago Press
    (2003) Remarks on "The methodology of positive economics." *Journal of Economic Methodology,* 10, 527–30.

Samuelson, Paul A. (1947). *Foundations of Economic Analysis.* Cambridge, MA: Harvard University Press

Simon, Herbert (1957). *Models of Man.* New York: John Wiley
    (1992). *Economics, Bounded Rationality, and the Cognitive Revolution.* Brookfield, CT: Edward Elgar
    (1997). *An Empirically Based Microeconomics.* Cambridge: Cambridge University Press

Snowdon, Brain and Howard Vane (1997). Modern macroeconomics and its evolution from a monetarist perspective. An interview with Professor Milton Friedman. *Journal of Economic Studies,* 24(4), 192–222

Solow, Robert (1971). Some implications of alternative criteria for the firm. In Robin Marris and Adrian Wood (eds.), *The Corporate Economy.* Cambridge, MA: Harvard Universtiy Press, 318–342
    (1997). How did economics get that way and what way did it get? *Daedalus,* 126(1), 39–58
    (2001). A native informant speaks. *Journal of Economic Methodology,* 8 (March), 111–112

United States v. Von's Grocery Co. (1966). 384 U.S. 270, 301 (Stewart, J., dissenting)

Von Neumann, John and Oskar Morgenstern (1953). *Theory of Games and Economic Behavior.* Princeton, NJ: Princeton University Press

Williamson, Oliver E. (1964). *The Economics of Discretionary Behavior: Managerial Objectives in a Theory of the Firm.* Englewood Cliffs, NJ: Prentice-Hall
    (1968). A dynamic-stochastic theory of managerial behavior. In Almarin Phillips and Oliver Williamson (eds.), *Prices: Issues in Theory, Practice, and Public Policy.* Philadelphia: University of Pennsylvania Press
    (1985). *The Economic Institutions of Capitalism.* New York: Free Press

10 Friedman's selection argument revisited

Jack Vromen

1 Introduction

Friedman's selection argument in his 1953 essay "The methodology of positive economics" (F53) received little attention in economic methodology. There may be several reasons for this. Friedman's exposition of the argument is so short and hidden in his lengthy defense of marginalism that it might easily have escaped the attention of economic methodologists. Alternatively, methodologists may have noticed the argument, but may have considered it to be too insignificant to Friedman's overall argument, too obviously just a rhetoric trick to savior marginalism, or simply as too obviously flawed to merit any discussion. Whatever the reason for this relative neglect by methodologists, the argument has not gone unnoticed in the economics literature. On the contrary, economists of different stripes and persuasion have taken up the argument and have bent it to their own purposes. Just the fact that this happened by itself warrants taking a closer look both at Friedman's original statement of the argument and the use that other economists subsequently made of it.

What exactly is there in Friedman's selection argument that has been found worthwhile to comment and elaborate upon? One of the aims of this chapter is to point out that different answers are given to this question. Different commentators have different ideas about what it is in Friedman's argument that warrants further consideration. As we shall see, the differences are vast. Different commentators concentrate on different *aspects* of the argument. Different commentators come up with different *interpretations* of the argument and of what the argument is meant to establish. And, last but not least, different commentators draw different *conclusions* as to what implications the argument has for economic theorizing. The chapter argues in particular that the implications for economic theorizing that most commentators impute to Friedman's argument may well be quite different from the ones Friedman intended. In this sense, this is a tale about *unintended consequences* of Friedman's selection argument.

257

2   The argument contextualized

Friedman's selection argument is part of a larger argumentative strategy to defend marginalism in general, and the profit-maximization assumption in the theory of the firm in particular, against critiques leveled by so-called antimarginalists. Based on responses to questionnaires, antimarginalists such as Hall and Hitch (1939) in the UK and Lester (1946) in the USA argued that marginal costs and revenues were no part of the decision-making of businessmen. Instead businessmen were allegedly observed to follow rules of thumb like the full-cost pricing rule. The antimarginalists concluded from this that the theory of the firm had to be discarded and had to be superseded by a theory with more realistic behavioral assumptions. Friedman's selection argument was specifically devised to bring home the point that even if antimarginalists were right that businessmen follow full-cost pricing rules, this does not jeopardize the usefulness and applicability of the (marginalist) theory of the firm. More precisely, the argument was meant to show that when it comes to assessing a theory of the firm it does not matter what decision rules and decision procedures businessmen follow. What matters is what businessmen actually do, not their motives, reasons, deliberations, and the like for doing so, let alone what they say they do (or what they themselves believe they are doing).

Friedman does not need many words to present his selection argument. Strictly speaking, Friedman dedicates no more than just one paragraph in the whole text of F53 to the exposition of the argument.

Confidence in the maximization-of-returns hypothesis is justified by evidence of a very different character. This evidence is in part similar to that adduced on behalf of the billiard-player hypothesis – unless the behavior of businessmen in some way or other approximated behavior consistent with the maximization of returns, it seems unlikely that they would remain in business for long. Let the apparent immediate determinant of business behavior be anything at all – habitual reaction, random chance, or whatnot. Whenever this determinant happens to lead to behavior consistent with rational and informed maximization of returns, the business will prosper and acquire resources with which to expand; whenever it does not, the business will tend to lose resources and can be kept in existence only by the addition of resources from outside. The process of "natural selection" thus helps validate the hypothesis – or, rather, given natural selection, acceptance of the hypothesis can be based largely on the judgment that it summarizes appropriately the conditions for survival. (F53, 22)

Presumably Friedman was the first to have developed this type of selection argument in defense of the theory of the firm. Although a similar argument appeared earlier in Alchian (1950), it seems that the first draft of Friedman's essay (which already contained the selection argument) was written before Friedman (as an editor of *the Journal of Political Economy*; Hammond 1991) came across Alchian's paper. In his essay Friedman notes that his own presentation of the argument is independent in origin of Alchian's.[1] Some ten years later Becker (1962) published a similar argument. Compared to Alchian's and Becker's versions of the argument, which are full-paper articulations of the argument, Friedman's is shortest and most cryptic. This might explain why in several discussions of the argument, Friedman's version is given short shrift or is even not mentioned at all. In his wide-ranging overview of earlier attempts in economics to import biological models, for example, Hirshleifer (1977) does not contain a single reference to F53. There is long discussion of Alchian (1950), Enke (1951), Penrose (1952), Simon (1955), and Winter (1964, 1971), but F53 is not mentioned once.

But Friedman was not the first to bring evolutionary considerations to bear on the antimarginalism controversy. In a somewhat forgotten paper Harrod (1939) already contains a few interesting evolutionary speculations.

Other lines of thought suggest themselves. It may be that certain procedures, of which application of the full cost principle is one example, are thrown up purely by chance in the first instance and survive by a process akin to natural selection in biology. New business procedures would then be analogous to new mutations in nature. Of a number of procedures, none of which can be shown either at the time or subsequently to be truly rational, some may supplant others because they do in fact lead to better results. Thus while they may have originated by accident, it would not be by accident that they are still used. For this reason, if an economist finds a procedure widely established in fact, he ought to regard it with more respect than he would be inclined to give in the light of his own analytic method. (Harrod 1939, 7)

The point Harrod is trying to make is different from, if not opposite to Friedman's. Friedman's argument was meant to persuade fellow economists that the issue of what the immediate determinants of firm behavior are is irrelevant for appraising the usefulness of the theory of the firm. By contrast, Harrod's point is that evolutionary considerations should caution economists not to be too readily dismissive of decision procedures observed in firms. The fact that some procedures and rules are observed widely may testify to their superiority to competing procedures and rules in prior selection processes. Whereas Friedman provided an evolutionary argument to show the irrelevance of the empirical findings of the

---

[1] The full footnote (14) reads: "This example, and some of the subsequent discussion, though independent in origin, is similar to and in much the same spirit as an example and the approach in an important paper by Armen A. Alchian, "Uncertainty, Evolution, and Economic Theory," *Journal of Political Economy*, LVIII (June, 1950), 211–21."

antimarginalists, Harrod sought to provide an evolutionary rationale for their relevance. In section 5 we shall see that in some relevant respects Nelson and Winter's evolutionary theory can be interpreted as a further development and articulation of Harrod's antimarginalist evolutionary line of thought.

It is not likely that Friedman himself thought that in his "*pro-marginalism*" case much hinged on his selection argument. For immediately after having presented his selection argument, Friedman continues as follows: "An even more important body of evidence for the maximization-of-returns hypothesis is experience from countless applications of the hypothesis to specific problems and the repeated failure of its implications to be contradicted" (F53, 22). Especially if we take Friedman to mean here that the "countless applications of the hypothesis" provide strong indirect testimony to its empirical record (F53, 23), this of course connects with the general methodological point Friedman is making in his essay. Economic theories should be appraised not on the basis of the realisticness of a theory's assumptions, but on the basis of the empirical accuracy of the theory's testable implications (or predictions). To some extent this makes the selection argument redundant in Friedman's defense of the hypothesis. Whether or not the selection argument is cogent and convincing, in the last instance the testable implications of the theory should be borne out by the facts. This suggests that Friedman holds that if the empirical record of the theory were poor, the selection argument by itself would never provide sufficient evidence to accept the theory.

Even with hindsight it is difficult to tell to what extent F53 helped restore or sustain the confidence of fellow economists in the marginalist theory of the firm in the face of the antimarginalist assaults. At any rate, the marginalist theory of the firm arguably did survive the antimarginalist assaults. Arguably this is all Friedman wanted to accomplish. So, we could say, Friedman's main mission has been accomplished. Case closed. For Friedman this means that economists now had their hands free to get on with their job and to move on to other, more interesting theoretical and empirical issues. This is indeed what many economists actually did. But there are also a few economists (and commentators) who singled out Friedman's selection argument for further consideration. This is surely not what Friedman intended and hoped for.

3   Evolutionary reinterpretations of economic theory

… under a wide range of circumstances individual firms behave *as if* they were seeking rationally to maximize their expected returns (generally if misleadingly called "profits") and had full knowledge of the data needed to succeed in this attempt; *as if,* that is, they knew the relevant cost and demand functions, calculated marginal cost and marginal revenue from all actions open to them, and pushed each line of action to the point at which the relevant marginal cost and marginal revenue were equal ... given natural selection, acceptance of the hypothesis can be based largely on the judgment that *it summarizes* appropriately *the conditions for survival.* (F53, 21–2; emphasis added)

Here we come across Friedman's notorious *as-if* methodology. What Friedman wants to make clear is that the theory of the firm is not committed to a particular view on the actual immediate determinants of firm behavior. In particular, the theory is not wedded to the view that businessmen actually conduct the marginalist calculations that the theory ascribes to them. The only thing the theory is committed to, Friedman argues, is that businessmen actually display the observable behavior predicted by the theory. Thus understood, the theory does not tell us anything about the actual determinants of firm behavior. This makes one wonder what are, or what could be, actual determinants of firm behavior. If it is not necessarily marginalist deliberations that make businessmen behave in the way they (allegedly) do, then what does ensure that they behave in the way they (allegedly) do? Friedman's selection argument can be taken to imply that it is ultimately "natural selection" in competitive markets that see to this. From here it is a small step to argue that what is suggested in the argument is that the theory of the firm should be reinterpreted along evolutionary lines. Appearances nothwithstanding, the theory is not really about motives, deliberations, and calculations of businessmen that make firms and industries behave the way they (allegedly) do. Instead it is about "natural selection" that makes firms and industries behave the way they (allegedly) do.

Friedman leaves no doubt that he ("of course") believes that businessmen do not actually and literally solve the system of simultaneous equations that the theory of the firm assumes they do. The hypothesis that firms maximize expected returns is similar in this respect, Friedman argues, to the hypothesis that leaves around a tree maximize the sunlight they receive and to the hypothesis that expert billiard players solve complicated mathematical equations to calculate the best shot possible.[2] The latter example of the expert billiard player was already introduced in Friedman and Savage (1948) to make the point that objections that the assumption (that expert billiard players solve mathematical equations before making their shots) is a patently unrealistic description of the behavior of expert

---

[2] Although Friedman consistently talks about "hypotheses," it is to be doubted that the examples he discusses can meaningfully be called hypotheses. Henceforth I shall use "assumption" instead of "hypothesis."

billiard players, though "natural and understandable," are "not strictly relevant" (Friedman and Savage 1948, 297). Friedman and Savage argue that "unless he was capable in some way of reaching approximately the same result as that obtained from the formulas, he would not in fact be likely to be an expert billiard player" (1948, 298). Recall that Friedman himself observes that this is similar to the evidence that justifies confidence in the maximization-of-returns assumption: "unless the behavior of businessmen in some way or other approximated behavior consistent with the maximization of returns, it seems unlikely they would remain in business for long" (F53, 22).

But is the evidence adduced on behalf of the expert billiard player assumption really analogous to that adduced on behalf of the maximization of returns assumption? In the case of the maximization-of-returns assumption, competition for resources is taken to be causally responsible for the (alleged) fact that firms display behavior approximating maximization of returns. In the case of the expert billiard player, is Friedman envisaging some similar sort of contest ensuring that the behavior of winners approximates perfect play? This is not clear. If Friedman has such a contest in mind, then it seems it does not follow that the winning billiard players necessarily play almost perfect games. A billiard player who made no mistakes in locating the balls, in solving the relevant mathematical implications, and in implementing the according shots would terminate each game in one turn. Even world champions do not succeed in doing so. Thus the behavior of winners of billiard contests may fall far short of perfect play. Alternatively, Friedman may simply be fleshing out what we understand by "an expert billiard player": by "an expert billiard player" we mean someone who is capable of reaching approximately the same results as that obtained by the formulas. But if this reading is indeed intended by Friedman, it may well be true that such an expert billiard player does not (and will not) exist. At any rate, both readings boil down to pretty much the same: there need not be any approximately perfectly playing billiard player around. Even if there were cutthroat competition, the behavior of winners may deviate not just slightly but significantly from perfect play.

What about the other example that Friedman takes to be similar to the maximization-of-returns assumption, that of leaves trying to maximize the amount of sunlight? Friedman argues that we of course know that leaves do not deliberately or consciously seek anything. Yet on the basis of the assumption we can "explain" (the quotation marks are Friedman's) that trees tend to have a higher density on the side that receives most sunlight. What is actually happening here is that there is a process of "passive adaptation to external circumstances" going on. The consequences of this selection or adaptation process are the same as those that would obtain if leaves were actually to maximize the amount of sunlight: trees have a higher density of leaves on the side that receives most sunlight.

It is tempting to argue that in one respect at least the leaves-around-the-tree assumption is more similar to the maximization-of-returns assumption than the expert-billiard-player assumption. Unlike in the expert-billiard-player assumption, in both the leaves-around-the-tree assumption and the maximization-of-returns assumption Friedman seems to believe that something like "natural selection" is actually driving the process, purportedly leading it to outcomes as predicted by the respective assumption. The disanalogy here of course is that whereas leaves do not actually deliberate and consciously seek anything, billiard players try to make the best shots and businessmen try to maximize profits. Note that Friedman is not denying that businessmen try to maximize profits. What he denies is that in their decision-making businessmen do exactly the things that the theory of the firm ascribes to them. But Friedman considers the whole issue of what are the actual immediate determinants of firm behavior – the mental processes businessmen go through before making decisions or displaying behavior (which includes their goals and motives) – to be irrelevant for the issue at hand. It can safely be assumed that firms behave *as if* businessmen go through all the mental operations ascribed to them in the maximization-of-returns assumption because only firms that do so survive "natural selection" in competitive markets.

Satz and Ferejohn's radical reinterpretation: rational choice theory as an external-structuralist theory

But if this is at the heart of Friedman's argument, then is not the correct interpretation of the maximization-of-returns assumption that it refers to "natural selection" in competitive markets? If in competitive markets the maximization-of-returns assumption "summarizes appropriately the conditions of survival" (F53, 22), and if these conditions are independent of immediate determinants of firm behavior, as Friedman argues, then can it be maintained that the assumption is really about the immediate determinants of firm behavior? Or should we conclude that this is only apparent and that the assumption is really about selection pressure in competitive markets? This is the line taken by Satz and Ferejohn (1994). Satz and Ferejohn argue that rational-choice explanations are most plausible in settings in which individual action is severely constrained.[3] For example,

---

[3] Satz and Ferejohn do not cite empirical support for this claim. There does seem to be some experimental support for the claim that rational choice theory does better in competitive environments. See, for example, Smith (1991).

the theory of the firm has been a far more productive explanatory theory than the theory of consumer behavior, Satz and Ferejohn argue, because consumers face less competitive environments than firms. Rational-choice explanations are argued to gain their explanatory power from features of the agents' environment rather than from the mental states or the psychological make-up of agents. This leads Satz and Ferejohn to plead for a *radical reinterpretation* of rational-choice theory.

The received interpretation is that rational-choice theory is a psychological theory, dealing with what is going on internal to agents, consistent with methodological individualism. By contrast, the interpretation Satz and Ferejohn favor is one in which rational-choice theory appears as an external-structuralist theory that is about external pressures that environments impose on agents. Satz and Ferejohn remark that evolutionary biology, which views nature as a selective structure, provides the crucial paradigm for their discussion (Satz and Ferejohn 1994, 81). They believe that there are social analogues to natural selection acting as powerful selective mechanisms. One such analogue is an environment of competitive capital markets acting as a selector on firms (1994, 79). On Satz and Ferejohn's reinterpretation, rational-choice theory carries no a priori commitments to a particular mental causal mechanism internal to agents (1994, 86). The assumed psychology of the agent is rather an entirely imputed one: "preferences" are derived on the basis of an agent's location in a social structure. This is why the interest of maximizing profits can be imputed to firms in competitive markets. Even though there can be many different motives and deliberations behind pursuing and attaining maximum profits (1994, 79), given their position in a competitive market it makes sense to ascribe the motive to make maximum profits to firms.

Binmore: memes as immediate determinants of behavior

A similar evolutionary reinterpretation of expected-utility theory is advocated by Binmore (1994). Binmore argues that leading utility theorists have long abandoned a literal interpretation of their theory. Utility theory does not explain observable behavior by referring to antecedently and independently identified preferences (or utility functions), expectations, and risk profiles of the agents in question. It is rather the other way around. Preferences, expectations, and risk profiles of agents are inferred from their observable choice behavior. In doing so, by identifying the agents' "revealed" preferences, expectations, and risk profiles, and by assuming that the agents maximize their expected utility, their observable behavior is rationalized. The assumption really is that agents behave, as Binmore puts it, *as though* they maximize their expected utilities thus derived. This of course is very much in line with Friedman and Savage (1948), for example, and with Savage's influential subjective interpretation of expected-utility theory in general.

Binmore goes one considerable step further by suggesting not only that what agents do, how they behave, is the outcome of processes of sociocultural evolution, but also that the latter view reflects the currently dominant or prevailing interpretation of expected-utility theory.

Stigler seems to me a windmill at which it is pointless to tilt. Not even in Chicago are such views given credence any more. I suspect that this is largely because a paradigm is now available that preserves optimization as the underlying mechanism, but no longer sees economic agents as omniscient mathematical prodigies. The new paradigm regards evolutionary forces, biological, social, and economic, as being responsible for getting things maximized ...
... mechanisms exist which could lead to behavior on the part of *homo sapiens* which mimics that of *homo economicus*, without requiring that *homo sapiens* necessarily thinks the same thoughts as those attributed to *homo economicus*. At his fireside, *homo sapiens* will tell different stories from *homo economicus*, and neither type of story need correlate very well with the actual reasons that the species came to behave the way it does. (Binmore 1994, 19–20)

The issue at hand here is whether *homo economicus* provides a useful model to social phenomena. Stigler's stance was that where self-interest (narrowly conceived) and ethical values conflict, self-interest prevails. Binmore argues that it is no longer assumed that *homo economicus*, current economic theory's depiction of human agents, is solely preoccupied with his own interests narrowly conceived. Modern *homo economicus* is an individual that is consistent in seeking to attain whatever his goals may be. Binmore maintains that nowadays most proponents of (and commentators on) expected-utility theory hold that sociocultural evolution sees to it that inconsistencies in human behavior are eventually weeded out. It is this belief, Binmore argues, that is behind the retention of *homo economicus* in current economic theory.

Binmore's contention that it is not omniscience of agents, but evolutionary forces that are responsible for getting things maximized is in line with Friedman's selection argument. But his further suggestion that the actual reasons for people to behave the way they do are *memes* is not in line with Friedman's argument. Following Dawkins (1976),[4] Binmore thinks

---

[4] In his controversial accounts of biological and cultural evolution, Dawkins makes it perfectly clear that his own talk about selfish genes and memes are convenient shorthands. "I expressed all these reasonings in terms of 'decisions' of individual animals but, to repeat, this is just shorthand. What is really going on is that genes 'for' maximizing grandchildren become more numerous in the gene pool. The world becomes full of genes that have successfully come down the ages" (Dawkins 1995, 137).

that believing that our behavior is molded by especially socioeconomic forces commits one to believe also that our behavior is determined by the memes, the units of socioeconomic evolution, that we, as their vehicles, are infected with: "to an observer, it will seem as though an infected agent is acting in his own self-interest, provided that the notion of self-interest is interpreted as being *whatever makes the bearer of a meme a locus for replication of the meme to other heads*" (Binmore 1994, 20; emphasis in the original). While Friedman prefers to remain silent or agnostic about the immediate determinants of behavior, Binmore contends that memes are immediate determinants of individual behavior.

Aumann: the evolutionary interpretation of the "Nash equilibrium" is the fundamental one

Besides Binmore, Aumann is one of the few game theorists to have explicitly addressed methodological issues.[5] Perhaps more than anyone else, Robert Aumann has sought to provide rationalistic foundations of solution notions in game theory, notably of the Nash equilibrium. Among game theorists, Aumann is well known for his staunch defense of the rationality postulate and of his rejection of weaker rationality assumptions. Indeed he has been criticized for taking such an unyielding stance by other prominent game theorists, such as the Nobel laureate Reinhard Selten. In his famous 1985 paper "What is game theory trying to accomplish?" Aumann argues that the Nash equilibrium embodies the most important and fundamental idea of economics, that economic agents act to maximize their utility (Aumann 1985, 43). Recently, in an interview with Eric van Damme, Aumann argues that besides this rationalistic interpretation, the Nash equilibrium also allows for an evolutionary interpretation. What is more, Aumann argues that the evolutionary interpretation is more fundamental than the rationalistic one (Aumann 1997, 18). Let us quote the relevant passages unabbreviated:

When there is a formal relationship between two interpretations, like the rationalistic (conscious maximization) and evolutionary interpretations of Nash equilibrium, then one can say, "oh, this is an accident, these things really have nothing to

---

[5] A more integral comparison between Friedman and Aumann would be interesting but has to await for another occasion. Suffice it to say here that although Aumann favors a type of formalistic economic modeling that Friedman presumably disavows, and although Aumann's predictive accuracy of models should be subordinate to the comprehension that they yield, Aumann is remarkably close to Friedman's methodology on other points. Aumann also holds that assumptions do not have to be correct, that the usefulness rather than the truth of theories is important, and that one can tell the usefulness of some solution concept, for example, from the extent to what it is actually used by economists.

do with each other." Or, one can look for a deeper meaning. In my view, it's a mistake to write off the relationship as an accident.

In fact, the evolutionary interpretation should be considered the fundamental one. Rationality – Homo Sapiens, if you will – is a *product* of evolution. We have become used to thinking of the "fundamental" interpretation as the cognitive rationalistic one, and of evolution as an "as if" story, but that's probably less insightful.

Of course, the evolutionary interpretation is historically subsequent to the rationalistic one. But that doesn't mean that the rationalistic interpretation is the more basic. On the contrary, in science we usually progress, in time, from the superficial to the fundamental. The historically subsequent theory is quite likely to *encompass* the earlier ones. (Aumann 1997, 18)

A superficial glance at this quote might suggest that Aumann's stance towards the notion of Nash equilibrium is similar to Satz and Ferejohn's radical reinterpretation of rational-choice theory. Both seem to argue that the "rationalistic" interpretation of "Nash equilibrium" and rational-choice theory respectively, albeit preceded by the evolutionary interpretation, is not the fundamental interpretation. Since evolutionary pressures and processes rather than processes of "rationalistic" conscious deliberation do the bulk of the explanatory work, it is the evolutionary interpretation that is the fundamental one. But appearances are deceiving here.[6] In calling the evolutionary interpretation of "Nash equilibrium" the fundamental one, Aumann does not want to convey the belief that convergence to Nash equilibria is due to evolutionary mechanisms rather than to conscious maximization. In this he differs from Binmore. Binmore argues that to the extent that people act rationally, they do not do so because of omniscient maximizing. They do so because their actual reasons are the products of evolutionary mechanisms. Upon closer inspection, it turns out that what Aumann wants to convey here is that rationality, or rather the capacity for human beings to act rationally, is itself a product of evolution. The evolutionary interpretation is fundamental in the sense that prior (or antecedent) evolutionary processes have laid the foundation for current maximizing behavior.

Aumann argues that paying attention to its evolutionary origins enables us to see that it is the *function* of our capacity for conscious rational utility maximization to adapt flexibly to complex environments (Aumann 1997, 21). Following Mayr's (1961) distinction between proximate and ultimate causes of behavior, Aumann posits that there are in principle two different

---

[6] Aumann seems to be wrong in suggesting that the evolutionary story is often treated as the more facile, "as if" one. In all the invocations of "natural selection", or evolutionary forces, we have come across thus far the cognitive rationalistic interpretation provides the as if story.

explanations for our behavior. Conscious rational utility maximization is an answer to the question *how* we arrive at our behavior.[7] But if we want to understand *why* we behave the way we do, we must be looking at the evolutionary origins of this capacity or mechanism for conscious rational utility maximization. The general idea here, that ancient evolutionary processes have resulted in conscious utility maximizing *as an immediate determinant of human behavior*, has recently been worked out in more detail by, for example, Robson (1996, 2001a, 2001b) (see Vromen 2003 for a critical discussion). Although it is not clear whether Aumann believes that conscious rational utility maximization means that individuals actually go through the calculations ascribed to them in utility theory, it is clear that Aumann's fundamental evolutionary interpretation of "Nash equilibrium" involves a particular view on the immediate determinants of behavior. In this he differs from Friedman.

Let us take stock. We have seen that there is no shortage of radical reinterpretations of "standard economic theory" along evolutionary lines. Yet we have also seen that the reinterpretations shift in subtle, but significant ways. The only thing Friedman wanted to argue, it can be maintained, is that in spite of all the antimarginalist criticisms there is nothing wrong in continuing the ongoing practice of applying the maximization-of-expected-returns assumption in the theory of the firm. Friedman saw no need for further reflections on the issue of whether his selection argument invites an evolutionary reinterpretation of utility theory.[8] He neither saw a need to identify immediate determinants of behavior. Yet this is what the authors discussed here undertake. Satz and Ferejohn argue that if evolutionary pressures in competitive markets are to carry the explanatory burden, as Friedman suggests, then the theory is best understood as a theory about the outcomes or results of "natural selection" in competitive markets. Binmore can be understood as adding to this a hypothesis about proximate causes, or actual immediate determinants as Friedman calls them, of human behavior. Whereas Friedman seems to prefer an agnostic stance towards these, and argues that there is no need to identify them, Binmore suggests that, the self-understanding of people notwithstanding, memes are in control of their behavior. Aumann, finally, argues that conscious maximizing can be resuscitated as the proximate cause of human behavior on evolutionary grounds.

---

[7] Aumann does not argue that we always engage in conscious rational utility maximization: "to the extent that we *do* calculate, it may be a result of evolution" (Aumann 1997, 32).

[8] Friedman would approve of the license that the evolutionary reinterpretations provide for continued use of equilibrium analysis. But he presumably would have less sympathy for "formalistic" uses of (Nash) equilibrium analysis in game theory.

4   Evolutionary game theory: checking the validity of the argument

Thus far it has been tacitly assumed that the evolutionary processes envisaged in the reinterpretations indeed do lead to the results and outcomes that standard economic theory predicts. Is this assumption warranted? Let us first look once again at the relevant crucial passage in Friedman's argument.

… given natural selection, acceptance of the hypothesis can be based largely *on the judgment* that it summarizes *appropriately* the conditions for survival. (F53, 22; emphasis added)

Friedman suggests that the evidence that "natural selection" in competitive markets provides for the continued use of the maximization-of-returns hinges crucially on the judgment that the assumption at least roughly gets the conditions for survival right. If firms that do not attain maximum returns can survive "natural selection", then the argument breaks down.

So the judgment that the maximization-of-returns assumption summarizes approximately the conditions for survival must be correct for the selection argument to carry any weight in favor of the assumption. Is it correct? Friedman apparently believed that no further argument or examination is needed to see that the judgment is correct. Others saw this differently. Friedman's selection argument incited many attempts to examine and scrutinize this judgment critically. Not surprisingly, different examiners with different persuasions came to different conclusions. The disagreement here is not only due to differences in persuasion, predilections, and the like of the examiners, however. It is also due to the fact that it is not perfectly clear what the judgment is actually about. What exactly is claimed? Note, for example, that "the conditions for survival" is ambiguous. Are the conditions *necessary* or *sufficient*? Is it claimed that attaining maximum returns is necessary for firms to survive? Or is the claim that attaining maximum returns is sufficient for firms to survive? The former claim is stronger than the latter. The former claim rules out a possibility that the latter claim leaves open: firms earning less than maximum returns may survive. Most examiners seem to assume that Friedman is making the stronger claim that only firms earning maximum returns can survive.[9]

Many commentators have rightly observed that what Friedman is really arguing is not that the theory of the firm gets phenomena at the level of

---

[9] I think there is some textual evidence favoring this interpretation, as Friedman argues that firms that happen not to earn maximum returns will tend to disappear.

individual firms right, but that the theory gets phenomena at the aggregate level of markets and industries right. An example of the type of *ultimate* claim Friedman is making is presented by Alchian (1950): the average labor/capital ratio in some industry rises if the (relative real) price of labor falls *ceteris paribus*. This suggests that the claim that only firms earning maximum returns survive is just an *intermediary* step in making and substantiating the latter ultimate claim (Langlois 1986; Vromen 1995). Sometimes the intermediate claim Friedman is making is discussed under the label of *as-if rationality*, or of *as-if maximizing* (Kandori 1997). The ultimate claim Friedman is making is sometimes discussed under the label of *as-if optimality*. As Alchian's example makes clear, what is at stake is whether competitive markets lead to productive efficiency. More generally, what is at issue, it seems, is whether competitive markets lead to Pareto-optimality.[10]

In order to examine or scrutinize Friedman's claims systematically, some formal structure is needed to model "natural selection" explicitly. This again leaves room for different approaches. What formal structures or techniques to apply? Several structures and techniques have been applied (Matthews 1984; Witt 1986; Hansen and Samuelson 1988; Schaffer 1989; Hodgson 1999, to mention just a few). Of all the attempts made to scrutinize Friedman's claims systematically, two stand out in terms of perseverance and faithfulness to his selection argument, I think: those by Sidney Winter (1964, 1971, 1975) and by Lawrence Blume and David Easley (1992, 1995, 1998). For reasons that will become apparent, I shall devote a whole section (section 5) to Winter's (and Nelson and Winter's) work. In their examination of Friedman's selection argument, Blume and Easley adopt an evolutionary general equilibrium model. In their model, if factor demands and supply evolves, prices (the firms' environment) also change.[11] Blume and Easley show that although natural selection in markets favors profit maximization, equilibria need not converge to competitive (Pareto-optimal) equilibria. They argue that "The weak link in the natural selection justification for the normative properties of competitive markets is not the behavioral hypothesis of profit maximization but the implication from profit maximization to Pareto

---

[10] Note that although Friedman's essay is about positive economics, these are normative issues.

[11] Blume and Easley note that this allowance for endogenous price change differentiates their approach from that of Nelson and Winter (1982). In passing, it is interesting to see that in their examinations many "mainstream" economists (such as Blume and Easley) refer to the work of the "heterodox" economists Nelson and Winter. This suggests that the neglect of heterodox economists by "orthodox" ones may not be as massive as is sometimes argued.

optimality" (Blume and Easley 1998, 2). Blume and Easley furthermore argue that if capital markets are added, natural selection does not favor profit maximization. Introducing capital markets in the picture may disturb the process in which the growth rate of firms is determined solely by the portion of their revenues (earnings) that are invested in them. The latter process, Blume and Easley argue, is the one Friedman has in mind when referring to "natural selection." Firms have to earn their own resources and the higher their relative revenues, the more they invest and expand.

Are Pareto-optimal Nash equilibria invariably selected?

The conclusion that there is more support for Friedman's intermediate claim than there is for his ultimate claim seems to be drawn also in *evolutionary game theory*.[12] Arguably, evolutionary game theory has become the prevailing modeling strategy to scrutinize claims and arguments like the one Friedman is advancing (for useful overviews, see Weibull 1995 and Kandori 1997). Apparently, many believe that evolutionary game theory naturally lends itself for such examinations. There nowadays seems to be a consensus among game theorists that evolutionary game theory by and large supports Friedman's selection argument. This might explain why many game theorists seem to believe that Binmore and Aumann have a point in their proposals to reinterpret standard economic theory along evolutionary lines. But before we conclude prematurely that evolutionary game theory supports Friedman's argument and claims, let us have a closer look at what exactly it is that evolutionary game theory does and does not establish.

Let us concentrate on George J. Mailath's (1998) "Do people play Nash equilibrium? Lessons from evolutionary game theory," since that paper provides an accessible and (at that time) comprehensive overview of the sorts of results obtained in evolutionary game theory that bear on Friedman's selection argument. In the Introduction Mailath remarks that "a common informal argument is that any agent not optimizing – in particular, any firm not maximizing profits – will be driven out by market forces" (1998, 1347). Mailath argues that evolutionary game theory is suitable both to render the argument formal and to check its validity. One of the things Mailath sets out to do in his overview is to find out to what extent evolutionary game theory supports the claim made in the argument. For Mailath this claim, properly understood, is that agents

---

[12] In Vromen (1995) I argued that Friedman's intermediate claim, if true, would validate his ultimate claim. The work discussed here calls this into question.

eventually converge to play Nash equilibrium.[13] The conclusion Mailath arrives at is that evolutionary game theory gives qualified support for this claim: "In a range of settings, agents do (eventually) play Nash. There is thus support for equilibrium analysis in environments where evolutionary arguments make sense" (1998, 1348).[14]

What does it mean to claim, as Mailath does, that evolutionary game theory provides qualified support for the central position that the notion of Nash equilibrium takes in non-cooperative game theory? It effectively means that any stable state that the evolutionary processes as depicted in evolutionary game theory can converge to is a Nash equilibrium. Or, to use slightly more precise and technical parlance, "any asymptotically stable rest point of an evolutionary dynamic is a Nash equilibrium" (Mailath 1998, 1371). If some evolutionary dynamic, such as the so-called replicator dynamic,[15] drives a process in the direction of a rest point (a state that, once reached, is left unchanged by the dynamic), and if this point is asymptotically stable (which means that any path that starts sufficiently close to the rest point converges to that rest point), then this outcome of the evolutionary dynamic is (and cannot be but) a Nash equilibrium. This might be understood as implying that any enduring state evolutionary processes (as depicted in evolutionary game theory) can result in must be a Nash equilibrium. This result certainly is reassuring for (Nash) equilibrium analysis. The main reason why Mailath argues that evolutionary game theory provides support for equilibrium analysis is that in many asymmetric games (games in which agents play different roles), the Nash equilibria available are not asymptotically stable rest points.

Mailath's conclusion here seems to bear more on Friedman's intermediate claim than on his ultimate claim. Play of Nash equilibrium is often seen as the embodiment of the idea that economic agents are rational (Aumann 1985, 43). What lessons, if any, are there to be drawn from evolutionary game theory about Friedman's ultimate claim? The asymptotically stable rest points identified by evolutionary game theory need not be optimal. In games in which there are multiple equilibria, for example, it is possible that evolutionary processes get stuck into a Nash equilibrium that is Pareto-dominated by another Nash equilibrium. This

---

[13] In his unpublished PhD dissertation, Nash (1950) himself suggested a population-statistical interpretation of his own equilibrium concept (Leonard 1994).

[14] See also Cressman (2003) who reports that this is dubbed the *Folk Theorem of Evolutionary Game Theory* by Hofbauer and Sigmund (1998).

[15] The replicator dynamic basically says that the growth rate of a strategy's share in some population is proportional to the degree in which it does better than the population's average. What is said here also holds for more general dynamics such as monotone dynamics.

means that some (and perhaps all) agents would have been better off (without there being someone who is worse off) had they all played their parts in the other Nash equilibrium that did not materialize. So the fact that in (symmetrical) games evolutionary dynamics produce Nash equilibria does not imply that agents will eventually be best off. In general it may crucially depend on the initial state of the population what asymptotically stable rest point some evolutionary process will converge on. If the evolutionary process starts in the basin of attraction of a Pareto-dominated equilibrium, it may remain locked into it. The fact that evolutionary game theory can account for this phenomenon of *path dependence* is generally welcomed by evolutionary game theorists as one more important and attractive feature of their theory (see Mailath 1998, 1360 and 1368).[16]

Thus evolutionary game theory seems to lend more support to Friedman's intermediate claim than to his ultimate claim. If evolutionary processes converge to enduring, stable rest points then these are Nash equilibria. This is taken to support Friedman's intermediate claim that only rational, optimizing behavior survives. Friedman's ultimate claim, that productive efficiency and Pareto-optimality are thereby safeguarded, is in general not supported. Asymptotically stable rest points that the enduring states evolutionary processes converge on may be Pareto-dominated Nash equilibria.

Are we still discussing Friedman's original claims?

One might rightly wonder, however, whether it really is Friedman's intermediate and ultimate claims that are addressed in evolutionary game theory. One has to take quite some liberty in interpreting Friedman's claims for evolutionary game theory to bear on them. It seems that Friedman's argument has tacitly been turned into another one and that it is at most this transformed argument that gets support from evolutionary game theory. This transformation involves three aspects: *mechanisms, conditions,* and *results.* In Friedman's argument the alleged mechanism is "natural selection," which refers to a process in which the relatively most profitable firms expand their market share at the expense of less profitable firms. In current evolutionary game theory the driving mechanism is learning. Individual agents are assumed to learn either individually or socially in a boundedly

---

[16] See also Young (1996). It has to be noted, however, that the evolutionary game theorists who embrace path dependence have also tried to show that at least in some games with strict equilibria, path dependence need not be forthcoming in the ultra-long run (see Foster and Young 1990; Kandori, Mailath, and Rob 1993).

rational way. Evolutionary game theory is about individuals and populations, not about firms and industries. This difference in mechanisms stipulated should not be exaggerated, however. The monotone dynamics mostly posited in evolutionary game theory seems to be compatible with Friedman's rudimentary ideas about the nuts and bolts of "natural selection." In both the central idea is that the share or frequency of some type of "individual" (whether it is a firm or a human agent) tends to be proportional to its relative performance.

The differences with respect to the other two aspects, conditions and results, may be less reconcilable. As to conditions, Friedman seems to have competitive markets in mind. "Competitive markets" refer to a *parametric* setting or context in which the behavior of the one firm (or individual) does not affect the profitability (or the payoffs) of others.[17] The profitability of each firm depends only on its own activities (Hansen and Samuelson 1988). By contrast, game theory by definition deals with *strategic* settings in which the payoffs obtainable by the one individual at least partly depend on the behavior displayed by others. Like theories about perfect competition, evolutionary game theory deals with large populations. Populations are so large that the share of each individual in the population is negligible. But mostly the assumption is that interactions are pairwise. What the opponent does directly affects the payoffs that one can obtain. For some evolutionary game theorists this is sufficient reason to call the sorts of situations they are analyzing non-competitive (Banerjee and Weibull 1995).

Friedman's intermediate claim is that the result or outcome of "natural selection" is that eventually only firms survive that earn maximum returns. The only survivors display behavior that can be said to be rational in the sense that it coincides with the choices that a fully informed, faultlessly calculating maximizer would make. Evolutionary game theory points out that, with a few exceptions, evolutionary processes tend to converge to Nash equilibria. Do individuals display optimal behavior when they play a Nash equilibrium? The definition of "Nash equilibrium" implies that they display optimal behavior *if* other individuals play their parts in the equilibrium. If other players do not play their parts in the equilibrium, the optimal behavior of an individual may also well be not to play his or her part in the equilibrium. It is possible that individuals would be better off in out-of-equilibrium situations. Furthermore, as Kandori argues "One prominent reason why irrational behavior may survive is that

---

[17] To put it more accurately, the profitability of some firm does not depend *directly* on the behavior of others. The behavior of others can affect the profitability of the firm indirectly, however, via changed prices.

commitment to a suboptimal strategy pays in strategic situations" (Kandori 1997, 258). In strategic situations, individuals that are, for example, emotionally committed to play a particular fixed strategy may outperform individuals that are not similarly committed (Frank 1988). Thus, *pace* Mailath, it is questionable that demonstrating that the use of Nash equilibria is (almost fully) justified can count as a substantiation of Friedman's intermediate claim.

There is ample reason to believe that Friedman would not be particularly fond of attempts made by evolutionary game theorists to check the correctness of his judgment (or claims). For one thing he simply saw no reason to do this. For another he would not have liked what probably is the main reason underlying these attempts. Mailath seems to be looking for the best possible justification for the standard practice in game theory to treat Nash equilibrium as the solution concept. He argues that of all the candidate justifications offered thus far learning seems to be the least problematic (Mailath 1998, 1354). As evolutionary game theory is argued to offer a particularly attractive approach to learning, he seems to present this as an argument in favor of evolutionary game theory. Use of the Nash equilibrium is not defended on Friedmanian grounds, namely that it works well for some particular purpose at hand. Such an eye on usefulness seems to be entirely lacking in Mailath's argument. Some evolutionary game theorists seem to analyze dynamic models with no other purpose in mind than to gain a better understanding of the properties of some stipulated dynamic in some particular game.[18] The issue of whether the understanding thus gained has any relevance for a better understanding of concrete phenomena in the real world does not seem to bother them at all. This is the type of formalistic, blackboard economic theorizing, which perhaps can be called Walrasian, that Friedman has little sympathy for.

5   Evolutionary economics: taking observed decision procedures seriously

Let the *apparent immediate determinant of business behavior* be *anything at all* – habitual reaction, random chance or whatnot. Whenever this determinant happens to lead to behavior consistent with rational and informed maximization of returns, the business will prosper and acquire resources with which to expand; whenever it does not, the business will tend to lose resources and can be kept in existence only by the addition of resources from outside. (F53, 22; emphasis added)

---

[18] It is clear that other economists working in this area, such as Nobel laureate Reinhard Selten, have other aims in mind, such as a greater realisticness of game theory.

The emphasis is here put on the fact that Friedman argues that certain results of "natural selection" obtain, no matter what apparent (or actual) immediate determinants of firm behavior there are. Immediate determinants of firm behavior are argued to be non-consequential for selection outcomes. Following Nelson and Winter (1982), evolutionary economists believe that this part of the argument is flawed. Immediate determinants of firm behavior do make a difference. What decision procedures firms follow matters a great deal for what outcomes are selected.

Winter (1964) is well known as one of the first and one of the most systematic and profound examinations of the selection argument. The conclusion Winter arrives at is that "to the extent that selection considerations support the use of traditional economic theory, they do so only under special circumstances and for a restricted range of applications" (Winter 1964, 268).[19] In other words, what Winter establishes is that the support that evolutionary considerations lend to traditional economic theory, and notably the theory of the firm, is quite limited. Winter discusses several circumstances under which selection considerations do not support traditional economic theory. For example, he argues that a theory of the firm, which is to yield refutable predictions about the behavior of individual firms or aggregates of firms, should be distinguished from a theory of entry and exit, which is to yield refutable predictions about the appearance and disappearance of firms. When it comes to assessing the selection argument, a theory of the firm should be supplemented by a theory of entry and exit. Thus if an industry initially consists of profit-maximizing firms, these firms may nevertheless be outcompeted by non-profit-maximizing firms that have the compensating benefit of increasing returns to scale.[20] The result may be a mixed industry rather than an industry consisting only of profit-maximizing firms. Another condition to be met for evolution to produce an industry solely consisting of profit-maximizing firms is that differential profitability of firms should translate into a proportional differential growth rate. If this condition is not met, if relatively profitable firms rest content with paying out their extra profits in higher dividends while remaining at the same scale of operation, for example, then less profitable firms will not be driven out of business (Winter 1964, 244).

Winter furthermore argues that if information may be imperfect and costly to gather, profit-maximizing firms need not be the ones surviving "natural selection": "If such a situation obtains, reliance on rules of thumb may, in a restricted range of 'normal' situations, be more viable

---

[19] See also "The preceding section provides examples of combinations of initial conditions and sets of possible organization forms for which this conclusion is not valid" (248).
[20] See Hodgson (1999) for a further discussion of this condition.

than profit-maximizing" (1964, 258). In this vein, Winter argues that a "full-cost" pricing rule might survive at the expense of a maximizing rule which goes through extensive and expensive calculations to find the price–output combination that equated marginal cost and marginal revenue (1964, 263). Thus again this presents an example of a situation in which non-profit-maximizing firms need not be weeded out by "natural selection." Note that this is reminiscent of Harrod's (1939) idea that observed business procedures, such as the "full-cost" pricing rule, are prevalent because they supplanted others in a selection process.

Note also that "profit maximizing" is understood here as a particular, time-consuming decision procedure. Winter assumes that what Friedman's selection argument purports to establish is that only firms with profit-maximizing decision procedures survive "natural selection." Strictly speaking, this misrepresents Friedman's argument. He does not argue that only firms with particular decision procedures survive "natural selection." What Friedman argues is that only firms that approximately make maximum profits survive, no matter how they do this. It is possible that firms that do not follow any decision procedure or decision rule can make maximum profits (due to sheer luck, for example). As argued earlier, for Friedman the issue of decision rules, or immediate determinants as he himself calls them, is essentially a non-issue. Whether or not firms follow some fixed decision procedure or rule does not matter, if they fail to make maximum profits they will be selected against.

Yet it is quite understandable why Winter reads Friedman in this way. Winter states that any theory of selection requires the assumption that individuals (in this case, firms) have fixed behavioral characteristics (Winter 1964, 251). If we want to develop a theory of selection in order to see what firms, or better, what types of firms, survive selection, then we must assume that firms have some fixed behavioral characteristics. Although it remains to be seen whether Winter is right in arguing that without such an assumption there can be no theory of selection, it seems he has a point here. To see this, let us get back to Friedman's argument. It is easy to see that Friedman's argument that immediate determinants of firm behavior do not matter is sound in some sort of *"Judgment Day"* *scenario*. The argument is sound, that is, if at the end of the day it is decided once and for all on the basis of the amount of resources that firms themselves earned thus far what market share each of them gets. Then, but only then, it does not matter whether the immediate determinant of the behavior of some firm is random chance, for example. The only thing that counts then is indeed what resources the firm has earned at the end of the day. And by pure chance or sheer luck it could be the case that the firm happens to have made maximum profits. But this is not how "natural selection" in competitive markets is supposed to work, even on Friedman's own view. Note that Friedman is arguing that firms that do not succeed in making maximum profits (returns) will tend to lose resources. In other words, it is suggested that there are repeated selection moments rather than one ("one-shot") decisive selection moment. If there is a sequence of selection moments, then what matters is how well firms perform in subsequent periods in time. And it is highly unlikely that the firm with the random chance determinant that was lucky enough to have earned maximum profits in one period will also be as lucky in subsequent periods.

This is exactly the point Winter is making: "If the immediate determinants of behavior are 'habitual reaction, random chance, or whatnot,' there is no reason to believe that the firms which take actions consistent with profit maximization at one time will also take actions consistent with such maximization at all subsequent times" (Winter 1964, 240). It could be retorted here that although its probability may be close to nil, the possibility cannot be ruled out that one and the same firm can be lucky all of the time. But the more fundamental problem Winter is drawing our attention to, I guess, is that if firms can change their behavior in unpredictable ways, it is hard if not impossible to trace what firms do relatively better consistently, that is over extended periods of time. If we want to know what firms perform relatively best in an ongoing process of economic "natural selection," then we may be at a loss if firms change their relevant operating characteristics faster than the rate at which they undergo selection effects.

Nelson and Winter's evolutionary theory in a nutshell

In any event, what started out as a "forced move," as an assumption made to meet the alleged requirements of selection theory, later grew into one of the three cornerstones of Nelson and Winter's evolutionary theory. Winter (1964) coined the slightly misleading expression *organization form* as the functional relationship between the state of the world and a firm's actions. Nelson and Winter (1982) talk of *routines*. Nelson and Winter argue at great length that firm behavior is better understood in terms of rigid routines than in terms of flexible, deliberate choice. Their catchphrase *"routines as genes"* amply makes clear that they believe that in certain relevant respects routines of firms are like genes of organisms. A firm's routines instruct or program the firm's behavior in much the same way as the genes of an organism instruct or program the organism's behavior. Most of the time this works in an automatic fashion, without the intervention of conscious volition. Nelson and Winter refer to

Friedman's example of the expert billiard player. Like the expert billiard player, businessmen "just figure out" what to do. There is not much deliberate choice involved in this. Routines are like genes also in another respect. Just like genes, routines embody wisdom or knowledge acquired and accumulated in the past.[21] The type of knowledge involved here is tacit knowledge. Moreover, it is know-how rather than "knowing-that" that can be fully articulated.

A second cornerstone of Nelson and Winter's evolutionary theory is "natural selection." Already in Winter (1964) it is clear that he does not examine the workings and consequences of "natural selection" just to see whether Friedman's argument is valid. Winter takes "natural selection" to be one of the crucial forces working in competitive markets that determine what firms and what industry structure prevail. In passing, we already came across what Winter believes "natural selection" amounts to: firms expand proportional to their profitability. Nelson and Winter set out to model this process explicitly. In doing so they put into practice what Enke (1951) and Koopmans (1957) pleaded for. Enke (1951) advances a selection argument similar to Alchian (1950). But he draws a conclusion from the argument opposite to the one Alchian draws: marginalism should give way to what Enke called *viability analysis*. Arguably this is exactly what Nelson and Winter want to develop. Koopmans (1957) argues that if "market selection" is indeed the basis for the belief in profit maximization, as Friedman argues, then that basis should be postulated and not profit maximization, which it is said to imply in certain circumstances. In their evolutionary theory, Nelson and Winter follow up on this.

Nelson and Winter are clearly *realists* about their own evolutionary economic theory.[22] Or alternatively we can say that their preference for an explicit evolutionary economic theory is ontologically grounded. They prefer modeling selection processes in which routine-following firms are involved explicitly over using equilibrium analysis in which maximizing agents figure, because they believe that that gives a more adequate representation of what is actually going on in market economies. This longing for realism (or realisticness) also shows in the third cornerstone in their evolutionary theory. Following Schumpeter, Nelson and Winter argue that endogenously engendered innovations are characteristic of capitalist economies. They posit that firms are induced to search for better routines in the face of adversity. Innovations are argued to be similar to mutations

---

[21] To the extent that present circumstances differ markedly from the one in which routines evolved, the resulting behavior can well be maladaptive.

[22] For a more detailed discussion of this, see Vromen (2001).

in evolutionary biology. At first sight this seems to conflict with their belief that firm behavior is routine. "Routines as genes" seems to imply that "mutations" can only emerge as copying errors, or something of the sort. But Nelson and Winter stress that rigid routines do not necessarily make for rigid behavior. Routines may have a conditional structure allowing for different behavior in different circumstances. Furthermore, firms may engage in efforts to search for better routines if extant ones cease to yield satisfactory results.

Nelson and Winter argue that their own evolutionary theory is superior to "orthodox" theory. Their theory is superior not just because of its alleged greater realism (or realisticness). They argue their evolutionary theory is superior also because of its greater *generality*. Nelson and Winter believe that their own evolutionary theory is more general than orthodox theory in several respects. In its own domain of application, they argue, orthodox theory demonstrably only covers limiting cases. Orthodox theory correctly predicts what happens at the aggregate industry level only under restricted conditions. Nelson and Winter's evolutionary theory is also argued to cover more ground than orthodox theory. It addresses phenomena that fall outside the purview of orthodox theory, such as Schumpeterian competition, technological innovation, and disequilibrium phenomena and processes. On top of that it is also more general in that it aims at descriptive accuracy not just at the aggregate level of industries and markets, but also at the level of individual firm behavior. Friedman argues that a theory of the firm should only be concerned about empirical accuracy at the aggregate level of industries and markets. Winter, by contrast, argues that ideally a satisfactory theory of the firm should also be descriptively accurate about individual firm behavior. From a methodological point of view it is interesting to see that Winter defends the superiority of a more general theory in this sense on Popperian grounds. Winter explicitly refers to Popper's *Logic of Scientific Discovery* in his argument that Friedman's "auxiliary hypothesis" is unacceptable that the theory of the firm should only be tested against market phenomena, and not against phenomena that pertain to the level of individual firms (Winter 1964, 232). The empirical content of the theory of the firm would be increased if testing against the latter type of phenomena were taken seriously: "We would certainly prefer a theory which predicted the market behavior of firms and the results of direct study of their decision processes to one which predicted only the former" (1964, 233).

Nelson and Winter took up the challenge posed by Friedman's selection argument, ran away with it, and ended up with something that seems to be the opposite of what Friedman intended. Winter (1982) makes it abundantly clear that he rejects the use that Friedman wanted to make of his selection argument.[23] Instead of licensing the continued use of the maximization postulate, Winter argues that taking "natural selection" seriously implies both that evolutionary processes in economies should be modeled explicitly and that observed decision procedures should not always be rationalized as instances of maximizing behavior. With their explicitly evolutionary theory Nelson and Winter appear as allies of the antimarginalists. They seem to provide the sort of evolutionary underpinning of decision rules such as the full-cost pricing rule that Harrod (1939) was hinting at.[24] Furthermore, Nelson and Winter take realism (or realisticness) to be a legitimate criterion for theory appraisal. They insist in particular on the realisticness of behavioral assumptions in a satisfactory economic theory. In all this Nelson and Winter seem to move away further from Friedman's intentions than any of the other authors discussed in this chapter.

6   Conclusions

The interpretations of the proper implications of Friedman's selection argument for economic theorizing that are discussed in this chapter have been seen to differ not only from Friedman's own interpretation but also from each other. Friedman maintained that the argument provided some (but not conclusive) evidence in support of the marginalist theory of the firm and left it at that. What the argument was meant to establish in particular is that even if antimarginalist findings were reliable, i.e. that businessmen follow particular decision rules and procedures in their decision-making rather than that they contemplate marginal costs and revenues, economists are justified in disregarding them. Some commentators argue that Friedman is right that standard economic theory can be retained, but add to this that the argument suggests an evolutionary reinterpretation of standard economic theory. Others qualify the claims Friedman makes in his argument by arguing that standard economic theory can be retained under some but not all conditions. Especially Friedman's ultimate claim that "natural selection" in competitive markets guarantees productive efficiency and Pareto-optimality has been shown not to be tenable in general. Still others draw conclusions from evolutionary considerations that are opposite to the ones Friedman draws. Explicit models of evolutionary dynamics that may help explain why

[23] Winter prefers an interpretation that he names after Armen A. Alchian in which evolutionary processes, rather than maximization postulates are treated as fundamental. Winter is trying to drive a wedge between Alchian and Friedman here that I think is not actually there. Given his intervention in the roundtable discussion Alchian seems to agree.

[24] Remarkably, Nelson and Winter (1982) do not mention Harrod (1939) in their list of antecedents.

widely observed decision rules and procedures are prevalent should supersede standard economic theory.

With the possible exception of the evolutionary reinterpretation, it is not likely that Friedman was happy about the directions in which his commentators took his argument. It seems Friedman's argument had some sort of boomerang effect. In the end his argument raised more worries and doubts about the economic theory he favors than it was able to put to rest. That at least some commentators may have misrepresented Friedman's argument is not of much avail here. It also remains to be seen whether faithfulness in representation should be a supreme goal in this case. Friedman's somewhat cryptic exposition of the argument leaves considerable room for different interpretations. More importantly, given the fact that Friedman himself indicates that not too much hinges on the validity and cogency of the argument, why would we believe that he is very careful and precise in his exposition of the argument? Perhaps it does not matter too much whether or not the interpretations of the implications of Friedman's argument for economic theorizing discussed here get the gist of his argument right. They have yielded insights that are interesting in their own right.

References

Alchian, Armen A. (1950). Uncertainty, evolution and economic theory. *Journal of Political Economy*, 58, 211–22

Aumann, R. (1985). What is game theory trying to accomplish? In K. J. Arrow and S. Honkapohja (eds.), *Frontiers of Economics*. Oxford: Blackwell

(1997). On the state of the art in game theory: an interview with Robert Aumann (taken by Eric van Damme). In W. Albers, W. Güth, P. Hammerstein, B. Moldovonu and E. van Damme (eds.), *Understanding Strategic Interaction: Essays in Honor of Reinhard Selten*. Berlin, etc.: Springer Verlag, 8–34

Banerjee, Abhijit and Jörgen Weibull (1995). Evolutionary selection and rational behavior. In Alan Kirman and Mark Salmon (eds.), *Learning and Rationality in Economics*. Oxford: Blackwell, 343–63

Baumol, W. J. (1983). Book review of Nelson, R. R. and Winter, S. G. (1982). *Journal of Economic Literature*, 21, 580–1

Becker, Gary S. (1962). Irrational behavior and economic theory. *Journal of Political Economy*, 70, 1–13

Binmore, Ken (1994). *Game Theory and the Social Contract*, vol. I: *Playing Fair*. Cambridge, MA: MIT Press

Blume, Lawrence E. and David Easley (1992). Evolution and market behavior, *Journal of Economic Theory*, 58, 9–40

(1995). Evolution and rationality in competitive markets. In Alan Kirman and Mark Salmon (eds.), *Learning and Rationality in Economics*. Oxford: Blackwell, 324–62

(1998). Optimality and natural selection in markets. EconWPA, report-no: cae-001

Cressman, Ross (2003). *Evolutionary Dynamics and Extensive Form Games.* Cambridge, MA: MIT Press

Dawkins, Richard (1976). *The Selfish Gene.* Oxford: Oxford University Press
(1995). God's utility function. In *River of Eden.* London: Phoenix, 111–55

Enke, S. (1951). On maximizing profits: a distinction between Chamberlin and Robinson. *American Economic Review,* 41, 566–78

Foster, Dean P. and H. Peyton Young (1990). Stochastic evolutionary game dynamics. *Theoretical Population Biology,* 38, 219–32

Frank, R. H. (1988). *Passions within Reason.* New York: W.W. Norton and Co.

Friedman, Milton and Leonard Savage (1948). The utility analysis of choices involving risk, *Journal of Political Economy,* 56, 279–304

Friedman, Milton (1953). The methodology of positive economics. In *Essays in Positive Economics.* Chicago: University of Chicago Press, 3–43

Hall, R. L. and C. J. Hitch (1939). Price theory and business behavior. *Oxford Economic Papers* 2

Hammond, J. D. (1991). Early drafts of Friedman's methodology essay. Unpublished paper

Hansen, R. G. and W. F. Samuelson (1988). Evolution in economic games. *Journal of Economic Behavior and Organization,* 10, 107–38

Harrod, R. F. (1939). Price and cost in entrepreneurs policy. *Oxford Economic Papers* 2, 1–11

Hirshleifer, Jack (1977). Economics from a biological viewpoint. *Journal of Law and Economics,* 20, 1–52

Hodgson, Geoffrey M. (1999). Optimization and evolution: Winter's critique of Friedman revisited. In *Evolution and Institutions: On Evolutionary Economics and the Evolution of Economics.* Cheltenham, UK, and Northhampton, MA: Edward Elgar, 175–95

Hofbauer, J. and K. Sigmund (1998). *Evolutionary Games and Population Dynamics.* Cambridge: Cambridge University Press

Kandori, M., G. J. Mailath, and R. Rob (1993). Learning, mutation, and long run equilibria in games. *Econometrica,* 61, 29–56

Kandori, Michihiro (1997). Evolutionary game theory in economics. In David M. Kreps and Kenneth F. Wallis (eds.), *Advances in Economics and Econometrics: Theory and Applications – Seventh World Congress of the Econometric Society,* vol. 1. Cambridge: Cambridge University Press, 243–77

Koopmans, Tjalling (1957). *Three Essays on the State of Economic Science.* New York: McGraw-Hill

Langlois, Richard (1986). Rationality, institutions, and explanation. In Richard Langlois (ed.), *Economics as a process.* Cambridge: Cambridge University Press, 225–55

Leonard, Robert J. (1994). Reading Cournot, reading Nash: the creation and stabilization of the Nash equilibrium. *Economic Journal,* 104, 492–511

Lester, R. A. (1946). Shortcomings of marginal analysis for wage-employment problems. *American Economic Review,* 36, 63–82

Mailath, George J. (1998). Do people play Nash equilibrium? Lessons from evolutionary game theory. *Journal of Economic Literature,* 36, 1347–74

284   *Jack Vromen*

Matthews, R. C. O. (1984). Darwinism and economic change. *Oxford Economic Papers (Supplement)*, 46, 91–117

Mayr, Ernst (1961). Cause and effect in biology. *Science*, 134, 1501–6

Nash (1950). Non-cooperative games. Unpublished PhD dissertation, Princeton University

Nelson, Richard R., and Sidney Winter (1982). *An Evolutionary Theory of Economic Change*. Cambridge, MA: Harvard University Press

Penrose, E. T. (1952). Biological analogies in the theory of the firm. *American Economic Review*, 42, 804–19

Robson, Arthur J. (1996). A biological basis for expected and non-expected utility. *Journal of Economic Theory*, 68, 397–424

    (2001a). The biological basis of economic behavior. *Journal of Economic Literature*, 39, 11–33

    (2001b). Why would nature give individuals utility functions? *Journal of Political Economy*, 109, 900–14

Satz, Debra and John Ferejohn (1994). Rational choice and social theory. *Journal of Philosophy*, 71–87

Schaffer, M. E. (1989). Are profit-maximizers the best survivors? *Journal of Economic Behavior and Organization*, 12, 29–45

Simon, Herbert A. (1955). A behavioral model of rational choice. *Quarterly Journal of Economics*, 69, 99–118

Smith, Vernon L. (1991). Rational choice: the contrast between economics and psychology. *Journal of Political Economy*, 99(4), 877–97

Vromen, Jack J. (1995). *Economic Evolution: An Enquiry into the Foundations of New Institutional Economics*. London: Routledge

    (2001). Ontological commitments of evolutionary economics. In Uskali Mäki (ed.), *The Economic World View: Studies in the Ontology of Economics*. Cambridge: Cambridge University Press, 189–224

    (2003). Why the economic conception of human behavior might lack a biological basis. *Theoria*, 18 (special issue on Darwinism and Social Science), 297–323

Weibull, Jürgen W. (1995). *Evolutionary Game Theory*. Cambridge, MA: MIT Press

Winter, Sidney G. (1964). Economic "natural selection" and the theory of the firm. *Yale Economic Essays*, 4, 225–72

    (1971). Satisficing, selection, and the innovating remnant. *Quarterly Journal of Economics*, 85, 237–61

    (1975). Optimisation and evolution in the theory of the firm. In R. H. Day and T. Groves (eds.), *Adaptive Economic Models*. New York: Academic Press, 73–118

    (1982). Oral contribution to general discussion: Evolution and human behavior. In R. P. Zerbe (ed.), *Research in Law and Economics* 4. Greenwich, CT, and London: JAI Press Inc, 131–65

Witt, Ulrich (1986). Firms' market behavior under imperfect information and economic natural selection. *Journal of Economic Behavior and Organization* 7, 265–90

Young, H. Peyton (1996). The economics of convention. *Journal of Economic Perspectives*, 10, 105–22

11   Expected utility and Friedman's risky methodology

Chris Starmer

1   Introduction

In this chapter my aim is to offer some reflection upon Friedman's methodology, focusing in particular upon his work relating to the theory of risky choice. With this objective in mind, I revisit two key papers in which Friedman and Savage (1948, 1952) discuss the empirical support for expected-utility theory (EUT).[1] In these papers there are clear traces of the methodological position set out in Friedman's 1953 essay (henceforth F53). For instance, a recurrent theme is that EUT should be judged in terms of its predictive accuracy relative to its intended realm of application. At the same time, both papers are motivated by the scarcity of "direct" empirical evidence, and in light of this each paper suggests some remedy. My interest will focus especially on the second of these contributions, which argues that the normative appeal of EUT axioms can be read as a source of "indirect" evidence for the hypothesis.

I will argue that this claim is methodologically problematic partly because the argument set out in the joint 1952 paper fails to successfully forge an explicit link from normative appeal of EUT axioms to predictive success of the hypothesis. A key question addressed in this chapter is how, if at all, such a link could be established. I suggest the issue is of more than passing historical interest because there has been an apparent tendency in modern economics for the selection of descriptively oriented theories to be guided by normative criteria. Put differently, at times economists behave as if they believe that normative appeal is a form of empirical

I am grateful to Robin Cubitt, Roberta Muramatsu, and Robert Sugden for helpful discussions leading to the development of this paper. I am grateful to Uskali Maki and participants at the Conference "The Methodology of Positive Economics: Milton Friedman's Essay at 50" at EIPE, Rotterdam, December 12–13, 2003. I am grateful to the Leverhulme Trust for financial support (award number: F/00 204/K).
[1] For compactness I will refer to these two papers as FS48 and FS52 respectively.

evidence and I illustrate this with a particular example in the contemporary theoretical literature on risk.

2   Development of the expected-utility hypothesis

EUT is an extremely widely used piece of economic theory. In one respect it is easy to see why. Risk is a pervasive aspect of the economic world and for some time now, EUT has been the standard approach to modeling decisions involving risks. But, although the theory dates as far back as Bernoulli (1738), it did not find much favor with modern economists until the 1950s. This may be partly explained by the fact that, in the form presented by Bernoulli, the theory presupposes the existence of a cardinal utility scale; an assumption which did not sit well with the drive towards ordinalization during the first half of the twentieth century. FS48 suggests that, prior to that, a firm (but mistaken) belief in the principle of diminishing marginal utility may have been a significant impediment to its acceptance.[2] Whatever the precise historical reasons for disinterest, it is clear that economists became much more interested in the theory following the demonstration by von Neumann and Morgenstern (1947) that the expected-utility hypothesis could be derived from a set of "appealing" preference axioms.

It will be useful for what follows to provide a thumbnail sketch of key ingredients in a typical axiomatization. A common approach has been to model risky alternatives as "prospects" or lotteries. I will use bold face letters to represent prospects and any prospect $\boldsymbol{p} = (p_1, x_1; \ldots p_n, x_n)$ is a probability distribution over a fixed set of n consequences where p_1 represents the probability of consequence x_1 and so on.[3] The expected-utility hypothesis can then be derived from three axioms on preferences over prospects: ordering, continuity, and independence. Ordering requires there to be a complete and transitive pairwise ranking of prospects;[4] the

---

[2] "The rejection of utility maximization as an explanation of choices among different degrees of risk was a direct consequence of the belief in diminishing marginal utility. If the marginal utility of money diminishes, an individual seeking to maximize utility will never participate in a 'fair' game of chance... But this implication is clearly contradicted by actual behavior.

Marshall resolved this contradiction by rejecting utility maximization as an explanation of choices involving risk. He need not have done so, since he did not need diminishing marginal utility – or, indeed, any quantitative concept of utility – for the analysis of riskless choices." (FS48, 280)

[3] Take it throughout that, for all prospects, $p_i \geq 0$ for all i, and $\Sigma_i p_i = 1$.

[4] More precisely, this axiom entails that: (1), for any pair of prospects q, r: either $q >\sim r$ or $r >\sim q$ or both, where $>\sim$ represents the relation "is (weakly) preferred to"; and (2) for any three prospect q, r, s, if $q >\sim r$ and $r >\sim s$, then $q >\sim s$.

addition of a continuity principle[5] is then sufficient to guarantee that preferences can be represented by *some* function V(.) which attaches a real-value to every prospect.[6] The independence axiom of EUT[7] adds a restriction of the following form. Consider two compound prospects $q' = (q, p; s, 1{-}p)$ and $r' = (r, p; s, 1{-}p)$, where q' is itself a probability mixture of two prospects; it results in q with probability p otherwise s. Similarly, r' is a mix of r and s and notice that the probability of s is the same (i.e. $1{-}p$) for both compound prospects. Independence implies that the common component of the two compound prospects (in this case the $1{-}p$ chance of s) is irrelevant to their relative ranking which should depend purely on the ordering of the simple prospects q and r.[8] Given this additional assumption, preferences can be represented by the familiar expected utility function $V(p)=\Sigma_i p_i.u(x_i)$, where p is any prospect, and $u(.)$ is a "utility" function defined over consequences.

Where lies the alleged appeal of this set of axioms or, equivalently, the appeal of EUT so axiomatized? One, I think enlightening, way to reconstruct it is as follows. The standard method of modern economics has been to understand behavior through the lens of optimization, that is, to assume that agents are rational actors moved along by coherent and stable preferences. Hence, to assume the existence of some preference function over prospects $V(p)$ is essentially to apply the standard method of economics to decisions over risks. But what justifies, from a normative point of view, the added restriction of independence?

A classic answer is provided by Samuelson (1952), who argues firmly that the type of independence condition entailed by EUT is itself a compelling normative principle of rationality. The nub of the argument is essentially this. Suppose you have to choose between q' and r' as defined above and suppose, for the sake of illustration, that $p=0.5$ with the compound lotteries resolved by a coin flip which determines the outcome to be s if "tails" comes up. Samuelson argues that, if tails does come up, you won't care which option you chose (because you get s either way) so you can safely ignore this common element of the prospects when choosing between q' and r', just as independence requires. Once it is

---

[5] Continuity requires that for all prospects q, r, s, where $q >{\sim} r$ and $r >{\sim} s$, there exists some probability p such that there is indifference between the middle ranked consequence r and the prospect $(q, p; s, 1{-}p)$.

[6] $V(.)$ represents preferences in the sense that $V(p) \geq V(q)$ if, and only if, prospect q is not preferred to p.

[7] Whenever I refer to "independence" principles later in this chapter, note that I have in mind Expected Utility Independence conditions and not other types of independence condition that feature elsewhere in economic theory.

[8] More formally, the independence axiom of EUT entails that for all prospects q, r, s: if $q >{\sim} r$ then $(q, p; s, 1{-}p) >{\sim} (r, p; s, 1{-}p)$, for all p.

conceded that the outcomes associated with tails can be ignored, it then seems plain that an agent should choose between the compound prospects on the basis of their ordering over the simple prospects q and r.

The argument for ignoring the tails outcome, and for (EUT) independence more generally, turns on the proposition that there can be no (rationally justifiable) *complimentarity* between the outcomes within a prospect because they are *mutually exclusive*. If this is conceded, and independence is accepted as an implication of rationality, then EUT has much more significance than simply being just one amongst many possible models of risk preference; EUT then has a claim to be interpreted as the logical extension of rational economic analysis to the realm of risk. Whether or not individual axioms of EUT can be defended as requirements of rationality has, of course, been a matter of much debate.[9] Fortunately, we need not enter these tricky debates because my primary concern will be to examine what follows granting, for the purpose of the argument, that the axioms of EUT *can* be taken as appealing principles of rationality.

To the extent that its axioms can be justified as sound principles of rational choice to which any reasonable person would subscribe, the axioms provide grounds for interpreting EUT *normatively*; that is as a model of how people ought to choose. Some writings have placed emphasis on this normative interpretation of EUT. For example, Savage (1954) presents what has become one of the most celebrated derivations of EUT explicitly as an attempt to extend logical reasoning to situations of uncertainty. His primary aim is not to provide an empirical theory for predicting human behavior, but instead to develop logical tools for deciding between alternative courses of action:

Decisions made in the face of uncertainty pervade the life of every individual and organisation. Even animals might be said continually to make such decisions, and the psychological mechanisms by which men decide may have much in common with those by which animals do so. But formal reasoning presumably plays no role in the decisions of animals, little in those of children, and less than might be wished in those of men. It may be said to be the purpose of this book, and indeed of statistics generally, to discuss the implications of reasoning for the making of decisions. (Savage 1954, 6)

That said, Savage does accept that EUT may also have some potential as a simple – if "crude" – empirical theory for predicting human behavior, albeit in a "suitably limited domain."[10] It is to the interpretation of EUT as an empirical theory that I now turn.

---

[9] For the reader wishing to explore these debates a good place to start is Sugden (1991).

[10] "[EUT] can be interpreted as a crude and shallow empirical theory predicting the behavior of people making decisions. This theory is practical in suitably limited domains, and everyone in fact makes use of at least some aspects of it in predicting the behavior of others" (1954, 20).

3   EUT as an empirical hypothesis

In two now classic papers coauthored by Friedman and Savage (FS48, FS52) – and published shortly before Savage's *Foundations of Statistics* (1954) and F53 – there is much more focus on the empirical interpretation of EUT. Both papers interpret EUT explicitly as an empirical hypothesis and present these papers as "crude" tests of it. The tests are crude, partly because of the limited supply of direct evidence suitable for testing the theory. Nevertheless, the two papers propose complementary strategies for crude testing.

So how does EUT stand up to empirical scrutiny? In FS48 they argue that, given a suitable specification of the utility function over wealth, the theory can explain a set of stylized facts about how people respond to risk, particularly in the context of gambling and insurance. They present a set of five stylized facts to be explained and they propose a functional form for the utility of wealth that is shown to be consistent with the presented facts. A crucial feature of their proposal is that the utility function contains both concave and convex segments. As such it allows the same individual to express both risk-averse (insurance) and risk-seeking (gambling) behavior – one of the key stylized facts they set out to explain.

It is the argument of the second paper (FS52), however, that will be my primary focus. This paper also presents EUT as an empirical hypothesis to be evaluated relative to the "evidence," but it brings a new and interesting twist by introducing an explicit distinction between *direct* and *indirect* evidence. Direct evidence comes from comparing the implications of theory with observations generated within the *intended domain* of application, while indirect evidence relates to phenomena that are not in the "primary" domain of interest. So, to the extent that EUT is intended to explain market phenomena such as gambling and insurance decisions, FS48 is in good part an evaluation of EUT on the basis of direct evidence.

In contrast, the main purpose of FS52 is to articulate indirect support for EUT. An interesting feature of the argument is that it seeks to license reading the normative appeal of EU axioms as a source of empirical support. I will refer to this maneuver as the *FS-twist*. The argument goes like this. There is, FS52 argue, "indirect evidence rendering it plausible that the hypothesis will continue to fail to be contradicted, in at least some important domains" (FS52, 466). The primary source of this evidence is "the plausibility of a set of postulates that are sufficient for derivation of the hypothesis" (FS52, 466).[11] The postulates are a set of axioms

---

[11]   They also suggest as an aside that "Coherence with rest of economic theory" (FS52, 466) may count as indirect evidence for EUT.

essentially equivalent to those discussed above. The question I wish to pursue here is how "the plausibility of postulates" translates into (indirect) empirical support for EUT? At first blush this seems slightly mysterious, but some insight is provided by the following passage from FS52:

> In saying that these postulates are more plausible than the hypothesis to which they are logically equivalent, we mean that the postulates immediately call to mind a host of implications (or predictions from the hypothesis) susceptible to casual observation. With respect to the class of phenomena to which these implications relate, the hypothesis has had many opportunities for contradiction and has repeatedly failed to be contradicted. The evidence is indirect because this is not the class of phenomenon we are primarily interested in using the hypothesis to predict (FS52, 466)

The suggestion that the "postulates immediately bring to mind a host of implications" seems very reasonable at least partly because the axioms make explicit particular formal properties of EUT which may be less than transparently obvious from a statement of the hypothesis. For instance, once I see and comprehend a statement of the independence principle, it then becomes clear that it is implicit in EUT that common components of prospects under consideration should be irrelevant to my choice among those prospects. The argument, however, involves two further claims that strike me as less obviously justified. One is the assertion that implications which the postulates bring to mind are "susceptible to casual observation," the second is the assertion that such casual observation has broadly supported the hypothesis.

A difficulty arises in relation to both of these latter assertions because it is not obvious what to understand by "casual observation" in this context. Perhaps the most natural interpretation would be to think that casual observations refer to instances of behavior thrown up by choices that people happen to make in the world. But if we put aside, for the moment, observations from specifically designed experimental tests of axioms, it is doubtful that the world throws up much data bearing on the validity of EUT axioms. An important reason for this is that the axioms are (for the most part) propositions about *consistency* between choices, and as such they do not typically tell us how individuals will choose in specific decision problems. Because of this, it is far from obvious that casual observations of decisions in the world generate rich opportunities for testing EUT axioms. For example, if we know that an agent prefers some prospect a over b, and b over c, we can test transitivity if we can also observe their preference between a and c. But it seems to me that casual opportunities for collecting such observations are rather infrequent.

Another possibility is that "casual observation" is to be understood as arising from introspective thought experiments, that is from personal reflections of roughly the form: would I violate the transitivity principle in this setting; or would I violate the independence principle in that setting; etc., etc.? Such introspections, however, could hardly be regarded as providing objective tests of what the agent's *behavior* would be. If an agent is, or tends to become convinced of the proposition that "I would not deliberately violate choice principle x," it seems that further introspections of the form "would I violate x in this specific case" can no longer be considered independent observations. To the extent that the agent is concerned to reason coherently, it seems the cognition that "I would not deliberately violate choice principle x" will move them to conclusions consistent with this, in thought experiments.

There is, however, another potential argument articulated in FS52 to motivate the FS-twist. This works in two steps. The first is to argue that the axioms are "introspectively very appealing" (FS52, 468) and seeks to persuade the reader that each principle "is not one he would deliberately violate" (FS52, 469).[12] It seems reasonable to suppose that many people would so endorse the principles. The second step is to assert that the introspective appeal of the axioms is "some reason for supposing that people do actually tend to avoid flagrant violation of the principle" (FS52, 469).[13] This second step appears to involve a questionable leap from propositions about the intuitive appeal of choice principles to propositions about choice *behavior*. In order to make this leap explicit, consider propositions P1 and P2:

(P1) the agent accepts axiom x as a principle they would not deliberately violate
(P2) the agent probably behaves in accordance with axiom x

As I read it, this part of the FS52 paper essentially asserts that because P1 holds, P2 is likely. But while P1 and P2 are not inconsistent, in the absence of further premises, P2 is not implied by P1. P1 is a proposition about normative judgments, while P2 is a proposition about behavior. In order to generate the implication suggested by FS52 it is necessary to introduce some premise linking normative beliefs with behavior. For example:

---

[12] While in FS52 Friedman and Savage discuss each of the EU axioms, a key part of their argument is concerned with justifying the independence axiom. This seems natural given that this was and continues to be the most controversial element of the EUT system: it is also the assumption that gives EUT most of its empirical content.

[13] Although the claim here seems a moderate one given the qualification that normative appeal is just "some" reason, I take it there is meant to be a substantive claim here given that the main argument of the paper seeks precisely to use normative appeal as a source of evidence.

(P3) agents rarely behave in contradiction with principles they believe they would not deliberately violate

Notice, however, that it is not enough just to assume P3: for it to do the job of converting normative appeal to evidence, it has to be empirically valid or at least plausible. How would one assess whether this is an empirically plausible claim? I can think of at least two possibilities. One would be to refer to a theory of the choosing mind. If one could point to some model of human mental processes which implied that normative beliefs govern choice behavior, and show that there is satisfactory empirical support for it, that would be one way to motivate a principle like P3. This strategy, however, would involve a major departure from the "as-if" methodology famously set out in F53.

It is clear that Friedman and Savage do favor an "as-if" interpretation of EUT. For instance, F48 provides this methodological aside with respect to evaluation of EUT:

> An objection to the hypothesis just presented that is likely to be raised by many, if not most, readers is that it conflicts with the way human beings actually behave and choose. Is it not patently unrealistic to suppose that individuals consult a wiggly utility curve before gambling or buying insurance, that they know the odds involved in the gambles or insurance plans open to them, that they can compute the expected utility of a gamble or insurance plan, and that they base their decision on the size of the expected utility?
>
> While entirely natural and understandable, this objection is not strictly relevant. The hypothesis does not assert that individuals explicitly or consciously calculate and compare expected utilities. Indeed it is not at all clear what such an assertion would mean or how it could be tested. The hypothesis asserts rather that, in making a particular class of decisions, individuals behave as if they calculated and compared expected utilities and as if they knew the odds. The validity of this assertion does not depend on whether individuals know the precise odds, much less on whether they say that they calculate and compare expected utilities or think that they do, or whether psychologists can uncover any evidence that they do, but solely on whether it yields sufficiently accurate predictions about the class of decisions with which the hypothesis deals. Stated differently, the test by results is the only possible method of determining whether the as if statement is or is not a sufficiently good approximation to reality for the purpose at hand. (FS48, 298)

This clearly has a great deal of resonance with the methodological position Friedman sets out in F53: we should not count it against EUT that its assumptions appear "unrealistic"; EUT is not to be interpreted as a model of conscious human decision processes but as an "as-if" model with the purpose of predicting behavior; as such, the only relevant test of the theory is taken to be its predictive performance, though note the important caveat that predictive performance is to be judged relative to the theory's domain of application.

This "as-if" strategy entails that theories *not* be judged in terms of whether they are defensible models of mental processes. So to invoke a model of mental process as a defense of the theory would not seem to provide an interpretation of the FS-twist which is consistent with F53 (or FS48).

Another possibility would be to interpret P3 as a purely empirical (but untheorized) principle. This, I suggest, provides an interpretation which is more consistent with F53 but it is not unproblematic. Part of the problem with this reading is that evidence from behavioral research runs against a general claim that peoples' behavior satisfies principles that most would take to be normatively appealing. To support that claim, here are two illustrations.

A.   *Savage and the Allais paradox*

A significant part of the debate about independence has centered on the well-known Allais paradox. Consider the following action/state payoff matrix where each row represents one of four risky actions (*g1* to *g4*), and columns represent possible states of the world (with probabilities given at the top of each column). The numbers in the matrix are to be read as the state contingent payoffs to each (in, say, 000s $).

Consider a choice between *g1* and *g2*. The independence axiom implies that since these two actions give the same consequence in the third state of the world, that third state must be irrelevant to that choice. The same argument applies to the choice between *g3* and *g4*. Notice that if the third column is blanked out, the choice between *g1* and *g2* is identical to the choice between *g3* and *g4* (i.e. 0.11 chance of 500 vs. 01. chance of 2500). Hence, independence implies that if *g1* is (not) preferred to *g2*, *g3* is (not) preferred to *g4*. There is considerable evidence that many people faced

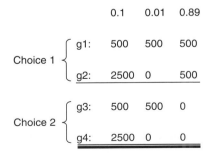

Figure 11.1 Action/state payoff matrix

with pairs of choices with this general structure choose *g1* over *g2* and *g4* over *g3* in violation of independence.

It is a matter of historical interest that Savage himself, in chapter 5 of *Foundations*, conceded that he also violated independence when first confronted with the Allais paradox. He reports that having once recognized the inconsistency, he reflected upon the situation and came to the conclusion that his belief in the normative appeal of independence was unshaken. Consequently, he determined that he must have made some error in one of his initial choices. Re-examining the choices, Savage applies independence, hence reducing both decisions to the choice (0.11 chance of 500) vs. (01. chance of 2500). Then, "Finally, consulting my purely personal taste, I find that I would prefer the gift of $500,000 and, accordingly, that I prefer Gamble 1 to Gamble 2 and (contrary to my initial reaction) Gamble 3 to Gamble 4" (Savage 1954, 103). On Savage's own account, his initial choice of *g4* over *g3* was an error which the application of normative reasoning allowed him to detect and correct.

This account seems unproblematic in relation to the argument of S54. In that context, Savage is explicitly concerned with developing a normative theory which may be used to "police decisions." The fact that real decisions may depart from the normative is a prerequisite for there to be any interesting policing role for his axioms. However, the example provides a counterargument to the proposition that being normatively committed to a decision principle implies conforming behavior, and the example seems especially compelling when the person concerned is an eminent decision theorist violating a principle which is the most important in his own normative theory.

B.   *Framing effects*

One possible defence against this example would be to suggest that Savage's mistake lay not in his choice, but in his adoption of independence as normative. An alternative interpretation of the Allais paradox is that it shows that independence is not a compelling normative principle (indeed, this is Allais's own reading). Someone who took this line would have the option of arguing that the Allais paradox does not demonstrate any inconsistency between compelling normative principles and choice behavior. That argument, however, could be quickly dismissed by pointing to violations of *description invariance*. By description invariance I mean the proposition that preferences between choice alternatives should not be altered by redescriptions of the alternatives which leave the objective choice set unchanged. I take this to be a very basic proposition implicit in normative decision theories (so basic that it is rarely explicitly stated as a proposition). There is, however, considerable evidence that very minor changes in the presentation or "framing" of decisions can have dramatic impacts upon the choices of decision-makers: such effects are failures of *description invariance*. Here is one famous example due to Tversky and Kahneman (1981) in which two groups of subjects – call them groups I and II – were presented with the following cover story:

Imagine that the US is preparing for the outbreak of an unusual Asian disease, which is expected to kill 600 people. Two alternative programs to combat the disease have been proposed. Assume that the exact scientific estimate of the consequences of the program are as follows:

Each group then faced a choice between two policy options. One group chose between A and B:

If program A is adopted, 200 people will be saved.
If program B is adopted, there is a 1/3 probability that 600 people will be saved, and a 2/3 probability that no people will be saved.

   The other chose between C and D:

If program C is adopted, 400 people will be die.
If program D is adopted, there is a 1/3 probability that nobody will die, and a 2/3 probability that 600 people will die.

The two pairs of options are stochastically equivalent. The only difference is that the group I description presents the information in terms of *lives saved* while the information presented to group II is in terms of lives lost. Tversky and Kahneman found a very striking difference in responses to these two presentations: 72 percent of subjects preferred option A to option B, while only 22 percent of subjects preferred C to D. It seems hard to deny that different behavior in the two problems is normatively unsound. Yet similar patterns of response were found amongst groups of undergraduate students, university faculty, and practicing physicians. Real people it seems, do not in general behave consistently with normative principles, even those that find very common assent.

4   Market selection and the FS-twist

Taken at face value, the evidence from simple choice experiments seems to tell against the FS-twist. Yet, one might accept that it is possible to construct experimental situations where people violate normative principles, but raise doubts about whether such violations would be common features of the wider world. One reason for such doubt might be connected with Friedman's famous "natural selection" argument. In F53, he argues that part of what may explain the success of the profit maximization hypothesis is that market forces will promote the survival (demise) of firms using strategies closest to (furthest from) profit maximization. The predictive success of the theory of profit maximization then relies partly on features of market processes, not explicitly modeled in the economic theories of firms and markets.

Analogous arguments could be constructed to suggest that EUT might have better predictive success in a marketplace, relative to laboratory tests, perhaps by virtue of the existence of market mechanisms that punish deviations from it. Indeed, widely rehearsed "money pump" arguments seem to have just this character. Such arguments typically work by suggesting that agents who fail to satisfy normative decision principles lay themselves open to exploitation. Consider, for example, an agent who has non-transitive preferences of the form $q >\sim r$, $r >\sim s$ and $s >\sim q$. Suppose they are initially endowed with q. Repeatedly trading according to these binary preferences could lead them to: (i) pay to swap q for s; (ii) pay to swap s for r; and (iii) pay to swap r for q, and so on. This agent has then been money pumped because they have paid for several trades only to find themselves returned to their original endowment (minus some cash).

One might argue that if agents were exploitable in this way, we should expect to see other people exploiting them. The lack of evidence of money pumps in operation in the world might then be taken as evidence that on the whole people must have preferences conforming at least roughly with normative presumptions most of the time. I think these arguments are unconvincing as attempts to suggest empirical support for EUT axioms not least because careful theoretical analysis seems to defeat the claim – central to money-pump arguments – that agents will be money-pumpable unless their preferences satisfy EUT. Contrary to this view, Cubitt and Sugden (2001) show that agents can have preferences which satisfy few, if any, of the standard normative criteria, yet still be money-pump proof.

But even if money-pump arguments fail as a convincing blanket defense of EUT, it is not entirely unreasonable to suppose that some market mechanisms might actually promote conformity with EUT. While it is currently hard to find much direct support for that conjecture, there is evidence that at least some preference anomalies do appear to decay in the context of some market mechanisms. One of the clearest examples relates to contingent valuation methodology: a standard methodology for assigning money values to non-marketed goods. The two most widely used valuation measures are willingness to pay (WTP) and willingness to accept (WTA). Standard preference theory based on indifference curve analysis implies that these two measures should generate similar valuations, but in practice WTA is typically much bigger than WTP. But further research has shown that the gap between WTP and WTA tends to be eroded as a consequence of exposure to some market mechanisms, particularly the second-price variant of the Vickrey auction (see, for example, List and Shogren 1999; Shogren *et al.* 2001).

While the existing literature suggests that more than one causal mechanism may lie behind the convergence of WTA and WTP in repeated auctions, there is some basis for thinking that part of the explanation involves subjects learning to behave more consistently with principles of rationality. For example, one factor sometimes cited as a possible account of the WTA/WTP disparity is that bidders may approach a market with a tendency to behave "cautiously" by underbidding when buying and over-asking when selling relative to their true values. Such a tendency may be rationally justified in some market contexts, for instance in markets where prices are negotiated through some process of haggling. In Vickrey auctions, however, revealing true value is a weakly dominant strategy and bidders operating cautiously may miss valuable opportunities to trade (e.g. by asking too high and then failing to sell at a price which is above their value). A possible explanation of the convergence of WTP and WTA is that missed opportunities of this sort cause agents to reflect on their behavior and consequently adjust towards the optimal bidding strategy. Some support for this explanation of convergence has been found in a study conducted by Loomes, Starmer, and Sugden (2003).

In principle, then, selection reasoning is a genre of argument that might work to forge, what seems to me, a missing link in the FS-twist argument of FS52 by giving some account of how normatively appealing principles may come to be manifest in market behavior even though they are widely violated in simple choice experiments. While Friedman's use of this kind of reasoning in F53 suggests that he may have been sympathetic to this strategy, the text of FS52 provides no obvious indication that Friedman and Savage had such a link in mind in this context. Even if they did, the link would remain weak in the absence of more explicit (theoretical and/or empirical) support for selection processes in markets specifically promoting behavior consistent with EUT.

5   Normative notions in descriptive dialogues

Let us take stock. In FS52 Friedman and Savage seek to argue that because EUT can be restated in terms of normatively appealing axioms, this provides a source of indirect support for the model as an empirical theory of behavior. This is what I have called the FS-twist. I think that is a questionable claim for at least three sets of reasons. First, the connection from norm to decision, at least in FS52, seems mysterious. Second, while it might be possible to articulate some connection, say by specifying a model of decision process with that feature, my impression is that the literature which does seek to model decision processes would typically point in the opposite direction: in general, models of decision process provide many varied reasons for thinking that behavior will deviate from normatively appealing criteria.[14] Thirdly, I have pointed to experimental evidence against the presumption that normative appeal implies empirical validity. At the end of the last section I did concede that selection arguments might in principle provide a missing step. The link made in that way, however, would remain an extremely tenuous one, absent a clearer theoretical statement of it and an assessment of its empirical plausibility.

The argument made by FS52 is of more than passing historical interest however. Indeed, it seems to me that developments in the economic theory of risk behavior, over recent decades, have been influenced in significant ways by a widely presumed (but I think misconceived) connection between normative principles and actual behavior. For example, since the late 1970s, numerous alternatives to EUT have been proposed (largely motivated by empirical counterexamples such as Allais's examples).[15] In these developments, it seems clear that economists have paid almost no attention to modeling phenomena that are inconsistent with principles that most economists take to be normatively compelling. For instance, although there is evidence that people violate principles like monotonicity and description invariance, economists have not been busy attempting to explain these findings.

Moreover, theories which have had the potential to explain violations of normative principles have been heavily criticized in the literature. For example, most would agree that the principle of monotonicity is a normatively appealing property in a theory of risky decision-making. Simply put, monotonicity means that objective improvements to a prospect (e.g. increasing at least some of its payoffs, holding others constant) should not reduce its attractiveness. Some non-expected-utility theories, however, do predict failures of monotonicity, though in these cases the prediction has usually been a by-product of the model: an unintended consequence of the theoretical structure adopted to explain some other phenomenon.

---

[14] For example, in Payne, Bettman, and Johnson's (1993) model, agents may draw on a wide variety of heuristics based on tradeoffs between "accuracy" and "effort." But while here there is an economizing motive, there is no reason to expect the degree of coherence in choice implied by EUT. Similarly, in Gigerenzer and Selten (2000), agents are conceived of as adopting "fast and frugal" heuristics.

[15] I review some of these developments in Starmer (2000).

One example is the model that extends EUT by attaching simple decision weights to probabilities such that agents are assumed to maximize a function of the form: $V(\boldsymbol{p}) = \Sigma w(p_i)u(x_i)$. This is essentially the type of value function assumed in prospect theory of Kahneman and Tversky (1979) and they show that the Allais paradoxes can be explained by non-linearities in $w(p_i)$. But this strategy for explaining the Allais examples has the side-effect that predicted choices among at least some prospects will violate monotonicity. This has generally been regarded as a fatal flaw sufficient to damn theories of this type. Arguments to this effect have been made by Fishburn (1978), Machina (1982), and Quiggin (1982), each of them heavyweights in the arena of choice theory.

No doubt conscious of these potential criticisms, Kahneman and Tversky propose an editing heuristic which eliminates dominated options, so long as they are detected (the *dominance heuristic*). This strategy for inducing monotonicity, however, has attracted further criticism from some economists. Quiggin (1982, 1993), for example, has criticized the approach on two counts. First, he argues that by appropriate specification of the preference function the dominance heuristic can be rendered redundant. Second, he criticizes the Kahneman and Tversky strategy for imposing monotonicity because it has the further spin-off effect that the theory then admits violations of transitivity in pairwise choice. Quiggin (1982, 327) describes this as an "undesirable result."

What is the basis of this latter claim? It is not, I contend, based on sound empirical evidence. First of all there is well-established evidence – Tversky (1969) produced some of the earliest – that cyclical choice is a robust and reasonably general phenomenon (for later evidence see Loomes *et al.* (1989, 91)). It is true that the form of intransitivity predicted by prospect theory is of an unusual kind and distinct from other forms of intransitivity. That, however, presents a useful opportunity for testing a novel prediction of prospect theory. Starmer (1999) reports an experiment which tests for the specific form of intransitivity implied by prospect theory and finds very strong evidence of it.

Notwithstanding this evidence, the economics literature continues to be dominated by models built on transitivity and other empirically questionable but normatively attractive principles. In light of this, I am inclined to the view that economists' reactions to evidence, in the theory of choice under risk, have been mediated by certain theoretical pre-commitments. In particular, a pre-commitment to preference theories which satisfy normatively appealing criteria such as monotonicity, etc. This pre-commitment has, in my view, delimited certain problems as interesting (i.e. those that appeared at least potentially soluble in terms of the pre-committed assumptions) and others as uninteresting or outside the realm of economic inquiry.

If it is granted that such a pre-commitment has been at work, is that a bad thing? I am not certain that it is. Some philosophers of science, among them Kuhn and Lakatos, provide strong arguments for thinking that some kinds of theoretical pre-commitments may be prerequisites for healthy, ongoing, scientific inquiry. On a Lakatosian interpretation, for instance, principles of rational choice like monotonicity and transitivity, might be taken as part of the hard core of the research program of choice under risk. What is questionable, however, is any tendency to mistake such a pre-commitment for evidence in favor of it.

6   Conclusion: reflections on positive economics

Friedman's 1953 essay is a remarkably rich and enduring piece. And, while it is long, and complex, and deals with many subtle issues, it sets an apparently clear line on certain methodological principles: positive economics is fundamentally empirical and should involve confronting theories with evidence from the world; the predictive ability of a theory (in its intended domain of application) is the key test of a theory's success; attempting to assess the realism of assumptions is not a meaningful test of any theory.

While F53 is primarily an exercise in abstract normative methodology, the papers which have been the primary focus of this discussion (FS48 and FS52) are *methodology in action* in so far as they involve explicit attempts to evaluate a particular theory, specifically, EUT. The contrast between the abstract and applied methodology is both striking and interesting. The abstract F53 essentially bids the economist, qua positive scientist, ask one primary question of a proposed theory: *how well does it fit the facts in its intended domain of application?* When it comes to the theory of risk, however, while Friedman and Savage explicitly endorse the key principles of positive economics (à la F53), its application appears complicated by the scarcity of a crucial ingredient: that is, direct evidence bearing on the predictive success of EUT in domains of intended application. This looks like a significant hurdle to get over if Positive Economics is to work in the domain of risky choice behavior. I suggest that both FS48 and FS52 can be read as attempts to respond to this, albeit in rather different ways. I have focused on the argument of FS52 not least because that paper involves strategies that might seem to present marked contrast with the prescripts of F53, such as appeals to indirect evidence, to casual observation, to introspection, and to the intuitive appeal of axioms.

The simple fact that economics in action (that is the business of constructing and evaluating theories of economic behavior) turns out to be more complex and messy than Positive Economics à la F53 need not necessarily undermine faith in its key methodological assertions. All must surely accept that theorizing necessarily involves simplification and abstraction from complex reality whether it be theory about the ideal behavior of an economy, or theory about the ideal behavior of economists, or whatever. Yet the persuasiveness of Friedman's methodology might be reduced to the extent that his own economics in action were plainly at odds with the prescriptions of F53.

An obvious question then is whether the FS-twist ultimately coheres with the Positive Economics of F53? One difficulty in assessing this arises from the fact that the FS-twist is not fully articulated in FS52: that is, the paper does not provide a clear account of why we should expect behavior to conform with normatively appealing axioms. I have argued that there may be different ways of forging such a link and I have discussed two particular possibilities: one way would be to develop a theory of choosing mind, another would be to invoke a theory of selection. I have suggested that the second of these routes would provide a reading of FS52 which coheres much more naturally with F53. On this reading, does the FS-twist then provide a satisfactory empirical defense of EUT? I think not as it stands, because it begs a further question about whether there are, in fact, selection mechanisms which operate in domains of interest to promote conformity between behavior and normative decision principles. I take it that this, in turn, is a question susceptible to positive economic analysis and not something simply to be taken on faith.

References

Appleby, L. and C. Starmer (1987). Individual choice under uncertainty: a review of experimental evidence, past and present. In J. Hey and P. Lambert (eds.), *Surveys in the Economics of Uncertainty*. Oxford: Blackwell

Bernoulli, Daniel ([1738] 1954). Exposition of a new theory on the measurement of risk. *Econometrica*, 22, 23–6

Cubitt, R. and Sugden R. (2001). On money pumps. *Games and Economic Behavior*, 37, 121–60

Fishburn, P. C. (1978). On Handa's "New Theory of Cardinal Utility" and the maximization of expected return. *Journal of Political Economy*, 86, 321–4

Friedman, Milton (1953). The methodology of positive economics. In *Essays in Positive Economics*. Chicago: Chicago University Press

Friedman, Milton and L. Savage (1948). The utility analysis of choices involving risk. *Journal of Political Economy*, 56, 279–304

(1952). The expected-utility hypothesis and the measurability of utility. *Journal of Political Economy*, 60, 463–474

Gigerenzer, G. and R. Selten (eds.) (2000). *The Adaptive Tool Box*. Cambridge, MA, and London: MIT Press

Kahneman, Daniel and Amos Tversky (1979). Prospect theory: an analysis of decision under risk. *Econometrica*, 47(2), 263–91

List, J. and J. Shogren (1999). Price information and bidding behavior in repeated second-price auctions. *American Journal of Agricultural Economic*, 81, 942–9

Loomes, G., C. Starmer and R. Sugden (1989). Preference reversal: information-processing effect or rational non-transitive choice? *Economic Journal*, 99, 140–51

(1991). Observing violations of transitivity by experimental methods. *Econometrica*, 59, 425–39

(2003). Do anomalies disappear in repeated markets? *Economic Journal*, 113, C153–66

Machina, M. (1982). "Expected utility" theory without the independence axiom. *Econometrica*, 50, 277–323

Neumann, J. von and O. Morgenstern (1947). *The Theory of Games and Economic Behavior*, 2nd edition. Princeton: Princeton University Press

Payne, J., J. Bettman, and E. Johnson (1993). *The Adaptive Decision Maker*. Cambridge: Cambridge University Press

Quiggin, J. (1982). A theory of anticipated utility. *Journal of Economic Behavior and Organization*, 3(4), 323–43

(1993). *Generalized Expected Utility Theory*. Dordrecht: Kluwer

Samuelson, P. A. (1952). Probability, utility, and the independence axiom. *Econometrica*, 20, 670–8

Savage, L. (1954). *The Foundations of Statistics*. New York: Wiley

Shogren, J., S. Cho, C. Koo, J. List, C. Park, P. Polo and R. Wilhelmi (2001). Auction mechanisms and the measurement of WTP and WTA. *Resource and Energy Economics*, 23, 97–109

Starmer, C. (1999). Cycling with rules of thumb: an experimental test for a new form of non-transitive behaviour. *Theory and Decision*, 46, 141–58

(2000). Developments in non-expected utility theory: the hunt for a descriptive theory of choice under risk. *Journal of Economic Literature*, 38, 332–82

Sugden, R. (1991). Rational choice: A survey of contributions from economics and philosophy. *Economic Journal*, 101, 751–85

Tversky, Amos (1969). Intransitivity of preferences, *Psychological Review*, 76, 31–48

Tversky, Amos and Daniel Kahneman (1981). The framing of decisions and the psychology of choice. *Science*, 211, 453–58

(1986). Rational choice and the framing of decisions. *Journal of Business*, 59(4), pt. 2, 251–78

12   Milton Friedman's stance: the methodology of causal realism

Kevin D. Hoover

1   The God of Abraham; the methodology of Marshall[1]

The philosopher Bas Van Fraassen opens his Terry Lectures (published as *The Empirical Stance*) with an anecdote: "When Pascal died, a scrap of paper was found in the lining of his coat. On it was written 'The God of Abraham, Isaac and Jacob, not the God of the philosophers'" (Van Fraassen 2002, 1). Pascal's God talks and wrestles with men; Descartes's God is a creature of metaphysics. Analogously, with respect to the "Methodology of positive economics" (F53) there are two Friedmans. Most of the gallons of ink spilled in interpreting Friedman's essay have treated it as a philosophical work. This is true, for example, for those who have interpreted it as an exemplar of instrumentalism, Popperian falsificationism, conventionalism, positivism, and so forth. And it is even true for those critics, such as Samuelson (1963), whose credentials as an economist are otherwise secure. Mayer (1993a, 1995, 2003) and Hands (2003) remind us that Friedman was philosophically unsophisticated, and in the essay Friedman tried a fall with other economists, not with philosophers. The origin of the essay was the quotidian practice of economics, not abstract epistemology. To know the Friedman of the economists, I propose to read the essay in light of Friedman (and Schwartz's) *A Monetary History of the United States, 1867–1960* (1963a) and "Money and business cycles" (1963b), perhaps his most characteristic economic investigations.

My point is not that there is a particular philosophers' position that can be contrasted with a particular economists' (or even Friedman's)

[1] I thank Uskali Mäki, Thomas Mayer, and the participants in the F53 Conference at the Erasmus Institute of Philosophy and Economics, Rotterdam, December 12–13, 2003 for comments on an earlier draft. I also thank Ryan Brady for research assistance. J. Daniel Hammond (1996) wrote an important book that examines Friedman's economic thought from a causal perspective. While I intentionally did not reread that book in trying to develop my own views somewhat independently, I could not help but be influenced by it.

position. After all, Pascal surely recognized that there were a variety of views of God among the philosophers. Nor would I suggest that philosophy has nothing valuable to say about, or learn from, Friedman's essay nor Friedman about or from philosophy. It is rather a matter of approach. Friedman cares most about doing economics and is largely innocent of the interests of philosophers and, equally, of the distinctions and nuances that philosophers routinely employ. If we – either as economists or philosophers – insist on reading the essay as a philosophical work addressed to philosophers, we must misread it.

The most infamous passage in Friedman's essay runs: "Truly important and significant hypotheses will be found to have 'assumptions' that are wildly inaccurate descriptive representations of reality, and, in general, the more significant the theory, the more unrealistic the assumptions (in this sense)" (14).[2] Samuelson (1963, 232–3) sees this as the extreme version of Friedman's general proposition that "[a] theory is vindicated if (some of) its consequences are empirically valid to a useful degree of approximation; the (empirical) realism of the theory 'itself,' or of its 'assumptions,' is quite irrelevant to its validity and worth," which he stigmatizes with the shorthand *F-twist*.[3]

The view that Friedman does not care about the truth of the assumptions faces a serious difficulty. After recounting the detailed evidence on the cyclical behavior of money and the real economy, Friedman and Schwartz (1963b, 213–14) raise the question, how we can be sure about the direction of influence?

It might be, so far as we know, that one could marshal a similar body of evidence demonstrating that the production of dressmakers' pins has displayed over the past nine decades a regular cyclical pattern; that the pin pattern reaches a peak well before the reference peak and a trough well before the reference trough; that its amplitude is highly correlated with the amplitude of the movements in general business. It might even be demonstrated that the simple correlation between the production of pins and consumption is higher than the simple correlation between autonomous expenditures and consumption; that the partial correlation between pins and consumption – holding autonomous expenditure constant – is as high

---

[2] Except where context would render it ambiguous, references to F53 will be referred to hereinafter by page numbers only.

[3] Replacing Friedman by his initial is an indication that Samuelson (1963, 232) is aware that the F-twist may be "a misinterpretation of [Friedman's] intention." While Samuelson rails against Friedman's apparent abandonment of truth and realism, Frazier and Boland (1983) turn it into a positive virtue. They interpret Friedman as an instrumentalist and defend instrumentalism as a logically sound doctrine. My suggestion here is that they have misinterpreted Friedman – he is not an instrumentalist – and my suggestion in Hoover (1984) is that Frazer and Boland's version of instrumentalism is not sound doctrine.

as the simple correlation; and that the correlation between consumption and autonomous expenditures – holding the production of pins constant – is on the average zero ... [B]ut even if [these statements] were demonstrated beyond a shadow of a doubt, they would persuade neither us nor our readers to adopt a pin theory of the cycle.

But why not? In Friedman and Schwartz's thought experiment, the pin theory of the cycle has implications that are confirmed facts. Why should the same variety of evidence that supports a monetary theory not equally well support a pin theory? "Primarily, the difference is that we have other kinds of evidence" (Friedman and Schwartz 1963b, 214): (i) pins are a trifling element in the economy, and "[w]e expect the effect to be in rough proportion to the cause," but money is pervasive in economies that experience business cycles; (ii) with money we can, and with pins we cannot, conceive of channels through which large autonomous changes in them might affect the economy; (iii) in contrast to a monetary theory, no serious student of business cycles has ever seriously suggested a pin theory.

It is not good enough for Friedman that a pin theory implies the facts. His criticisms are based on evidence relevant to the truth of its assumptions. The *Monetary History* can be seen as a detailed marshalling, not only of the facts implied by Friedman's monetary theory, but of the evidence for the truth of its underlying mechanisms and initial conditions: its assumptions. A partisan for the assumptions-don't-matter interpretation of Friedman's essay might argue that there is a flat contradiction between his rejection of the pin theory and his methodological position. That would be too easy and too lazy. To say that Friedman does not care about the truth of the assumptions is wrong. On the contrary, Friedman's methodological stance in the essay is best described as *causal realism*, which can be defined as the view that the object of scientific inquiry is the discovery through empirical investigation of the true causal mechanisms underlying observable phenomena.

One object of this chapter is to support this controversial claim. To do so, I propose to read Friedman's essay charitably – not as the work of an amateur philosopher but as the work of an economist, one whose methodological reflections are consistent with his intellectual antecedents and with his own empirical practice. Friedman's most important intellectual antecedent is Alfred Marshall. Marshall's writings are Friedman's economic Bible. When, after a long and illustrious life, Friedman finally passes on, he may well leave a scrap of paper pinned to the lining of his coat on which will be written: "The Methodology of Marshall, not the Methodology of the philosophers."

2   The absence of causal talk

If Friedman is a causal realist, there surely is a puzzle in his work: he rarely talks about causes. In the 814 pages of *Monetary History*, a work that I maintain is an exemplary piece of causal realist research, the words "cause" or "causal" are used – as far as I can tell – only nine times, and four of those nine are attributed to agents of the Federal Reserve (see table 12.1).[4] Similarly, Friedman's claim that the effect should be proportional to cause cited earlier is one of only two instances of causal talk in "Money and business cycles." What is more, Friedman is conscious of his own unease with respect to causal talk. Tobin (1970, 301) asserts that Friedman claims that changes in the money supply are the principal cause (sometimes unique) of changes in money income. In reply, Friedman (1970, 319) not only denies the accuracy of Tobin's claim, but assails the imprecision of Tobin's causal talk. Friedman (1974, 101) writes: "I myself try to avoid use of the word 'cause' … it is a tricky and unsatisfactory word" (cited by Hammond 1992, 91–2, as part of interview with Friedman).

There is less here than meets the eye. Friedman routinely employs a large variety of synonyms and circumlocutions, so that he clearly engages in causal talk, even when explicit causal words are not in play. Instead of *A causes B*, Friedman frequently writes: *A produces* (or *influences, engenders, affects, brings about*) *B*; *B reflects* (or *is a consequence of, is a result of, is an effect of*) *A*; *A is a dependent variable, while B is an independent variable*. Instead of *causal chains* Friedman writes of *chains of influence*. Table 12.2 gives a number of examples from the *Monetary History*, which plainly show that, while Friedman and Schwartz have avoided the use of "cause," "causal," and etymologically related terms, they use a variety of words that must be regarded as synonyms.

Friedman's avoidance of explicit causal talk in the face of clearly causal intent might be dismissed as a mere quirk. I will argue subsequently that it is of a piece with his overall Marshallian methodology. But first we must examine that methodology somewhat more closely.

3   The F-twist in the light of Alfred Marshall

In describing Friedman's intellectual relationship to Marshall, the metaphor of the Bible was not chosen lightly. Methodologically Friedman is like a fundamentalist Christian who constructs his theological position by direct quotation from scripture. Once one has read Marshall's essay,

[4] My count is as accurate as I could make it on a single reading of the text, but I cannot warranty that I have caught every instance. Causal language would be exceedingly uncommon in the *Monetary History* even if I had shortened the count by half a dozen instances.

Table 12.1 *Uses of causal language in Friedman and Schwartz's* Monetary History of the United States, 1867–1960

"The **proximate cause** of the world price rise was clearly the tremendous outpouring of gold after 1890 that resulted from the discoveries in South Africa, Alaska, and Colorado and from the development of improved methods of mining and refining." [p. 137]

"And, of course, the Board also took the position that the expansion in the stock of money was **a result, not a cause**, of rising prices." [p. 223]

"[The Federal Reserve Board] argued that changes in U.S. prices were **effect rather than cause**, that the Reserve Board was powerless to do more than adapt to them, and that the Board's policies had prevented financial panic at home and moderate the price changes." [p. 237]

"Doubtless there were effects both ways **and common causes as well**." [p. 288]

"By relevant standards, the discount policy was abnormally tight, not easy. The System regarded the lack of discounting as a reflection of the large accumulation of excess reserves and hence as a lack of need for accommodation. That view no doubt had some validity, but **the causal chain ran the other way as well**." [p. 514]

"To his directors, he [Governor George L. Harrison of the Federal Reserve Bank of New York] pointed out in December that 'most of the executives of the Reserve System do not believe that monetary action would afford relief in the present business situation, regardless of whether **the causes of the recession** are monetary or non-monetary but rather that it was felt that improvement in the business situation would be more influenced by actions of the Administration.'" [pp. 528–9]

"Precisely the same is true of a draft of a memorandum prepared at the New York Federal Reserve Bank by John H. Williams in answer to the question **whether the reserve requirement changes caused the 1937–38 depression**." [p. 544]

"Consideration of the effects of monetary policy on the stock of money certainly strengthens the case for attributing an important role to monetary changes as a factor that significantly intensified the severity of the decline and also probably **caused it to occur earlier than otherwise**." [p. 544]

"Again, if the common movement of the stock of money and of money income and prices is not coincidental **or the consequence of a common cause**, the direction of influence must run from money to income." [p. 687]

Notes: emphasis in bold type added; page numbers in square brackets. The table attempts to identify every use of explicitly causal language in the *Monetary History*. It was, however, constructed from a single reading, so that completeness cannot be guaranteed.

"The present position of economics" (1885), the methodological antecedents of Friedman's essay and his other well-known methodological work, "The Marshallian demand curve" (1949b), are obvious and fairly complete. The word in Cambridge used to be "It's all in Marshall." This appears to have been true in Chicago as well.

I take the identity of Friedman's and Marshall's methodological positions as a postulate. In juxtaposing arguments from their two essays, I do not aim to persuade anyone of that identity. Rather I explicate what I take to be their commonly held views.

Table 12.2 *Examples of synonyms for causal language from Friedman and Schwartz's* Monetary History of the United States, 1867–1960

"[The *Monetary History*] traces changes in the stock of money for nearly a century, from just after the Civil War to 1960, examines the factors that accounted for changes, and analyzes **the reflex influence** that the stock of money exerted on the course of events." [p. 3]

"That outcome was widely regarded as, at least partly, **a delayed reaction to** the large wartime increases in the stock of money." [p. 13]

"As a matter of economics, there can be little doubt that [the contrast between a rise of 1.1 per cent per year in the money stock and a decline of 3.5 per cent per year in prices] **reflects primarily** a rise in output." [p. 34]

"On this interpretation **the chain of influence** ran from the attempted deflation to the economic stagnation." [p. 41]

"Not only did [the deflation of 50 percent in the decade and a half after 1865] **not produce** stagnation; on the contrary it was **accompanied and produced** by a rapid rise in real income." [p. 41]

"the amount of high-powered money is **a dependent rather than an independent variable**, and is not subject to governmental **determination**." [p. 52]

"Such shifting expectations could **affect** the price of gold *only* as they **affected** the demand for and supply of foreign exchange ..." [p. 58]

"the government **did succeed in bringing about** a minor reduction in the stock of high-powered money ..." [p. 81]

"The **major channel of influence** was from the stock of money to the level of money income to the level of prices, and thence to the rate of exchange between the dollar and other currencies, though undoubtedly some **influences** ran in the other direction." [p. 89]

"These measures, in turn however, **had offsetting effects**, since debt redemption reduced the amount and raised the price of bonds available to serve as backing for national bank notes, and so **led to a reduction** in national bank notes from a peak of some $350 million in 1882 to a trough of some $160 million in 1891." [p. 128]

"there was no evidence on the length of the lag **between action and effect**." [p. 239]

"the decline in the stock of money and the near-collapse of the banking system can be regarded as **a consequence of** nonmonetary forces in the United States, and monetary and nonmonetary forces in the rest of the world." [p. 300]

"if it did initiate a worldwide disturbance, it would inevitably be **affected in turn by reflex influences** from the rest of the world."

"the rapid rise in the money stock certainly **promoted and facilitated** the concurrent economic expansion." [p. 544]

Notes: emphasis in bold type added; page numbers in square brackets.

Van Fraassen (2002) refers to a "stance" as a kind of commitment to a creed that is maintained by faith. Within the "empirical stance," certain kinds of empirical evidence have force, but the stance itself cannot be justified by evidence of the same kind. Friedman's stance is Marshallian. But Friedman sees himself to be in a kind of Babylonian exile, singing Marshall's song in a foreign land, while other economists sacrifice at the altar of strange gods. Baal in this parable is Walras. Friedman sees the Walrasian stance as the requirement that, to know anything, one must know everything. A theory must articulate a structure that can accommodate every economic actor in its full particularity. The Walrasian economist recognizes the impracticality of doing this completely. Instead, the Walrasian offers the perfect general-equilibrium model as a transcendent ideal from which one can criticize the compromised and inconsistent realities of applied economics. Walras's is truly the Methodology of the philosophers.

The Walrasian approach suggests viewing the whole economy from an Olympian height. But Friedman denies that there is any such standpoint or that anyone could grasp the economy in its totality. Marshall argues that "[t]here is no use in waiting idly for [a unified social science]; we must do what we can with our present resources." He goes on, "common sense does not deal with a complex problem as a whole. Its first step is to break the problem into its several parts ... the human mind has no other method of inquiry than this (Marshall [1885] 1925, 164).[5] For Friedman knowledge is the product of sweaty labor among gritty facts. Marshall (p. 171; cf. Friedman [1949] 1953b, 90) writes that the economist "must stand by the more laborious plan of interrogating the facts in order to learn the manner of action of causes singly and in combination." Friedman's and Marshall's object, then, is the acquisition of causal truth. The barrier is the complexity. Marshall (157) writes that economic "causes often lie below the surface and are likely to be overlooked by the ordinary observer." Similarly, in his essay Friedman (33) writes:

A fundamental hypothesis of science is that appearances are deceptive and that there is a way of looking at or interpreting or organizing the evidence that will reveal superficially disconnected and diverse phenomena to be manifestations of a more fundamental and relatively simple structure.

The *Monetary History* can be seen as an attempt to put that hypothesis to the test. In the "Summing up" at the end of the book, Friedman and Schwartz (1963a, 676) echo the Marshallian methodological conclusion: "In monetary matters, appearances are deceiving; the important relationships are often precisely the reverse of those that strike the eye."

Opposed to a naive empiricism, Friedman and Marshall give theory a special role. "[F]acts by themselves," writes Marshall, "are silent. Observation discovers nothing directly of the action of causes, but only sequences in time" (166) ... "[T]he most reckless and treacherous of all theorists is he who professes to let the facts and figures speak for themselves ..." (168;

---

[5] Except where context would render it ambiguous, references to Marshall ([1885] 1925) will be referred to hereinafter by page numbers without dates.

cf. Friedman [1949] 1953b, 90). In the essay, Friedman concurs: "A theory is the way we perceive 'facts,' and we cannot perceive 'facts' without a theory" (34).

What is a theory? Friedman ([1949] 1953b, 91) draws his interpretation of "theory" directly from Marshall:

Economic theory, in this view, has two intermingled roles: to provide "systematic and organized methods of reasoning" [Marshall, 164; cf. F53, 7] about economic problems; to provide a body of substantive hypotheses, based on factual evidence, about the "manner of action of causes" [Marshall, 171]

Theory, or what Marshall (164) calls the "economic organon" is "not a body of concrete truth, but an engine for the discovery of concrete truth, similar to, say, the theory of mechanics" (Marshall, 159; quoted in part by Friedman [1949] 1953b, 90). The ideal theory for Marshall is universal, saying nothing about particulars, and needing to be supplemented with particular facts if it is to be useful. Economic theory, however, has not yet reached universality so that it is necessary "to sacrifice generality of form to some extent" (Marshall, 160).

In the essay, Friedman characterizes theory as, in part, "a 'language'" (7), an "analytical filing system" (11) constituted of tautologies that are useful in "organizing refractory empirical phenomena" (12) and, "[i]n part, a body of substantive hypotheses designed to abstract essential features of complex reality" (7).

Both Friedman and Marshall conceive of theory as a purely deductive system, whose claims are universal. Even the particulars that, on the one hand, fill the lacunae of incomplete theory and, on the other hand, tie that theory to empirical applications are strained and filtered to pick out what is "essential": the color of the wheat-trader's hair or number of members of his family are not relevant particulars (F53, 32). There is little difference here between Cartwright's (1999, ch. 2) treatment of theory as fables in the sense of Lessing or some accounts of theories as idealizations (Nowak 1980; Hoover 1994) – views which are compatible with realism. Friedman (F53, 36) himself refers to perfect competition and monopoly as ideal types, the application of which to concrete cases requires judgment about their suitability and about the objects of the analysis.

Cartwright thinks that fables are true; Nowak thinks idealizations get to the genuine heart of the matter. So what do we make of Friedman's famous denial that the realism of the assumptions matters? The key is to read Friedman's claim carefully. What he actually argues is that checking the realism of the assumptions does not provide a test in addition to the empirical implications of a theory. He does not claim that those assumptions are immune from indirect tests (F53, 14, 23). A theory for

Friedman is a deductive system in which some propositions are taken as axioms (or postulates) from which others can be deduced (F53, 23). The axioms are part of "conceptual world or abstract model" simpler than the real world and tied to it through rules for a class of applications and correspondences (F53, 24). The parts of a theory are interdeducible, so that what may, from one point of view, be taken to be an axiom may, from another point of view, be taken to be a theorem (F53, 26–7). How to classify various theoretical propositions is mainly a matter of finding the most economical mode of stating them (F53, 23). Economical axioms need not themselves be superficially obvious nor tied individually directly to reality.

Friedman's view of the status of theoretical axioms is virtually identical to that of Bertrand Russell (1918, 145–6):

When pure mathematics is organized as a deductive system – i.e. as the set of all those propositions that can be deduced from an assigned set of premises – it becomes obvious that, if we are to believe in the truth of pure mathematics, it cannot be solely because we believe in the truth of the premises. Some of the premises are much less obvious than some of their consequences, and are believed chiefly because of their consequences. This will be found to be always the case when a science is arranged as a deductive system. It is not the logically simplest propositions of the system that are the most obvious or that provide the chief part of our reasons for believing in the system ... Electro-dynamics, for example, can be concentrated into Maxwell's equations, but these equations are believed because of the observed truth of certain of their logical consequences.

Friedman subscribes both to Russell's claim that axioms are often not obvious ("appearances are deceiving") and that they *are* supported by indirect evidence. In dismissing as futile "Walrasian" criticism of the realism of assumptions, Friedman is attacking *naive theoreticism* – the idea that a theory should (or must) mirror casually parsed facts about the world. Instead, Friedman argues that a theory needs to get to the essence of the matter. Generally, that requires the creation of categories of entities that are not directly observable, governed by rules that omit irrelevant details, whose success is to be judged holistically.

In his monetary analysis, Friedman illustrates this strategy. The *velocity of circulation of money*, for instance, is a theoretical construct that can be observed only indirectly (= *nominal GDP/money* or = 1/*money holdings expressed as a number of weeks' income*). Friedman treats velocity as a causally significant, real category. But the evidence that he offers for its causal and ontological significance (in the *Monetary History* or in Friedman 1959, 1966, or Friedman and Schwartz 1982) is the general empirical stability of the entire analytical schema of which it is but one part.[6] What is more, Friedman treats velocity as a variable that measured in one context can be transferred to another context.

Permanent income provides another – and perhaps more compelling – example. Like velocity, permanent income is not directly observable, but is indirectly measured and validated in the context of the consumption function. Permanent income is not only a causally significant category in this context, but Friedman regards it as sufficiently freestanding and independent of its original context, that he routinely uses the measured quantity in other contexts. For example, Friedman takes permanent income to be a causal determinant of the demand for money (i.e. *permanent velocity = permanent income/money*).

Critics who hold that Friedman does not care about the truth of assumptions or even positively endorses their falsehood in some unqualified sense overlook Friedman's claims about the import of indirect evidence. In a famous example (F53, 20), Friedman talks about leaves of a tree arranging themselves as if they were maximizing received light. Since trees do not maximize, this is often taken to mean that the truth of the assumption does not matter. But Friedman goes on to say that we should prefer an explanation in terms of the mechanisms that make the tree behave as if (counterfactually) it were a conscious maximizer. Finding and elaborating such mechanisms is useful. First, a theory that encompasses those mechanisms will be more general and, therefore, more fruitful in making predictions about a wider variety of phenomena. Second, evidence for the predictive power of such a theory in other domains lends *indirect* evidence in favor of the prediction based on the assumption that trees act as if they maximized received light. The assumptions underlying such a theory may also be unrealistic in Friedman's peculiar sense of not giving us a photographically accurate description of reality, but that does not make them untrue. And, just as for Russell, the more accessible implications of a theory lend support to the logically more primitive, but inaccessible "assumptions."

4   Friedman's anti-realism reconsidered

If Friedman is a causal realist after all, what then are we to make of statements in which he denies the necessity of realistic assumptions and even seems to promote the desirability of unrealistic assumptions?

The goal of science for Friedman (F53, 7) is to construct theories that yield "valid and meaningful ... predictions about phenomena not yet

---

[6] As an economist, Friedman does not think or write explicitly in these metaphysical terms.

observed."[7] Such theories are generalizations, which necessarily omit many particular and, implicit in the theory, irrelevant details. This lack of particularity or "realisticness" (to use Mäki's apt coinage) is probably the sense of realism in play when he attacks the need for a theory to provide "photographic descriptions of reality" (Friedman [1949] 1953b, 91). "Lack of realism" for Friedman is just another (and for many philosophers, perhaps paradoxical) way of referring to the desirable property that a theory captures the essence of a deep relationship.

Marshall (166), in arguing for a theoretical approach to empirical phenomena, notes that "every event is the complex result of so many causes, so closely interwoven that the past can never throw a simple and direct light on the future." In much the same vein, Friedman (F53, 25) argues that a model is a half-truth: although "there is nothing new under the sun" (that is, generalization is the essence of the model), "history never repeats itself" (all generalizations omit particularities). Yet, both Marshall and Friedman see the immersion of the theorist in the particularities of factual inquiry as the source of further generalizations. The more the theorist is successful at eliminating necessary reference to particularities, the more general and more powerful the theory becomes, and the more nearly it approaches Marshall's ideal of a universal economic doctrine (Friedman 1953b, 159; Marshall, 14). Paradoxically, it is unrealisticness that serves and underwrites Friedman's realism with respect to the deep causal mechanisms.

Marshall, of course, did not claim that universal economic doctrine was ready to hand. Friedman (F53, 34) sees the complexity of economic phenomena as itself an argument for the incompleteness of economic theory. To accept the complexity of phenomena as an irreducible fact is to deny "the tentative state of knowledge that alone makes scientific activity meaningful." By way of illustration, he heaps scorn on John Stuart Mill's claim that the laws of value (in 1848!) were complete and required no future development. Economic theory is unrealistic in the sense that it is incomplete. But the only completeness that is valuable scientifically is that which reduces its particularity and simplifies the complexity of phenomena.

The essence of Friedman's Marshallian stance is that the pursuit of substantive knowledge cannot be stymied by the incompleteness and, therefore, "unrealism" of theory. We cannot have a complete, realistic theory first and apply it to concrete phenomena afterwards. Nor can we start with atheoretical facts, for there are none; facts are theory-laden. All we can do is to work back and forth between theory and facts, starting with the primitive and highly tentative and working toward the sophisticated

---

[7] Friedman (F53, 9) is clear that by prediction he means the inference of the unobserved from the observed, and not only forecasts of the future from the past.

and more secure. In this process, we can tolerate a large lack of realism in another sense. Predictions based on theoretical assumptions that are only approximate and, therefore, unrealistic may be as accurate as we can use given our ability to measure or as accurate as we need for some practical purposes (F53, 15–17).

Lack of realism in all the senses just discussed is perfectly compatible with the project of a constructive causal realism – that is, with the project of seeking to identify the true mechanisms underlying observed phenomena. Friedman's implicit commitment to such a project is clear in his empirical practice as a monetary economist. Most obviously, what would be the point of Friedman and Schwartz's massive historical project, not only of the *Monetary History*, but of its sister volumes, *Monetary Statistics of the United States* (1970) and *Monetary Trends in the United States and the United Kingdom 1867–1975* (1982), if somehow it were possible to be unconcerned about the accuracy of the antecedents of economic inferences? One might think of history as just a giant testbed for Friedmanian models with unrealistic assumptions, but that would miss the *modus operandi* of Friedman and Schwartz as historians: far from merely collecting data on which to test predictions, they seek detailed accounts of the institutions and even the sociological or psychological bases for the actions of particular actors; in other words, they seek to describe the actual mechanisms that generated the behavior of the economy accurately and realistically.

In Friedman's Marshallian methodology, it is possible to have causal knowledge without knowing all of the links, yet filling in the gaps is a positive virtue. In his essay (42), Friedman argues that the static monetary theory is satisfactory, but that we are largely ignorant of dynamic monetary theory. One of the promises of detailed empirical investigations is to seek new generalizations to amplify theory. His point is not merely methodological. In Friedman and Schwartz (1963b, 222) it is elaborated:

> We have little confidence in our knowledge of the transmission mechanism, except in such broad and vague terms as to constitute little more than an impressionistic blueprint. Indeed, this is the challenge our evidence poses: to pin down the transmission mechanism in specific enough detail that we can hope to make reasonably accurate predictions of the course of a wide variety of economic variables on the basis of information about monetary disturbances. (Cf. Friedman and Schwartz 1963a, 678–9.)

The dual call for realistic elaboration of the assumptions of the theory and, simultaneously, for securing breadth of generalization could not be clearer.

In principle, any theoretical propositions are at risk of being overthrown in the face of predictive failure. Although the collapse of a bridge might be taken as evidence by some of a failure of the theory of mechanics, Marshall (159–60) cautions that the theory ought to be regarded as secure in this case and its application questioned.

Friedman maintains a similar position with respect to elementary economic theory. He is well known to have attacked the utility of elaborating price theory with a theory of imperfect competition (F53, 34–9). This is an empirical claim of the lack of fruitfulness of imperfect competition. It could not, consistent with Friedman's own principles, be upheld if imperfect competition were discovered to underwrite better predictions. It is important to understand that Friedman does not dismiss criticism of analysis that divides the world into either perfect competition or monopoly, only because good predictions can be had by acting *as if* these assumptions were true. Rather Friedman makes a conceptual claim that the alternative assumption, imperfect competition, undermines the practical division of the economy into distinct industries and that, without this division, practical testing of the hypothesis is impossible. Since every case would be *sui generis*, imperfect competition could not support a general rule needed for prediction. Friedman does not deny the desirability of true assumptions in this case, instead he questions whether certain assumptions lend themselves to even indirect inquiry into their truth. For both Friedman and Marshall facts are theory-laden: the choice of theoretical assumptions helps to define what constitutes the facts. Friedman argues for one set of assumptions and against another set of assumptions on the basis of each set's effectiveness as a potential servant of the truth.

Friedman's deepest theoretical commitments are in principle, but not in practice, at risk in theoretical inquiry. Auxiliary assumptions are, in contrast, very much at risk. One nice example is provided by Friedman and Schwartz's comparison of the banking crises in the contractions of 1907–8 and 1929–33. The assumptions underlying their analysis of each recession are adjusted to fit the facts of the other. Such adjustments provide the basis for conjectural histories in which one can speculate how things might have gone differently under different policies. Such conjectures are grounded in common assumptions about the mechanisms governing different episodes. Friedman and Schwartz (1963a, 168) conclude:

all truly analytical history, history that seeks to interpret and not simply to record the past, is of this [conjectural] character, which is why history must be continuously rewritten in the light of new evidence as it unfolds.

Friedman and Schwartz practice what they preach. The *Monetary History* provides numerous examples of counterfactual analysis, the most famous example of which is their extended analysis of how the US economy might not have collapsed so deeply in the early 1930s had Benjamin Strong, the influential (and, to Friedman and Schwartz, right-minded) President of the Federal Reserve Bank of New York, not died in 1928 (Friedman and Schwartz 1963a, ch. 7). Counterfactual experiments of this sort make no sense without a commitment to the reality of a causal structure that can be faced with alternative initial conditions (see Hoover 2001, esp. chs 2 and 4).

5   Effects, not causes

We must now revisit the puzzle of why, if Friedman is a causal realist, he is so averse to using causal language. In his interview with Hammond (1992, 92), Friedman said: "The problem that bothers me about cause is that it almost invariably leads into a problem of infinite regress. There is no such thing as *the* cause of anything." Friedman sees every "proximate cause" standing in a chain of influence. What is more, influences between two variables can go in both directions. While much of Friedman and Schwartz's work has aimed to document the dominant influence of money over income and business activity, they have candidly acknowledged that influence runs from income and business activity to money as well (e.g. Friedman and Schwartz 1963a, 695; 1963b, 214; Friedman 1970, 321). It is not only the existence of causal chains that concern Friedman; he also worries that independent factors might influence any variable at one time and that there are no unambiguous ways to count causes (Friedman 1970, 319).

Friedman's squeamishness with respect to causal language can be seen as consistent with his Marshallian stance. The problem with talking about causes is that, working backwards in time, the chain never ends and, working contemporaneously, the array of causes is (perhaps infinitely) wide. Causal talk could be regarded as the enemy of Marshall's strategy of analyzing problems in manageable units: where do we draw the lines delimiting the scope of our causal interests? To think in causal language is to risk losing focus.[8]

As table 12.2 shows, Friedman frequently replaces talk of causes with circumlocutions that concentrate on effects. One might argue that effects are necessarily correlative to causes, so that this circumlocution is point-less. But that would miss the asymmetry of causation. Effects are defined as a terminus. From the point of view of an effect, the whole world and all of history spreads out around and behind us as potential causes. From the point of view of the cause, the effects lie in relatively compact lines. This is

---

[8] This interpretation is drawn from Hoover 2004, which concerns the use of causal language in econometrics in the postwar period.

obvious in tracing genealogies: it is a relatively manageable task to trace the descendents of a particular man; it is a completely open-ended task to trace his ancestors. Friedman is by no means alone. In his account of causal analysis, the statistician Paul Holland (1986) argues that we should attempt to assess the effects of a cause and not the causes of an effect, on the grounds that the first will produce stable knowledge, while the second is necessarily always an incomplete task. Holland adds, on top of Friedman's worries, that anytime we assign a proximate cause to an effect, we place ourselves hostage to future research that may find a more elaborate causal chain lying between the (now obviously not proximate) cause and the effect. In contrast, once the effect of a cause is established, further knowledge elaborates the mechanism perhaps, but does not threaten the truth status of the original claim. Friedman is clearly thinking along similar lines when he claims that changes in nominal income are an effect of money, while at the same time calling for investigation into the transmission mechanism that would elaborate that channel as well as others.

There is, as he himself recognizes (Hammond 1992, 97) a large element of semantic choice in Friedman's avoidance of explicit use of "cause" and etymologically related terms. It is a semantic choice that reinforces, and is reinforced by, his Marshallian stance. His usage is not, however, substantive in that it in no way undermines his general commitment to causal realism, which is the commitment to the existence of structures governing the causal influences among economic variables.

6   Milton Friedman's causal legacy

My reading of "Methodology of positive economics" turns large amounts of Friedman scholarship upside down. Most methodologists and most practicing economists have read Friedman's essay as offering a rationale for being unconcerned for the truth status of the assumptions of a theory. What matters is not whether markets are perfectly competitive or whether people form rational expectations, but whether they act *as if* they do.[9] Hutchison (1992, 2000) and Blaug (2002a, b) have taken Friedman to have licensed the rise of formalism in economics on the basis of such an interpretation of the essay. Hands (2003) argues that Friedman does no such thing and that Hutchison and Blaug misinterpret his essay (see also Mayer 2003). While Hands is likely right that Friedman should not be regarded as licensing formalism, the average economist interpreted it along the same lines as Hutchison and Blaug and probably regard it as a defense

---

[9] See Hammond (1992, 93) for Friedman's own criticisms of the rational-expectations hypothesis.

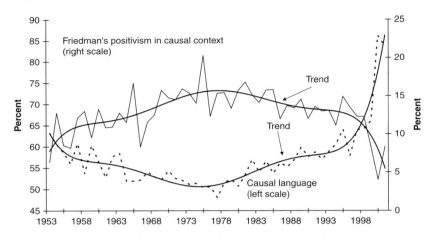

Figure 12.1 The reception of Friedman's positivism and the fate of causal language in econometrics

Notes: Each series based on counts of articles in the JSTOR archive of economics journals 1953–2001. *Causal language* shows articles in the econometric family and causal family (= "cause," "causes," "causal," "causally," "causality," or "causation") as a fraction of the econometrics family (= "econometric(s)," "regression(s)," "structural model(s)," "estimate," or "estimation"). *Friedman's positivism in a causal context* = "Friedman" (and "positive economics" or "as if") and causal family and econometric family expressed as a fraction of articles using the econometrics family and causal family. Heavy, smooth lines are sixth-degree polynomial trends.

against criticism of formalism. That widespread understanding of Friedman's methodology may have had implications for the history of causality in economics.

Figure 12.1 uses the proportion of articles available through the JSTOR journal archive that use a family of terms associated with causality and a family of terms associated with econometrics as a proportion of all articles that use the econometrics family.[10] It shows that causal language fell during the postwar period to reach a nadir in about 1980 and to revive subsequently. The figure also shows the proportion of articles that use "Friedman" and either "positive economics" or "as if" in the same article as a proportion of all articles. The rise and fall of the proportion of such references to Friedman strikingly mirror the fall and rise of causal language in econometrics.

[10] Figure appears as figure 6 in Hoover (2004).

The relationship in Figure 12.1 is itself not necessarily causal. I find it hard to believe that Friedman's own fastidiousness about the use of causal language was either directly influential or even shared widely in the economics profession. But I have argued at length elsewhere that the fall and rise of causal usage is connected to the rise and fall of formalism in econometrics, which is itself closely connected to the rise and fall of formalism in economics generally (Hoover 2004). Thus, to the extent that the common interpretation of Friedman's essay set the stage for over-valuing formalism in economics, we are left with an ironic conclusion: "The methodology of positive economics" is best read as advocating causal realism. At the same time, it was a contributing cause in the suppression of causal language in economics.

References

Blaug, Mark (2002a). Ugly currents in modern economics. In Uskali Mäki (ed.) *Fact and Fiction in Economics: Models, Realism, and Social Construction.* Cambridge: Cambridge University Press

(2002b). Is there really progress in economics? In S. Boehm, C. Gehrke, H. D. Kurz, and R. Sturn (eds.), *Is There Progress in Economics?* Cheltenham: Edward Elgar

Cartwright, Nancy (1999). *The Dappled World.* Cambridge: Cambridge University Press

Frazer, William J., Jr. and Lawrence A. Boland (1983). An essay on the foundations of Friedman's methodology. *American Economic Review,* 73(1), 129–44

Friedman, Milton (1949). The Marshallian demand curve. In *Essays in Positive Economics* (1953b), 47–99

(1953a). The methodology of positive economics. In *Essays in Positive Economics* (1953b), 3–43

(1953b). *Essays in Positive Economics.* Chicago: Chicago University Press

(1959). The demand for money: some empirical and theoretical results. In Milton Friedman, *The Optimum Quantity of Money and Other Essays* (1969). Chicago: Aldine, 111–40

(1966). Interest rates and the demand for money. In Milton Friedman, *The Optimum Quantity of Money and Other Essays* (1969). Chicago: Aldine, 141–56

(1970). Comment on Tobin. *Quarterly Journal of Economics* 82(2), 318–27

Friedman, Milton and Anna J. Schwartz (1963a). *A Monetary History of the United States, 1867–1960.* Princeton: Princeton University Press

(1963b). Money and business cycles. *Review of Economics and Statistics* 45(1, part 2: supplement). Reprinted in Milton Friedman, *The Optimum Quantity of Money and Other Essays.* Chicago: Aldine, 189–236

(1970). *Monetary Statistics of the United States: Estimates, Sources, Methods.* New York: Columbia University Press

(1982). *Monetary Trends in the United States and the United Kingdom: Their Relation to Income, Prices and Interest Rates 1867–1975*. Chicago: University of Chicago Press

Hammond, J. Daniel (1992). An interview with Milton Friedman on methodology. In W. J. Samuels (ed.), *Research in the History of Economic Thought and Methodology*, vol. 10, 91–118. Greenwich, CT: JAI Press

(1996). *Theory and Measurement: Causality Issues in Milton Friedman's Monetary Economics*. Cambridge: Cambridge University Press

Hands, D. Wade (2003). Did Milton Friedman's methodology license the formalist revolution. *Journal of Economic Methodology*, 10(4), 507–20

Holland, Paul W. (1986). Statistics and causal inference [with discussion]. *Journal of the American Statistical Association* 81(396), 945–60

Hoover, Kevin D. (1994). Six queries about idealization in an empirical context. *Poznan Studies in the Philosophy of Science and the Humanities*, 38, 43–53

(2004). Lost causes. *Journal of the History of Economic Thought*, 26(2), 149–64

Hutchison, Terence (1992). *Changing Aims in Economics*. Oxford: Blackwell

(2000). *On the Methodology of Economics and the Formalist Revolution*. Cheltenham: Edward Elgar

Marshall, Alfred ([1885] 1925). The present position of economics. In A. C. Pigou (ed.), *Memorials of Alfred Marshall*. London: Macmillan, 152–74

Mayer, Thomas (1993). *Truth versus Precision in Economics*. Aldershot: Edward Elgar

(1995). *Doing Economic Research: Essays on the Applied Methodology of Economics*. Aldershot: Edward Elgar

(2003). Fifty years of Friedman's "The methodology of positive economics." *Journal of Economic Methodology* 10(4), 493–4

Nowak, L. (1980). *The Structure of Idealization: Towards a Systematic Interpretation of the Marxian Idea of Science*. Dordrecht: Reidell

Russell, Bertrand ([1918] 1972). *The Philosophy of Logical Atomism*, ed. David Pears. London: Fontana

Samuelson, Paul A. (1963). Discussion. *American Economic Review*, 53(2), 231–6

Tobin, James (1970). Money and income: Post hoc ergo propter hoc? *Quarterly Journal of Economics*, 82(2), 301–17

Van Fraassen, Bas C. (2002). *The Empirical Stance*. New Haven: Yale University Press

13 On the right side for the wrong reason: Friedman on the Marshall–Walras divide

Michel De Vroey

1 Introduction

In 1949 Milton Friedman published an article on the Marshallian demand curve (Friedman ([1949b] 1953) which is still frequently quoted, less for its main argument than for its short final section entitled "Alternative conceptions of economic theory" in which he launched a fierce attack on Walrasian theory. Drawing a contrast between the Marshallian and the Walrasian approaches, Friedman expressed his regret that the latter had superseded the former. In his oft-quoted words, "We curtsy to Marshall but we walk with Walras" (Friedman [1949b] 1953, 89).

Eminent Friedman scholars, such as Roger Backhouse (1997), Mark Blaug (2003), Michael Bordo and Anna Schwartz (2004), Dan Hammond (1996, 2003), Abraham Hirsch and Neil De Marchi (1990), Kevin Hoover ([1984] 1990), and Tom Mayer (1993, 2009), have endorsed Friedman's claim about the Marshall–Walras divide.[1] The following quotation from Hammond summarizes the gist of their argument:

The hallmark of Friedman's methodology is Marshallianism. With this label he sets his view apart from the Walrasians'. In the 1940s the differences in the two methodologies were recognized, and as we have seen, they were not Friedman's creation. As time passed, the Walrasian approach ascended to a position of dominance in both micro and macroeconomics, with the virtues of the general equilibrium approach and mathematical qualities of elegance and generality taken for granted by most economists. (Hammond 1996, 43)

[*] This work was supported by the Belgian French-speaking Community (Grant ARC 03/08-302) and the Belgian Federal Governement (Grant PAI P5/10). The author is grateful to Mark Blaug, Milton Friedman, Dan Hausman, Dan Hammond, Kevin Hoover, Robert Leeson, Tom Mayer, Ivan Moscati, and Roy Weintraub as well as to the participants at the Duke Workshop on the History of Political Economy for their comments on an earlier version of this chapter.
[1] Nonetheless the prevailing view, which can be traced back to Hicks, is that the Marshallian and Walrasian approaches are complementary. Cf. De Vroey (2009).

The aim of this chapter is to assess the validity of Friedman's claim, first by studying the argument offered in section V of his 1949 article and, second, by comparing it with his other contemporary methodological papers – his reviews of Robert Triffin's *Monopolistic Competition and General Equilibrium* (Friedman 1941) and Oscar Lange's *Price Flexibility and Employment* (Friedman ([1946] 1953), his comment on Christ's assessment of Lawrence Klein's econometric model (1951), his famous "Methodology of Positive Economics" essay (F53) and finally his review of William Jaffé's translation of Walras's *Elements d'économie pure* (Friedman [1955] 1993).

Most of these papers pursued a critical aim. As will be seen, Friedman had many foes at the time – the concept of indifference curves, Hicksian demand analysis, Henry Schultz's, work aiming at measuring interrelated demands, macro-econometric models *à la* Klein, monopolistic competition, Keynesianism *à la* Lange. To Friedman, the common thread in all these disliked models was their connection to Walrasian theory. Hence his attack on the latter – and the commentator's difficulty in assessing whether his target was Walrasian theory per se or the models he associated with it. His positive hero was Marshall, whose insights, he felt, had been unduly discarded, and his indictment of the "Walrasian" models rested on their alleged departure from the Marshallian agenda.

The questions that I wish to address in this chapter ensue from these observations. Was Friedman right in wanting to draw a contrast between the Marshallian and the Walrasian approaches? Did he characterize it in an apposite way? Should we follow him when he claims that the Marshallian program was good and the Walrasian bad instead of simply opposing them as alternatives? What did he actually understand by the "Walrasian" modifier? Why was he so strongly anti-Walrasian in his 1949 article and less so in his 1955 piece?

A complete discussion of these issues must evolve at two levels, concerned respectively with the "politics" underlying Friedman's stance and the contents of his arguments. The first is a tale of a group of Chicago economists (Milton Friedman, George Stigler, W. Allen Wallis, and Aaron Director) gradually taking the reins of the University of Chicago community of economists, with the aim of implementing a defence of free-market economic liberalism's agenda.[2] A twofold offensive, external and internal, was implied. The external fight opposed Chicago and Harvard and concerned the relevance or otherwise of the monopolistic competition theory put forward by Chamberlin.[3] On the internal front, one enemy was Walrasian theory as upheld within the Department first by Henry Schultz

---

[2] Cf. Stigler (1988, 150).   [3] See Leeson (2000).

(who died in 1938) and later by Oscar Lange. Adhesion to the Walrasian approach was also the hallmark of some prominent economists (such as Tjalling Koopmans, Jacob Marschak, and Lawrence Klein) on the Cowles Commission (which had been relocated in Chicago in 1939). While they were only residents in the University's Department of Economics, their presence might be viewed as a threat to the laissez-faire agenda since, in the wake of the debate on the possibility of socialism, Walrasian theory was associated with collectivism, or at least with social democracy. So, when studying what was going on in Chicago in the 1940s and 1950s at the level of ideology and politics, a possible shorthand answer to the question "What did Friedman mean by 'Walrasian'?" is "socialism."[4]

While, for all its bluntness, I may sympathize with this interpretation, it does not provide a complete assessment of the issue. Whatever Friedman's motivation for entering into the fray and attacking Walrasian theory, his objections ended up being expressed as theoretical statements whose intrinsic validity needs to be examined. The shortcoming of Mirowski and Hands's work (Mirowski 2002, Mirowski and Hands 1998), which provides vivid narratives of the contextual-historical dimension, is that they fail to discuss this validity. The aim of this chapter is complementary to their work, in that its exclusive concern is an assessment of Friedman's theoretical arguments.

2   The Marshall–Walras divide in Friedman's early writings

2.1   Friedman's 1941 review of Triffin

Triffin's *Monopolistic Competition and General Equilibrium* (1940) was based on his doctorate, written under the supervision of Chamberlin. As far as can be judged from its introduction and first chapter, its aim was to integrate monopolistic competition and Walrasian theory:

Monopolistic and imperfect competition theories have evolved in the United States and in England alike along the lines of the theoretical tradition dominant in both countries: the particular equilibrium of Alfred Marshall. What we might well do now is to restate the whole problem in terms of the Walrasian, general equilibrium system of economic theory, so much more influential in economic thought on the continent of Europe. We shall find with happy surprise that monopolistic competition begins to bridge the canyon which has for years separated two schools of theoretical thought. (Triffin 1940, 3)

---

[4] As stated by Mirowski and Hands, "In the minds of many at Chicago, Walrasian mathematical theory became conflated with socialism, crude numerical empiricism, and politically naïve welfare economics" (Mirowski and Hands 1998, 268).

However, going beyond rhetoric, not much of this programme ended up being realized. While Triffin's book contains many scattered references to Walrasian theory, they concern particular points rather than Walras's general system. No model of a general equilibrium incorporating imperfect competition is present. The bulk of the book rather consists of a comparison of different imperfect competition models. Still, one claim that could not but attract Friedman's attention stands out, namely that as soon as product differentiation is introduced, the notion of an industry ceases to be relevant. Only the notions of the firm, on the one hand, and the economy as a whole, on the other, remain relevant.

In his two-page review of Triffin's book, Friedman (1941) did not evoke the Marshall–Walras opposition. Actually, Walras's name was not mentioned. Friedman's main complaint was that "Marshallian tools have been thrown away too light-heartedly" by imperfect competition theorists (1941, 390). He had in mind the notion of industry. While, like Triffin, he considered the notions of monopolistic competition and industry antagonistic, he drew the opposite conclusion – for Friedman, the notion of monopolistic competition had to be abandoned and that of industry maintained. The underlying reason was his enduring concern for practical issues. The latter, he believed, were to be grasped at the level of the industry instead of that of the firm or the economy as a whole (Hammond 2003).

2.2   Friedman's 1946 review of Lange's Price Flexibility and Employment

The aim of Lange's (1944) book, whose inspiration was Hicks's *Value and Capital* (1939; 2nd edition 1946), was to examine the Keynesian issue of whether a decrease in the money wage could restore full employment in the face of involuntary unemployment. Lange's interest lay in the persistence of underemployment, rather than in the study of the logical existence of a state of equilibrium with involuntary unemployment. Not surprisingly, his conclusion was that Keynes had been right:

Only under very special conditions does price flexibility result in the automatic maintenance or restoration of equilibrium of demand for and supply of factors of production. (Lange 1944, 83)

Lange's book started with a rejection of partial equilibrium analysis on the grounds of its narrow range of validity. Although Lange did not refer to the industry notion, it is clear that he had no sympathy for it. This was certainly not to please Friedman. Yet his criticism was not directly addressed to this point. Rather Friedman wanted to indict Lange's analysis, for consisting of "empty tautologies" or being mere "taxonomic theorizing" ([1946] 1953,

277). He concluded that Lange was just "enumerating theoretical possibilities, not describing the real world" ([1946] 1953, 271) and that his work lacked any empirical anchorage – no fact-gathering at the initial stage of the inquiry, no refutable predictions at its end stage.

> Lange largely dispenses with the initial step – a full and comprehensive set of observed and related facts to be generalized – and in the main reaches conclusions no observed facts can contradict. His emphasis is on the formal structure of the theory, the logical interrelations of the parts. He considers it largely unnecessary to test the validity of his theoretical structure except for conformity to the canons of formal logic. His categories are selected primarily to facilitate logical analysis, not empirical application or test. (Friedman [1946] 1953, 283)

This was the very criticism that Friedman was later to address to the Walrasian approach. Yet at this juncture, no reference was made to Walras.

A further, yet less emphasized, reason for Friedman's dissatisfaction with Lange's work concerned its policy conclusion. In Lange's paper, general equilibrium theory was used as a vehicle for making a Keynesian case. That general equilibrium might serve the purpose of dismissing the working of the invisible hand did not bode well for it in Friedman's eyes.

2.3   Friedman's 1949 paper on the Marshallian demand curve

Like the Triffin review, Friedman's 1949 paper on the Marshallian demand curve was a complaint about the turn taken by economic theory, a regret that Marshallian tools had been thrown away too airily.[5] The object of Friedman's dissatisfaction was the mutation that Marshallian demand theory had undergone. He felt that the newly prevailing interpretation of the Marshallian demand curve was unsatisfactory and needed to be replaced by an alternative more faithful to Marshall's interpretation.

> The currently accepted interpretation can be read into Marshall only by a liberal – and, I think, strained – reading of his remarks, and its acceptance implicitly convicts him of logical inconsistency and mathematical error at the very foundation of his theory of demand. More important, the alternative interpretation of the demand curve that is yielded by a literal reading of his remarks not only leaves his original work on the theory of demand free from both logical inconsistency and mathematical error but also is more useful for the analysis of most economic problems. (Friedman [1949] 1953, 48)

While some readers may be at a loss to see who Friedman had in mind when speaking of the "current interpretation," his target was actually well

---

[5] This theme is also visible in Friedman's lecture notes for his 1940s Economics courses at the University of Chicago (Hammond 1996, 31).

defined: the ideas developed by Hicks in his analysis of demand in part I of *Value and Capital* and expanding on Hicks and Allen (1934), on the one hand, and Henry Schultz's work (his 1935 article his book, *The Theory and Measurement of Demand*, 1938), on the other. Both Hicks and Allen, and Schultz had independently rediscovered views that had been put forward by Slutsky in a 1915 *Giornali degli Economisti* article.[6] Hicks's views soon gained wide recognition. Although Hicks and Schultz shared the same insight about building demand theory on the apparatus of indifference curves, they pursued different purposes. While Hicks was interested in pure theory without aiming at measurement, Schultz's aim, in contrast, was to make the new demand theory amenable to empirical testing. Friedman wrote his master's dissertation at the University of Chicago under Schultz's supervision. He was also Schultz's research assistant for a year. Yet at the end of the day he barely adhered to Schultz's views.[7] He was not alone in this respect. Critiques of Hicks's conception had already been delivered by Stigler (1939) and Knight (1944),[8] and in the 1942 Festschrift edited by Lange *et al.* in memory of Schultz, Friedman himself had already written an article (jointly with Wallis) criticizing the indifference curve notion (Wallis and Friedman, 1942).

Hicks's aim was to rebuild the Marshallian theory of demand while disposing of the idea of diminishing marginal utility. Beginning with the case of two goods, Hicks studied the effect of the variation in the price of X on the demand for Y, the nominal income of the agent under study being fixed. The renowned distinction between the substitution effect and the income effect ensued. The analysis was subsequently extended to the case of a great number of goods.

The contrast drawn by Friedman between the Hicksian reconstruction of Marshallian theory and what he believed to be its proper interpretation is as follows. In Hicks's model the money income and the price of every other commodity is fixed, on top, of course, of tastes and preferences. The real income is changing due to the eponymous effect. In contrast, Friedman argues that the real income should be considered fixed as well as the price of all close substitutes for, and complements of, the particular commodity.

---

[6] For a study of the relationship between these authors, see Chipman and Lenfant (2002) and Moscati (2004).

[7] Hammond (1992, 223) gives a vivid account of Friedman's opinion of Schultz. See also Stigler (1994, 1200).

[8] Knight introduced his paper as follows: "The objective of this paper is largely negative – to criticize certain recent innovations in the treatment of demand which have been generally hailed as representing an advance but which, in the writer's opinion, constitute a movement in a backward direction. The particular reference is to the treatment of demand and utility by J. R. Hicks, pioneered by E. Slutsky, and also followed, and more or less independently worked out, by Henry Schultz and many others" (1944, 289).

Whenever a change in the price of the good considered occurs, the average level of prices of unrelated goods needs to be changed in such a way as to freeze the purchasing power of money. Adopting Friedman's stance amounts to eliminating the income effect, thus leaving only the substitution effect to be active. Therefore, the Marshallian demand curve *à la* Friedman is necessarily negatively sloped, which is untrue for the Hicksian demand curve.

Friedman was critical of the indifference curve apparatus in general, but his precise target was its use by Hicks, i.e. employing the substitution effect while keeping utility constant – that is, consumers are compensated by just enough money to bring them back to their initial indifference curve. Friedman dismissed this view on the grounds that indifference curves were not an observable phenomenon. In contrast, he endorsed Slutsky's formulation, where the substitution effect gives the agent enough money to get back to his or her initial level of consumption. Slutsky was thereby tilted towards Marshall's side.[9]

In defence of his interpretation, Friedman claimed that it was more modest ("because it does not try to take account of all prices in the system, not even by keeping them constant" (Yeager 1960, 54)) and more "useful" than its rival when it came to practical problems.

A demand function containing as separate variables the prices of a rigidly defined and exhaustive list of commodities, all on the same footing, seems largely foreign to this [Marshallian] approach. It may be a useful expository device to bring home the mutual interdependence of economic phenomena; it cannot form part of Marshall's "engine for the discovery of concrete truth". The analyst who attacks a concrete problem can take explicit account of only a limited number of factors; he will inevitably separate commodities that are closely related to the one immediately under study from commodities that are more distantly related. (Friedman [1949] 1953, 57)[10]

Friedman went to great lengths to convince his readers that his interpretation was more faithful to Marshall than the Hicksian one. In effect, most of the paper is devoted to this task. While I doubt that Friedman was able to make the point, I will refrain from entering into this issue, and turn at once to the paper's penultimate section.[11]

---

[9] "On my interpretation, Marshall's demand curve is identical with the constructions introduced by Slutsky in his famous paper on the theory of choice, namely, the reaction of quantity demanded to a 'compensated variation of price,' that is, to a variation in price accompanied by a compensating change in money income. Slutsky expressed the compensating change in money income in terms of observable phenomena, taking it as equal to a change in price *times* the quantity demanded at the initial price" (1949] 1953, 52–3).

[10] See also Friedman ([1949] 1953, 85, 91).

[11] Let me nonetheless give a quotation from Aldrich that is rather dismissive: "Friedman's essay did not generate new economic theory but it established Marshall's demand theory

For all its brevity, section V develops several distinct themes. Instead of trying to paraphrase what Friedman wrote, I find it preferable to quote at length from this section.

A difference in purpose and method between Marshall and Walras

The important distinction between the conceptions of economic theory implicit in Marshall and Walras lies in the purpose for which the theory is constructed and used. To Marshall – to repeat an expression quoted earlier – economic theory is "an engine for the discovery of concrete truth" ... Economic theory, in this view, has two intermingled roles; to provide "systematic and organized methods of reasoning" about economic problems; to provide a body of substantive hypotheses, based on factual evidence, about the "manner of action of causes." In both roles the test of the theory is its value in explaining facts, in predicting the consequences of changes in the economic environment. Abstractness, generality, mathematical elegance – these are all secondary, themselves to be judged by the test of application. The counting of equations and unknowns is a check on the completeness of reasoning, the beginning of the analysis, not an end in itself. Doubtless most modern economic theorists would accept these general statements of the objective of economic theory. But our work belies our profession. (Friedman [1949] 1953, 90)

Friedman's indictment of the Walrasian approach

According to Friedman, the Walrasian approach must be indicted on several grounds:
(a) Means – i.e. "abstractness, generality, and mathematical elegance" – have become ends in themselves (Friedman [1949] 1953, 91).
(b) The Walrasian approach is flawed because it gives precedence to the realism of assumptions over their predictive ability:

> Facts are to be described, not explained. Theory is to be tested by the accuracy of its "assumptions" as photographic descriptions of reality, not by the correctness of the predictions that can be derived from it. (Friedman [1949] 1953, 91)

(c) It eliminates the industry notion and takes the monopolistic competition line, a blind alley:

> From the "Walrasian" viewpoint, to take another example from recent developments in economic theory, it is a gain to eliminate the concept of an "industry," to take the individual firm as the unit of analysis, to treat each firm as a monopoly, to confine all analysis to either the economics of the individual firm or to the general equilibrium analysis of the economy as a whole. From

as a topic for historians of economic thought. Its bold thesis and its detailed attention to what 'Marshall really meant' were provocative. It set a pattern: the subject text is tortured until a confession is produced that can be corroborated by modern theory" (1996, 212).

the Marshallian viewpoint this logical terminus of monopolistic competition analysis is a blind alley. Its categories are rigid, determined not by the problem at hand but by mathematical considerations. It yields no predictions, summarizes no empirical generalizations, provides no useful framework of analysis. (Friedman [1949] 1953, 91–2)

The difference between the two approaches is not a matter of partial versus general equilibrium

The distinction commonly drawn between Marshall and Walras is that Marshall dealt with "partial equilibrium," Walras with "general equilibrium." This distinction is, I believe, false and unimportant. Marshall and Walras alike dealt with general equilibrium; partial equilibrium as usually conceived is but a special kind of general equilibrium analysis – unless, indeed, partial equilibrium analysis is taken to mean erroneous general equilibrium analysis. Marshall wrote to J. B. Clark in 1908: "My whole life has been and will be given to presenting in realistic form as much as I can of my Note XXI." Note XXI, essentially unchanged from the first edition of the *Principles* to the last, presents a system of equations of general equilibrium. (Friedman [1949] 1953, 90)

Praising Keynes

Section V ends with Friedman praising Keynes on the ground that he was a real Marshallian:

Of course, it would be an overstatement to characterize all modern economic theory as "Walrasian" in this sense. For example, Keynes's theory of employment, whatever its merits or demerits on other grounds, is Marshallian in method. It is a general equilibrium theory containing important empirical content and constructed to facilitate meaningful prediction. (Friedman [1949] 1953, 92)

2.4   Friedman's 1951 comments on Christ's article

In a paper presented at a NBER Conference on Business Cycles, Christ (Christ 1951) set himself the task of testing Klein's econometric model. The conclusions he reached were rather negative.

Friedman's comment on it is interesting for my purposes, because he took the opportunity to plead against using simultaneous equation models aiming at representing an entire economy to make short-term predictions. In Friedman's eyes, Christ has shown that Klein's model was a failure. This was music to his ears. He then raised the question of what to do next. "Does it not then follow that despite the unsatisfactory results to date, the appropriate procedure is to continue trying one after another of such systems [of general equilibrium] until one that works is discovered?" (Friedman 1951, 112). No, was his answer, for "the probability that such a process [of constructing a model for the economy as a whole] will yield a meaningful result seems to me almost negligible" (Friedman 1951, 113). Instead, his proposed line was to return to the study of industries:

> The direction of work that seems to me to offer most hope for laying a foundation for a workable theory of change is the analysis of parts of the economy in the hope that we can find bits of order here and there and gradually combine these bits into a systematic picture of the whole. In the language of model builders, I believe our chief hope is to study the sections covered by individual structural equations separately and independently of the economy. (Friedman 1951, 114)

Friedman might aptly have evoked the names of Walras and Marshall in this discussion. In effect, studying the individual structural equations separately was nothing other than doing Marshallian industry analysis, while Klein's attempt at grasping the economy as a whole suggested a Walrasian affiliation. Yet he did not do so.

2.5   The 1953 *"Methodology of positive economics"* essay

While the Marshall–Walras opposition was not mentioned in Friedman's celebrated 1953 paper (F53), two related themes were nonetheless broached. First, Friedman engaged in a criticism of empty tautologies, taking up the theme developed in his Lange paper ([1946], 1953). Second, as in the Triffin review (1941), he crossed swords with imperfect competition theory.[12] It is to the latter that he resorted when criticizing the realism of assumptions view:

> The relevant question to ask about the "assumptions" of a theory is not whether they are descriptively "realistic" for they never are, but whether they are sufficiently good approximations for the purpose in hand. And this question can be answered only by seeing whether the theory works, which means whether it yields sufficiently accurate predictions … The theory of monopolistic and imperfect competition is one example of the neglect in economic theory of these propositions. The development of this analysis was explicitly motivated, and its wide acceptance and approval largely explained, by the belief that that the assumptions of "perfect competition" or "perfect monopoly" said to underlie neoclassical economic theory are a false image of reality. And this belief was itself based almost entirely on the directly perceived descriptive inaccuracy of the assumption rather than on any recognized contradiction of predictions derived from neoclassical economic theory. (F53, 15)

---

[12] According to Leeson, "his methodology of positive economics was formulated as a 'reaction' to Robinson and Chamberlin" (2000, 62). On this, see also Hammond (2003, 13 ff.).

2.6 Friedman's 1955 review of Jaffé's translation of Walras's Elements

Friedman's tone regarding Walrasian theory was more positive here than in his Marshallian demand curve article, as witnessed by the following statement: "The *Elements* is a great work which marked an important step forward in the development of economics as a science" (Friedman [1955] 1993, 19). His review started with the recognition that Walras was pursuing an aim different from Marshall's – to "give a bird's eye-view of the economic system as a whole" instead of trying to solve concrete issues – yet of no lesser importance.

Walras solved a different, though no less important, problem. He emptied Cournot's problem of its empirical content and produced a "complete and rigorous" solution "in principle", making no pretence that it could be used directly in numerical calculations. His problem is a problem of form, not of content: of displaying an idealised picture of the economic system, not of constructing an engine for analysing concrete problems. His achievement cannot but impress the reader with its beauty, its grandeur, its architectonic structure; it would verge on the ludicrous to describe it as a demonstration of how to calculate the numerical solution to a numerically specified set of equations. ([1955] 1993, 23–4)[13]

Walras was thus to be credited with having given economists "a framework for organizing their ideas." Nonetheless, it was time, Friedman claimed, to return to the more serious business of "meaningful theory" ([1955] 1993, 27).

Substantive hypotheses about economic phenomena of the kind that were the goal of Cournot are an essential ingredient of a fruitful and meaningful economic theory. Walras has little to contribute in this direction; for this we must turn to other economists, notably, of course, Alfred Marshall ... All these [factors] have combined to favor the Walrasian emphasis on form, to make it seem not only an essential part of a full-blown economic theory, but that economic theory itself. This conception – or misconception – of economic theory has helped to produce an economics that is far better equipped in respect of form than substance. In consequence, the major work that needs now to be done is Marshallian rather than Walrasian in character – itself a tribute to Walras's impact. (Friedman [1955] 1993, 27)

In writing the above, Friedman fell back on Stigler's opinion as expressed in *Production and Distribution Theories*:

---

[13] The same more balanced view is to be found in his *Debate with his Critics* (Friedman 1974, 145–6).

Indeed the general equilibrium theory has contributed little to economic analysis beyond an emphasis on mutual dependence of economic phenomena: the problems are far too complicated to be grasped *in toto*. Yet this particular theory describing the nature of general equilibrium was essential: such an idea had to appear before rigorous study could proceed. It was Walras's greatest contribution – one of the few times in the history of post-Smithian economics that a fundamentally new idea has emerged. (Stigler 1941, 242)

Note finally that, in spite of his praise to Walras, Friedman still stuck to his "empty tautologies" indictment, as the following excerpt makes clear:

In his final sentence, Jaffé speaks like a true Walrasian in methodology. One first constructs a pure theory, somehow on purely formal considerations without introducing any empirical content; one then turns to the "real" world, fills up the empty boxes, assigning numerical values to constants, and neglects "second-order" effects at this stage. As I have argued extensively elsewhere, this seems to me a basically false view. ([1955] 1993, 29 note 6)

3   Friedman's subsequent views

Two main claims were made in Friedman's 1949 article, first that there existed a better alternative to Hicks's account of demand theory, second, that the Marshallian and the Walrasian approaches were poles apart. Since Friedman continued to contribute to economic theory for almost a century, it is worth raising the question as to whether he stuck to his earlier views. The answer is yes.

As to demand theory, it suffices to turn to the first chapter of his *Price Theory* essay (1976, second edition; first edition 1962). It starts with the exposition of the "old" Marshallian conception of demand and includes the different concepts which Hicks wished to ban. As in the 1949 article, the "ordinary" demand function is criticized "because changes in real income are not rigorously excluded" and contrasted with a favored alternative "in which the real income, in the sense of money income divided by the purchasing power of income, is held constant" (1976, 29).

A concession to orthodoxy, Friedman broaches the notion of indifference curves – an apparatus fiercely criticized in Wallis and Friedman (1942) on the grounds of its separating preferences from prices and income. Yet when it comes to deriving demand functions from indifference curves, he falls back on the wedge between Slutsky and Hicks, with the former being the "good" and the latter the "bad" guy! Thereby, the earlier contrast between a conception of demand that is somewhat loose yet lends itself to empirical work and another, which for all its possible higher rigor fails to do so, turns up again:

The advantage of the Slutsky measure, even though in one sense it is an approximation which the Hicks measure is not, is that it can be computed directly from observable market phenomena and behavior, namely prices and quantities purchased. The Hicks measure cannot; it requires knowledge of the indifference curves. (1976, 50)

Likewise, there is little doubt that Friedman remained faithful to his earlier views as to the existence of a divide between Marshall and Walras. Two testimonies suffice to support this view. The first comes from Friedman's interview with Snowdon and Vane, one of several interviews in which he was invited to develop his current views on economics,

Question: Kevin Hoover has drawn a methodological distinction between your work as Marshallian and that of Robert Lucas as Walrasian. Is that distinction valid?

Answer: There is a great deal to that. On the whole I believe that it is probably true. I have always distinguished between the Marshallian approach and the Walrasian approach. I have always been personally a Marshallian. That doesn't mean that the Walrasian approach is not a useful or appropriate approach. Peoples' temperament and attitudes are different I guess. (Snowdon and Vane 1997, 202)[14]

---

[14] Unfortunately, when asked to delve into the reasons why he endorsed the Marshall–Walras divide, Friedman's testimony has been of little help, as the following extract from Hammond's interview makes clear:

Hammond: In "The Marshallian demand curve" you echo Marshall's description of economic theory as an "engine for the discovery of concrete truth." You compare the Marshallian conception of economic theory with the Walrasian conception of what theory should be and should do… Do you have a sense of how you first came to make this distinction and how or why you saw it as important?

Friedman: I don't really have the sense of how I first came to make the distinction or why I said it was important. I haven't thought about the question, and offhand, in thinking about it, I really don't know. It is a distinction I made fairly early on…

Hammond: You made it early, and I've come to think that it may be one of the keys to your methodology and perhaps…

Friedman: I suspect that came from Burns. That's my guess; but I really couldn't document it – because he was so imbued with Marshall. You see, he was very much a disciple of Marshall on the one hand, and Wesley Mitchell on the other. And Wesley Mitchell would have impelled in him aversion to the pure abstract Walrasian, while Marshall would have impelled in him his problem-seeking approach. I suspect that that's where it comes from, but I really can't say. That's just pure rationalization. (Hammond 1992, 226)

The second testimony is the well-known discussion between Friedman and his critics organized by Gordon (Friedman 1974). Section 3 of Friedman's *Debate with his Critics* is entitled "What explains the difficulty of communication?" (between Tobin and him). His answer to this question was that "the difficulty is a different approach to the use of economic theory – the difference between what I termed a Marshallian approach and a Walrasian approach in an article I wrote many years ago" (1974, 145). Friedman went on quoting extensively from his 1949 article. Later on, when discussing Patinkin he returned to the same theme of the contrast between Marshall and Walras:

> ... Patinkin, even more than Tobin, is Walrasian, concerned with abstract completeness, rather than Marshallian, concerned with the construction of special tools for special problems. (1974, 159)

4   A criticism of Friedman's section V argument

Friedman's 1949 paper section V raises a host of questions. Had Friedman's claim that Walrasian theory dominated the profession any plausibility at the end of the 1940s? Did Friedman mean that the Marshallian and the Walrasian approaches differed in purpose or in their implementation of a common purpose? Was Friedman right when stating that the divide was not a matter of partial versus general equilibrium? Can his portrait of the Walrasian approach be considered fair and well documented? Finally, how does his 1949 article relate to his other pieces?

The alleged dominance of the Walrasian approach

Considering the time at which he was writing (the end of the 1940s), Friedman's fierce attack on the Walrasian approach is surprising. "We curtsy to Marshall but we walk with Walras" is definitely a powerful image, but is it a correct account of what was going on? I doubt it.

At the time, Walras's *Elements* had not been translated into English. Arrow and Debreu had not started their collaboration. Only a few sources (e.g. Stigler 1941) and the works of Cassel and Wicksell were available to economists who wished to become acquainted with Walrasian theory while being unable to read French. Admittedly, a revival of Walrasian theory, triggered by Hicks's *Value and Capital*, was effectively under way. A few works of mathematical economics had seen the light of day, led by authors such as Moore, Hotelling, and Schultz.

Their aim, which could not but have looked odd to Walras, was to render the Walrasian conceptual apparatus statistically operational. Thus, their perspective was poles apart from the line pursued by Arrow, Debreu, and Mackenzie, which I for one view as being more faithful to Walras's own methodological precepts. It is also true that Friedman was in direct contact with some of the few Walrasian American economists and enjoyed many opportunities to confront them with his views when attending seminars at the Cowles Commission.

Yet, all in all, these economists were a definite minority in the profession. Therefore, Friedman's image is totally inappropriate. At the time, the majority of economists were not walking with Walras.

A fair portrait of the Walrasian approach?

The Lausanne economist would hardly have recognized his brainchild in Friedman's sketchy portrait. Take the statement that to Walras "facts are to be described, not explained." Assuming its meaning is clear, which is questionable, I do not see how it relates to Walras's methodology. Likewise, having Walras ranked as a defender of the realism of assumptions looks odd. Ascribing to him the view that a "theory is to be tested by the accuracy of its 'assumptions' as photographic descriptions of reality, not by the correctness of the predictions that can be derived from it" (Friedman [1949] 1953, 91) indicates a total ignorance of his methodological principles. It is true that, unlike Friedman, Walras did not believe that economic theory needed to be gauged by its predictive capacity. Yet, he never viewed the realism of its assumptions as the criterion by which to assess it. Finally, another indication of Friedman's ignorance of Walrasian theory is his claim that Walras adhered to monopolistic competition and treated firms as monopolies. In fact, nothing was more alien to Walras than such a view.

Furthermore, on reading section V it is unclear whether Friedman had in mind that the Marshallian and the Walrasian approaches were pursuing different purposes or whether he indicted the Walrasian approach for having lapsed from some purpose that would have been common to both of them. He started by asserting that they pursued different purposes. Yet, when it came to documenting this difference, he shifted toward denouncing abstractness, mathematical elegance, and means becoming ends, all of which suggests that Walrasian theory had derailed from the supposed common purpose of economic theory.

Even this derailment claim is poorly supported. Friedman's opposition between mathematical elegance and relevance has little grounding. While mathematical elegance has indeed been a distinctive feature of neo-Walrasian theory – which, remember, had not seen the light of day at this time – Walras's own work can hardly be characterized in this way. If anything, Walras's mathematics was, as noted by Harrod (1956), "clumsy and tortuous."

Friedman's claim that the Marshall–Walras divide is not a matter of partial versus general equilibrium

Can Friedman be taken at his word when he claims that Marshallian analysis is a fully fledged general equilibrium theory? I do not think so.

The most plausible definition of general equilibrium analysis consists of stating that a model can be considered as "general equilibrium" as soon as its object of study is an entire economy rather than a fraction of it. The immediate implication is that all models that fail to meet this criterion must be considered as partial equilibrium models. The joint study of two markets (for example, the market for a given good and the markets for its inputs) constitutes partial equilibrium even if it is concerned with an interdependency phenomenon. As soon as this definition is adhered to, the matter is settled: Marshallian analysis *à la* Friedman, centered on the study of an industry, is partial equilibrium.

Unfortunately, Friedman refused this characterization. The underlying reason, I believe, is a matter of territorial claims. The term "general equilibrium" has positive connotations of completeness, while the term "partial equilibrium" suggests an admission of incompleteness. Hence the struggle to stop the Walrasian camp having a monopoly over the positively connoted field.

As soon as it is accepted that general equilibrium must be equated with the analysis of an economy as a whole, Friedman's stance can be ascertained unequivocally: he is against it. It suffices to return to his comment on Christ's assessment of the Klein model, where he argued that industry analysis has advantages of its own that are lost when the economy as a whole becomes the object of study. Therefore, Friedman's rationale for calling his preferred approach "general equilibrium analysis" is hard to understand. Does it mean that admitting that one is not doing general equilibrium analysis amounts to an unbearable stigma? Be that as it may, nothing but confusion is to be gained by such a semantic move.

As to Friedman's claim that Marshall's Mathematical Note XXI generalized his partial equilibrium into a general equilibrium analysis, it breaks down as soon as the line between general equilibrium and non-general equilibrium is drawn along the above lines. Marshall's note is concerned with the phenomenon of joined and composite supply and demand. Clearly an element of interdependency is involved. Yet widening the scope of the analysis from a single market to a group of related markets cannot be viewed as tantamount to analyzing the entire economy. Likewise, the fact that Marshall wrote to John Bates Clark that all his life had been devoted to giving flesh to this note should not be taken for more than it was, a declaration of intention. Authors must be judged on their theories rather than on their metatheoretical comments.

Three main lessons can be drawn from my survey. First, it is surprising to see how numerous Friedman's foes were at the time. The concepts or works that he disliked and felt the need to attack ranged widely: indifferences curves, Hicksian demand theory, Schultz's statistical demand curves, econometric models aiming at representing the economy as a whole, monopolistic competition, and Lange's Keynesianism. All this conveys the image of Friedman as an outcast, or at least as somebody fighting against the tide. Positively, he had one hero, Marshall, and to him this meant three associated features: (a) the search for concrete truth and an under-standing of the ordinary business of life; (b) the need to focus on the study of particular industries; and (c) the need to resort to concepts that were directly operational, i.e. measurable. The second lesson is that Friedman seems to have believed that all the models he disliked were "Walrasian." The third lesson is the difference in tone between Friedman's criticism of Walrasian theory in his 1949 and 1955 articles. In the latter, he is still dismissive of the Walrasian approach, but in a far less vehement way.

Two tasks ensue from these observations. The first is to assess whether there are good grounds for characterizing all the above models as Walrasian. That is, what might the "Walrasian" modifier have meant for Friedman, and does his understanding of it stand up retro-spectively? The second is to elucidate his change in tone between 1949 and 1955.

5   Friedman's understanding of the "Walrasian" modifier

As I see things, Friedman's characterization of Walrasian theory can be summarized in the following five points:

(1) Walrasian theory aims at discovering fundamental principles governing abstract economies.
(2) Walrasian models comprise theoretical concepts that have no direct measurable counterparts.
(3) Empirical measurement and prediction-making and testing are no part of the research program.
(4) Walrasian models are concerned with the economy as a whole rather than with a part of it, such as an industry.
(5) The Walrasian approach is formalized; whenever necessary, relevance will be sacrificed to rigour.[15]

On all these points, the Marshallian approach is supposed to stand in sharp contrast to the Walrasian. Moreover, to Friedman, bringing out a contrast between the Marshallian and the Walrasian approaches was tantamount to pleading for the superiority of the former over the latter. So all the above features were considered by Friedman as flaws and reasons to condemn any model which adopted them.

The question must be asked as to whether such a characterization stands up to a retrospective test – would a present-day defender of the Marshall–Walras divide agree with Friedman's way of putting the issue? As expected, the answer is not clear cut. Positively, Friedman's characterization of the scope and aim of Walrasian theory is acceptable. Negatively, three critical observations come to mind. First, Friedman insists too much on broad methodological traits such as those above, failing to realize that the contrast between the two approaches is also a matter of narrower methodological choices, the effect of which is to put the theoretical construction on divergent tracks. These bear on the notion of equilibrium that is adopted, the role of money, the trade organization and information assumptions, the treatment of time, etc.[16] Second, the fifth criterion, on which Friedman insisted, has failed to pass the test of time. Accepting that game-theoretical and industrial organization models can be considered neo-Marshallian, it has turned out that the Walrasian approach no longer has a monopoly over formalization. Finally, Friedman's manicheist stance must also be questioned. In my opinion, no one approach should be considered superior to another. They are rather alternative research programs, each having its pros and cons.

In order to qualify as Walrasian, a given model must abide by the above criteria.[17] Let me then ask whether there are good reasons to consider

---

[15] Some further traits mentioned in section V of Friedman ([1949] 1953), such as the monopolistic nature of Walrasian theory, have been dropped because they are patently mistaken.
[16] On this, see De Vroey (1999a, 1999b, 2003).
[17] Henceforth, I will consider only the first four conditions, eliminating the fifth one.

the models criticized by Friedman as Walrasian according to his own definition.

Hicks's demand theory

Unlike Friedman (and myself), Hicks saw no fundamental reason for opposing Marshall and Walras. To him, these two authors held complementary approaches (Hicks ([1934] 1983). He viewed the study of the Marshallian market as a first step in the analysis of the economy as a whole.[18] Be that as it may, separating the elements of Hicks's *Value and Capital* (1946) that are Marshallian from those that are Walrasian is quite easy. The very fact that part II of the book is entitled "General equilibrium analysis" indicates that part I, entitled "The theory of subjective value," where Hicks develops his demand analysis, is not a general equilibrium theory. In effect, Hicks's recurrent reference in the chapters composing part I of *Value and Capital* is Marshall. So Hicks's demand theory analysis belongs to the Marshallian part of the book rather than to its Walrasian part.

It may be argued that the fact that every commodity composing the economy is individually listed in the Hicksian demand theory makes it Walrasian.[19] Yet this is not a sufficient condition. For example, the category of income as understood by Hicks in these chapters – a quantity of money that agents have at their disposal before entering the goods markets and which accrued to them from their antecedent sale of inputs – has no place in a Walrasian framework.

Finally, comparing Hicks's demand theory with the set of conditions above, it turns out that it abides by conditions (1), (2), and (3), but definitely not by condition (4).

To conclude, it is dubious whether the Hicksian demand theory can be characterized as specifically Walrasian. Friedman's dissatisfaction with it may well rest on a trait that he associates with the Walrasian approach – basing the analysis on concepts having no observable counterparts – yet this association is far from compelling. The dispute between Hicks and Friedman is one that takes place within the Marshallian partial equilibrium framework rather than opposing the Walrasian and Marshallian approaches. As a result, Friedman's transition from the discussion of

---

[18] "If a model of the whole economy is to be securely based, it must be grounded in an intelligent account of how a single market functions" (Hicks 1965, 78).

[19] This is the step taken by Hirsch and De Marchi: "In comparing two demand curves, one of which he calls Walrasian (the conventional one) and of which he refers to as Marshallian (constant real income) Friedman gives us an example of how he applies the Marshallian–Walrasian distinction in a specific case" (1990, 23).

demand theory in sections I to IV of the 1949 article, where he discusses demand theory, to section V, devoted to the broader Marshall–Walras contrast, is far from straightforward. While there is a link between these two parts of the article, they are hardly part and parcel of each other. In fact, they could be split without harming the argument in either.

Schultz

Schultz was an author who claimed to be part of the Walras–Pareto lineage while pursuing the aim of making Walrasian concepts statistically measurable, a project that Walras would have refused to consider as his. Be that as it may, Schultz cannot be considered Walrasian according to Friedman's criteria. His agenda fails to abide by conditions (1) and (3), and possibly also condition (2). Friedman might have been expected to credit Schultz with having breached the Walrasian reluctance to enter into empirical work, but this was not the case. In Friedman's eyes, something more than merely engaging in empirical work was needed, namely that the empirical results exerted a feedback on the theoretical structure.[20]

Moreover, Schultz's work shows that there is many a slip 'twixt cup and lip. To achieve his aim of measuring Walrasian concepts, Schultz had to go through many twists as, to give just one example, his transmogrification of the Walrasian notion of endowment into the Marshallian notion of monetary income witnesses. While the theoretical and empirical parts of Schultz's paper and article are excellent contributions on their own, the link between them is virtually non-existent.[21]

To conclude, there is more to Friedman's dislike of Schultz's work than its Walrasian character. Moreover, Schultz should not be considered a fully fledged Walrasian economist.

---

[20] This is evidenced in a letter that Friedman wrote to Edwin Wilson in 1946 in which he criticized Schultz in the following terms: "Schultz took the theory as fixed and given, and tried to measure what he thought were essential functions in the theory. He imposed extremely high standards of care and thoroughness on the measurement process – but he nowhere attempted what seems to me the fundamental important task of reformulating the theory so that it would really generalize the observable data; he also tried to wrench the data into a pre-existing theoretical scheme, no matter how much of a wrench was required" (Stigler 1994, 1200).

[21] This has led Mirowski and Hands to conclude that "it is seldom recognized that [Schultz's] book is essentially a swan song for Walrasian economics: Schultz bravely reported the empirical debacle in detail and then produced a litany of excuses why things had not worked out as hoped" (1998, 264).

Lange

Price Flexibility and Employment was an attempt to combine Walras and Keynes, two authors to whom Friedman was strongly opposed. Was there then some domino process at work, Friedman's dislike of Keynes spilling over to Walras? Actually, the matter is more complicated than that. Recall Friedman's hailing of Keynes as a genuine Marshallian in section V of the 1949 article. In other words, while Friedman was opposed to Walrasian theory because of its methodological principles, his opposition to Keynes had no such groundings. Keynesian theory was to be rejected, not, like Walrasian theory, because of its faulty methodological basis, but rather because it had been contradicted by empirical evidence.[22] So, Friedman's target in his criticism of Lange's book is less the Keynesian than the Walrasian element of the proposed Keynes–Walras alliance.

The irony here is that, while Walras's name does not appear in Friedman's review of Lange, of all the authors attacked by Friedman he was the only one who really deserved the Walrasian label. And, in effect, his theory abides by the criteria set up to this effect.

Triffin

Two reasons may explain Friedman's hostility to Triffin's project. First, it amounted to shelving the study of industries. The second objection has a more ideological nature. Triffin claimed that a deep affinity linked imperfect competition and Walrasian general equilibrium, to the effect that a synthesis between them was within reach. This could not but displease Friedman on the ground of a bedfellows argument – any friend of any enemy must also be an enemy. Friedman did not question Triffin's cooptation of Walrasian theory. Saddled with such a bedfellow, Walrasian

---

[22] The following extract from Friedman's *Theoretical Framework for Monetary Analysis* makes this clear: "Keynes was no Walrasian seeking, like Patinkin and to a lesser extent Tobin, a general and abstract system of all-embracing simultaneous equations. He was a Marshallian, an empirical scientist seeking a simple, fruitful hypothesis. And his was a new, bold, and imaginative hypothesis, whose virtue was precisely how much it could say about major problems on the basis of so little. Of course, his assumptions were not in literal correspondence with reality. If they had been, he would have been condemned to pedestrian description; his whole theory would have lost its power. Of course, he could be wrong. There is no point to any scientific theory that cannot be. The greater the range of evidence that, if observed, would contradict a theory, the more precise are its predictions and the better a theory is provided it is not, in fact, contradicted. I believe that Keynes' theory is the right kind of theory in its simplicity, its concentration on a few key magnitudes, its potential fruitfulness. I have been led to reject it, not on these grounds, but because I believe that it has been contradicted by evidence: its predictions have not been confirmed by experience. The failure suggests that it has not isolated what are 'really' the key factors in short-run economic change" (Friedman 1974, 134).

theory could hardly look congenial to him. However, what he failed to see was that the synthesis between Chamberlin and Walras evoked by Triffin was just wishful thinking. Triffin's thesis hardly took the first step toward constructing such a synthesis. If the Marshall–Walras divide makes sense, it would be better to put monopolistic competition on Marshall's side (as argued in De Vroey 2004).

The general lesson to be drawn from this quick assessment is that, with the exception of Lange, the reasons for Friedman's dissatisfaction with the models he rejects actually have little to do with their alleged Walrasian character.

6   Friedman's 1949 account of the Marshall–Walras divide and his review of Jaffé's translation of Walras's *Elements*

Finally, let me compare the 1949 article with the 1955 review. While the former is virulent, the latter, although still dismissive, is milder in tone. In particular, the Jaffé review improves on the 1949 article by bringing out the difference in purpose between Marshall and Walras more satisfactorily. Walras is no longer assessed through a Marshallian lens. The specificity of his project is recognized.

Two factors may be evoked to explain the difference between the 1949 and the 1955 articles. A first one is the bad company explanation. Yet, as seen, it played only for the imperfect competition / Walrasian theory connection. In 1949, Friedman might still have believed that Triffin was right in arguing that Walrasian theory and imperfect competition were compatible.[23] At the time, he had only an indirect knowledge of Walrasian theory, while the works against which he felt it necessary to react were claiming a Walrasian affiliation. Professor Blaug's testimony can be called in support of this view, as he has written to me that Friedman told him that the first time he read Walras was when he reviewed Jaffe's translation.[24] Once Walras's *Elements* became available in English, Friedman realized that Walrasian theory did not carry the associations which Triffin and Lange had wanted to impose upon it. It was still not his cup of tea, but at least he recognized its specificity and was ready to give it due credit.

---

[23] An extract from Hammond (2003) is worth quoting in this respect for it reveals that Friedman's mistake is still being made: "So the impetus of Friedman's discussion of methodology with George Stigler was the challenge posed by *Walrasian monopolistic competition* to Marshallian industry analysis" (2003, 16; my emphasis). Treading in Friedman's footsteps, Hammond wrongly takes it for granted that Walrasian monopolistic competition existed and raised a challenge to Marshallians.

[24] This point was confirmed to me by Professor Friedman in private correspondence.

The second factor relates to the political dimension evoked in the introduction. On the one hand, the Cowles Commission had left Chicago. On the other hand, the socialist debate had petered out, and on reading Walras's *Elements*, Friedman must quite rightly have discovered that no plea in favor of socialism was to be found in it.

7   Concluding remarks

My aim in this chapter has been to assess the validity of Friedman's claim, made in his 1949 article, as to the existence of a Marshall–Walras divide. I have shown that Friedman's arguments in favor of it stand up to scrutiny only partially. I have also put forward the view that when he criticized specific models for their Walrasian flaws he might have had in mind other targets for which the Walrasian label served as a proxy. The change in tone, from a vehement to a softer anti-Walrasian stance, between Friedman's 1949 article and his 1955 review of Jaffé's translation of Walras's *Elements of Pure Economics* has also been brought out. While keeping his Marshallian affiliation, he followed Stigler to a position combining praise for Walras's achievement with the conviction that it was not the right line to take. Thus, to my mind, the 1955 article is a better embodiment of Friedman's definitive view as to the relationship between Marshall and Walras than the 1949 article.

My judgment that Friedman's justification of the Marshall–Walras divide was unsatisfactory should not be taken as meaning that he was wrong in believing that the two approaches were poles apart. On the contrary, he should be credited for having blazed the trail for the recognition of this divide, which in my opinion constitutes a clue for understanding the development of economic theory over the last century. He was right in perceiving the need to draw the Marshall–Walras divide yet unable to give a solid argumentation as to its grounding. The task ahead is to fill in this lacuna.

References

Aldrich, J. (1996). The course of Marshall's theorizing about demand, *History of Political Economy*, 28, 171–217

Backhouse, Roger E. (1997). The rhetoric and methodology of modern macroeconomics. In Brian Snowdon and Howard Vane (eds.), *Reflections on the Development of Modern Macroeconomics*. Cheltenham: Edward Elgar, 31–54

Baranzini, R. and P. Bridel (2003). Echange et utilité: Walras, versus Pareto. *Communication au X Colloque de l'Association Charles Gide pour l'étude de la Pensée Economique*, Grenoble, September 2003

Blaug, Mark (2003). The formalist revolution of the 1950s. *Journal of the History of Economic Thought*, 25, 145–56

Bordo, M. and A. Schwartz (2004). IS-LM and monetarism. In M. De Vroey and K. Hoover (eds.), *The IS-LM Model: Its Rise, Fall and Strange Persistence*, annual supplement of *History of Political Economy*, 36, 217–39

Buchanan, James (1958). *Ceteris paribus*: some Notes on Methodology. *Southern Economic Journal*, 24, 259–70

Chipman, J. and J.-S. Lenfant (2002). Slutsky's 1915 article: how it came to be found and interpreted. *History of Political Economy*, 34, 554–97

Christ, C. (1951). A test of an econometric model for the United States, 1921–1947. Paper presented at the 1949 NBER Conference on Business Cycles, 35–105

Clower, R. and A. Leijonhufvud ([1975] 1984). The coordination of economic activities: a Keynesian perspective. In D. Walker (ed.), *Money and Markets: Essays by Robert Clower*. Cambridge: Cambridge University Press, 209–17

Colander, David (1996) (ed.). *Beyond Micro-Foundations: Post-Walrasian Macroeconomics*. Cambridge: Cambridge University Press

De Vroey, Michel (1941). Review of *Monopolistic Competition and General Equilibrium Theory* by Robert Triffin. *Journal of Farm Economics*, 23, 389–91

　([1946] 1953). M. Lange on price flexibility and employment: a methodological criticism. In *Essays in Positive Economics*. Chicago: University of Chicago Press, 277–300

　([1949] 1953). The Marshallian demand curve. In *Essays in Positive Economics*. Chicago: University of Chicago Press, 47–99

　(1951). Comments on Christ, *Conference on Business Cycles*. New York: National Bureau of Economic Research, 107–13

　(1953). The methodology of positive economics. In *Essays in Positive Economics*. Chicago: University Chicago Press, 3–43

　([1955] 1993). Léon Walras and his economic system. In J. Cunningham Wood (ed.), *Léon Walras, Critical Assessments*. London: Routledge, vol. I, 19–29

　(1968). The role of monetary policy. *American Economic Review*, 58, 1–17

　(1999a). The Marshallian market and the Walrasian economy: two incompatible bedfellows. *The Scottish Journal of Political Economy*, 46(3), 319–38

　(1999b). Equilibrium and disequilibrium in economic theory: a comparison of the classical, Marshallian and Walras-Hicksian conceptions. *Economics and Philosophy*, 15, 161–85

　(2002). Equilibrium and disequilibrium in Walrasian and neo-Walrasian economics. *Journal of the History of Economic Thought*, 24, 405–26

　(2003). Perfect information à la Walras versus perfect information à la Marshall. *Journal of Economic Methodology*, 10, 465–92

　(2004). The history of macroeconomics viewed against the background of the Marshall–Walras divide. In M. De Vroey and K. Hoover (eds.), *The IS-LM Model: Its Rise, Fall and Strange Persistence*, annual supplement of *History of Political Economy*, 36, 57–91

　(2009). Marshallian and Walrasian theory: complementary or alternative approaches? *History of Political Economy*, forthcoming

Friedman, Milton (1974). *Milton Friedman's Monetary Framework: A Debate with his Critics*, ed. R. J. Gordon. Chicago: University of Chicago Press

(1976) *Price Theory*. Chicago: Aldine

Hall, R. E. (1979). A theory of the natural unemployment rate and the duration of employment. *Journal of Monetary Economics*, 5, 153–69

Hammond, J. Daniel (1992). An interview with Milton Friedman on methodology. In Bruce J. Caldwell (ed.), *The Philosophy and Methodology of Economics*, vol. I. Cheltenham: Edward Elgar, 216–38 (interview took place on May 24, 1988)

(1996). *Theory and Measurement: Causality Issues in Milton Friedman's Monetary Economics*. Cambridge: Cambridge University Press

(2003). Predictions as the goal of economic analysis. Paper presented at the Conference *Milton Friedman's Essay at 50*, Erasmus Institute for Philosophy and Economics, December 2003

Harrod, Roy F. (1956). Walras: a re-appraisal. *Economic Journal*, 46, 307–16

Hausman, Daniel (1990). Supply and demand explanations and their *ceteris paribus* clauses. *Review of Political Economy*, 2, 168–86

Hicks, J. R. ([1934] 1983). Léon Walras. In *Classics and Moderns: Collected Essays on Economic Theory*, vol. III. Oxford: Basil Blackwell, 85–95

(1946). *Value and Capital*, 2nd edition. Oxford: Clarendon Press

(1965). *Capital and Growth*. Oxford: Clarendon Press

Hicks, J. R. and Allen, R. G. D. (1934). A reconsideration of the theory of value. *Economica*, 52–76, 196–219

Hirsch, Abraham and Neil De Marchi (1990). *Milton Friedman, Economics in Theory and Practice*. New York: Harvester Wheatsheaf

Hoover, Kevin ([1984] 1990). Two types of monetarism. In J. Cunningham Wood and R. N. Woods (eds.), *Milton Friedman: Critical Assessments*, vol. III. London: Routledge, 527–51

Jaffé, William ([1980] 1983). Walras's economics as others see it. In Donald A. Walker (ed.), *William Jaffé's Essays on Walras*. Cambridge: Cambridge University Press, 343–70

Knight, Frank (1944). Realism and relevance in the theory of demand. *Journal of Political Economy*, 52, 289–318

Lange, Oskar (1944). *Price Flexibility and Employment*. Bloomington, IN: Principia Press

Leeson, Robert (2000). *The Eclipse of Keynesianism: The Political Economy of the Chicago Counter-Revolution*. Basingstoke: Palgrave

Mayer, Thomas (1993). *Truth versus Precision in Economics*. Aldershot: Edward Elgar

(2009). The influence of Friedman's methodological essay. This volume

Mirowski, Philip (2002) *Machine Dreams. Economics Becomes a Cyborg Science*. Cambridge: Cambridge University Press

Mirowski, Philip and D. Wade Hands (1998). A paradox of budgets: the postwar stabilization of American neoclassical demand theory. In M. Morgan and M. Rutherford (eds.), *From Interwar Pluralism to Postwar Neoclassicism*, annual supplement to *History of Political Economy*, 30. Durham, NC: Duke University Press, 260–92

Moscati, I. (2004). History of consumer demand theory 1871–1971: a neo-Kantian rational reconstruction. *European Journal of the History of Economic Thought*, 14, 119–56

Schultz, H. (1935). Interrelations of demand, price and income. *Journal of Political Economy*, 43, 433–81

(1938). *The Theory and Measurement of Demand*. Chicago: University of Chicago Press

Slutsky, E. (1915). Sulla Teoria del bilancio del Consumatore. *Giornale degli Economisti*, 3, 1–21

Snowdon, Brian and Howard Vane (1997). Modern macroeconomics and its evolution from a monetarist perspective: an interview with Professor Milton Friedman. *Journal of Economic Studies*, 24(4), 192–22

Stigler, George (1939). The limitations of statistical demand curves. *Journal of the American Statistical Association*, 34, 469–81

(1941). *Production and Distribution Theories: The Formative Years*. New York: Macmillan

(1988). *Memoirs of an Unregulated Economist*. New York: Basic Books

(1994). Correspondence on methodology between Milton Friedman and Edwin Wilson; November-December 1946. *Journal of Economic Literature*, 32, 1197–1203

Triffin Robert (1940). *Monopolistic Competition and General Equilibrium*. Cambridge, MA: Harvard University Press

Wallis, W. A. and M. Friedman (1942). The empirical derivation of indifference functions. In O. Lange, F. MacIntyre and T. Yntema (eds.), *Studies in Mathematical Economics and Econometrics. In Memory of Henry Schultz*. Chicago: University of Chicago Press

Yeager, L. (1960). *Methodenstreit* over demand curves. *Journal of Political Economy*, 68, 53–64

Part 5

Concluding perspectives

14 The debate over F53 after fifty years

Mark Blaug

"The methodology of positive economics" (F53) is a classic text in economic methodology and like any classic text it can be read in or out of context. Its original context, as Roger Backhouse reminds us in chapter 8 of this volume, was that of antimarginalist attacks on profit maximization by heterodox economists using survey data to demonstrate that businessmen do not calculate marginal costs and benefits. Much of the essay is easier to understand when we keep that context in mind. But as time passed, that particular context became irrelevant and the essay was increasingly read in the light of Friedman's subsequent career as a monetarist, leading opponent of Keynesian demand management and outspoken advocate of free-market fundamentalism. After, say 1970, few economists could read the essay as simply a methodological defense of patently "unrealistic" assumptions in economic theories because the rest of Friedman's message was always in the back of their minds. In short, in examining interpretations of what F53 really meant, it is important to take account of the year the interpretation is advanced. To underline that point, let me briefly reminisce.

I first read F53 for a 1955 Yale University seminar organized by Tjalling Koopmans when he was writing the second of his *Three Essays on the State of Economic Science* (1957). Koopmans was quite skeptical of the essay, saying it apologized too much for the lack of realisticness of standard price theory, but I myself, knowing no better, thought it was a remarkably effective defense of standard theory and I was totally convinced by the idea that the assumptions of a theory did not really matter provided the theory predicted accurately. The now familiar proposition that there is something wrong with a black-box theory that predicts accurately but provides no mechanism to account for those predictions did not occur to me at the time. Besides, I was impressed by Friedman's fall-back argument that the beliefs of businessmen do not matter anyway, because competition is a Darwinian selection mechanism for weeding out firms that fail to maximize profits in accordance with the marginal-cost-pricing rule of orthodoxy. In other words, standard theory predicts accurately because it captures the essential consequences of a survival mechanism that produces results that are indistinguishable from those of perfect competition.

It was some years later that I read Sydney Winter's PhD thesis at Yale, which argued that standard price theory is a precisely stated static theory, whereas the Darwinian selection mechanism is a vaguely stated dynamic theory. That is to say that Friedman employed a radically different evolutionary explanation to justify his original contention about the accurate predictions of comparative static reasoning. It seems perfectly obvious now but, with tremendous efforts, I can still recall my confusion about all these issues fifty years ago. Fifty years ago? Was it really that long ago? Why, that is longer than the years that separate World War I from World War II, or the publication of Marshall's *Principles* from Keynes's *General Theory*.

When I came to take another look at F53 in the late 1970s in preparation for my *Methodology of Economics* (1980), it was easy to read Friedman as yet another weak-kneed Popperian who would not practise what he preached. After all the fuss about judging theories by their predictions and not their assumptions, he finally reached the disappointing conclusion that "An even more important body of evidence for the maximization-of-returns hypothesis is experience from countless applications of the hypothesis to specific problems ... This evidence is extremely hard to document; it is scattered in numerous memorandums, articles, and monographs concerned primarily with specific concrete problems rather than with submitting the hypothesis to test" (F53, 22–3). Really? Not even one concrete prediction? For example, that advertising will never be observed in a perfectly competitive market and therefore that the more nearly the market structure of an industry approaches that of perfect competition, the less is the quantity of advertising we will observe; or, that a rise in the money wages of a particular category of labor will reduce the volume of employment of that type of labor, if not in the long run then certainly in the short run. Whatever the evidence for both propositions, is there really nothing we can do to marshal that evidence, and if there really is no such evidence, does that not tell us something very significant about the theoretical beliefs of the economics profession?

By 1980, Friedman's monetarism had arrived – but was not yet gone – and again it was all too easy at that time to agree with Lawrence Boland (1979) that Friedman was an "instrumentalist" who cared little about the truth-value of theories but more about their utility in devising solutions to practical problems. Besides, even Friedman himself endorsed Boland's interpretation (Boland 1997, 41–51; 2003).[1] But ignoring the context in which F53 was written and even the heated macroeconomic debates surrounding Friedman's views on money in the 1970s, it is difficult to see any explicit endorsement in F53 of the old Mach–Poincaré philosophy of instrumentalism. Uskali Mäki (1986) is quite right, it seems to me, to reject Boland's claim that when F53 is read carefully it will be found to be "both logically sound and unambiguously based on a coherent philosophy of science-instrumentalism." Actually, it is at once wonderfully ambiguous and incoherent. One can find in it echoes, and sometimes much more than echoes, of Popper, Kuhn, Quine, Toulmin, Laudan, and even Feyerabend – and that is precisely what made it one of the most influential texts in the methodological literature of twentieth-century economics.

One of the most memorable ideas in F53 is the notion that competition is an evolutionary selection mechanism weeding out businessmen who fail to maximize returns. Jack Vromen (this volume) dismisses the importance of this argument in F53 because Friedman expounds rather vaguely what I once called the Alchian thesis[2] and follows it almost immediately by the "countless applications " paragraph cited earlier. However, without something like a Darwinian selection mechanism, Friedman's frequent appeal to as-if reasoning lacks any grounding in a commonsense realist interpretation of economic behavior. This is a crucial point in the essay at which it does matter whether we read it as an exercise in the philosophy of realism or in the philosophy of instrumentalism because, as Uskali Mäki rightly observes in chapter 3 of this volume, we may argue that businessmen act as if they only maximize profits (but of course they do many other things) or that they act as if they maximize profits (but that they really don't). I side with Mäki and against Boland in this because Boland's reading implies an uncommonsensical philosophical sophistication on Friedman's part that rings false.

Besides, if we examine *Capitalism and Freedom* (1962) and *Free to Choose* (1980), the principal statements by Milton and Rose Friedman of the normative case for free markets, what we find is an informal dynamic argument about competition between independent self-interested individuals doing good as an unintended by-product of doing well; not for them the arid formalism of Arrow's First and Second Fundamental

---

[1] Boland modestly announced that he was the first to realize that Friedman was an instrumentalist while everyone else had pictured him as a sort of positivist. He also claimed to be one of the few methodologists who understood that Popper was no "falsificationist" but only a "critical rationalist", that is, one who believes that everything can be criticized including reason itself (Boland 2003, 26–8, 268–78).

[2] Vromen shows that Friedman's own presentation of the argument was made independently of Arman Alchian but it was credited to Alchian in F53.

Theorems of welfare economics (Arrow 1983).[3] In other words, they lean on something like a Darwinian selection mechanism.

This relates to one of the mysteries of F53, which is Friedman's (and Stigler's) deep-seated antipathy to the theory of monopolistic competition and the insistence that to understand the phenomena of the business world, all we need is a theory of perfect competition and a theory of monopoly, applying them alternatively as circumstances require. The trouble with the theory of monopolistic competition according to Friedman (F53, 34–9) is not the usual objection that the Chamberlin case of product differentiation without oligopolistic interdependence between firms is a quantitatively unimportant market structure in modern economies (Blaug 1997a, 376–9), but rather that it destroys the concept of an industry which is the bedrock of the Marshallian analysis of firm behavior. It is not always appreciated that Chicago-style economics regards real-world competition as so nearly resembling the textbook model of perfect competition as to be just about the same thing. Melvin Reder (1982) in his famous exegesis of Chicago economics labeled this the "good approximation assumption," which was a principal element in the "tight prior equilibrium theory" of Chicago economics. The state of perfect competition may be regarded by other economists (for textbook references, see Blaug 1997b) as an ideal, an unobservable analytical fiction, which nevertheless serves as a benchmark against which to compare real-world markets, but that is not how it is regarded by Friedman and company. To label Friedman an instrumentalist is to deny the real-world ontological status of his conception of what Marshall called "free competition" to distinguish it from a theoretical notion of perfect competition. This is a subtle distinction that is easily lost sight of if we reinterpret Marshall – and Friedman – in the light of the dominant Walrasian end-state conception of competition.

Now, economic theory, orthodox or otherwise, provides no measure of what would be a close or distant approximation to a perfectly competitive economy in which no firm has a price policy and all firms are grouped together with other firms producing the same homogeneous product. In other words, "tight prior equilibrium theory" involves a judgment about the real world that is incapable of being reduced to quantifiable elements. Ah, this argument is beginning to sound very similar to the judgment involved in appraising the predictive accuracy of the maximization-of-returns hypothesis. The idea of conclusions which are not quasi-mathematical proofs but fuzzy dynamic qualitative judgments is in fact a

---

[3] Although Arrow's Second Fundamental Theorem, permitting a divorce between equity and efficiency, turns up in the Friedmans as a proposal for a negative income tax.

principal feature of what Friedman calls the Marshallian, in contrast to the Walrasian, approach to economics.

So, how can anyone say, as I am supposed to have said according to Wade Hands, that Friedman licensed the formalist revolution? It is simply that those who read F53 remembered the fundamental thesis – that the realisticness of assumptions does not matter and all that does matter for the validity of economic theories is their predictive accuracy – and ignored everything else. Also, unlike Wade Hands (or Tom Mayer) they paid no attention to how Friedman went on to validate his favorite economic theory, the quantity theory of money. After all, Friedman gave no pre-scriptive advice in F53 on how best to validate economic theories. Should we use econometric evidence or historical evidence? Should it be a "thick" case-by-case examination of the evidence or a "thin" verification by a perfectly general demonstration? Friedman may have won some meth-odological battles with F53 but he lost the methodological war because he went on to write *A Monetary History of the United States, 1867–1960* (1963) with Anna Schwartz – a thick examination of the historical evidence for the theory that money causes prices and not the other way round – while the rest of the economics profession put its faith in thin corroborations by means of econometric regressions. So, Hands has a case when he argues that Blaug and Hutchison are examples of methodology-as-viewed-from-philosophy, while Mayer gives us methodology from the standpoint of the applied economist but, as usual, he overstates a good case. It is not Blaug and Hutchison but the profession as a whole that took from F53 the methodological message that suited them and simply ignored Friedman's subsequent practice.

References

Arrow, Kenneth J. (1983). An extension of the basic theorems of welfare econom-ics (1951). In *Collected Papers of Kenneth J. Arrow*. Oxford: Blackwell, ch. 2

Blaug, Mark (1997a). *Economic Theory in Retrospect*, 5th edition. Cambridge: Cambridge University Press
  (1997b). Competition as an end-state and competition as a process. In *Not Only an Economist*. Cheltenham: Edward Elgar

Boland, Lawrence A. (1979). A critique of Friedman's critics. *Journal of Economic Literature*, 17, 503–22
  (1997). *Critical Economic Methodology: A Personal Odyssey*. London: Routledge
  (2003). Methodological criticism as ideology and hypocrisy. *Journal of Economic Literature*, 10(4), 151–226

Friedman, Milton (1953). *Essays in Positive Economics*. Chicago: University of Chicago Press

(1962). *Capitalism and Freedom*. Chicago: University of Chicago Press

Friedman, Milton and Rose D. Friedman (1980). *Free to Choose: A Personal Statement*. New York: Harcourt Brace Jovanovich

Mäki, Uskali (1986). Rhetoric at the expense of coherence: a reinterpretation of Milton Friedman's methodology. *Research in the History of Economic Thought and Methodology*. 4, 129–43, Greenwich, CT: JAI Press

Reder, Melvin W. (1982). Chicago economics: permanence and change. *Journal of Economic Literature*, 15(1), 1–38

15   Final word

Milton Friedman

I have somewhat mixed feelings about the splendid conference that Uskali Mäki organized on my ancient methodology article. On the one hand, it is a source of great satisfaction that an article I wrote more than fifty years ago should still be regarded as worth extensive scholarly discussion. On the other hand, that very fact is a severe condemnation of the essay. Surely, if the essay had been really lucid, scholars should not today still be having different opinions about what it says.

I have myself added to the confusion by early on adopting a policy of not replying to critiques of the article. I decided that I had a choice: I could spend my time discussing how economics should be done – a worthy cause; or I could spend my time doing economics – in my opinion, if not a more worthy, a more attractive cause. That act of self-denial has quite unintentionally been a plus for the discussion of methodology. It has left the field open for all comers, and they have all come and produced a broad stream of commentary. The articles at this conference are a good example.

I have read them all and I am impressed with their high quality and intellectual seriousness. I would not have thought that my modest essay would have relevance to so many issues. I feel like a proud father who has a large brood of bright children – all of them right, all of them wrong, and all entitled to his or her own views. Yet I am also impressed that there is a common thread that runs through them.

I would like to close by offering my personal thanks to the authors of the chapters in this collection, for how responsibly you have taken your task of commenting on my essay. I have learned much from your essays about my own as well as about other ideas on methodology. I am sure other readers of the book will have the same experience.

Milton Friedman, February 19, 2004

Index